THE CITY
AND THE CATHEDRAL

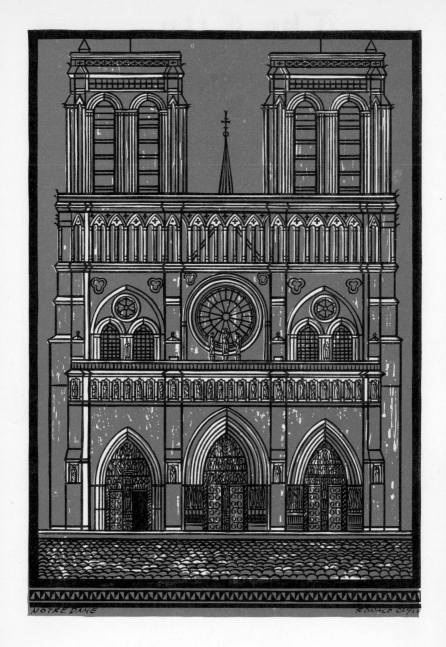

NOTRE DAME   RONALD CLYNE

Notre Dame of Paris

The City and the Cathedral

A Reflection of the Glory of the
Gothic and the Middle Ages at their
High Tide in the City by the Seine

by

ROBERT GORDON ANDERSON

Author of
"The Biography of a Cathedral"

LONGMANS, GREEN AND CO.

NEW YORK   TORONTO

1948

LONGMANS, GREEN AND CO., INC.
55 FIFTH AVENUE, NEW YORK 3

LONGMANS, GREEN AND CO.
215 VICTORIA STREET, TORONTO 1

Printed in the United States of America
Montauk Book Mfg. Co., Inc., N. Y.

To
Those Who Because
They Truly Loved France and Humanity
Suffered and Died in the Resistance

R. G. A.

*In grateful acknowledgment of the invaluable
and illuminating editorial counsel of Julie Kernan*

R. G. A.

Contents

The Paris of the Middle Ages

HERE IS BUT ONE PARIS. THERE NEVER COULD BE A SECOND, one patterned after her that would beat with her particular heart-beat or glow with her light. With three alone of history's great capitals, Jerusalem, Rome, Athens, she has earned, as far as mortal city can, the crowning word, "immortal."

Two thousand years of pilgrims have left testimony to her eternal spell in lovely lyrics out of the past whose music lingers still, in more books that have been written about her than of almost any other glamourous city or cross-roads in the world, and in innumerable portraits of her fair self in her every aspect, from where she sits by the palaces and beggars of the quais, laving her white feet in the Seine, to the great pearl of Sacré Cœur crowning her lovely head on Montmartre. Strangers have built within her walls schools that men may drink of her perennial springs. Aliens spend fortunes to remove from her beloved features the scars of war. And they make long journeys to see her again and again or lodge permanently in her magnificently appointed hotels or in her poor, heavenly little rooms way, way up under her blue-grey mansards or twisting chimney-pots.

For two thousand years and more they have been going that way. Wars have stopped the endless parade, except for the soldiers. Almost as soon as the drums, the trumpets have ceased, the legions of peace have entered again. It will be so when, in present or future wars, the high explosives are stilled, until the day—may God forever postpone it—when they turn this beautiful and so alive personality they call the City of Paris into a dead and mocking ruin.

Roman generals rested from their warfare by the Seine. Charlemagne rode to Paris to hear his school-boys sing. Dante sought more wisdom on the Street of Straw. Aquinas dwelt on Sainte Geneviève's Hill. At the Ile Saint Louis landed Cadet Napoleon, to the west gate came Josephine of Martinique. Homeless Heine, sea-trumpeting Paul Jones, Chopin, Karl Marx found asylum here. Unceasing is the parade to Paris of these lodgers for more than a night. A royal Stuart left his heart in an urn in her care. An American general simply could not stay away because near her, under white crosses rest his dead.

1

An Italian who adored her lies buried in the shadow of the Cathedral, at the feet of the flying buttresses.

Modern Paris, in the days of peace, is a serene and gracious city. She is spaciously spread out, in all her many-roofed, columned, bright river-girdled, and soft-foliaged beauty, over the valley and her four hills.

Mediaeval Paris too had an irresistible allure, but the city then was neither spacious nor serene. It was a cramped, elbow-rubbing, and most exciting gathering-place of hearty and vociferous human beings. They were so thickly crowded in that the houses often shut out the sunlight, the eaves frequently almost meeting five or six stories above the streets. These were tortuous and narrow. Not more than two mailed horsemen could ride abreast even down the royal highways of the city. It sometimes seemed as though the very city walls, had they not been firmly anchored to the earth with mighty masonry and scores of round towers, would have given way under the pent-up energy, the shove and thrust of all its robustious citizens.

And if Paris then was far from spacious, it had a stimulating and aspiring verticality. One looked up at so many interesting things on high. The energy of its residents and pilgrims found vent in escaping upward into a fairy, a great Gothic world of crazy ridge-poles, cone-capped towers, weathercocks and pinnacles, and an infinitude of spires. Those spires gave God's accents to a crowded city that throbbed and burned with enough of devil's desires. Something was lost to man when, in the New World, he let his towers of commerce surpass those of God. In modern Paris they raised the Eiffel Tower. But that is a silhouette only; the rest of Paris stays moderately low; and the spires and Cathedral towers still give character to the fair Paris sky-line. They dominated the mediaeval city.

There was more of splendour than of sanitation then, but there was that splendour. The citizens made all comers forget the mediae-val mire by the gorgeousness of their banners and pageants, all the bright blazonry of the high Gothic period. The very paint-brush and chisel served as outlets for their excess of spirits. With gaiety and gusto they decorated the house fronts, gave gold haloes and coloured robes to their statues. In their happy exuberance they added to corbel, torch bracket, inn signs the most captivating carved creatures. Every-where, fetchingly ugly gargoyles grinned over the church cornices. In form they expressed their joy in life, poured their hearts out in colour.

At noon cripples and beggars sought their little lozenge of sun in the gutters. But for those who wanted care there were legions of soft-voiced, gentle-handed nuns in the Hôtel Dieu, God's House of Healing, and in asylums and retreats all over the crowded city. Evil spread its nets in pestilential spots, sometimes near the holy places. Perhaps what one has to do in studying such alive history is to keep one eye on the social problems, the other on the human tragi-comedy. And Paris was possessed by such a turbulent, vivid crowd of sinners, mortal and venial, and a few saints, of fascinating, pathetic, mirth-provoking, mediaeval men, some of whom pursued a straight line to real objectives, but most of whom, like the moderns, were running around in circles, getting nowhere in particular. But they had a wonderful time in doing just that and presented a most engrossing and spirited spectacle.

And, too, if thieves and cozeners and harlots kept house in lanes all too near Our Lady's great home, her aisles were so often full, the church-bells forever kept going, the choirs singing, and the glory streaming from the holy panes. If, before the moral plague spots, the torches burned red and sinister all night, they were quenched with the dawn. The myriad lights by the altars of Notre Dame, by those of all the churches in the city, never went out. And in these one found the heart of Paris.

But the Cathedral of the City was more even than the soul of Paris, this idyllic reassurance, this sanctuary of peace. It was the top crest of the mighty tides of the Gothic Age that remained lifted up there against the sky forever for us, after those tides had ebbed. And it was the symbol of the greatest, the most inescapable of universal facts. As the illuminating mysticism of the Cross has an indestructible frame of logic, so this Cathedral of the City, built up in the form of that Cross, represents something that cut ruthlessly, magnificently across the whole life of Paris and the whole life of man.

In an earlier story, *The Biography of a Cathedral,* we viewed the march of civilization toward it and an even farther-off goal, and all the movements which affected the Cathedral, or which it affected, over twelve centuries. It was a long flight. But it was good to have that sweeping survey and gathering up of so many forces, so many strands, all being knotted in that lovely culmination, Notre Dame there by the Seine.

It should be said that the earlier story and this are not completely dependent on, though they support, each other. They are not sequels in too literal a sense, but rather, sister books. They need not be read in the order of the years. Each has a complete identity, her own individuality. Indeed, it is not necessary for clarity to know both sisters, though it is to be hoped that, since there is a mutual helpful relationship between them, knowing the one sister may make it agreeable sometime to meet the other.

But in contrast with that long range of the first book over the centuries, a long swan migration as it were, surveying the little doings of big men, the big doings of the little, this is not to be a long flight but rather a settling-down. But oh, such a busy, dynamic, galvanic settling-down in Paris principally, by the Seine, and never very far out of the shadow of the Cathedral. In carrying on this story of Notre Dame, Paris, France, mankind, we are going to observe all for the time from a truly neighbourhood viewpoint, a neighbourhood that then knew the highest in civilization, which was capital and epitome of all the neighbourhoods worth-while then in the world.

One then has to slacken his pace, narrow his range, to see things whole and perhaps gain greater wisdom. For Paris was such a packed-in city that these were very crowded hours. As in the landscape of a pioneer country in that earlier story (running from 52 B.C. to A.D. 1225 when they were just reaching the summits of the Notre Dame towers), the human habitations were farther apart, their top events, black deeds, shining achievements were fewer, though they were fascinating enough when they came. Men then set down scantier chronicles of them on clay, papyrus, parchment.

There was a glory in the early Christian Church right after the Founder, an earthly splendour in Augustan times, a grand and fetching gustiness in Clovis and Charlemagne. But recorded history, original documents that would have supported it, was covered by the shadowy cloak over Europe, lost or destroyed in the vast milling-about of many races and men. About so many movements, developings, emergings, was wrapped that mysterious, enveloping Dark Ages mantle. Cities that produced, discoverers, men that did really big things were lost oftentimes in a vast anonymity.

Oh, there were gleams enough then. In spite of the envelopment, the shrouding and darkness, it was a most colourful, fascinating march of man we saw, and particularly from that magnificent vantage-point, the rose window eye of the Cathedral.

But the archives are richer in this Gothic high tide, in this thirteenth century which we will look at now. More tongues were speaking, more pens setting things down. Institutions had multiplied. France, in the "Glorious Thirteenth" designed for herself a pattern of what in courts, parliament, body politic, she would one day more thoroughly be. She arrived now more nearly at her natural identity, matured into a personality that rather powerfully affected all of Europe.

Epical had been the heroes that strode on that early stage. Dazzling had been the pageant when it shone through the dark cloak. But Paris had now come into the greater and more varied glory of the Gothic, at its very height. This happened to be the busiest, the most productive as well as the most charming of cities. And it happened to be now in the most energetic of centuries, the one which, in spite of populations and tools of later eras, was the most colorful century of all. Also the richest not only in contagious gusto, and joy, but in vitality, raw human power, brain labour, visions seen, industrial brotherhood, and in the flowering of the Gothic—and of the power of God—in all that is lovely in art, above all, in faith.

When, the flight of this book over, we press on further in the story of the City, the Cathedral, and man, we shall come first into the ebb of the Gothic tide. It was redeemed only by the wisdom of Charles the Fifth of France, the invincible strength and immortal sweetness of Jeanne d'Arc. Then, and as the Renaissance comes glitteringly in, we shall sweep on more swiftly over more centuries, and at that earlier pace.

But when you walk within the covers of this book, you will walk pretty much within the walls of Paris, packed in, filled out almost to bursting with its dynamic citizenry. You will be occupied enough in a very active settling-down. Eyes and ears will find enough to take in, in this second Athens and labour stronghold of the thirteenth century, the capital of France and of the world of the Gothic, by the Seine.

I

Queen Eleanor, once of France, later of England, escorts Small Blanche of Castille over the Pyrenees to her Wedding by the Seine. . . . Blanche becomes "the White Queen," Regent of France, receives Proposals in Verse, answers them in Kind, but refuses All, to educate her Boy. . . . An Extraordinary Mother, she frustrates the Rebel Nobles and raises this Son, Louis the Ninth, to be the Ideal King.

1200 𝔄.𝔇.

𝔄S THE TWELFTH CENTURY, WHICH HAD SEEN THE BIRTH OF the Gothic Age, was dying and the thirteenth was coming in, a cortège glittering in the sun defiled through a high Pyrenees pass, headed for the Paris whose stirring life and torches drew all men. This cavalcade, for the moment poised in the high air between Spain and France, was going to a wedding by the Seine, from which it would proceed to the capital.

Thus marriage would be an international affair. The tall, hooded, elderly, but still beautiful woman in the center, Eleanor, once of Aquitaine, was Queen of England and had been Queen of France. She had come over from England—to further her own purposes of state—to the home of her grand-daughter in Spain. To make sure of the alliance, she was escorting this child, little Blanche of Castille, over the mountains and up through France. The groom, her grandson too, who would meet them in an assigned Normandy church, was to reign over France as Louis the Eighth. He was now thirteen, his bride twelve.

This child bride-to-be, Blanche of Castille, though a mere slip of a thing, rode well in the cumbersome, velvet and gold-tasseled saddle, with gauntleted hand held high, and a little sway of her pliant figure. Her youthful features showed a whiteness that just escaped the pallid because of the slightest underlay of olive. The eyes even then held promise of that burning, devotional and yet appealing quality which, when she was older, swayed so many. But they were still the eyes of a child, very deep and filled with thoughts and responsibilities that

6

should not have burdened one so young. Had not her father, Alfonso of Castille, and even more often her confessor told her of the great things she might do for Spain and France, God and Mother Church, should she leave her homeland and travel to that famous City of Paris of which she had heard so many good and so many fearsome things, and there give her hand in marriage to a boy she had never met?

Though she was so young, she and her famous grandmother had already frequently differed on the way up through the plains of Spain. It was a daring thing for the child princess to do. Eleanor was not only her august grandmother but one of the most famous women in the world. But one or two queens, like Cleopatra, Theodora or Sheba had ever matched her. Over her, down the centuries, there were to be several wars. Divorced from Louis the Seventh of France, because of a lovely eye that wandered too much during the second of his Crusades—no one ever knew just how much guilt had been mixed up with the charming guile, the compelling beauty of her—she had proceeded to marry Harry the Second of England. And she had torn out the great side of France, Aquitaine, Guienne, and other provinces, and had presented them to her new husband over the channel.

Queen Eleanor, though seventy-eight, was without age. She was not like the picturesque Jumièges and Tintern Abbeys over whose pathetically lovely ruins we sadly exclaim. She was a splendidly whole and articulating unit. Passers-by could see this, for Eleanor, disdaining a litter because of her years, rode gracefully by them on horseback. They did not say, "What a beauty she must once have been!" but rather, "What a grand and handsome-looking queen and woman!" There was still the suggestion of the litheness and grace of the leopard— and no aging one, either—about her. The hood she wore against the mountain winds concealed the frosts in which the bright glints of her hair had been buried. The years had not noticeably indented her features' lovely lines. The deep-set eyes could still blaze and compel men. All the way from Madrid, when knights had bent low in the saddle or peasants had knelt before her among their goats, they felt warmed by the fires of the afterglow of her beauty. No wonder they sang songs about her—"Elinor, Eléanor, Aliénor"—with glamourous phrases that men could not get out of their heads or their hearts.

In history both Eleanor and Blanche would be known as imperious queens, but with such a difference. Eleanor attracted all men, from regal and feline vanity, from the desires of her wilful heart. Perhaps the one great and good thing she would ever do was what she was doing at this moment—escorting this child to the marriage she had arranged. This, through its effects, would in part make up for the great woe she had brought on her one-time country, France. The little Blanche, grown, would compel men enough, yet always for a cause: for her God or her son. But slight, immature as she was now, rising and falling in the huge saddle as they rode over the rocky way, she seemed at such a disadvantage physically with her august grandmother, match-maker and duenna. Then all at once she did not. She flashed the power over men she would one day wield. Without asking permission she halted suddenly in the path and thrust up her little gauntleted hand. It was a truly regal gesture. And it did curious things to the long, colourful, sun-smitten cavalcade climbing the rocky trail behind them. In the train were knights, ladies-in-waiting, soldiers in yellow and red and blue and with leather head-pieces, fatherly priests, a corded monk or two, a motley group of pilgrims from Saint James' shrine at Compostella, and an immense following of cooks with huge wheeled kitchen-wagons filled with produce, two ladies' litters which queen and princess had scorned, muleteers with lashing whips, whistling browned jackanapes of ostler boys, belled mules, and sturdy little donkeys whose grey backs were like shaggy isthmuses between great bays of sacks, packs, and studded trunks. These were loaded with utensils for cooking in camps by the way, warming-pans for overnight stays in cold inns or convent cells, and a great wealth of gowns, fineries, fans, mantillas, even feather mattresses, and priceless presents of lace, fabrics, damascened Toledo blades, and the finest goldsmith work for all the new royal in-laws and court dignitaries in France.

A little lower down the ascent, the deep gorges had been musical with a melodious Babel of waterfall thunder, the drinking songs of the soldiers, the ostlers' piercing whistles, and the tintinnabulation of all the mules' bells. But as, straining, they had neared the top, they had been silent. The little Princess Blanche herself had reached it, and suddenly realizing, perhaps, that from there she would see the last of her native land, she had shot that gauntlet up as she wheeled on her horse. The gesture brought to a shock stop all her train which had been moving along like some coloured dragon, but one whose vertebrae did not articulate well, so varied were the strides and the paces and the gaits and the swayings of the little donkeys and mules. But they were brought to so sudden a halt that men and animals bumped into each other all along the line; and boulders and a mule or two, with a cart and driver tangled in the harness and traces, plunged with an awesome clatter down into the ravine.

This saddened the little princess, who had been unhappy enough already at leaving her native land. She rode to the edge to see if anything could be done for the victims, but they lay crushed far below in the abyss. Then she turned to look back at her Spain. There behind her in the distance a great section of it stretched: the tawny, savagely-hued ravines and mountains; the yellow rivers; the dusty grey-green olives and fruit; and the round towers and toothed turret tops in the azure distance with that fabled and romantic look with which story had clothed all the castles in Spain.

In the south of her country would be shown, just about two hundred years later, a rock called "The Last Look of the Moor." Here, in the high thin air over the Pyrenees, Blanche of Castille took her last look at her home. The lot of the famous children of history is often very hard. She wiped a tear from the corner of her eye, crossed herself, said a little prayer, then turned to leave forever her home and mother and all she knew, for a strange country. Her father confessor, at her side, looked at her with sorrow and sympathy and yet with approval. For all the mist in her eyes, one could tell from the little chin held high, the firm tiny hand which turned her donkey, that there burned in that child's staunch heart the wish to go whither the good God had sent her, to do the hard things He had bidden her.

So they turned their backs on the familiar, the violently-hued landscape of her country, and descended to the lush valleys, the ranked forests, and the full-bodied rivers of France.

The children were married in Portmont, a town in that part of France still so incongruously owned by England. Eleanor, having seen her intrigue, her matrimonial venture consummated, and for once in her life having helped France, departed in the sunset of her beauty for Windsor. Then the young couple with what was left of their train rode up the Seine Valley, to the west Paris gate. To a flaring of trumpets and a ruffling of tabours, they rode up the banner-hung street. With curiosity and an initial courtesy the citizens welcomed this pale imperious child who bore herself very well. But she would be on sufferance, as all alien queens are, for a long time before she would quite win their love.

So, passing over the north bridge across which Charlemagne had come joyously riding, she entered, on the middle of Paris Isle, the low-lying, grim palace by the Seine, descendant of the old one of the Roman governors, whose latest edition we know as the Palais de Justice. This was to be her home for fifty-two years more, except on those short journeys which she courageously undertook to help her husband or her son. It was a somewhat overpowering one for so young a bride, but kings' daughters were used to that. In winter the palace seemed cold from the frosts and the sharp breath rising from the foun-

tains' occasional ice, and the great black, over-realistic Spanish crucifixes she, in her piety, installed. However, it was warmed by Crusade
carpets from the East, the colours of the hangings, the costumes of the
court, and great rosy, leaping fires on the capacious, carved, hooded
hearths.

She did very well by her husband, this little Blanche. It is a question
whether or not she had much romantic love for him. It is very difficult
for a girl of twelve to adjust herself with perfect emotional normality
to an unknown husband just arrived at puberty. This is especially true
when one has a very set, if handsome, grandmother writing her directions and cues from far-off England, and when one has a consuming
passion for doing her duty for God and the Church. She bore Louis
the Eighth enough children, so many indeed that historians have lost
count, some saying a round, others a baker's, dozen. All this came to
pass as she increased in stature, devoutness, and inner power of personality. She had beauty of the austere, the pallid sort, but her brooding eyes could flash dark fires. Meantime, her figure lost some of its
willowyness and yet none of its essential pliancy and grace. She still
rode well—and on dangerous expeditions for her husband.

He turned out a short, thin, orderly, somewhat austere man,
devoted too to his duty, though this sometimes made him harsh to the
border-line of the cruel. He did not a little killing of the Albigenses
down around Toulouse. This was not a one-sided story. The Albigenses and their main corps, the Cathars, were a sober though fanatic
people, of very estimable conduct at times. Not always, though. They
murdered a papal legate, which touched off all these wars. And they,
despite Saint Dominic's long efforts at conciliation, kept on villifying
not only ignorant and incompetent priests, such as are found in any
fold, but the whole sacred mystery of the mass, so beloved of most of
Europe. They had, too, many weird beliefs which will be gone into
a little later. And they had one peculiar and devastatingly revolutionary major tenet: physical marriage, all child-bearing, was a sin; the
only one who could get to Heaven was a virgin, male or female, or
one with a post factum chastity. To prevent this wholesale swallowing
up of both Church and State in the vast vortex of race-suicide (though
English and French politics too entered in) the well-meaning Louis
the Eighth took himself to the South to wage war against the heretics.
Altogether he was much away in the saddle and at his wars; and even
more than his councillors, in his absence, Blanche of Castille ruled his
France profitably and well.

And then Louis the Eighth must undertake an invasion of England.
It is a puzzling convention of patriotic Englishmen to speak of the last
invasion of their Isle as the one of 1066. There have been others. And

what should have been the English pride was that all these others were driven off. Louis' came in 1216 just one hundred and fifty years after the completely successful one of William the Conqueror. His lasted a few months. He gained quite a foothold while he was there with his many thousands of French knights. Blanche rode to the sea-coast and herself superintended and hurried on the gathering of two great fleets to act as escorts for the various contingents and a second large army for reinforcements. In the end, the English who had favoured the French (another little by-product of Queen Eleanor) turned coat again. And finally, though he sailed back to France, he carried off a nice little fox's brush of a fair indemnity.

On all these adventures, thin Louis grew more *maigre*; and at last he caught a dangerous dysentery in the siege of Avignon, and left the kingdom of France to Blanche, as regent for her twelve-year-old son. She mourned Louis with dutiful decorum if no agonized heart-break. Most of her twelve or thirteen children had died somewhere along the way. It was a curious characteristic of parents in that century and in most of the ages since, through the Victorian, that, like the prolific Bachs, Schumanns and Mozarts, it did not matter how many children one lost as long as some, like little olive plants, survived. They did not seem to mourn the little vanished ones after the hour, so long as they had been baptized. It was "God's way." Others came trooping along and their unfortunate little predecessors were unwept and forgotten. In the new shoots God had blessed the parental tree. And He had blessed this couple in their middle age with this survival named Louis, now the Ninth. For he was to become one of the very, the truly, great in history. For him, then, Blanche was to reign during his minority, and to fight for him too. She did this with wit and bold-ness, great gallantry, profound piety, and a dash of coquetry.

But first she had concentrated on the education of her son. More often than any court sage or philosopher was she his preceptor. Very early she told him stories of good men and great, made him familiar with the deeds of the noble kings and the saints. Plutarch was a con-stant companion. The pictures she etched deep on the sensitive plate of his mind she hoped would arouse his burning emulation when he was past his minority. In the deep vibrant tones of her beautiful voice she read him *The Song of Roland,* all the *chansons de geste,* the more decorous tales of the troubadours, Saint Gregory's *History of the Franks,* written in Tours, hero tales of her own Spain. By day she set him to studying the bright letters in a jewelled *Book of Hours.* So he learned his alphabet, picking up pure thoughts by the way. Often his mother would come upon him copying with delight the Gothic script of the text. Setting up at his slanting desk, on his little sheet of parchment, the regiments of privates, the plain letters, and the gaily coloured officers of capitals was more fun for the little king than the parade of lead soldiers for the modern boy.

As soon as he was able to comprehend them, she gave him practical lessons in the application of the ideals in the books by calling attention to the pious deeds of the saints, or the gallant achievement of some crusading knight of their own time. She took him on visits to her homes for the poor and instructed him in the common-sense giving of alms. She was the especial patroness of homes for daughters of the peasants who had been wronged by the haughty nobles. And it is nice to know that the tiny king who accompanied her on these rounds proved, when he grew up, a grand partner in the founding of refuges, hospitals, and asylums.

She saw to it, of course, that other tutors instructed him in more physical pursuits, except in horsemanship at which she herself was so adept. Hunting he tolerated, hawking he did not much care for, but he strove sturdily at all exercise with the sword, boy's size of course, and with the battle-ax. He himself longed to perform worthily heroic deeds like those of the great men whose achievements she had recited to him by night. There was nothing he desired more than to please his beloved mother, wherefore to please God and the Blessed Virgin, since that would delight her most. And often she could look down in the court and see him engaged with the master of fence, hacking away at an oak post or learning to guard himself, and taking stoutly the severest thwacks of the flat sword on his new leather jerkin or suit of chain-mail, expressly made to fit him by the palace armourer.

Even when the boy was very small, she always took him on Maundy Thursday to watch the Bishop of Paris washing the beggars' feet, in the crossing of Notre Dame. She even arranged to have the little king take his towel and cleanse the feet of one of the outcasts, in preparation for what would be his royal duty at Eastertime when he became sovereign complete. Once a beggar put out his hand to stroke the yellow head, then thought better of it. The little king would not have minded. Nor would the proud Blanche have cared on such an occasion. The glory from the two transept roses streamed on the little kneeling figure with his white linen and little silver basin, as he bent over the gnarled body of the battered mendicant, who too was glorified by the light, the royal service of the small fair-haired monarch attending him, and the beautiful, concluding benediction.

Blanche did not transmit much of the Spanish to Louis. He was to grow up as French as a man could who remained so wholly individual. Her piety and devotion in greatest measure she handed on, but, although when he grew older he could lay on mightily enough with the battle-ax in conflict, he never had quite that fervour of hers which was edged now and then with almost a Spanish savagery. For the piety and maternality of this slender white queen with the dark, deep-set, brooding eyes had something of the purity yet intensity, the almost primitive fierceness, which characterizes the emotions of the noblest blood of Spain, even her saints.

A striking instance and illustration of this intense fervour of piety and motherhood commingled was etched deep and ineradicably on the boy king's memory when he woke one night to see her standing over him, a little Pompeian-like lamp, with spout, vegetable oil, and wick swimming in it, in her white hand. Suddenly she set the light down, sank on her knees, stretched out her arms, clutched him tight to her breast with an anguished cry that startled him, "My son, my son, I would rather see you dead here in my arms than that you should some day commit mortal sin."

Why this horrid contingency had occurred to her in the late night watches, when all along the boy had been sweetly tractable and naturally devout, is puzzling. Of course, sin meant much in those days where in these it means all too little. Souls occupied the attention glands did later. For the mediaeval men universal as well as mechanical processes entered into the picture. Possibly too Queen Blanche had fallen into one of those reactions, the near neuroses, to which intense and deeply religious natures are liable. To save him, she had been ready to sacrifice her son, then with that sudden gesture of her arms, her whole body, her beautiful hair falling down enveloping him, she had feverishly tried to snatch him back from the imagined death of her high-strung fancy. That night the boy too never forgot.

But Blanche, with all this burning zeal, had regal imperiousness, the lovely all-embracing charity we have already noted as she went her rounds, and a definite humour and charm when she chose to use them. In her first years in Paris she had failed to win completely the hearts of the people. They gave her cheers sometimes when she rode abroad with husband or son, but these were never full-throated. Like some other queens who would live in and love Paris, she was an alien, on trial, and had a little betraying accent in her otherwise impeccable mediaeval French. But she was determined—for her son's sake—to win them. One year after her husband's death, two years before the strange Notre Dame penance, she had her chance.

The famous and fashionable Counts of Bar, Brittany, Lusignan, Champagne, and De la Marche had thought the time opportune, with the king so small and a woman holding the reins, to swell their estates and revenues at the expense of the Crown. They met and mobilized at Corbeil, where Abelard had once taught. The Queen, at Montlhéry with little Louis and a small company, fearing that they might be captured, sent messengers to the capital for help. A result so triumphant she could not have expected. Half the population of impulsive Paris poured out to rescue her. Companies of horse led the way, followed by men-at-arms, smiths with huge hammers, armourers with long blades from their shops. The peasants crowded to the roadside and joined in the cheers for the little king and the mother who would fight for her son. Those lusty soldiers, the earthy peasants, sang religious hymns almost all the way up from Montlhéry. Those in Paris who had not gone out could hear them coming while still far off. At the gates they welcomed the parade with tumultuous cheers. It was even more impressive than the entry over flower-strewn bridges into banner-hung streets of the boy's grandfather, famous Philippe Auguste, after he had beaten the Germans so roundly at Bouvines. For Blanche it was a happy day. She felt she would now have—and she was right—the love and confidence of the people of Paris.

But those ambitious nobles would not let her rest. Of course, they did not want too much fighting themselves. Wars those days, except in the Crusades where there was man's work, were made up of a day's fighting to many weeks of truce, formal or informal, when the armed men returned to farm, manage their estates, collect their rents, or merely to hunt, fish or talk. In the contests of diplomacy, of wits, Blanche came out best. Twice they made bold attempts to kidnap the boy but she foiled them and managed, in spite of them all, to see her son crowned with costly ceremonies at holy Rheims. Often she came off with prize treaties that added provinces or purses of size to France.

There was one day, however, when her fearlessness got her into trouble. She had ridden down, with a small retinue, to meet a band of the titled rebels. Astonished to see her so inadequately convoyed, the armour-gleaming, accoutrement-clashing nobles came to a halt, their restless horses pawing the ground. They stared at her spirited figure, but no one ever stared Blanche down. Her eyes could fall in humility before the King of Kings in prayer but before none else on earth. They were uneasy, perhaps (let us give them the credit) a little guilty over their fighting a woman and a small boy.

Then suddenly the eyes which would not fall or falter softened. She threw into the fray her reserves—her charm, all the appeal those eyes knew so well how to speak—also, it is possible, a little coquetry.

"By my faith!" she said—a strong oath for a mother as scrupulous in her speech as later would be her royal son—to the once hearty and now embarrassed nobles in the highway. "Why are you here, proceeding against my son? Remember, *messieurs,* how our son, the King of France, went to your aid"—she always spoke as though the youngster were responsible for her own achievements—"when your rivals from Languedoc would have burned your crops and your barns to charcoal, your own hides to crisp."

The famous Count of Champagne was not so careful of his speech. "By God, madam," he said, and something more. He was very fat, and his armour sweated him hard. But he was great of heart and quick of tongue and pen. Very lightly for him he leapt from the saddle to the ground, bowed low at her stirrup and finished him out:

"Not only my body but my soul too is yours to command. There is nothing which you desire that I will not perform, if you will only ask me."

After a council the nobles rode back the way they came. She herself turned north for Paris. She had won the day, but then there began for her the siege perilous. Count Thibaut simply could not forget that regal and handsome, that so pure white face. He was to do more than any other to fasten on her the famous soubriquet "the White Queen," to make famous her complexion as matching the camelia, a report which has come down to us today. Soon his horsemen began pounding the white roads down from his native Champagne to Paris. All bore messages of love. He was portly but a poet. Those messages sang, burned. It was more than she had reckoned on when she, knowingly, had used those eyes of hers.

Now hers was no passive beauty, even when she was in her brooding, profound, contemplative calm. Often when she had been younger she had been quick with capable movements, akindle with fiery energies, fierce ambitions and resolves within. The chief difference now was that these were, as a rule, beautifully controlled. And she recognized that in spite of her alluring femininity, for which she cared not a whit and would willingly have resigned as a bride of Christ had it not been for the will of God, the Church and her son, she possessed that quality which would have been called masterfulness in a man. She knew well how potent that masterfulness could be if allied with feminine finesse and the charm she knew well how to turn on—when she had a point to gain—said point, of course, always being for one of her triune objects of adoration, God, the Church, and her boy. Remorseful as she had been for it at the confessional, on the *prie-dieu,* she had used her unique equipment, almost meretriciously, her conscience told her, to make compliance with her wishes not only very agreeable to men, but something devoutly to be desired. So she had used her man's power in a woman's way. And now she had Count Thibaut, with others, bewitched, the count unfortunately well beyond the period when she had need for his bedazzlement.

Some even said that he became physically as well as sentimentally her lover. This was downright scandal and foolishness. Though she had taken no vows she was too much the *dévote,* the wholly religious soul, for that. He had proposed to her and in verse. And here, to tell the truth, she had yielded to a most venial little temptation. She had refused him, but she had answered him almost too playfully in kind, in verse. Widows, even those with pious resolves, can be lonely at times, even if they have lovable sons, and for a month or two she rather enjoyed the epistolary companionship and the exercise of her own metrical ingenuity.

Thibaut wrote that he was dying of love in phrases as weighted with amorousness as he was with pounds.

"By my faith!" she had versified back—and it is odd to find Blanche chuckling even in a letter—"What is this you say? You must be as far from death as you are very, very far from being thin!"

When it had grown a little too hot for Blanche, a courtier, Raoul of Soissons, stepped in. An amorous dithyramb of Thibaut's had fallen by chance into his hands. It cried to all the heavens and the world how much he, poor Thibaut, was to be pitied. And now he had gotten below his accustomed chivalry, had gotten indeed below the queen's white face whose praises he had sung, and much, much too far for Blanche. Now he longed, forsooth, to "embrace her fair white body"!

Sniggering, Raoul wrote, showing it to all the court. "Why, you big oaf of a lover, Thibaut, I'd like to see you embrace her! You are as wide as your arms are long. With your huge, puffed-out belly you couldn't get near enough even to touch her."

This letter and a crusade that happened along took fat Count Thibaut away, though later he came back as King of Navarre. His was one of the many distinguished proposals—the rest were in prose—that Blanche refused, to devote herself to her son.

II

Little Louis receives his Hardest Lesson. . . . A Noble is stood up without his Breeches before the Last Judgment Portal. . . . The Beautiful Rake-hell Giant King Peter, and a Mighty but Mixed De Montfort. . . . The most Disorderly Orderly, Immoral Moral, and Gently Murderous Folk in History. . . . A Little French Teacher gives his Life's Savings to build a House for Dominic on Sainte Geneviève's Hill.

1229 A.D.

WHEN LOUIS WAS FOURTEEN, HIS BEAUTIFUL, DEVOTED, devout, and sometimes difficult mother gave him his harshest lesson, much harder than any at the rough single-stick he loved. She took him to Notre Dame to see a noble stood up without his breeches before the beautiful but forbidding Last Judgment Door. We will see the Cathedral in many a lovelier aspect. And, after all, this was no aspect of her at all, only of man. Forever he is bending her pure straightness to suit his ideas.

The victim must have been cold, standing there on the paving, clad only in his shirt, when the royal pair passed through the crowd gathered in front of the Cathedral. Their greeting of Blanche was respectful enough. A gleam of affection, however, in the eyes of most there, followed the boy.

Some restraint too showed in her acknowledgment. She smiled, but her handsome eyes were a little cold for them, try as she would. They were warm only for Our Lady at her portal, the beautiful Christ by the central pier, and for the boy. Even then was the silver cord showing.

She sat on her chair throne with no pity for the victim—from the South—showing in the markedly southern, imperious aquilinity of her countenance. The boy king, a thin lath of a lad, his blue silk robe accentuating further his ganglingness, sat uneasily at her side, with the shadow of distress on his open, kindly face. He was sad and embarrassed to see an upstanding man, who did not look unlike the heroes his mother held up to him as examples, thus humiliated. Not only that, but apparently he would be consigned, not to the happy

17

fate of the saints up there, but to the penalty in the middle panel. And the fires there were so real, carved even to the very licking of the flames.

The crowd edged near the thrones. Other spectators looked down from the painted, half-timber houses opposite. But, except for the shufflings, a few phlegmy coughs, and titters from nervousness, there was a great silence in the square. Not even the beggars jeered to see one so lordly reduced to worse than their own tatters. Penance was an awesome thing, heresy a crime abhorrent. So, within and without the beautiful Cathedral, Count Raymond of Toulouse, with a fine dignity for all his bare shanks, the shadow of a supercilious smile on his dusky yellow face, went on with the prostratings, breast-beatings, lighted candles, the *Mea culpa, mea maxima culpa,* the horrendous Latin intonings of the Bishop in all his gorgeous vestments, and the prolonged sonorous chanting of trailing penitential psalms.

The small depressed blue-eyed king, at *dejeuner* in the palace afterwards, asked the eternal boy's "Why?"

"He had defied God and the Church," Blanche said.

The explanation would have satisfied her dutiful self as a child. It came near being the only answer for her now, so long had she accustomed herself to look only for the ecclesiastical whites and blacks. But, after all, was it quite so simple? Could she tell a fourteen-year-old that it all came—that this Count Raymond who looked so fine was there stood up breechless—because of a gentle and murderous people, the most disorderly orderly, the most moral and yet, in the final analysis, the most immoral people in the world? Why had this cultivated count with his maddening smile gotten mixed with them? Béziers—Carcassonne—their counts too? And this the gravest threat to the Church since the Moslems had reached as far as Poictiers? The more deadly threat too, because these "Albigenses" (most of them, at least their leaders, came from around Toulouse) had mixed in decent Christian prayers and benedictions with all their wizardry and obscene purity.

She did not have to go South, away from Paris walls, to know all this. Her husband Louis the Eighth had gone down there; and the boy was fatherless. She decidedly had a personal grievance too against Raymond, against the whole fanatical lot.

Furthermore, a very great man had brought her first-hand news. Illustrious men had forever been coming up Sainte Geneviève's Hill, where was kept burning the torch of ancient Greece, with some new, leaping, illuminating flames all Paris' own. That immortal parade had started before Caesar, even before Aristotle. It would go on for man forever. This herald with the news from the South was the second of the nine very great men of this century to ascend that hill. His name was Dominic—not yet Saint.

It had happened some years before, in 1219, when the boy had been five. That southern trouble had been going on a long, long time. Dominic had come through the Paris gates, had knelt in the Cathedral, then had ascended the hill with that long ground-covering stride his endless missionarying had given him, the long black mantle billowing around his fast-meagre, work-emaciated form. His foes said he was fanatical in appearance. His followers said he was holily fervent. Both were right. He was fiery of look, flaming of tongue. His eyes were both soft and hard. The first for the sinner who would turn; the second for the sinners who after ten years of his cruelly hard work down there in Languedoc, Provence, still spurned and jeered at his Christ message of love. He was the most ardent of mediaeval Peters catching souls with the net of his sermons and prayers. The net, his Order of Preachers, he had started in 1206, down Toulouse way, at Prouille. Preaching was the great and incessant *means* of his great order of friars, the Dominicans; the saving of souls was the magnificent end.

The meshes of his net were multiplying. He hoped that one day it would cover the world. He was not far wrong in his hope. But in 1219, when Blanche as Queen Regent met him, Saint Dominic had come up to Paris to see that new mesh, netted just the year before. It was the first Paris Dominican chapter-house, the later famous Saint Jacques Convent on the very top of Sainte Geneviève's Hill.

Dominic came later to the palace. The atmosphere in which they talked was a little overcast for a child but five years old. Rather naturally, for it was evoked by the Saint with sandals worn, his body wracked, but not one little tongue of the flame of him quenched, his eyes often like dark volcanic lakes shot through with fire; the Queen with her darting black eyes in the white of a face from which the dusty Tagus yellow had long since vanished; the giant black Spanish crucifix near the two as they so fierily conferred. It was lightened for the child, or a painter, by the colour of a salver, two silver plates and knives, by a sliced melon golden in hue, of which with two bread crusts they sparingly ate, and by a little orange African bird, the same colour as the melon, singing over against the crucifix.

What Blanche did not know (and this was not so much) the Saint, not too partially, supplied. In the first place, it was crazy to call this crowd with which the Languedoc counts had to a great extent allied themselves, Albigenses, when not Albi but Toulouse was their main fomenting place. Cathars were what they really were. They might, Dominic admitted, have a little kinshop with a Lyonnais sect who lived purely enough but who had vaguely distorted Christian tenets. And these Cathars were nothing new. As Paulicians, Bogomils, what not, they had showed up before, all through the centuries. All believed in two gods, one of Good, the other of Evil. That of Good did not have the might of Him of the Christians. The two sort of check-mated each other. Man was the offspring, the result of that primeval conflict up on the heavenly plains somewhere between the Angels of the Light and the dark ones of Prince Lucifer. The latter had tumbled to the earth as men, and were forever wanting to get back to their real selves, their former soul-selves up in Heaven.

Men and women both could be what in authority and prestige, if little else, corresponded to Christian priests. These were the real Cathars, a name meaning "the Perfect Ones," though the term was applied to all ranks of the sect when the misleading name of Albigenses was not used. These only had received the "Holy Spirit," Christ in entirety, as they saw it, into their hearts. They only could recite the Pater Noster of the Cathedral. And "the Credentes," the lower rank Cathari, or imperfect "Perfect Ones" must prostrate themselves before those of this higher order.

To gain this high rank, the perfectly "Perfect Ones" had to give up much: not only the family ties, wife and children, forsaken by the Catholic priest, but all relations with sisters, brothers, fathers, mothers too. They had a peculiar kind of Eucharist, and often carried about their bodies for years fragments of the holy bread.

Those who sought to rise out of the lower rank into the higher must renounce too their home life in every phase. In many of their practices and beliefs there was much that was good. This is what puzzled Dominic more than it did the religiously forthright Blanche, for whom there was but one way out for heretics. The whole puzzle, except for the results, makes a fascinating study. It is not worth here a foray into the South, since we have pledged ourselves to remain within Paris walls, and we want to watch Louis grow up into that exceptional, ideal king. But the whole movement, crazy as it seemed, was the gravest threat to Paris since the Moslems got as far north as Poictiers with their scimitars and the crescents with which they wanted to replace the crosses on the two parent churches of the Cathedral. It therefore warrants our following for a moment or two the conferring great personalities, the Queen and the Saint, in their harassed unravelling of this sect which could not be called Christian, but was a wild extraterritorial venture beyond the confines of Christianity.

They often were good, these "Perfect Ones" or Cathars. But in their very goodness was a sort of dynamite. They had all south France now and north Italy by the ears. It was not only these things that upset people: Their ritualistic departures. Their turning our bodies into homes for the refugees of Lucifer's fallen army, trying desperately to find our original selves back somewhere up there. A thorough acceptance of transmigration. Nor even that major distortion in demoting God from His high place of Fatherhood and turning Him into an equally matched duellist with the Devil. But they also disobeyed all civil oaths, and spurned hierarchical and civil authority. There were, as Dominic knew (it was one of the reasons for his establishing his new preaching order), incompetent, even corrupt, parish priests. But the misguided, wild-eyed Cathars disregarded the truly devout ones, made a blanket indictment of all, covering even Mother Church, shouting to the passers-by on the country roads, on the city street corners, that she was a harlot. It was a wonder that the Church for generations, so long a time had this been going on, had remained so patient.

State and Church were very closely intertwined in those days, in spite of the imperial-papal quarrel. Indeed, it was the State that punished heresy, when it was punished. Until this war over the falsely-called Albigensian, and really Catharist, crazy-quilt religion that didn't even make sense, there were not many relentless expeditions and inquisitorial prosecutions.

The Church had started as a democracy and yet a theocracy, one with the authority regnant that was passed on by the founding Christ. Paul punished heretics like Alexander and others. In the Church of his time they held what were really restrained inquisitions. It was devoutly believed in the Middle Ages, when the flock had increased to such tremendous and often illiterate proportions, that there had to be discipline or the whole Church would run "hog-wild," as the moderns put it. That was just what these good fanatics, these obscene pure ones, were doing now.

Except for these sadder Toulouse incidents, this was not a prosecuting, persecuting century in the main. The cruelty would come in with the fifteen and sixteen hundreds, in the splendour of the humanistic Renaissance, when men turned really inhuman. Of course, we can never be satisfied with men in any age; but the Gothic was robust, not cruel. This is true, even though we must except the blood of the Crusades. And there was a mediaeval logic there. They were risking their heart's blood to take from the foes of Christ His precious Tomb.

In any event, we can be grateful that in our Paris stay in this century it was not a cruel Paris.

Of course, in that cabinet over the flowing Seine, looking out on the palace garden, with the centuries-stained heavy furniture, the black crucifix, and the little singing canary, the Saint did not discourse on these last matters. He talked on, with his flowing gestures, in which one wondered at the extraordinary pliancy of his hands, of all the phalanges of them, his deep eyes giving to the place and meeting the dark tones of a great Flemish painting. But Church discipline, authority, inquisition, all, all, the two accepted. What puzzled Blanche later, in her effort to explain cause and effect to the boy at the unbreeching before Notre Dame, was the crux of the whole matter that Dominic, coming as near frothing as a holy man could, touched on now: their insane stressing of celibacy, of abstinence as the soul-cure for the world. That celibacy which Christ had commended for those who thought to give Him and His Church complete service, with these Cathars had turned sour.

All mating, even proper husbanding and wiving, was corrupt. It had been so ever since Eden. The controlling "Perfect Ones" abstained from it themselves. They insisted on this eventually, the sooner the better, for all the others. With them, the only decent people, both sexes, were virgins. Men, on earth, like the angels in Heaven, were not to be given in marriage. Marriage was fornication, child-bearing a process to be eschewed and abhorred.

Of course, in the way of all religious folk running amuck, they were inconsistent. Like so many extreme modern sects who place a premium on virginity, they winked at deviations on the part of the lesser people, the lower ranks, the *"Credentes."* All these "Believers" had to do was to accept nominally the main principle. They could go on with this accursed process of procreation, provided they agreed ultimately to accept chastity. Sometime. Any time. When at death's door. When the Dark Angel was about to make them forever incompetent, they could become continent and so get into Heaven—just under the wire. Insane! Demented! Diabolical! cried Blanche. Her teeth, in her anger, sank into her lips. On them little red beads appeared, foretaste of the red wrath that was to come.

Why so many nobles accepted such theses it was hard, and yet not hard, to say. Blanche could swear that in the main none of them did more than smilingly assent to the principle. Complete chastity was not for those cultured counts, playing their viols, wooing their mistresses in their love courts. To be sure, they did not want any interference from the outside. And it might, she suggested, be a novelty now, to discuss the value of complete abstinence, between kisses on the grass amidst the roses and the laurel. And then—and then—Dominic insisted, with that wave of his expressive hands, one had to admit that these Cathars, the "good men," as they were called, could be very attractive. Orderly. Kind. The southern counts seemed to want to protect them. They had some very beautiful prayers. Like those of the early Christians. Some most excellent things they had retained. If only they had retained Christ's teachings complete, instead of compounding them with such fiendish innocence.

And hark to this: John the Baptist, they said, was a "renegade Jew." The Jordan baptism was not lawful. The only valid one was theirs they called "of the spirit." Meat they could not eat; they would be swallowing a brother. Besides, animals were so carnally begotten. Fish, because of their "innocent fertilization," were all right. Never milk! That came from the same frightening copulation. Eggs, cheese too were lewd products.

Why, they had made nature so abhorrent that they could not bear even the thought of the womb. They had Christ conceived, not as Matthew and Luke have told us, but by the Holy Ghost's piercing of Mary's ear!

And then right out of that purity and goodness the dynamite exploded. They began to insist that this celibacy, even for the lesser ones, counts too, should be more than academic or merely taken up *in extremis*. Marriage which the Church solemnized as a sacrament and an institution blessed of God was for them anathema. They preached this everywhere. Whole populations should become abstinent *en masse*. The earth was evil, of the God of Evil. No children should be born into it any more.

Now State and Church did indeed have to take notice. Missionaries, legates, through the generations had been sent first to preach, to persuade them out of their silly error. Those "generations" were proof of the gentleness of the Church, said Dominic. Knowing men, wise Blanche was confounded. The priests had had to be so lenient with human frailties. And here were great hordes of husky Provençal peasants and Languedoc lovers, frustrating nature, bridling their passions, or certainly shelving them, not to save any souls, as did the celibate clergy, but at the frenzied behests of deranged fanatics claiming all nature, processes designed by God and followed by them through the ages, to be downright sin.

The point, of course, was obvious. The clergy could stand the personal insults hurled at them from roadside and market-place and nave. Priests worth their salt welcomed such persecutions as somehow paralleling their Saviour's. Mother Church, in her magnificent innocence and purity, could stand being called a harlot. They had called her so before and would again. What was threatened now by these upside-down-turned folk was a mass race suicide. State and Church were to go out, to be extinguished.

Since all progeny was to be ciphered out, all the race erased, perhaps one life did not matter. Still, these gentle Quaker-like folk up and murdered a papal legate.

Tirelessly Dominic had wrestled with this problem, after he had been unwillingly brought up from Spain because of the mission ordered by the Pope. Well he might have hesitated, though he didn't, for the issue had remained unsettled for so long. Dominic had pleaded, persuaded, prayed for ten years. There was this process in the purest of theological minds that must be accepted: the erring must be reasoned with, wrestled with, endlessly and in love. But when these gentle methods failed, they must be succeeded by the punishment, all the way from that unbreeching, even to death.

Out of his heart Dominic had explained this to the White Queen in the palace by the Seine. For his own sake—as well as others'—to save his soul, the incorrigible sinner had to be dealt with, in the end. Grave heresies like this, threatening Church and State and race extermination, with no end of absurdities besides, were devils' leprosies. He who persisted in this spiritual leprosy would carry it further, destroying himself and many others besides.

That he dreaded the final penalties Blanche knew. She was acquainted with his family, which too came from Spain. Several of them ordained, the rest indefatigable lay workers, fervently loving God and profusely generous to the poor, they made up as holy a family as any outside the Holy Family may be. This transmitted nature had been further moulded by an extraordinary conviction, consecration, the awareness of a great mission—his establishment of the great Order of Preachers, the Dominicans, whose good works still beautify the world.

When he spoke of his love for these Languedoc and Provençal sinners, and his voice, indeed the whole self of him, seemed to tremble, she knew his love for them came from the very depths of his soul. She looked again over the mantle, worn and beginning to show holes, the broken sandals, but knew, underneath, the unbroken spirit of him, the flame unquenched. She observed too the tears in those eyes which could be both hard and soft. She would completely have agreed with a nineteenth-century Protestant critic who would have this to say of this remarkable, this often attacked, man: "Dominic was a noble personality of the purest religious faith. His nature was so gentle that frequently he shed tears in sympathy for his foes. In the genuineness, the sincerity of his intentions, in the fervour and spirit with which he tried to carry out his objectives and ideals, he must be ranked with Saint Francis himself."

So sides were fantastically drawn in this Albigensian War, whose issue would save Notre Dame as she was for Paris, and Paris as she was for the little boy king. Those southern counts sided with the Cathars. They did not want outsiders like the King of France, Simon de Montfort, the Norman-French-English Earl of Leicester coming in. They preferred home rule, were locally patriotic, and had not a little fondness for their deluded countrymen even after their official murder of the legate, their civil insubordination, and general sex nuisances. Curiously, the local bishops impeded the chastising army. They too seemed to favour home rule, resenting the missionaries sent by Rome.

An incongruous champion too took up the Cathar cause. King Peter of Aragon did not want to see Frenchmen and Englishmen fussing about his borders. And he was a great help, physically, if not ideologically. For all that mass Cathar continence King Peter seemed to make up, as a champion at concupiscence. But this rake-hell of a blond giant, resplendent in shining armour, was also a champion on the battle-field. It was unfortunate his morals and his cause were so bad, he would have made such a grand figure for the pantheon of heroes Blanche built up for the boy.

And Peter's death was far from exemplary. True, he died on the battle-field for that curious Cathar cause. But the night before the fray, he, the squire reported afterwards, had made a sort of record with wine and women. They had had to drag him to the battle mass at dawn and help him up in the saddle.

They found King Peter once so magnificent in stature, good looks, and shining armour, among the corpses. This royal giant, reprehensible in so many ways, had had a way with him. It seemed to have softened even the grim destroying angel, he touched the king so lightly in passing. Looking down on him, many wept. Even in death, Peter was so very beautiful.

The military chief of the avenging army, Simon de Montfort, had a worthier, if at times war-cruel, life, and a more exemplary death. A curious mixture, though not so unusual in mediaeval times, he was, in his personal dealings, absolutely upright, aggressive in his conquests, kind to his own, ruthless to his foes, and an indefatigable observer of his religious duties—and this, strange as it may seem to modern liberals of the Mother Church, was as sincere a side of his nature as the warlike one. Simon de Montfort greatly loved the Church in his hard, devoted way, although she was surely better served in his time by the gentle Francis, by Dominic with his mission, and since by Jeanne, Vincent de Paul, and such great military leaders as Foch and De Gaulle.

On his last day, too, De Montfort attended mass. Just as the sacring-bell signalled the Elevation, the trumpets outside sounded the warning of an assault. The besieging armies had forced the gates. Aides rushed into the church, begging De Montfort to come. He shook his head, remained on his knees. Not until the *"Ite missa est"* would he leave, to rush with battle-ax and sword into the fray. Under an avalanche of steel and horse he went down. His pious delay had caused his death.

Dominic himself was credited with the decisive victory at Muret in 1213. Not through the sword, but his own prayers. For ten long years he had served Love, all up and down the hills, the high roads, in the cities of Languedoc and the South. They had spurned his teachings, spewed him out of the very churches. All this, returning love for hate, constantly turning the other cheek, he had borne. Whatever the conviction of the other side, he felt this love very deeply in his heart. But it was the hour now, he felt, to call down a little victory. So all the night preceding the battle and through the daylight hours of struggle, when the tide ebbed this way and that, he remained in prayer in the church. None could persuade him to rest or eat. At last over him came a great peace. He left the church to sleep. Comparing notes with the priest afterwards, De Montfort said that moment was the very one when the tide of battle finally turned.

Victory! Yes. And so again, as ever He does, Christ walked the battle-fields, weeping because all along, down two thousand years, man has not yet learned his simplest lesson told to the songs of the angels in the alphabet of the Bethlehem stars.

There were, of course, more massacres with which only the generals, never Dominic, had anything to do. Afterwards, the Cathar movement sporadically flickered up, but finally went out. In a way, the "Perfect Ones" had had their way. They wanted the race ciphered out through abstinence. *They* had been. So too, in the struggle, vanished much of the beautiful Languedoc culture, famous ever since great Romans had sent their boys for education to Toulouse. In the Treaty of Paris of 1229, there had been other clauses besides the one requiring Raymond to be stood up, breechless, before the Cathedral. France got some territory from the counts for her boy king. The year after his death, she was to get all Languedoc.

Fascinating and picturesque as history-lovers consider this long-drawn-out mixup in which, through man's stubbornness, ignorance, and conceit, the main strands of politics and religion got fouled, it is something of a relief to look, not there, beyond Paris walls, but *within* this peaceful, bustling city. To see that boy grow up into the mighty man, that ideal kingdom develop! But while Blanche was stepping out of her educating and mothering and devotions long enough to give *congé* to all her suitors in prose or rhyme, and humanly enjoying it perhaps as a relief to her graver hours, a little incident occurred about the time of Dominic's stay that shows eloquently, if quietly, why it is so agreeable to walk in this wonderful century in its most magical city, Paris.

A generous gentleman on the faculty of the University of Paris had built, with his lifetime's savings, a hill-top college which he himself was to head. This college Messire Jean de la Barastre—his name should always be remembered in Paris—now turned over, free and clear, to Matthew of Paris as the first Dominican chapter-house in the city. This Convent of Saint Jacques overlooking Paris was to make history. We shall see more of it later. The Saint's great Order of Preachers grew fast. Before Saint Louis departed on his first Crusade, as we shall see a little later on, there were chapter-houses in many of the great cities of Europe. And three thousand members! A great number when you consider the three thousand were all trained, seasoned, very competent men of a highly consecrated calibre.

Louis was six when Saint Dominic died. It was at Bologna, in 1221. Blanche was glad to learn that when he was ailing, not long before the end came, he had paid a visit to Fanjeaux Abbey. He must, poor man, have been so tired. And there, in his cell, quite as they had attended His Master long before, angels came and ministered unto him. Indisputable was this celestial evidence. She recounted the heavenly visit to the little boy who was much impressed. And yet he said he would like better to be a soldier like his father and grandfather.

III

Louis dispenses Justice, seated on a Little Carpet in his Palace Garden. . . . He settles the Boundary Disputes of the Little Pasture People, the National Disputes of Kings. . . . The Silver Cord. . . . The King even gives up Lands to the Astonished English. . . . He cleans up, paints up, refurbishes his Palace and City. . . . The Same Old Story, even though a Royal One— Mother-in-Law versus Daughter-in-Law. . . . The Hall of the Lost Footsteps. . . . Queen Blanche puts Little Singing Birds in Every Chamber of the Palace.

1229-1248 A.D.

S O THE YEARS OF HIS INTENSIVE EDUCATION PASSED AND LOUIS the Ninth became king indeed. More time passed and he who had been the thin lath of a lad, with the serious face and the lovely manners to all of high or low degree, grew up into the gentlest, the most forceful, and the greatest king in the world.

Most of the first families of the court could scarcely realize this. His eccentric way of administering justice, the old hats he wore, his odd, kindly ways blinded them to what he really was. But Blanche, at every step of the long course of her regency, had known that this would come. She had prayed for and expected his goodness and his fame. On the very morning of the day before he was to leave on his first Crusade she did not think it at all strange that so many of the great, counts and dukes from her side of the channel, envoys and princes from beyond it, were coming to Paris to taste—and to test— that wisdom and justice for which he already was renowned.

On this morning of the day of his farewells, in 1248, Louis was thirty-four, Blanche sixty. Few would have thought that, so young she seemed, as she sat in a window of her apartment of the palace on the Island of Paris and watched the renowned visitors come through the arch and into a very queer place for a court, the palace garden. Sometimes he chose the great hall which he had had newly redecorated with lilies and gold stars and pillars, and crimson and blue paint,

again an oak in the park near his castle at Vincennes just east of the
city, and quite often this palace garden where he dispensed justice
al fresco, among the legumes, the flowers, the bee-hives and the
blossoming fruit-trees.

Knots of people, turning their horses over to servitors, were entering under that heavy Gothic arch; others in embroidered surcoats or
in rough peasant wool—with King Louis it made no difference—
stood all around, conversing and gesticulating in the freshness of the
garden and the morning. Fragments of their talk of assaults on shepherds and on castles, of the disputed boundaries of tiny little farms
and mighty kingdoms, of withheld pasturage fees and abbey accounts
that would not balance, and of king's ransoms came up to her.
Now if she was no longer Louis' teacher she was his counsellor and
ally. Though she sat in the window above the vernal fragrance and
the hum of the court and the bees, she was no mere spectator. Some
of these matters he had talked over with her in advance, others he
would explore with her later. Often now he would glance up at her
from his seat for approval or in comradeship; and sometimes it
seemed as if there were actual thought-transference between this saint-
like and most extraordinary and capable mother and her great and
famous son, later to be actually canonized.

Except for an occasional obeisance, a stranger might not have
guessed that Louis was the king. His brown taffeta tunic, the dark
blue coarse silk mantle over it, appeared poor beside the brilliant
dress of his court. And though when ceremony demanded it he could
be stately enough, he had that incorrigible liking for old hats. The
whole cast of his countenance was gentle with reassuringly strong
planes. The mouth showed shrewdness and twitched, though almost
imperceptibly, with humour as he warned a debtor haled before him,
"Never borrow, for repayment appears so very, very disagreeable to
all human beings," and then rallied the grand constable on his new
vermilion-lined mantle with voluminous gold markings, saying the
chanticleer of France would soon be lost in the coxcomb.

His location too was scarcely royal. He sat, not on a throne, but
under an espaliered pear tree which dropped white petals on his
mediocre costume, and on a figured carpet whose manufacture he was
then encouraging in France. A strange throne, this carpet among the
onions, the leeks, and the lilies. But this Louis the Ninth in whom only
his mother, the Bishop, and the poor saw the coming saint, was no
ordinary king. Though the very first man in Europe, no country priest
could have been simpler or more natural. He said that in the *plein air,*
with the birds and the cherries and the little springing beans so dear
to his countrymen, all the stuffy lawsuits of the nobles would get a

good airing. And since so many of his subjects worked in the soil, a seat on the good earth was the proper place from which to hear their pleas. Indeed, the Bishop of Paris observed that innocence and justice seemed once again to have come to earth to reign in a garden like that of our common forefather before the fall.

The return of this first estate was symbolized by a clear fountain in that garden. It gushed inexhaustibly in the soul of the king himself expressing itself in little jets of humour, sparkling bon mots that cleared up in a twinkling knotty judicial points, and in refreshing, gracious courtesies for all. If ever there was on earth a man of good will to whom the Bethlehem angels addressed themselves, it was this Louis.

Even when he was seated on the figured carpet the strangers from overseas could see that he was tall. When he rose, he loomed half a head over the famous Crusaders and the princes from the north who prided themselves on their stature. He came of a tall race. Grandfather Philippe Auguste, who had beaten English and Germans and rebel nobles alike, and some of his grandsons would be men of impressive height. Though spare of frame he was not weak. There was not an extra ounce on him, no superfluity of flesh about his midriff. Like Grandfather Philippe Auguste, though just a trifle thinner, he was slender and very fit and very powerful. Courtiers who had seen him laying on helm with his sword or driving it into a solid oak block knew this. A very important thing about that wise judge, stout warrior, patron of the poor, builder of churches, abbeys, hospitals, and colleges, was that with great arms and shoulders he had the great heart to back his ideals. And he had a tremendous indefatigability on which he could call nine-tenths of the time. Like many great men, however, he was susceptible to strange fevers, unaccountable indispositions which worried his mother and his councillors. But from these, even when appearing at the very verge of death, he would suddenly rise to strike out on some undertaking that would require the maximum of his strength.

That those eyes, so gentle and seeming to bestow a blessing on all, could blaze with lightnings the stranger-princes now saw when the King swung on a choleric crusader because of an oath. "I tell you," he said, "I will have no foul mouths in my kingdom!" Saint Louis was surely the forerunner of the Society of the Holy Name. Never had anyone heard him, even in the most trying of ordeals, use a stronger expletive than "Truly!" Indeed, so adamant had this loving King been that he had ordered pierced with red-hot awls the tongues of his subjects who persisted in uttering particularly shocking blasphemies before the churches. Two or three cases came to the carpet that morning. With one plaintiff who testified that he had been worsted in a duel of words over the Trinity with an atheist, near Saint Louis' Sainte-Chapelle too, he had little patience.

"I tell you, never argue with witty and wily unbelievers. Leave that to the scholars of the University. With those strong shoulders of yours, you should prefer action to dialectics. It is a wonder to me that you did not run him through."

And to another:

"There, my friend, you did wrong. Caution the foul-mouthed twice, thrice. Then, if he continue to insult God and Mother Church, see how far through him your sword may go."

Reverence toward God and with it purity of speech had become such an obsession with him that he went sometimes to extraordinary lengths. Later in the Holy Land, hearing a man-at-arms uttering a stream of ribald blasphemies at high Heaven, not knowing, of course, that the King was so near, Louis had him put in the stocks on the beach. Then he had him smothered up to his mouth in pig-guts.

In all of which you have a key to the man himself. Saint Louis, of course, did not know, any more than the scholars then, our chemical elements and the many combinations of them. But he had a peculiar sensitivity to combinations of the elements we call characters or letters. These elements, innocent of themselves when alone, could make devastating unions. Four—L O V E—could melt an immense hardness. Another quartet—H A T E—could act as a tremendous explosive. And quite as some of our chemicals joined can have malodorous effects, so certain letters forming words which call up impure images and associations could make a most terrible smell. The old adage that "Sticks and stones can break my bones but names [or words] can never hurt me," had no place in Saint Louis' belief. He knew they could have all the unwholesome, unholy, deleterious and hateful effects mentioned above. He took very much to heart a certain injunction, not only spiritually but psychologically wise, which was to disappear almost entirely from the consciousness of the twentieth century. It had been handed down twelve centuries before him, nineteen before us, by Saint Paul: "Whatsoever things are true, whatsoever things are honest, whatsoever things are just . . . pure, lovely, of good report, if there be any virtue, if there be any praise, think on these things." Continually did this King who exercised so strong and absolute a justice, who rode a horse so splendidly, and who so mightily wielded his shining and tremendous battle-ax, think upon them.

But harsh as he was with the foul of mouth he was as far from being cruel as ever king was. He didn't even punish *lese majesté* against himself—only that against the King of Kings. For that he would never stand. Right by the staircase of his own palace but the other morning, an old woman, a character of the town, named Saurette had screamed at him:

"You are not fit to be a king! We had better get us another. For you are king only with the permission of friars, priests, and frocked clerks. Men in petticoats! It is a pity and a wonder that the people of Paris have not driven you out of the kingdom."

The sergeant of the guard had made a motion with his weapon, but the King had waved him aside.

"You speak the truth, Saurette," he said. "I am far from being worthy to be king. If only it had pleased God to have given you another ruler who would have understood how to govern France better, I would have been very happy." And he crowned this graciousness to the dissolute old woman by giving her a gold coin.

Now, in the garden, noting on the faces of the stranger-princes a look of incredulity, almost of scorn, that he had been so severe with what they took for mere ways of speech—the English themselves being known to the mediaevel French invariably as the "Goddams"— he said to his councillors in as near wrath as ever he showed, a sad sort of wrath:

"They don't understand. I do not hate these I punish. I would willingly be pierced through my own tongue, could I by so doing stop all the foul words and particularly the cursing in my kingdom." And he meant it.

But the fine little lines at the corner of his eyes crinkled with humour and delight when a bishop from the Loire brought word to him of the result of some highly original advice he had given to two abbots at a previous session. The two abbeys had splendid choirs and, according to the royal suggestion, the matter was left to be solved by song. In the meadow of their dispute, the two robed choirs had met, singing first against then with each other. In song, in the sun, their wrath soon melted and the meadow was peaceably halved.

"It is always easy, once you get people together," said Louis over-joyed with this practical proof of what he himself preached and practised. "It is as easy to co-operate as to contend with a neighbour." Then he added to his council and court:

"You remember those other two abbeys down in Poitou? They had chosen two champions to settle their quarrel by ordeal of battle. They met in a neutral ground, the parish church of the village near by, for the vigil the night before the duel. But when they were both on their knees, so near each other, it seemed very foolish to fight in a quarrel with whose issue they had no concern. Instead, they embraced in the church, and at the inn broke bread and drank wine together in the dawn. True brotherhood is not so hard to achieve as some people think."

These vernal court sittings of Louis the Ninth, long remembered in history, were called "the Pleadings at the Palace" or "the Gate." There was the justice of *Parlement* and that of the Provost of Paris, who handled many crimes, but petitioners with long-drawn-out suits and victims of tyranny preferred to come into this garden for "the Justice of the King."

Particularly did Louis welcome into this spot between the grim walls, so lovely it seemed indeed a sanctuary, the lowly and the poor. With him they came first. The visiting princes now had to wait on a crook-backed, bow-legged tiller of the soil with deep gashes showing through the rags, as he crawled on the carpet where he would have kissed the King's foot had not Louis raised him up. The foreigners, however, were glad enough to attend. Would not he, the simplest and the greatest man in the world, render them the most unbiased justice? Were not the very terms of the treaty which they had come to discuss, and to which he had already agreed, astonishingly generous?

So, coldly studying him nonetheless, they watched Louis as with trembling mouth he looked down on the serf whom he called "my poor child." Then those gentle, vision-seeing eyes blazed—now at the landowner who had wielded the lash and whom the sergeants of the guard brought in. The justice dealt out to this cruel offender was not light, that to the poor serf a healing balm. Louis was continually freeing thousands of them in his domains.

The English princes, though they expected to fare so well, still did not understand him. They were baffled by, and a little suspicious of, him. At Taillebourg and Saintes, in two fierce battles two days running, in which the battle-ax swinging down from his great height had told mightily, he had badly trounced the English and the rebel nobles. Then came a most extraordinary thing. In the hour of victory he had turned back to the English some of the spoils he had won, together with land around Perigord and Limousin (which was to add a word to our modern vocabulary) which his own grandfather had wrested from them. Angrily his council and generals had protested.

"We marvel, sire, that you should thus generously give to the English so great a slice of your realm and acres which your ancestors fought for and won. If this is logical and right should you not go the whole way and return to them every region of France which they have ever invaded?"

"Milords," Louis had replied, then as almost always keeping his patience, "it is not that the English have legal claim to these acres.

I hand them over not for any claim binding on me, but to breed love between my own children and those of the King of England, all being, as you know, blood cousins."

So Louis had smiled and gone his own sweetly stubborn way. Perhaps on this point the council and the grand constable of France had greater earthly caution, if they were not so heavenly wise as he. The liberality did not breed that cousinly love Louis intended. As much as the wilfulness and vanity of the beauteous Queen Eleanor who had gone over to England, his nobly-motivated policy bred later wars between the kinsmen.

That is one way of looking at it. For another, Louis had shown shrewdness. If he did not insist on gaining all he might have had, by a later treaty he secured from England Maine, Anjou, Normandy, Poitou, and Touraine. So his quixotic way paid Caesarian dividends. And he had gained a point in feudal law since, in accepting the returned provinces, English Henry must now do him homage.

"Besides," he had added to his dismayed generals, "as it now stands, Henry is not my liegeman at all. If I turn over to him these lands, he, the King of England, will owe lealty to France and to me, as the King of France."

This was not too prophetic foresight. Feudalism was on its way out. Those feudal as well as the cousinly ties were soon to be sundered.

But this must be remembered: slightly mixed as may have been his motives, his millennial idealism was a far, far greater factor than any opportunism or political shrewdness. He longed truly for love not enmity between individual rivals and neighbouring nations. He wanted a policy to be right, not merely profitable. To Spain and to other countries he had been as amazingly decent as he had been to England.

The feudal practice of settling disputes by bloody duels he had tried to reduce, if he could not quite stamp it out. For checks he had established the king's truce, and a forty days' cooling-off period, seven centuries before modern parliaments would try that method in labour disputes. A fight, he said, did not necessarily or invariably determine justice. Unhappily the Davids did not always win against the corrupt Goliaths. He tried to extend to the royal throne the same high morality that he imposed upon the baronies and duchies. The reforms he was establishing among the little land units he endeavoured to establish among the great kingdoms too. He was the first of all kings really to want to buttress kingly rule with moral power. Alfred the Great had tried it in a smaller way; others like Albert the Good of Belgium would follow his example. Few have been very energetic and consistent about it. But there is no doubt that he established the prestige of the kings of France so that the glamour of the throne shone out in distant generations even when the incumbent was not a monarch after Louis' own heart. And there is little more doubt that in showing the world what the ideal king might be he made later generations remain satisfied with kinghood, expecting all the time that another Saint Louis might come to reign in their lands.

Knowledge of his spirit, his aims, warmed Blanche's heart as she looked down on the foreigners advancing with their heralds toward him. In this son, the then greatest man in the world, her lessons, her prayers, her hopes, her battles had borne magnificent fruit. Never did mother, never did woman enjoy greater vicarious delight. His career was but an extension of hers since she had come over the Pyrenees on the little donkey's back. Her maxims, principles, piety, battles against the nobles, abounding charity, utter belief in God were being intensified in him, although without her fierceness and the occasional sharpness and asperity which she showed in spite of all her beauty and charm.

She remembered, too, that other occasion so astounding to all of his court who witnessed it, when he had patched up a bitter quarrel between two factions of the nobles against whom his mother had fought so hard. Then the Constable of France had indeed been wild.

"Why, sire, do you not let them fight it out? So you would let them weaken and impoverish each other. Now they will join forces and turn on you."

"On the contrary," Louis had explained it in his charming, patient, adamant, and sometimes maddening way. "If they should see I was willing to let them fight it out when I might stop them, they would believe I did it for purposes of my own. It is then that they would stop fighting each other and turn on me."

Then he had quoted what was really a living law of his life: "Who was it, my friends, that said, 'Blessed are the peacemakers'?"

To their practical minds the worst of it was that never could they detect in the King any smuggery which would have enabled them to circumvent him. He considered others as naturally as men breathe or the sun shines. Of one thing his own people of Paris were sure: The good King Arthur might have been born in Brittany. But he was living now in Paris.

This home reputation did not prevent some of the visiting princes and envoys from being suspicious of him, even as they brought to him their own quarrels. They trusted him and they didn't trust him. One of the chief delights in history lying in finding parallels in different scenes and ages, it should not take one too violently out of the mediaeval mood of that garden assize to apply a sentence of twentieth-century slang to the attitude of those thirteenth-century cynics—it fits so—"What's his racket?"

It was odd how when all the royalties of Europe chose lions, leopards, unicorns, and clawed and combative animals for their symbols, Louis had taken three simple flowers. They of England, with the lions on their heralds' tabards, now advanced in their toes-out, high-stepping, lordly English way but their eyes, glancing right and left, showed an ordinary cat-like caution. They were followed by the yellow and scarlet envoys of Spain, the furred ones of Denmark. Invariably when they came in turn to the royal carpet and listened to his incisive interrogations, his weighing sentences, and calming pronouncements, they all went away somewhat as the Pharisees had left the Temple after trying to bait Him Whom this Saint followed.

So through all this morning before the fateful one on which he would leave her perhaps forever, the queen mother sat in her window a little tired, not so much in her tireless body as in her heart. Seldom did she take her eyes off this son of whom she was inordinately proud. It was the sin of which she most often unburdened herself in the confessional. But what mother would not have been exultant as she saw those of humble and those of lordliest estate, from far distant lands, waiting there among the roses and the rasps, for the one man in all the world who could settle their petty hedgerow and their grand national quarrels.

As if mindful of what the coming separation might mean to them both, often he would look up at her—the merely spiteful said, for cue. Each time one would wonder afresh at that slender height of him. And when he removed that most unroyal-looking old hat, letting the summer breeze play with his receding and thinning hair, one could remark afresh too how well his character was carried out in his face, all its lovableness, its gentleness supported by those strong planes. The visitors from overseas often glanced from one to the other. Well they might. It was not often if ever in history that one could see so remarkable and complementary a mother and son. In that high carved Spanish chair, in the reflection of the lights from the precious things in the apartment behind her, she would have been an alluring subject for a painter that morning, and for the psychologist at any time: those fathomless dark eyes in the unfading camelia face, now brooding in religious meditation, now calculating matters of state; her figure which at sixty her prodigious maternity had not perceptibly harshened; her unconsciously regal and imperious pose from which she unbent so easily when she looked down on the poor beaten serf. So delicate looking yet strong, austere yet passionate in piety and love for her son, cool to the point of frostiness at times, with great charm for such men as touched the affairs of Louis. Most admirably jealous *for* her son and her religion, most reprehensibly jealous *of* her daughter-in-law.

She was the one fly in the ointment, poor Margaret of Provence, whom, in 1234, Louis had married in the cousin cathedral of Notre Dame, Sens. A great catch she had been considered, being one of the four daughters of the Count of Provence, all of whom married sovereigns. Had it not been for Margaret, life for Blanche, with her son, even in this grim palace would have been idyllic, especially since now he had brightened up the pile for her. It was a morbid and an unfortunate triangle. And Margaret too had her parts. She bore him about the same number of children as Blanche had borne Louis little brothers and sisters—thirteen. And she could show spirit enough. In a galleon at sea, a lady-in-waiting had deposited a filmy gown—queens as well as peasants those days often slept naked—too near the night light in her cabin. It had caught fire. The lady screamed. But Queen Margaret had leapt up naked as she was, and had carried the flaming cloth stuffs out of the door and to the rail, flinging them overboard and into the waters, to the admiration of the crew who had had no orders like those given the citizens of Coventry.

The palace household might have been happier, and it would have been better for Louis if he had been a trifle less filial and a little more uxorious. But—it was one of the faults of a great and good king—he paid little attention to any ideas Margaret might have. And—it was one of the few unadmirable things about a most admirable woman—Blanche got into the habit of constantly criticizing the poor queen. She would even call Louis away from *têtes-à-têtes* with his wife. So far did this incomprehensible mother-in-law's interference go that she ventured to detach him even from the queen when she was brought to bed of a child. Then Margaret, poor lady, rebelled. She forgot her royal dignity and like any slum woman screamed and shouted. Deliberately she put on a scene. For once she won. Louis went back to her. That display helped a little to clear the royal atmosphere. Never afterwards were Louis or Blanche so completely oblivious and inconsiderate.

There was still, of course, some domestic duelling. Margaret had often chided him for that plainness of dress for which he was noted. Once she begged him, if he loved her at all, to don raiment equal in quality to the fine silks and ermine and jewels she wore. He had agreed. Pleased, she had turned away, when he grasped her by the arm.

"Wait! Turn-about is fair play. I will appear tonight in royal

raiment like any butterfly, and you will appear attired simply, as
I am."

Chagrined, she left. No more than any commoner wife could she
change her husband's sartorial habits. He had a humour which some
called wintry. Others said it had a quality like fine dry wine. It was
too dry that day for the queen.

He had replied on a higher plane when bantered by De Joinville
(faithful retainers like old favoured housekeepers sometimes take
liberties) on a particularly uninspiring outfit from the court tailor:
"I prefer my extravagance in charity rather than in dress." This was
true. His abbeys, his blind, his poor were the reasons for the frequently meagre board in the royal household as well as for his near-
shabby wardrobe. It was a noble parsimony.

Still Queen Margaret, despite her artificial love of dress and display, had helped him with her reasonableness when he had been
exhausted from devotions more intense even than his mother's, and
his usually superb common sense appeared to have deserted him.
Once, after a prolonged night vigil, he had even proposed that he
become a monk, she a nun.

"A monk," she had replied, "does much, God bless him, for God's
glory. But as for yourself, is it not apparent that you can do more
for Him as well as for your people as a sovereign ruling over and
moving among your many subjects than as a solitary, alone in your
cell?"

Margaret was not in or near the garden that morning. It was
always Blanche who was on hand or at his side. It was a pity that
Louis and his queen were incompatible, that the three should not
have gotten on. Two were truly great and noble people ninety-eight
per cent of the time and Margaret was really a very nice and competent person. But even at court, triangles of any sort rarely work
out. Mothers-in-law, though illustrious queens, should not dwell
under the honeymoon roof even though it be that of a palace. The
situation is quite as bad as in a cottage.

The proceedings in the garden were now drawing to a close. The
foreign nobles, pacified and making pleased obeisances to the king,
were withdrawing to go to the hotels assigned to them in the city.
A dark vinegary duke had agreed to restore expropriated lands to the
prior in miniver. Two barons whose swords had been drawn were
swearing eternal friendship. Two shepherds, bandaged from blows
from each other's crooks because of a pasturage feud, had their arms
around one another. So in this vernal court, amidst the flight of
butterflies and wasps and winged things, the petal fall of the plum

trees and the pears, the pungency of thyme and rue, the fragrance of roses and lilies, there came these judgments that might have been handed down in our first garden by the four rivers of Paradise. Each day, visiting violent men were astonished by these bloodless triumphs of personal integrity, naturalness, and the love for his brethren of a great king who happened to be a thoroughly good man.

The king now rode out under the garden arch with some of the abbots who had come to the "Pleadings." There were a host of abbeys which he had founded within or near Paris walls, Saint Anthony of Paris, Grey Friars at Saint Cloud, Célestins by the *quais,* one at green Longchamps, two dedicated to his mother at Melun and Pontoise, a high one on Montmartre, lovely Saint Martin in the Fields, the "Brethren of the Bag" by Saint Germain, the "White Mantles" near the Temple, and many others, all of which had made terrific inroads into his purse. But though the abbots rode part way with him through the city streets, it was not they whom he was going to visit on this his last day before he left for the Crusades. He wanted to see once more, perhaps for the last time, his new fish markets, his holy chapel, his blind men, the minstrels by the bridge, and the Cathedral of Our Lady.

Queen Blanche now started on a housekeeping tour of the palace, of which, though there was a queen consort now, she still felt herself the chatelaine. She wanted particularly to visit the cuisine, to see the head palace cook, the Grand Quex, to make sure that the king would have the things he liked for his last supper. He never bothered much about what he ate, but he was very fond of eels boiled in milk. Great lady and stateswoman though she was, she was as much concerned that he should have these before he left for the Crusades as any twentieth-century mother of a midwestern manufacturing town would be that her son had his home-made apple pie for their farewell meal together, before he sailed to fight overseas.

The palace was a rambling, low, brown-gray pile with creneled ramparts around it, the walls of its buildings narrow-slitted, and with guarding cone towers and a long low parapet wall that served for a river walk along the Seine. And it was the ancestor of the many-annexed pile, the Palais de Justice, which we see there today midway on the Isle of Paris, by the Boulevard du Palais and Money-changers Bridge, still with three ancient towers and many another historic unit in it.

Enclosed then within its outer ward walls were courts, among them that garden, part of which edged out into what we now call the Place Dauphine. In others were many dependencies. As she walked through her own apartment dark with the huge black armoire, rich wood coffers, a high hanging ebony crucifix from Spain; bright with a few precious things, embroidered arras, and in place of the old rushes the new gay carpets, Blanche's aristocratic nose could tell the nature of the industry of each court: the barkish smell of a tanning-vat, the sharp one of a pickling house, the hotly humid one of the court armourer's white-hot steel plunged hissing into the cooling tub, also, unfortunately, the acrid odor of a necessary house improperly placed, and then the wholesome aroma of wheaten bread browning in great ovens, the juicier smell of spitted sizzling roasts mingled with the fragrance of the flowers and herbs of the royal garden.

Running east and west with the river was the great Hall of the Lost Footsteps to which Saint Louis had just given new pillars, royal statues, and gilded stars and his own modest flowers painted. By the river and below were the great high vaulted kitchens and guard-rooms which we still see. Near by and above was his bedroom, and, adjoining, a closet in which he kept a dozen of his favourite books, adorned with emeralds, topazes, and rubies, bright enamel on their vellum or leather covers, curious clasps, and the bright scenes of places like his own garden transferred by the illuminators and minia-turists on the pages within. Ancient palaces and castles might have faulty drains and drafts, but for the hardy soul with a zest for life they were exceedingly colourful, thrummingly active, and vastly in-teresting places to live in.

For Blanche this was the old, ancestral Capetian mansion. She had shivered at it when, a girl bride, she had arrived from her native Spain after the long journey over the Pyrenees. Now she loved it as her own home, not because of her husband but for her son and the familiarity of almost fifty years' usage. This day she walked through it, thinking of housekeeping improvements, like the laying of those carpets in place of the rushes which had had to be sprayed so often with perfume—a wicked economic waste. But also she was mindful of its memories as any chatelaine of the manor-house of an English county-house might be when showing the picture gallery and the ghosts. And well she might be. No palace in the world had had such a long and continuing history, had seen so much glorious and terrible and rousing life. Every room of the place, every yard outside, was layered deep in history. Always there had been, always there would be, changes from sieges and fires, or necessary expansion. But traces of the former life that had been there would always remain in the tower tops, the foundations, the walls, or buried underneath, like the Roman hall which with its black paint, green festooning, and carved ornaments of the time of Christ would be unearthed in the Sainte-Chapelle court-yard by excavators in the nineteenth century.

Everywhere in Paris, traces of remote ages lie side by side with the evidence of the new. In living there one must maintain this parallel view of the past, the present, and the future beyond the period at hand (in this case 1248 when Blanche walks through her son's rooms). So, there will be no violation of mood in passing from one epoch to another. For Paris is the city of continuity if there ever was one. It is the place for looking around in space and time, forward and back, on the moment's notice, at the signal of a suddenly-glimpsed tower or spire or fountain, at the sound of a church-bell, a phrase of *argot*, or a street song of long ago.

So the White Queen was crowded every step of the way by the ghosts. In Saint Symphorien, near the outer ward wall, Saint Denis had been imprisoned. There Eloi had made gold coins for Dagobert. Out of that gate Charles Martel had marched with his battle-ax. Under that arch Charlemagne had come riding and Founder Hugh with his little cape. In this room her great-grandfather-in-law, Fighting Louis the Sixth, had died; in the one next, grandfather-in-law, Louis the Seventh, who had started Notre Dame. From crenels on the wall on which now she walked, Count Eudes had poured boiling lead, stripped from church roofs, on the Normans. From that tower at evening her husband's grandfather, Philippe Auguste, had gazed on his rising city wall. Where Blanche stood, Geneviève had stretched forth her arms, for God's help, to the hills.

And there was an infinity of ghosts to come. In the Hall of the Lost Footsteps, on the great marble table, Fête Dieu revelers would recite their verses, the men of Burgundy would carve up the men of Orléans. In that court, for a diamond necklace De la Motte would be branded; in that room the child Voltaire would read; in a waterside wing Dreyfus would be absolved; over there black Laval, the ill-starred Petain of Verdun would be tried for treason. Two little slips of islets then lay before the prow of the Île de la Cité itself. Later the three would be joined together and on this new-made land, beyond the royal gardens, Molière would be played on an outdoor stage; Madame Roland would go to school; Henry of Navarre, Berenger, Anatole France would dine. Her son's very bedroom would become drenched in historic memories. The handful of precious books he loved would multiply into the five million of the great Bibliothèque Nationale over on the Rue Richelieu. The bedroom would become first the council-chamber into which Louis the Fourteenth would stride, cockily announcing that he himself was the State, then the Revolutionary court in which a queen, one more of the long line of alien queens with alien accents like her own, would be cruelly tried. In a cell near the grand kitchens her son had just constructed, that same unhappy queen, behind a skirt hung up to shield her from the jailer's eyes, would change to the shift she had saved to go clean to the guillotine. In another cell there, the Girondins would bravely sing out their last night on earth. In the tower at her left, which like the kitchens is still there, grim-mouthed Fouquier-Tinville would each night make out his bloody list of the tumbril passengers for the next dawn.

From the ramparts for a moment, before going down into those kitchens to give the Grand Quex the menu for the evening meal, Blanche surveyed her son's capital which he was to leave for so long.

The city was an irregular pudding-shaped circle, half a mile wide at best, almost five miles around its outlining city walls. It was slashed by the shining river into three slices: the north or Right Bank slice of roofs, on the plain, the Left Bank which included Sainte Geneviève's Hill, which too was within the walls; in between lay the also-walled little slice of island with the palace, twenty churches, and the Cathedral.

Out of that five miles of wall rose a hundred towers. Within the walls of these slices, the big ones north and south, the little one encircled by the silver of the river, was a fascinating jumble: high fortresses at east and west gates and at the bridge-heads. Houses crowding the bridges too. Nobles' mansions rising painted and escutcheoned and turreted. Clusters of abbey settlements with bits of orchard and garden green perking up the uniform grey. A snarl of twisting streets. Without-rhyme-or-reason-leaning blocks of high-up tenements. And enough needle spires pricking the blue to turn Paris into a fascinating giant pincushion, with the two just-finished Cathedral towers like a blessing over all.

One hundred and twenty-five thousand citizens were thus cramped and yet happily belted in. Their songs, dances, street cries, love-making, even their brawls showed how happily they enjoyed their picturesque congestion.

So much water had flowed under that bridge since the Romans passed over it, since she herself had come over the hills, the bride of a dozen years, to marry a boy of a baker's dozen and to bear him a baker's dozen children, including the one worth all the rest to her. She turned her steps when she saw him riding over the bridge below for his farewell tour of the city. Then suddenly there broke forth from the palace, everywhere pouring through arrow slits and windows, a great chorus of song. It came from no church canons but from feathered songsters. When Saint Louis had started to expand and beautify his palace, she also did her part. With her own white hands she had hung gold cages in all the rooms of the palace, and in them had placed birds of every clime and colour: nightingales from the Rhine, bullfinches from Provence, bulbuls of Persia, azure, emerald, yellow and crimson minstrels from Africa and the Aegean. Like their melodious counterparts of today in the bird markets of the Quai de la Mégisserie, just across the river from where Blanche stood that afternoon, and of the birdstalls of the Rue de la Cité where Abélard once walked with Heloise, these songsters seemed to express in notes what her son's new church, Sainte-Chapelle, expressed in its exquisite deep-dyed colours. So it always seemed to Saint Louis of the high heart, and the child's, when he heard the songs of these birds of his White Queen Mother.

IV

Saint Louis visits his New City Hall, his Recently Erected Markets, and reads to his Blind Men. . . . He sets up Just Officials throughout his Kingdom, builds Colleges, and Violet and Crimson Sainte-Chapelle for the Crown of Thorns. . . . Things of God and those of Caesar. . . . The Great Provost of Paris, Etienne Boileau. . . . New Blood of the Guilds, and a Rising Mercantile Aristocracy. . . . No Mediaeval Merchant sells Shoddy, gives False Weight, or kicks his Servants. . . . A Golden Age of Labour. . . . Louis feasts Every Night, wherever he is, Four Hundred Beggars. . . .

1248 A.D.

HILE BLANCHE WAITED, NOT ONLY TO GIVE HER SON HIS favorite dishes but to discuss the new plot for a college a Robert de Sorbon wanted to build on the hill, and the challenge of the Church by the German Emperor and other delicate matters, and what she should do in his absence, Louis proceeded to say good-bye to his Paris. Etienne Boileau, the provost who had done much for the town, the quiet but brilliant architect Pierre de Montereau, the Grand Constable and the Sire de Joinville, who was never far from the king's side either at court or in stormy battle and who so often wore green, went with him. As he proceeded over the historic north bridge between the shops of this lively little water settlement, the merchants and the gossips from the windows between the half-timbers above hailed him with delight. There was no doubt that he was a people's monarch.

He proceeded on foot. Often he went about town without any escort excepting one sergeant. He said that in that way he got to know his people better. In this he was like another king, two Louises farther on, with a few Philippes and a John and a Charles or so in between—Louis the Eleventh. He was like him too because they both consolidated France and both were inconspicuous dressers. But there the similarity ended. The eleventh Louis was a sinister as well as a shabby figure. Saint Louis, in spite of the little the court tailors did for him, was a truly royal and benignant monarch. The two Louises were like the obverse and reverse sides of a medal, the one shining, the other dark.

Walking over the paving with which that conqueror and innovator, Philippe Auguste, his grandfather, had replaced the old Roman cobbles, he came to the old Chapel of the Innocents, then to the new markets, Les Halles, which his grandfather had also put up but to which he had just made valuable additions. With that continuity which is both the wonder and the charm of Paris, these markets with later expansions would supply Paris with its food for seven centuries. Where mediaeval housekeepers purchased butter and eggs from the farms roundabout and fish from the Seine for their mercer husbands who let down their counters out of the house walls themselves, modern *concierges* would come with black bags and baskets for cheese, snail, and the eternal *veau* and *haricots verts* for twentieth-century tourists and students at the university which Saint Louis was just then founding.

In the new commodious and airy sheds he moved among the white-smocked hucksters, ensanguined butchers, silver-scaled fishmongers, with friendly, not condescending, greetings, as any small-town mayor might when visiting his constituents, though Saint Louis needed no votes. Once he suddenly stopped at a suspicious-looking place and asked Etienne Boileau to have the weights tested, so insistent was he on maintaining standards throughout his kingdom. At others, he smilingly inspected the great tubs of deep mottled-green *langoustes,* or lobsters, the knots of vividly green *aiguilles,* or eels, of which he was so fond, or the vermilion gills of a fish struggling in his hand, praising the stall keeper when he slitted his wares to show the firm pink-and-white flesh.

He had so many calls, official and friendly, to make these last few hours that he hurried on now—his head six inches over the tallest of the little band of celebrities with him, his long stride ever in advance of theirs—to the eleventh-century Priory of Saint Martin in the Fields, just outside the north loop of the city wall, to which De Montereau, the architect of the group, had just added a fine refectory. Louis wanted to be sure that the priory books were in order before he left for the Holy Land.

The accounts in abbeys under his immediate patronage were usually well kept. But there was a deal of trouble elsewhere. Books too often would not balance. Frequently the outside auditing, required by church law, was forgotten. Mistakes were usually due to carelessness or to absorption rather than cupidity. Sometimes, of course, a lay brother would pilfer from the abbey stores; but that was hardly dealt with. Second offences brought excommunication with staff and lighted candles. The pope once ordered a monk found dead with money in his bed buried in a dunghill.

Now it must not be inferred that Louis was antagonistic to, or interfered too much with, the abbeys—he built too many for that— or to the Church. He did give that uncannily wise suggestion that certain abbey petitioners settle their feud with song. Abuses of authority he checked. When some prelate was too free with excommunications for minor infractions he would reason with him. But that disposition whose kindliness was so notable did not always prevent resentment among the more narrow. Never in the heart of Louis. He recognized that the bigoted as well as the frail would be found in the ranks of the Church quite as they had been in Christ's pioneer band. Had not Judas kept his mind too much on the money-bags and later betrayed Him, only to go out and hang himself? Had not Peter denied Him, not to go out to self-destruction but to be transformed into the Rock of the Church? Was there not even petty striving for priority among them, by Galilee, before they came into the true humility of the Lord? Louis had learned that very early.

But though many of the over-ecclesiastical ecclesiastics bore him ill will and libelled him, Louis, with his love for mankind, never fought them. Sometimes he even forbore to claim his royal rights for the sake of peace.

"I cannot but remember," he said, "all the mercies God and Mother Church have shown me. I prefer to yield some of my sovereign rights rather than to start contention within the fold."

In a more important dispute than those about excommunications, equity, and auditing, in the greatest over-all quarrel of the age between Frederick the Second and the popes, Louis had shown wise statesmanship. Frederick, ruler of what was left of the old Roman Empire, was trying with one hand to hold down the German princes, with the other to control all Italy, even as he reached out to take over Sardinia and Sicily. This astigmatic, bald, red-bearded monarch was widely read, cultured, hot in his loves for women, calculating in his politics, the founder of the University of Naples, the keeper of an extensive harem, now the respecter, again the challenger of the Church. In bishops' elections he interfered, incited others against the popes, and through his extension of his power down through the Italian boot, hemmed in the little domain reserved for the popes, the Papal States.

Now all of the five walking over the cobbles, through the mire, between the bright houses, on the Rue Saint-Martin—the minivered provost, the green chevalier, the thoughtful architect, the labour leader in sober attire, the King in his unroyal-looking hat—were of one mind in the matter. This masterful red-beard had his side but he should not have belled the Church. Occasional prelates might be ambitious—had not John and James and their mother, until they had been enlightened of Our Lord, wanted those first places in high Heaven? But the Church was not to be blamed for that any more than a good ship for having taken on an inept pilot, particularly when there had been so many great ones to steer the ship. And the great, the magnificent, the true and heavenly bark that was the Church, they agreed, always, in spite of its crews, steered by the stars, kept to its celestial course. Again, that the Church, though the Kingdom it represented was invisible, should have a capital, some rank and dignity, a little domain, was only decent. And since the kingdoms of this world ran their affairs through diplomats and treaties, when not at war, it was only practical that the Church should have representatives, instruments of diplomacy, to negotiate with these earthly leaders, to make treaties, to have that status that would enable her to look out and arrange for the safety of her flocks in other lands when trouble threatened. If, said Saint Louis, there was thought to be some pomp in all this, why, the courts of the world had enough to spare for Mother Church. Besides, such majesty as there was in Rome was more than offset by the humility, the poverty, of thousands of poor friars and parish priests and nuns walking the hard way for Christ.

And always there had been the grand underlying conception of the founders in Jerusalem and throughout the Near East and Rome, of the great leaders like Augustine, that though Caesar's things were Caesar's and God's God's, Caesar's—the world—could only make any ultimate sense, win out to any order and peace, by adopting Christ's precepts and following His ways. The Church, went on Saint Louis, was the mystical body of Christ projected throughout the world. Who, then, was better fitted than the head of the Church, and those ordained by, trained in, and devoted to His teachings, to advise about the practical application of His teachings in this world?

So he had tried, with all the wisdom and tact and friendliness he possessed, to keep the audacious little red emperor from encroaching too far on the proper papal power. But if he was as loyal a son as Mother Church ever had, he was also ruler of France. And he showed a little of that independence in ecclesiastical relations that rulers of France have always displayed; a few, like Philip the Fair and Napoleon, bullying the popes to the point of barbarity, others, like Saint Louis, using a wiser discretion. In his dealings with the Pope, in his interviews with his legates, in all his correspondence he endeavoured to see that the sovereign rights of France were not jeopardized by too sweeping a victory over the temporal power in the neighbouring empire, the results of which might extend to France. It was a conscientious middle course that this saintly and sincere king took in that tumultuous age. His prestige as a great statesman and king, peacemaker and warrior too, had helped to keep the quarrel from splitting Europe wide open.

The royal highway they took, though narrow, was the old Roman artery running north and south through Paris and the Île de France. Its continuation on the Left Bank was the Rue Saint-Jacques which ran, as it still runs, over Sainte Geneviève's Hill. Traffic in the Roman Imperial period could go from Orléans up, over that hill, the bridges and the island, and by this Rue Saint-Martin, to the north. In times of fêtes or triumphs it was gay and hung with banners. Even on this normal morning, though dubious in spots underfoot, it was bright at the sides. For Saint Louis had started, not a "clean-up week," such as modern towns advertise, but a redecorating decade. As he refurbished the grim old palace, reconstructed or built anew many an abbey, reared a new city hall and the glowing Sainte-Chapelle, the householders of the better quarters repainted every half-timber and corbel and the inn signs. All their corner *tourelles* and towers, grilles and brackets were runningly alive with fascinating creatures of the earth, legend, or their riotous imaginations. And traffic was sometimes congested as passers-by paused to study the details of the picture-books into which these house fronts, like the Cathedral, had been transformed.

The Rue Saint-Martin, however, was not as well sanitized as it was decorated, though Louis was adding drains, sluices, fountains, and running water everywhere he could. And some of the students, the housekeepers too, still showed a gypsy carelessness. From upper attic windows where, not aware that the king and his friends were passing underneath, they swept, or lunched on various viands, often clots of dust, or cheese and melon rinds, with handfuls of cherry pits were tossed down, to land on illustrious shoulders, making still more unroyal-looking the old hat of the king. This did not annoy him; he simply glanced up at the quaint, gabled heaven from which the strange shower came and laughed as he brushed himself off.

They rode through the north gate, under the high arch of the gate-house, under the iron-toothed portcullis, and over the Paris-encircling moat into the flowery meadows and the *enceinte* of Saint Martin's Priory. One with that parallel vision of history (which all should have to enjoy and understand it) should know that in that priory today, instead of cells and crucifixes and *prie-dieux,* there is a steam automobile which was built in France long before Ford and even the Declaration of Independence; Ader's 1893 plane—before the Wrights—is there together with the Blériot over-water one of 1907 and a host of fascinating historic objects. Entering De Montereau's just-finished, magnificently vaulted and columned refectory (which still stands) Saint Louis, with the prior and some of the chapter, in the rich light from the stained glass, went over the huge books with their calligraphy as exquisite as any carvings in the hall. Rapidly he turned the stiff pages, his eye running over the items: bottles and bees-wax, marjoram and haricots, towels for the monks' lavatories, cloth purchased at the Lendit and Saint Germain fairs, bundles of fagots, costs of charcoal, iron, and such conventual etceteras, with the most prodigious item of all, alms.

Returning toward the palace, he came into one of the few little open spaces which seemed to have been dug out of the packed-in masses of dwellings before important places like Sainte-Chapelle, the Cathedral, and here, the city hall. Quite small then, and hemmed in by lines of those pinched-up, peak-gabled, timber-crossed houses, it was not called the Place de l'Hôtel de Ville, as its enlargement is now, but the Place de Grève. Grève was for the gravel of the river strand on which it bordered; and later the term would be applied to the French labour strike because so many workers were accustomed to gather there. On this Place de Grève many historic and horribly ingenious hanging, tearing-apart, disembowelling executions would take place, down to modern times.

Nor was this new city hall known as the Hôtel de Ville as is now its palatial successor with its rows of pennoned knights on the roof. This pioneer hall, of which you will often read in mediaeval chronicles, was known as *"La Maison aux Pilliers."* It was a curious sequence of big pillars, with a long row of weird gables with stucco and diamond panes above. It bordered the square's east side. On the other three were drawn up irregular companies of those carved and painted mediaeval house-fronts. And here Louis entered in to see that not only this little city hall, the "House of Pillars," but his greater house of Paris, and the still greater one of France, should be in order before he set out with his mighty battle-ax to fight for Christ's Tomb. There was no one in the kingdom better equipped to take care of, or to assist the White Queen in looking out for, his capital than the great Provost Etienne, or Stephen, Boileau.

Now this term, *"Prévôt,"* or Provost, was to have many meanings which have been none too clearly explained in the hosts of historical novels of the Middle Ages. The *Prévôt des Marchands,* for example, selected from the membership of the Merchants' Guild, saw to the policing of the city and the river, collected taxes, and set those uniformed patrols Saint Louis saw everywhere that morning guarding the city gates and all the sections between the hundred towers of the city wall. As for the Provost of Paris, this famous Boileau, he was, after the King himself, the great royal judge of the city, sometimes the executant of that justice as well. The Royal Council often advised the King on affairs of state; the *Chambre des Comptes,* the kingdom's auditors, helped with the accounts; the *Parlement,* not then a body of law-makers but judges, assisted in the administration of justice. But Louis the Ninth was the Solon, the great law-giver of France, and Provost Boileau was a most excellent adviser.

Louis wanted to go over the appointee lists, the rounds of the new executive ladder he had framed for the nine great provinces: the *bailli* in each, superior trial and appeal judge, who too acted as the King's viceroy when the reigning noble of the province was away; the seneschal who exacted military service; the provincial provost, inferior but important judge; the mayors of the towns. Each, Louis had made solemnly to swear that he would not be guilty of simony, that is, the selling to bidders of offices, of taking bribes, or of nepotism, the giving of posts to relatives. If Louis' prestige had influenced all Europe, certainly it had raised very high the standards of justice and administration at home. Few appointees ever disappointed him. France, while he lived, saw a reign of law it was not to know again for many generations.

However, he was not idealistic to the point of the impractical. He had sent *Enquêters,* or inquirers, into the provinces to see that none of these sworn office-holders forgot those oaths. These overseers Louis too selected from disinterested groups, the Dominicans and Franciscans. He had watched these two new orders which had been founded in his own century and which were, like himself, to bring great glory to it; and he knew that their fresh, eager and zealous members had, almost invariably then, little thought of worldly advantage. And he, with his mother, had joined the Third, the lay, Order of St. Francis.

And he and Boileau had seen that in the reign of law his capital led the way. The Provost had strained the populace of Paris and had seen that the dregs, the sharpers, conies, pickpockets had been tossed out. And prostitutes did not infest the streets. But Louis wanted to be merciful. He said that many of these magdalens were ignorant, simple, and young. Men as well as women had a hand in such matters. Men should not go scot-free. So they had written into the code an ordinance that required that any who gave the prostitute a lodging, so that he might profit by her trade, should be fined a year's rent. And Louis gave large sums to his foundation, the House of Filles-Dieu or

Daughters of God, the reclaimed penitent prodigals of the Paris pavements. Nothing he ever did pleased his mother more.

The Provost now had set on a massive table before this King of moderate habits a little lunch, or *déjeuner,* of cheese, a long loaf, fruit, and a little wine. The sun shining through the stained panes, and the glass of wine which the King duly watered, cast bright lozenges and discs of dancing colour on the table, on the dark attire of the King and on the great *Book of Trades* which he had propped up beside him so that he might read as he ate. It was a very practical work and no book of the Middle Ages, not even the *Romaunt de la Rose,* written on the Rue Saint-Jacques, or Joinville's life of his friend and King, was more important. Provost Boileau had compiled it, and huge, cumbersome as it was, it was nonetheless a wonderful mirror into which one might look over the King's shoulder and see reflected the fascinating world of the mediaeval workmen.

In the earlier story of the Cathedral we watched the unfolding of the guilds, the merchants' and the crafts', in greater detail than can be given here. But this much at least should be ever kept in mind as our eyes, with the King's, run down the regiments of paragraphs in the copyists' script, which was a work of art in itself.

In the Dark and very early Middle Ages, the feudal *seigneur* had owed lealty, revenues, and military service to his superior lord, duke, count, or king, but in turn, over his domain, his villages, the chief town and the farms roundabout, he had exercised an almost absolute sway. In the twelfth century this power, through violent revolution, even more through peaceful and natural evolution, was seeping away. Workmen, smiths, armourers, masons, carpenters, weavers, tailors, and other artisans for a long time had lived in the castle wards or in the village nestling around the castle, and had worked only for milord. As these hamlets evolved into more sizeable towns, these workers began to branch out. They continued to work for milord, but added new customers from among the residents of the growing towns. Sometimes, nobles with an investment sense helped the enterprising workers by advancing them money to buy raw materials or by buying these themselves, thus becoming titled business men on the side.

But gradually the more aggressive and capable of the artisans began to get out from under the seigneurial employment and supervision. They set up independent establishments, hired corps of workers with less initiative and used them practically as retainers as well as workers, built fine mansions, hired guards, put them in showy livery, decked themselves out in rich apparel, adopted insignia, and flaunted banners. So a new order, a mercantile aristocracy, a Four Hundred of burgesses, was evolved. Gorgeous as butterflies sometimes, they still worked hard, on a higher level, in running their businesses and attending to civic duties. Meantime their bejewelled and beservanted womenfolk made the most of it.

Then their ranks closed for a front against the feudal *seigneurs*, though they took in with themselves the nobles who had turned commercial, and they formed strong Merchants' Guilds in every city of size. Their codes, standards, morals were noted in that earlier story, together with their charities such as the quaint one of doling out to the unfortunate, quart for quart, as much wine as they themselves consumed at banquets. And they had other provisions more salutary. But these Merchants' Guilds had teeth. Each prominent member had, in his armed retainers, a little private army of his own. All were employing artisans in numbers ever increasing with the city's prosperity. These too could be armed and drilled on the side, and were. Together they mustered quite a force for the inevitable conflict with their one-time employers, the old feudal *seigneurs*.

Naturally these lords, sometimes of ungovernable tempers, and always of pride strengthened by centuries of tradition and possession, would not take this lying down. There were gory conflicts like that with Gaudry the Gaudy at Laon. But more often than not the Merchants' Guild came out on top. Their task was easier, since the kings, seeing in these merchants' associations fine checks for the nobles who were forever bedevilling them and encroaching on their royal power, helped the guilds. Of course, it was in the name of the commune that the city would be taken over. But it was all one and the same. Commune and Merchants' Guild were practically synonymous. Lists of the members, of the officers of the two, were often identical.

They were more powerful in the north of France. In this era there were three kinds of cities that rode the wave toward more civic freedom. The "Franchised Town" (*Ville Franche*), found in many parts of France, had won its charter through king's award, by wresting it from the noble, or by more peacefully lending him mortgage money to pay his debts or to go on a Crusade. Bankrupt later, he could only liquidate by granting the charter. And this gave the citizen much liberty, in particular limiting the taxes and military service owed the *seigneur*. In the "Council City" (*Ville Consulaire*) of the south, the burghers elected their council but allowed nobles and bishops to sit in it. In the third city type, the "Commune Town" of the north, these dignitaries were left out in the cold. The Merchants' Guilds, through their alter egos, the communes, controlled these northern cities pretty thoroughly.

This town Paris which, at that luncheon, was the main concern of the King and Provost Etienne, was not a commune but a royal city.

Still, it had its magnificently carved and decorated Merchants' Guild-hall by the Seine, directly across from the White Queen's observation post that morning. And one could see everywhere evidences of the Merchants' Guild activities. There were so many Matthews of their body tax-gathering in all the wards of the city, collecting imposts at the massive city gates, on the *quais,* on the wharves from the heavy-nosed boats from Rouen, Britain, Cornwall. In every watch their *échevins,* sheriffs and under-sheriffs, stationed the sentries or held inspections on the different sections of the city wall between the hundred guarding towers.

These over-all Merchants' Guilds were both just and unjust stewards. Through their upbuilding of the commerce of the cities they brought wide employment and many comforts to the workers. They did not, however, favour the artisans' forming their own craft guilds. But the Merchants' Guilds could no more stop these craft unions than the old haughty *seigneurs* had been able to stop the merchants. Now these craft guilds were flourishing everywhere, especially in Paris, where they had taken over whole sections, each craft settling in a quarter of its own where all of that trade might work and manufacture and sell, have their shops and their houses too, and enjoy life with their families and apprentices.

It was the codes, ordinances, customs, of these crafts that Provost Etienne Boileau had woven into this revealing *Book of Trades,* whose giant pages were not only filled with this raw stuff of romance but were bright with the very colour of it, though he, conscientious man, anxious only to make a utilitarian book, was not aware how vivid a one he would leave behind him for us.

And these were a few of the recordings—some like our modern labour provisions, others, unhappily for us, so unlike our own—which Louis' eye ran down in both delight and haste, for he had to hurry if he was to see his old blind men and hear his minstrels:

First, Boileau had set down in his introduction his motive for com-piling this big book: "Recently there have been sold to foreigners visiting our Paris articles that were not as honestly made and of as good quality as they should have been."

Seldom in the history of trade and commerce has there been such care for aliens. *Caveat emptor* was no motto of mediaeval Paris. It must be remembered too that the statutes Etienne gathered together were, most of them, not of his own contriving. They had been willingly self-imposed by these craftsmen's guilds, the mediaeval unions. All that he had to do half of the time was but to collect and set down.

King Louis was smiling now at another: Such and such trades had to be "worked on the front of the street," that is, in the front of the shops or forges and near the streets, so that all passers-by who cared to look might see what material and workmanship went into the article.

Certain objects, like saddles, cradles, screens, the statues of saints, had to be displayed, to show the solidity of wood and leather, before the paint, the crimsons, blues, and gilts, could be applied. There was no such thing as painting over poor jobs.

The standards of the precious metals had to be maintained rigidly. So well were they followed that the goldsmiths of the Quai des Orfèvres, south of the Palace, boasted with justice that "Paris gold is the best in the world."

Purveyors of poor beer and spoilt edibles were severely dealt with. No mediaeval merchant in Paris dared sell shoddy. A candle-maker, the records show, was fined by his own guild for selling a candle that dripped grease on the Saint Gervais altar-cloth. Nor were they forever going to law, either. They took care of their own offenders. An arrow-maker by the Saint Ladre Gate was penalized by his brethren for fitting a bedraggled goose-feather to a shaft. The Brewers' Guild kicked out a member for kicking his pregnant wife. Even the old clo' men around little Saint Merri's asked modest prices from the students for cast-offs. And anyone coming out of the Cathedral from a Sunday mass was apt to see in the window of the Hôtel Dieu, close by, some tailor surlily sewing for the invalids. That was a penalty for spoiling a piece of cloth. On the Quai des Orfèvres, the goldsmiths closed all but one of their shops Sundays, each taking his turn in working on the seventh day. That day's profits entire were turned over to the Hôtel Dieu for a good Sunday dinner for the poor.

Sometimes these fine labour conditions, the fair hours and holidays, astonished English travellers on their way back from the Holy Land or Rome, or entering the famous colleges of the University. They took word of these innovations home, thus paving the way for what was later known as the "English" but was really the "French Week." The humanity of the ordinances baffled the men from over the channel. A master, for example, was required to look out for the hand's training and the soul's welfare of the boy bound to him. And they did not keep their apprentices down. Quite the contrary. They gave them a leg up. Often the apprentice from an indigent home married the boss' daughter—and not the ugly one, either. A poor boy could rise high, those days, in Paris. To have taken, of a Sunday evening, the roof off any painted, half-timbered weaver's house and shop on Rosebush Street, or any saddler's on Rue Sellerie, would have been to see master wife, family, apprentices, sitting around the board in Burns' "Cotter's Saturday Night" fashion.

And women were protected by ordinance from too long hours and too onerous work, those tasks that required endless polishing or too much back work and lifting. It further pleased the king that there was provision for charity chests and security funds, and no one really needed to urge these on the guilds; their contributions were abundant. Also, it was a practice, if not absolutely enjoined, for all self-respecting workers to attend mass. One and all the crafts, after the Cathedral was finished, continued to add canons' stalls, carvings, statues, windows, embroidery, jewels and other lovely things to enhance the beauty of Our Lady's house.

Other paragraphs protected "neighbourhood trade," and prevented "corners." None could go around the country-side with his huge-wheeled wagons and buy up all the geese, ducks, cheese, eggs, and ham in sight. "Because," wrote down Provost Etienne, "the rich might gather all the foodstuffs; there would be nothing left for the poorer; and the rich might charge any prices they liked."

There would have been little need for Theodore Roosevelt's "trust-busting" then. "Alliances" the trusts were called in Saint Louis' time. And merchants and owners could not form these "alliances" to raise prices. They could not form them, either, to lower prices in pioneer Standard Oil fashion, to squeeze competitors out. Nor could the workmen strike forcibly to raise wages or threaten those who were satisfied with working conditions and wages. That is, they could not in Saint Louis' reign. Two generations later, when the tall, handsome, arrogant Philip the Fair, Louis' grandson, came to the throne, this labour-management peace did not prevail. Many rich men had to pay three hundred dollars' fine (a huge sum those days) and spend sixty days in one of the Châtelets, that is, in jail, for forming these "alliances" or trusts.

As a matter of fact, there would have been as little need those days for the pathos of those two social-document novelists, Charles Dickens and Charles Reade, as for Theodore Roosevelt's "trust-busting." They would have found scant material for the pathos of their pens in the streets called "Of the Leather-workers," "Of the Ironmongers," "Of Glass-work," "Of Stone-breaking," and "Of Parchment-making," and in all the craft quarter lanes and passages whose names are still on the walls of the corner houses of the Paris we walk today.

Which does not mean that all industry was an *agape*, or love-feast. The aristocrats of that Burgher Four Hundred could certainly quarrel. But in these cities, under the over-all Merchants' Guild and the vigorous new craft guilds, in this thirteenth century, which was the flood of that glorious Gothic high-tide, there was a wider distribution among the common people of the manna of liberty.

Particularly in Paris, the home town of this benevolent and constructive king, no pickets were needed in that golden age. Then, with employer and employed, one's responsibilities weighed as much as one's rights in the great scale of human values.

What astonishes one sometimes in this code drawn up almost precisely seven centuries ago—in a time too which the unthinking would call backward—is the idealism which breathes through it and which brought it into being. No level was allowed to grab off something for itself. Invariably emphasis is laid as much on the quality of work and material as on the wages and labour conditions. Something like these standards were observed by the old pagan Roman builders until Roman life turned sour under staggering tax burdens, overplusage of slaves and rich and the vanishing of the middle class, emperor worship, luxury, and lust. Later the traditions were resurrected by the eighth- and ninth-century Lombard builders. But never had such idealism been shown as under Saint Louis. Then, in Paris, the trinity of master, worker, customer, was reverenced.

There is always a question about the exact relationship of any great leader to the significant movement of his age. Has he anything to do with the impulsion of that movement? Or does he, being in accord with it, simply mount and skilfully ride the top crest, giving the impression of guiding and directing it? Does the great dictator-conqueror himself clap on the flanks the Four Horsemen of the Apocalypse and send them forth? Or when Evolution unlooses them, does he leap on and stride them, riding them to the amazement of the world and invariably to his own destruction?

Perhaps it was simpler than that? Possibly it was just that there had come to earth one of those rarities, an exceptionally good and an exceptionally able and wise man. God may have sent him to show that the mould had not been lost or cast away.

It was not a long walk to Louis' house of the blind called, because of the number of its inmates, the "Quinze-Vingts"—the "Three Hundred." It was not far from the site where, in the next century, the Bastille would go up and, though the remains of the hospice now lie in the heart of the city, it was then outside the city walls. Fertile farmland lay all about, and the smell of maturing hay, of green growing things came through the arched windows of the hall which Saint Louis entered with his small party.

Though the old pensioners had as fair a measure of happiness as the king's providing of warm clothes, comfortable beds, and good food could bring, often their faces wore the fixed look of the blind which is the more poignant because of their eternal patience. But that look changed to smiles when they heard his step and his cheery, "Hail to all, in God's name."

All who ever accompanied Saint Louis on these visits were amazed to see how quickly and unobtrusively he put them all at their ease. Never were poor beneficiaries and eminent benefactor so nearly on a level. Instead of having them kneel to him, he had them all sitting around him. Instead of offering them a hand to kiss he often laid it on their shoulders, calling many of them by name.

On some visits he sat around the board with them and ate their fare. Once at Royaumont Abbey, when there was a shortage of lay help, he had gone to the kitchens to help carry in the food; and he had emerged with the borders of his mantle wrapped around his wrists and fingers to keep from being burned. In his haste he had done this awkwardly and the edges of the mantle trailed in the gravy.

Those who were too sick to come into the hall he visited in their cells, asking about their little ailments and troubles and appetites until all perceptibly brightened. This attitude of his toward all the world, except the blasphemers and the declared foes of his Lord, Christ, breathes out of a letter which he wrote later to his daughter who had married the King of Navarre:

"Ever keep, my daughter, a heart full of love and kindness for all whom you know or have heard to be sorrowing and unhappy. Help them wherever you can, practically with alms, or with consolation, whichever they most need at the time."

To the steward he observed, when they were alone in his bureau, that the shoes of many seemed worn. They should all have new ones with stout soles. And many hundred ells of *tyreteinne,* a strong cloth made by weaving linen thread on a wool warp, must be purchased. These shoes and the new gowns must be ready before the heavy weather of the autumn set in. And the steward should ask the mercers to give as good material as any they furnished to the folks of the court. He could trust his guildsmen. Just tell them it was for the blind men of the king and they would give as fine workmanship and goods as any they gave the rich.

Before he left, as a last attention to these old men, he drew from a cover his own *Book of Hours* which had been carried by a sergeant. The exquisitely wrought clasps, the precious gems he let them see with their all-seeing fingers. Then sitting among his beloved "Quinze-Vingts," while many crowded at the doors, and raising his voice so that those who lay sick might hear, he read from the great Book in his lap. There in the sun, with the fragrance of the meadows coming through the windows, he read to the old unseeing whiteheads clustered around him the simple yet exalted phrases on the pages decorated like the flowery meadows outside.

Then he left and the old blind men waved him off to his wars. . . .

Two bridges then spanned the north fork of the Seine to the island, the ancient one of Charles the Bald, built in the early 800's, and one two city squares' distance or so up-stream, a temporary affair of wood. The King seemed to like the rumbling thunder of its yielding planks when the heavy trade tumbrils passed over in one of those immemorial rhythms for the ear, which like those for the eye—the flow of the Seine underneath, the flight of the migrating birds above or the circling of those around the Cathedral towers—took one back to the beginning of things. Crossing over this and threading the narrow island streets, he came under the arch into a palace court to gaze up at the loveliest landmark of all he had erected in Paris, which would in distant ages be most closely connected with his name: the little shining Gothic jewel, Sainte-Chapelle, which he had made for the Crown of Thorns.

They came upon it, Louis, De Joinville, his confessor De Châtillon who had joined them, and the quiet Pierre de Montereau who had had the major hand in the designing. It rose up out of that court, and from the grey palace buildings and annexes all around it, like a loftier centre island looming above its ancient storm-beaten fellows, a heavenly beacon with its glowing glass. It might have been a little Mont-Saint-Michel set down in that court.

Inch for inch Sainte-Chapelle had cost more than any shrine in the world from Sancta Sophia on. Forty-thousand *livres tournois,* or, in the currency of Tours. Louis, not a half bad banker for a king, had to some extent stabilized the finances in his kingdom but he could not unify all the currencies in it. Nor, great man though he was, could he keep that *livre* from going down. The *livre,* ancestor of the *louis,* then the franc, was the equivalent then of England's pound, which had a tremendous purchasing power. Between this day when Saint Louis looked up at the fine church of his ordering and that when the Revolutionaries would smash all the royal insignia on it and tear its lead spire down, the livre-louis-franc would depreciate eighty times. And—a later tragedy for the poor tillers of the soil, the toilers up the city streets, to whom the franc meant blood and life—it was to go horribly toboganing further, down through the twentieth-century world wars.

The outlay for this little but tall and shining church was the equivalent of two million pounds or about ten million dollars in the First World War, a much larger sum in the Second. These millions had gone for labour and materials, including the matchless stained glass. All these innumerable panes with the hues deep in their hearts had been made in the pots, fitted together in the designs, and hung on the iron armatures with the little copper wires, by the Atelier of Paris, which had at last surpassed the school of Chartres. A king's fortune beyond that ten million had gone to the goldsmiths who fashioned the little temple-like shrine, with its infinitely delicate fretwork and the gleaming pinnacles, that housed the holy relics within the church. A piece of the True Cross, a Nail from it, the Lance-head, and particles of the Crown of Thorns—it was the most precious collection in the world. Some questioning it, Saint Louis sent his best scholars to investigate the Crown of Thorns. Two Emperors, Baldwin the Second of Constantinople and John de Brienne, the western-chosen King of Jerusalem, declared they were very sure. Baldwin, of course, had much at stake. He had deposited the relics of the Crown of Thorns in the Venetian Treasury as security for a large loan. Never had earthly gold been given such sacred collateral. From this commercialism Saint Louis longed to save it and to give it a beautiful home.

If some dismiss this as wishful if creditably pious thinking on the part of a good and great king, few of the informed are dubious about the genuineness of the piece of the True Cross. The members of the early Church, with their Apostle leaders, would long have kept green the memory of the little eminence on which their Founder died. Perversely, the Romans confirmed this by building a challenge to the Cross, a pagan temple, on that hill. In 326, as we have seen in the story of Julian, Constantine's mother while excavating on Calvary had come on the three crosses, carelessly tossed, in a hollow. The further fortunes of the little pieces of the True Cross (of pine, not Lebanon cedar), of their dispersal to various capitals, their wanderings to Constantinople, Persia, Rome, and all about the Mediterranean, with the testimony of chroniclers, historians, and saints from Ambrose to Sozomen, have been given in their fascinating and convincing sequence in that earlier story.

Often, after the event, Louis and Blanche would speak with shining eyes of the exaltation they had felt when, in 1239, they had ridden to Villeneuve-l'Archevêque, near Sens, to receive the relics and thence had borne them, in a tremendous procession, with banners flying and flowers being strewn, through the Paris gate and into Notre Dame. It was no wonder. They were receiving into their country the most precious souvenirs in all the world, one of which, if not all, had touched His body in the hour of His sacrifice, His tragedy and triumph, in memory of which Notre Dame—all the cathedrals—had been built, and which, even for those not openly acknowledging Him, would change the entire history of the world.

In Notre Dame they rested from 1239 until 1248, when lovely Sainte-Chapelle was complete. Later they would return again to the Cathedral, to lie near the sanctuary, with one fragment of Thorn, after the 1860's, in the great ball on the high *flèche*. Beautiful as was the shrine-chapel Saint Louis made, it was fitting that these mementoes of the Son who had lain under Our Lady's heart should rest in the heart of her great house. At the sanctuary rail, in the proper seasons, they have, through the centuries, been exposed for the adoration of millions from all parts of the world. If it chances that the pieces of the True Cross are the only relics indubitably proved real, that would be enough to kindle the imagination and exalt the soul. And to the others there has accrued a secondary hallowing, an associational sacredness through the adoration of the uncounted hosts of believing souls.

It was Pierre de Montereau, standing with Saint Louis that day, who had transformed Saint Louis' pious wish and his *livres* into that marvel of the Gothic in miniature. It was as though, after Notre Dame in all its majesty had been built, an omnipotent power had said, "Now, sons of men, see if you can reproduce something of that glory in the small." De Montereau had. Here, as in his changes in the Abbey Saint-Martin, his finishing of the Saint-Denis Suger had begun, he had worked quietly, never allowing any excess or architectural mannerisms to creep in, so that later authorities were baffled at not finding individual evidences of him in his lovely buildings. He is as striking an example as one can find of the unselfish anonymity (though in his case we do know his name), of the devotion to a cause, the consecration to religion and art that mark the designers, the masters-of-works, the architects of the Middle Ages.

De Montereau particularly had a genius for self-effacing achievement. The Gothic riches which had been left him by the architects and builders who had immediately gone before he ordered so well, blended with such harmony and perfection, that not this individual adapter, marvellous genius though he was, but the acme of the Gothic at which the race had at last arrived was evident. He turned his creative imagination into a mould into which he let flow all the splendid compound the Gothic men had brewed. He put in nothing self-exhibiting that could mar it. When the cast was ready, the creator could be forgotten, discarded. The cast was set up there, in that court, rising out of the surrounding isles of palace buildings, only one hundred and eighteen feet long, but one hundred and thirty-eight feet in height, with its encrusted lead spire adding to its Mont-Saint-Michel-like appearance of elevation, its glass richly glowing, its great congregations of carven apostles and saints so life-like they seemed actually joining in litanies or chants. The cast of the World's Seven Wonders may have varied from age to age, but somewhere along the line Sainte-Chapelle, the architectural jewel, should have been numbered among them.

The King looked inside, but for a few moments only. He must get through with his minstrels, Notre Dame, feeding two hundred beggars, the eels for himself, the final commissions to the White Queen, the last bedtime readings to the princes, some hours of prayer, and an hour of sleep before he left with his armies in the dawn. He was glad that Sainte-Chapelle had been completed before he left. On April 28th, that year (1248), the papal legate had dedicated the upper chapel to the Crown of Thorns, the Archbishop of Bourges the one on the ground-floor to the Blessed Virgin. Seventeen bishops had assisted, also the prize soloist canons of all the churches of the city gathered for the day into one great choir, accompanied by the new organ.

Louis was properly proud of this; it was such an improvement over the primitive instrument of the Dark Ages whose hydraulic apparatus often froze, winter nights, leaving the monks and canons musically unsupported at matins. The range, though, of the keys was still limited. These were four inches wide, cumbersome to strike. There were no semi-tones as yet, only the whole ones for the plainsong. And the power was supplied by large bellows requiring teams of blowers working in relays. Fortunately these were hidden so that the devotions might not be disturbed by the sight of their violent motions and consequent exhaustion.

It was a shining little world here within the church, with its many gay columns whose motives were fleurs-de-lis and gilt castles (honouring Blanche of Castille) on scarlet backgrounds, the pinnacled shrine of the Crown of Thorns like a bursting sunrise shooting its beams over the horizon, and the circling sunset splendour of the glass. This was, of course, its greatest glory. The wall partitions were so narrow between the vast stretches of violet- and crimson-hued glass that when the candles were lit it often looked to those in the court as though a three-dimensional section of the flower-strewn meadows of Heaven had been let down between the islands of that dark palace pile. For Louis, for Blanche, it was better than that. It was like having the living, throbbing, glowing altar of God at their very door.

Brothers of the Order of Sainte-Chapelle now marched in the vespers processional. The tall king knelt, crossed himself, joined in the "Magnificat" and the hymns with that rapt expression he sometimes had, which seemed to foretell his later canonization. "Oh, Star of the Sea . . . Gate of Heavenly Rest . . . Chase all evil from us. . . . Make our way secure . . . Till we find in Jesus our joy forever more." So the old Latin phrases of the sixth-century *Fortunatus* floated through the glorious panes, out through the court, and over the river.

While all the choir of Blanche's little birds in the palace chambers joined in the evensong, Louis came home to his supper. Margaret significantly, dined in her apartment. But the able prime minister ex-officio, that extraordinary mother of his, sat down with him. And around the table were that constant companion De Joinville, the Comte d'Artois, the king's brother, Milord de Coucy of the formidable castle, and Doctor de la Brosse, the remarkable fellow who had been the king's valet but was now also the illustrious Sieur de Châtillon, with many estates, he being one of Louis' few extravagances.

Amid the bustle of the servitors' bringing in the platters, ewers and bowls from the recently modernized kitchens, the clatter of knives —there were no forks—the gusty wiping of lips, the sipping of wine undiluted, while Louis watered his, the dipping of spoons into honey freshly gathered from the garden, and the splashing of the cleansing rose-water, Blanche watched her son. Those dark eyes, lovely, imperious, appealing, more deeply set now in the somewhat lined but still regally handsome camelia face, seemed never to leave him. She appeared at times to be enveloping him, this the greatest man in the world, with the pious yet fierce Castilian maternal solicitude she had shown when he was a little boy. His muscular slenderness did look a bit fine drawn, and he none too fit for the savage, years-long combat a Crusade often turned out. In her uneasy mood, evidenced by the tense interlocking of her still beautiful white hands, little things made her nervous. For one, Louis ate so tentatively now of those favourite dishes which she had expressly ordered for him: eels boiled in milk, lobsters with sauce, turtles, cinnamon rice, whey, cherries.

She questioned De la Brosse. Yes, the physician said, the King had eaten too little lately. And wading deep in gore in Palestine streets was hardly his prescription. And—would the Queen forgive him?—he did not favour so many night vigils. They were all right for the monk but they weakened the warrior. Last spring, the king had been getting up for matins just after midnight. Then he would lie down fully dressed to be ready for lauds at dawn. Three offices during the day he had attended, also vespers at five and compline at nightfall. He had lately reduced this schedule? Good. But she might save his life if she could get her son to doff that hair-shirt. It was marvellous that he showed no sign of irritation either of skin or temper; continued use might fatally deplete his vitality.

Those of modern temper who jeer at such self-imposed discipline should consider the motivation. It was imposed quite as a fighter inflicts hardships on himself—the punishing runs, the bouts, the swims in the icy river. Like the soldier, the King thought to harden his spirit, his mettle for the coming ordeal. Further cue to his char-

acter is found in a favourite prayer of his at this time: "Lord, grant
that we despise prosperity so much that we dread no adversity."

With this subjection of the body the devout Blanche was all of a
mind, but the mother in her was worried. She returned to the theme
of those strange visitations, the deathlike trances which overtook him
sometimes, as they have others of the gifted and great. They were,
the physician admitted, not promising for such hazardous adventures
as crusades. But then one could never tell about these geniuses. Louis
was apt to rise from what many would think his death-bed and ride
out and cut the Sultan in two and drive his armies into the sea. If she
remembered, it was one of these dangerous low states—in 1244 it had
been—that had led him to take this vow. No movement had been
visible at either breast or nostril. The Bishop of Paris had come to
administer extreme unction. They had even started to close his eyelids, draw up the sheet, when they noticed an inhalation. Then suddenly he had sat up. To do what? asked the doctor, baffled, disgusted,
awed. To seize the Bishop, crying: "Milord Bishop, I beg of you here
and now to place on my shoulders the red cross, the seal of the holy
Crusade, which binds me to fight for Christ's Tomb."

Crusades were hard things to get under way; and that had been
four years ago. There had been leisurely lulls now and then for
farming, the mending of political fences, the settling of feuds, the
making of wine, of love. But all that time ships had been gathering
in the ports, finances were being arranged, seneschals were seeing
to the mobilization, the *baillis* to the levies, nobles were selling their
acres to raise cash, others bargaining with the cities for franchises
in return for huge loans. But at last the pennons were floating from
the mastheads in the south and Saint Louis was eager to be off. So
eager, this last night, that after making sure that Blanche would
attend to the deed for Sorbon's new hill college he said little beyond
inquiring about the preparations. Had the grand constable the actual
number of soldiers ready to embark? Were the contracts for the grain-
loadings at Aigues-Mortes being promptly carried out? Had the
treasure promised by his son-in-law, the King of Navarre, arrived?
Were they sure enough smiths and armourers had been recruited?
They would need chain-links and horseshoes aplenty in the coming
battles to the east.

Absorbed, but with a salute to all, he rose and went to the window,
looking down on an inner court of the palace whence arose a tremendous racket of eating and chatter. A great throng of the beggars
he loved as much as his blind men and poor minstrels were having
the time of their lives with the cheeses, viands and pasties the cooks
handed out from the grand kitchens. One hundred and twenty—it

was an exact rule—had to be fed each night wherever he lodged. He always made sure of this number before he himself would sit down at the board. It had gotten so that the nobles up and down the country-side were uneasy when they saw the royal train approaching. The beggars were fed at his expense, but the haughty chatelaines feared theft and did not like so many tattered guests at their doors.

Everyone at the king's table had memories too of many Maundy Thursdays. As the ancient custom was, he washed the feet of the beggars, not already cleansed as they sometimes were, but in Christ's way, when they were actually dirty. And he himself was no self-conscious martyr, burdening others with his self-sacrifice. Though he did at times heckle the haughty, chide the lukewarm nobles, more often he spurred them on to some act of devotion or humility, simply with irony and dry humour. With all his vigils and hair-shirts, he somehow added this humour, and charm too, to his piety. He bore his outer vexations and inner tragedies with a sweetness of spirit that made even the hard religious way seem the natural one.

And again we must remind ourselves, when suddenly thinking of those pierced blaspheming tongues, that it was attacks on his Lord that he punished; those on himself he magnanimously forgave. If he was marching out in the morning to sail over-seas and bloodily kill infidels, it was not for their differing belief but because they had defiled something very dear to his heart, the resting place of Christ before He rose. The ideal king could go no farther in that era with its limitation of light. Within the framework of his age he was a great liberal, and lived and breathed the spirit of his Master. That he was far from bigotry removed, placing love above all observances and rites, Crusaders at that table were soon to learn in a Damascus street:

An old woman was carrying down the highway a bowl of fire in one hand, in the other a phial of water.

"I shall," she cried to the whole city, "with this fire burn down Damascus, with this water put out the fires of Hell."

"There is a lesson in that," said the king. "Even in her daftness she is wise. She preaches to outward followers of religion a burning sermon. And I myself would not have any man do right from either fear of Hell or hope of Heaven, only for love of God."

In spite of his four major mistakes—the first in quixotically leaving to England so much of France; his subordinating of Margaret, due perhaps to excess of filial devotion or some incompatibility; his assent, after objecting, to his brother's conquest of Naples; and his last Crusade which, with the toll that harsh self-discipline and his super-human activities had taken, would destroy him—his life was as grandly constructive as ruler's ever was.

But the diners missed him. He had left his stand at the window where he had been looking down on the happy feasting beggars and had gone upstairs to see his boys. Where later judges would put on their caps of doom, now small hose, mediaeval drawers, a stuffed falcon, toy cross-bows, laughable hobbledehoys lay about the room. The little princes gathered in the high-roofed bed, hands clasped about their hunched-up knees, as he told them ideal stories that brought wonder to their young eyes. When, at such hours, Queen Margaret happened to look in, observers were sure she felt a tenderness for the king she had seldom felt before—he was such a grand father. As for Blanche, though she was downstairs, she knew the picture well; and all at the table were aware that it brought both joy and sadness to her heart. Perhaps too she had a presentiment even then that she would not see her son again when he returned from the Crusade and his long captivity. But never did mother have cause for greater gratitude. His loyalty and love she had known, undivided. Her ideals, her very ambitions, the career she herself might have had, had been carried out in him. At that very moment he was telling her grandsons, his boys, the tales of heroes good and great which she had once told to him. . . .

V

The Great Cathedral in the Mid-Thirteenth Century. . . . The Minstrels and Tumblers stage a Farewell Performance for the King before Notre Dame, on the Eve of his Departure on his First Crusade. . . . On his Second Crusade, his One Great Mistake, Saint Louis dies. . . . "As an Author," says his Chronicler, the Sire de Joinville, "when his Book is done, adorns it with Red and Blue and Gold, so Saint Louis illuminated All his Kingdom."

1248 𝔄.𝔇.

ON TOWARD EVENING, THE MINSTRELS OF THE PETIT PONT, the ancient Little Bridge hard by the Hôtel Dieu and the Cathedral, were glad to see the King coming their way. They were very poor. Besides, he always greeted them like a comrade, as though he were one with them—which is a gift and a grace possessed by few even of the great.

When one walks in Cathedral Square, he is treading on holy ground. For here at the island's upper end, from time immemorial, the sons of men, from those of the Stone Age through Gauls, Romans, early and later Christians, according to their varying faiths, have worshipped. Today on the north side of this great open space stands Napoleon the Third's Hôtel Dieu, on the west the police barracks, on the south a long lawn and a mounted Charlemagne, and on the east the Cathedral.

Saint Louis, walking through a much smaller square, saw of this setting only the eternal, the immortal part: Notre Dame. North and west then were lined with those timber-crossed, old-world houses. South, lay the long parade of gables of the mediaeval Hôtel Dieu. Between the Cathedral, on the east, and the river alongside it, lay the bulky Gothic Bishop's Palace, its side just edging into the Square.

Now this Middle Ages Hôtel Dieu was but one link in a long continuity of hospitals, the oldest-going set in the world. Sainte Geneviève had nursed in one of them there, in the 400's. Saint Landry had extended it in the 600's. Back nearer Christ, the Ferryman, Saint Julien the Poor, had set up the first cots in a little hospice on the shore whither, the old chronicle tell us, he had brought the Christ. On a stormy night, he had ferried Him in the stern of his little boat across the Seine.

So that corner of the Square, with Cathedral, ancient Bishop's Palace, and immemorial Hôtel Dieu so near together, where the minstrels and jugglers were to perform, was a venerable, even holy, stage. And it was a very lively one with the inmates of the houses across the Square gathering at the windows, and the Hôtel Dieu invalids being helped to theirs so that they might look down on the entertainers, and, pressing into the Square, a throng of gold-chained merchants, much-draped housewives, floury-forearmed cooks, students with books, armed men of the watch, beggars dripping rags, gamins wriggling in and out, nuzzling lovers, old people with sucked-in mouths, and young mothers offering to grasping-fingered babes the coral-tipped white apples of their breasts. And there was a great and still audience too, on the lofty walls and roofs and towers of the Cathedral, gazing down out of that other world on this.

If these young mothers exposed their breasts unashamed before the crowd, if a student fondled a girl a little too low, or a juggler suddenly left the open-air stage to make a urinal of the outside of a Cathedral bay, why, it was all a very natural world. On the Cathedral capering animals mingled with the angels.

Though Louis preferred to stand, they brought tall chairs from the Hôtel Dieu. It was interesting for a layman, even a royal one, to see the preparations. Musicians were tuning up. Tumblers were limbering up by the north tower postern. Jugglers got out their coloured balls. A knife-thrower boasted he could shave the down off a cheek without drawing blood. Derisive comrades asked him where were last year's targets?

But the king, delighted as he was with all this, did not love all minstrels. The goliards, for example. Renegade clerks, impudent students, they loved to drink, dice, wench, above all to hear themselves talk and shock people. Saint Thomas Aquinas had taken time off to denounce them. But, strange exception in an age of authority, for decades they continued to recite their ribald and subversive lampoons of sacred things. Still, there were dragons to fight without worrying too much about gad-flies.

Austere saint and mystic though he was, Saint Thomas loved the sincere down-to-earth minstrels and highly commended their art. And had there not been truly great artists among them? The singing Taillefeur of the armies; Arnaud Daniel, Dante's favourite; Richard le Pèlerin and Peyre Cardinal; Bernard de Ventadour; Blondel;

Bertrand de Born; Giraud de Bornehl; and a host of illustrious others. They filled the courts, cloisters, castles, the very air of Europe with their sweet music, and, for our delight, the libraries and archives with ringing war chants, tender love songs, exquisite accompaniments to them, and deathless tales.

Still, these champions had no need of Louis' ready alms. And there were fortunate troubadours of the south, *trouvères* in the north, who had regular court posts. Others attached themselves to noble houses, drank the choicest wines, and had many shoes where these poor waifs of the Paris bridges counted themselves lucky, when Saint Louis was out of town, to have one whole pair. And many a minstrel eked out a living by working on texts and poems or helping the church choirs by making arrangements and variations for the chants.

Even among the little minstrel people, there was a distinction. For some made up their own songs and tricks, but most relied on the brains of others. Saint Louis, with all his wisdom and executive ability, had weaknesses springing out of his very goodness. And one was for the small-fry minstrels. Of course, he was the same with all the wandering and distressed. Vagabonds of our Far West chalk houses where they have been hospitably received, as a cue for comrades coming that way. It seemed as though the gypsy minstrels must have put a chalk mark on his palace and the Little Bridge. For sooner or later all the waifs, sometimes with good performers among them, came up to Paris.

The Romany gypsies had a great chronicler in one George Borrow. The mediaeval George Borrow of these minstrel gypsies, Rutebeuf, has told us vividly of the hardships of their sometimes gay, always irresponsible life. But though the lordlier entertainers scorned them, these grasshopper troupers added life and colour to the streets and to the castles of the country-side which they sometimes toured, hoping for luck.

To the audience, when the king was not there, the minstrels would bow and say, "We will show you, *messires et mesdames,* many fine tricks. We will enchant you with our magic." Then they would perform their juggling and songs and would also put on side-shows. Advice would be offered to the giggling love-lorn. And they would run a little shell-game played with snails.

When the king was on hand they would dispense with the more frivolous *divertissements* and stick to the main events: knife-throwing, juggling, tumbling, imitations, and jests and songs. Of the last they had quite a repertoire. Some were gay, others wistful, even poignant, not a few naïvely boastful. In their gaudy patches, they would proclaim the day when they would wear rich clothes and the itching straw of their dens would be transformed to goose-feathers, their torn mantles to silk coverlets. The hazards of their life, shelter, bread, shoes were ever on their minds.

> "There are ten thousand fires in Paris;
>   Is there not one to which I can come in?
> Will you not in the pity of your hearts unbar the door?
>   So that I may warm my hands for a little while,
>   So that they may not be too numb
> For me to play and earn a crust?
>   Then I will move on,
>   In the dark,
>   In the cold,
>   With my song."

Another, less pitiful and with a sardonic note in it, would tell plaintively how a poor singer had to pawn his lute for a loaf. Another berated a cruel landlord because he had forced a minstrel, who knew well he had no money when he ordered his drink, to pay for it by leaving behind his shoes. Quite literally these poor waifs had, year after year, to sing for their suppers. And there was another subtle little song they often delivered when, from the snows, they came into the hall of the great castle and its central fire:

> "Saddest of all men is the minstrel,
>   Playing and singing too his theme.
> He sings an appealing song,
>   As a minstrel courteous and worthy.
> Then, his little song ended,
> He bows and politely begs that you
>   *May help him to live a little while longer.*"

Thus clever, graceful, even delicate in a French way was their plea. As exquisite was this encore, weaving in with the hardship the lover theme:

> "These rhymes fall from heart,
>   As cherry blossoms from the branch,
> But branch and heart are bare.
>   Won't you please let me come to the hearth of your heart?"

A composite sigh arose from commoners and queens. Blanche and Margaret would have tossed them their purses at once. But the king restrained them. There was to be the climax of a farewell gift this night.

The wistfulness of the songs had been stressed by the shabby appearance of the singers. But suddenly there was a transformation. The porter lighted the torches of the Hôtel Dieu. The sacristan came out of the Cathedral and ignited those by the portals. Afterglow of the west, moon in the east over the towers, lent overtones. These crosscurrents of light brightened the worn stops of their flutes, regilded the great outflares of their sidewise horns, and dyed afresh the faded ribbons of the lutes and the weather-stained stripes of their hose and tunics. It was as though there had been a transfiguration. For the moment the poor bridge waifs were miraculously decked out to play for Christendom's greatest king.

Good showmen, they now changed the theme. And they put a little—not too much—daring in it:

> "When the emerald grass and the blossoms unfold in the orchard,
>   And the nightingale sings to its mate,
>   It much delights me to hear him and to smell the flowers.
>   So I am very content with myself
>   —But oh, so much more with my wife."

The Queens laughed delicately. The King threw back his fine head and chuckled. Then Blanche, eager for an old tale, requested one of the leader. From his rich store, appropriately he chose Blancheflor, "Whiteflower," which is as effective as any Percevel or Tristan and Iseut.

This softer note over, they reached back into the dark and pulled down from a flying buttress one of the night's stars, wearing an oriental fez, a Morisco jacket, and with a tight curl in his tail like that of an Ionic capital. This little *singe,* or monkey, was a great help to them not only in their performances but on their travels. When they came to a toll bridge, they paid "monkey money," *monnaie du singe,* a trick or two from him.

He even climbed up the arm of the King, who joined in the laughter. And, not to let the merry mood die, they put on a swift succession of acts. One borrowed a towel from the Hôtel Dieu, sprang from it into a somersault, and landed on its eight inches without a toe over. Two contortionists mounted a table and stood on their heads, then, sitting down, wrapped their legs around their necks. Finally they reversed the process, wrapping their legs around their necks as they stood on their heads. Thus looking out through their leg crotches, they winked at the King. For a clown could wink at a king, if that king happened to be Saint Louis.

Without a pause then, other mediaeval vaudevillians set up a mighty clamour before the majesty of the Cathedral, imitating cats, dogs, blackbirds, sheep, pigs, and the bellow of a bull heard miles off, and one clever fellow the angelus chimes, and the clarion hail of the sentries at midnight.

And now for the last act they moved over before the Last Judgment Door, and laid down a rug. Two jugglers got down on it on their backs, raised their legs, and soon fountains of balls kept rising and falling on their nimble feet. And the tumblers began more complex somersaults, oddly enough crossing themselves before the forward somersault when the back turn was more dangerous. When one was about to land badly but recovered with a neatly executed, improvised manœuvre, Saint Louis nodded sagely to De Joinville, pleased as a child to show that he saw through it all. Then, for the finale, two executed simultaneously a triple somersault, landing head up, bowing before the King.

So these wanderers did their turns and tricks and imitations before Notre Dame of Paris, playing their low comedy before the high tragedy of that Last Judgment Door. But it was all of a piece with the Cathedral. The builders put saints and gargoyles, devils and angels, earthly scenes and heavenly on that noble pile. All their tragedy was inwelded with comedy, thus making the Cathedral the composite it is of this life below and that to which we look above.

It was a magnificent, almost an historic *pourboire* Louis gave the minstrels. And he did not toss it to them as the "mighty" would have done. He gave it to the leader, placing his hand on his shoulder as though he, the King, were the comrade of them all. They would not need shoes now for a long, long time.

The King now stepped back and a little out in the Square, for a moment, to take a farewell look at the beloved features of a very great lady—Our Lady—Notre Dame of Paris.

His ancestors had worshipped in the two parents of Notre Dame, the two ancient churches that had stood there before. There were marks of his family all about. Over Saint Anne's Door, his great-grandfather, Louis the Seventh, with founding Bishop de Sulli, would forever pay tribute to Our Lady. By the high altar Grandmother Isabeau lay buried—you still can see her name in gilt letters on the choir screen. To that same altar Grandfather Philippe Auguste had marched his bloodied troops after Bouvines Battle. Soon they would put Saint Louis up in stone—above the Red Door.

There were still a few things missing. The transept doors were still to be carved, the last ring of chevet chapels to be added. There was no treasury. A central belfry stood on the roof in place of our *flèche*. These details do not matter. The body of the Cathedral was practically complete. That magnificent body, the familiar features, almost every one of her infinite number of graces that we see, Saint Louis gazed at, in the flooding moonlight coming over the twin towers.

This difference there was: she has now the mellowed, the imperishable beauty of age; Saint Louis saw her in the loveliness of her youth. One would scarcely know which to choose. The saints, now so gray and august of mien, wore gay painted robes of deep blue and crimson, and had gilt haloes. The tympan arches were resplendent with gold leaf. The stained glass now is enchanting with its tones which have been multiplied and deepened with the centuries. Then it had, as it were, *une virginalité de la verrerie,* an exhilarating virginal brilliance and radiance of colour.

A venerable patina now overlies the whole pile from storms, sieges, centuries, and—alas—machines and chimneys. It seems strange to us to think of Notre Dame as not only young but actually fresh of hue. She was then. The masons had laid the last stones on those tower summits when Saint Louis had not been long out of his 'teens. You can see what those stones were like if you watch them working on replacements in the *chantier* or workyard, back of the Cathedral, or see them derricking a piece of that cream-coloured Seine Valley limestone (or its equivalent when that is exhausted) into the old grey fabric of the Cathedral. Then, not only by day but at night, when the moonlight heightened the effect, Notre Dame was light, even creamy of hue throughout her long and lofty and beautiful body.

Well did Saint Louis know her points. Pierre de Montereau had told him what to watch for, all the effects usually overlooked. These were the more wonderful to recognize when one realized that the builders had but one-hundredth of the plans and elevations and detailed draughtings of a modern skyscraper. The few paper or parchment designs soon became so smudged that often they tossed them aside to work, in the large, from that wooden *molle* or model, with buttresses, arches, spires, and all, which we saw in the tent of the master-of-works in the earlier story of the Cathedral. And often they went ahead relying only on their memories and inspired artistic judgment. Yet, with all our tools and equipment and new processes, no one since has been able to match them.

It is with this understanding that our eyes, with Saint Louis' and those of the gallery, must sweep from left to right over that magnificent first story. Here, with that paucity of means, the builders achieved a magnificent effect. The four giant upshooting vertical buttresses, with the three deep-cut, high-arched, carved portals set between, give a noble proportion to that first story. The vast mass, the towering height you not only accept now, you expect, on that grand base.

You cannot pause now to study the superb wealth of carvings in and around those doors—they and their stories are for another day— or days. For your eyes are swept up from that grand base by the irresistible accents of those four buttresses, which not only assure you that the Cathedral will stand forever but carry you up to other beauties aloft. First, that second story where the twenty-eight kings range in majesty across the façade. It was the inspired way in which such horizontal features were related to the four giant vertical ones, with the treatment of the planes in between, that made the serene, gracious Notre Dame west front the noblest in the world of the West.

There is another horizontal banding over that row of kings, a delicate white balustrade. Climbing over this, the eye now comes into another plateau and, ignoring the high and white statues here and there and other details, it centres on what is the focal centre not only of that story but of the whole façade, the lovely western rose-window. The white figures of Our Lady, two angels, and the Child Who is the eternal point of it all, extend over the lower rim of the glass. And now as the lights go on within, that rose leaps into glory, becomes a living, throbbing jewel on Notre Dame's breast.

The eye swept up still, scaling the Cathedral heights, dwells on another beautiful horizontal feature, a row of arched, white, lace-like colonnettes, the loveliest open-air gallery in France. One last little climb then over a perfect cornice, a mounting of the last white balustrade, with grim monster sentries perched upon it where the buttresses end, and we have reached the towers. There, with their wise old louver eyes, they gaze out over the River, the Island, the City, and the Hills. We have scaled the Cathedral heights. There is nothing now between those tower summits but the transfigured clouds and the swimming moon.

And the bold climber is now in a mountain world. All round the sides of the towers are graceful little stone floriations like *edelweiss* blooms on the Alps. Grotesque monsters perch at all angles, like capering mountain goats on the heights. The towers, with their fresh creamy stone overlaid with moonlight, rise like snowy storied summits over the city.

But down below, the compline chants had succeeded the minstrels' merry notes; and the crusading ships were straining at their hawsers down in Aigues-Mortes Harbour. A moment Louis looked down the sides to see if still there were tethered to the Cathedral's great body those squadrons of titanic steeds, the flying buttresses. And there they were, shoring up on their great haunches the accumulated weight of the three lofty stories, the arch ranges within, vast roof, belfry, the regiments of pinnacles, dormers, spires, the angelic and the fantastic populations of the upper air, and the crowning towers. Yes, Our Lady's great house was safe for the night—for the ages. With easy mind, the King could go on his Crusade.

He went within. Under the exquisitely-wrought stone forest overhead, lighted by the three never-dying sunsets of the rose-windows, he knelt by the rail, the old hat on the floor beside him.

In the *"In manus tuas, Domine,"* "Into Thy hands, oh Lord, I commit my spirit," his lips moved tensely in his earnestness. Those eyes which had been so wise and humorous in the morning were filled with wonder and were shining. The greatest king in the world had become what his King had wished—as a little child. Then, with the age-old beautiful Gregorian canticle, *"Nunc dimittis,"* "Now Thou dost dismiss Thy servant, according to Thy Word, in peace," he went out into the night.

In the morning, in chain-mail and mounted, he was the warrior king. From a palace tower, the two queens watched the Crusaders march out. But the White Queen stayed there the longer. Her scarf waved for quite a while after Margaret had gone in.

The years now were filled with thrills, hardships, blood, misadventures. The green knight, robust De Joinville, who, though he admits refreshingly that he was often afraid, rarely was far from the King's saddle-skirts, tells us something of all these things in his little *anabasis* which was much more charming than any of Xenophon's or Caesar's or U. S. Grant's. And though Louis carried his religion ever with him, he must have enjoyed much of the excitement as did Napoleon Lodi Bridge or Theodore Roosevelt San Juan Hill.

To secure good fortune, he had ordered pieces of the True Cross brought down from Notre Dame. These the Bishop held over every little and big boat in the harbour of walled Aigues-Mortes.

"Strike up a chant in God's name!" he cried as he neared Egypt's shores. And he led them himself in the ninth-century hymn of Rabanus, *Veni, Creator Spiritus.* Never had it sounded grander than then as it came from the sailors hauling down the triangular sails, the lords on the poops, the mailed knights swaying with their weight of steel on dangling ladders above the tumbling waves, and the sailors racing with rhythmically rising and falling oars to the landing.

The dead were piled pretty high on that Crusade. Wind-rows of bodies were washed ashore by the tides, corpses were jammed up against the bridges. There were dizzying successions of horses running crazed, spears buried in their rumps; of knights with feet caught in the stirrups and throats cut being wildly dragged, bumping over obstacles; of the Saracens tumbling their very house roofs down on the Crusaders surging through the streets; of receptacles filled with flaming tow, pitch, gum, sulphur, charcoal, naphtha, the wild "Greek fire"—the new war device—streaking with flaring comet tails across the skies. Saint Louis himself was a glamorous enough figure, with gleaming sword swinging over his great height, and his helmet, with two gold lilies crossed, shining out over every battle-field.

But effective as are such pictures, it is a question whether this fine man did not show up better in those familiar and homely scenes when he feasted his scores of beggars as he ate, washed their feet on Maundy Thursday, sank on his knees in prayer in such utter sincerity, dispensed common sense on his rug in the garden, tested scales, weighed fish, drew up ordinances for women's welfare, made shepherds who had been battering each other with their crooks embrace, smiled at crusty insulting old hags, subsidized his minstrels, bought cloth for his old blind men and read to them and to his little boys in bed, and cared in so many ways for all the wandering and oppressed.

He had come home, after his imprisonment, to render justice in a grand general way, through his wise laws, national peacemaking and drawing up of treaties, and in his hundred and one little sympathetic personal ways. But somehow he was not the same man. His prodigious activities, his strenuous austerities had taken their toll. And mixed in with all that crusading glory, there had been a full measure of fevers, stinks, pestilences, imprisonment. But more even than these hardships, the death of Blanche while he was away had changed him. He missed her presence, advice, companionship, the wordless communication there had been between them, sometimes flashed by a look, often even without that, but ever eloquent, effective, unfailing.

It may have been because she was not there and because in his age his religious ardor blinded him, that he insisted on starting his second, that inept, ill-fated Crusade. Even the faithful De Joinville would not join. He did not like leprosy, he averred. For the King is was a blow. But maybe the gusty green chevalier was thus spared to write, when he was very old, that finest of tributes to his royal friend, his immortal little book.

The King had advanced no farther than Algiers when he was stopped. It was an ancient enemy that laid him low. Louis, recognizing him, sent for his son. We have seen this boy before. Up in Paris. With the toy cross-bows, suits of child armour, little mediaeval hose and drawers all around the stout-walled nursery of the old palace. He was sitting up in bed with some of his small brothers listening to the fascinating stories of heroes their father was telling. Most of those small brothers had gone. And it was he who came into that hot fetid room overlooking the African white walls and red roofs and green orchards, so far from the Paris his father had loved, to be, before he left it, the king—Philip the Third and Bold. He had been three years old that night in Paris, and very tiny. Now, twenty-five and of great stature, like most of his family, he looked down on his father who no longer was tall but looked shrunken on the pallet.

In the heat, with dissolution so near, it was difficult for this once great king and judge and mighty warrior even to draw a feeble breath. But he summoned that last residue of strength which the devoted and strong of spirit reserve for the farewell messages to those they love. And this is what the dying saint, the father, told the boy, the tall young man bending over him:

"Fair son, *win* the love of your people. I would rather an alien ruled them and well than that you, the native prince, should govern them badly.

"To that end, avoid feuds and strife, even to the point of dishonour, though not beyond. Do not speak that hot word. It may bring war, then death, not only to you who said it but to innocent thousands.

"Be sure that you attend with seriousness and devoutness all the offices of the Church. And choose only the company of men of tried character and proven worth, loving only the good. Be both firm and liberal with your people so that you always rule them justly. And, first before anything else, search yourself, and if you know you possess anything belonging to another restore it now. If you are uncertain about the ownership, start inquiry at once. Be economical in the royal household, at Paris, everywhere; above all, keep from starting wars. If these cannot be prevented, guard from harm the poor who always suffer most.

"Finally, dear son, have prayers said for my soul throughout the kingdom. And in spirit give me a special part in all the good deeds you may do after I am gone. For a beloved son, I give you all the blessings a loving father may give his child. May God grant you the grace ever to do His will, that He may be honoured by you, and you and I, after this mortal life, may be together with Him."

When the father, with failing lips but with all the passion of his soul, had said these things to the oncoming king, his boy, he signed to the attendants. Then, according to an old, old custom when a king was passing, they brought ashes. In a room next that Paris nursery, Louis the Sixth and other monarchs of the family when they knew the end to be near had lain down in ashes strewn on the floor, arms out in cross fashion. Nor was this any quaint gesture merely to be smiled at. It was mighty proof of a man's sincerity when, in his agony and extremity, he could order his wracked body so to express his humility and his reaching out to the King of Kings.

Saint Louis, now unable to move, had the ashes strewn not on the floor but on his bed. At his sign, they laid his arms out in the form of the cross on which had died the King he himself had so faithfully followed. And the battered body seemed to assume the old stature and commanding dignity.

So, calling on the name of the city he had just started on so futile a Crusade to save, the city over which his Lord had wept in Gethsemane, "Oh, Jerusalem, Jerusalem!" Saint Louis passed on.

It was years later that the Sire de Joinville set down his last words about his friend. They were his best. There he rose to the heights: "As an author, when his little book is done, adorns it with blue and crimson and gold, so Saint Louis adorned all his kingdom."

VI

Wise Men from the East, from the West, come up to Paris. . . .
The City now has one hundred and fifty thousand Souls in three
hundred and twenty-nine Streets. . . . Father Adam's Little Col-
lege on the Bridge. . . . The Housing Shortage on the Island is
acute, and most of the University moves over the Bridge. . . .
"The Five Nations" and the Chain of Colleges on the Hill. . . .
Students' Comfortable Unions and Dingy Attics. . . . Aristotle,
Boethius, Porphory, Peter Lombard. . . . College Courses in the
Middle Ages. . . . The Rich Mediaeval Bachelors of Arts wear Silk,
have Orderlies, and fight on Saint Germain Green; the Poor empty
Slops and write Love-Letters to pay their Way. . . . The Greater
European Universities. . . . The Mighty Mustard Seed, the Little
Sorbonne, and the Flaming Torch of Theology in Paris.

The University Years

OTHERS BESIDES THIS IDEAL KING ON HIS WAY TO THE CRUSADES
helped to make glorious mediaeval Paris and their century,
at which men still look back nostalgic for the great deeds, the
banded expressions of brotherhood, the bright blossoming in arts,
crafts, book, song, and all the splendid energy and urges of that
historic high-tide.

Genghis Khan too was of that time and with his grand-scale arson
was making a great blaze in the East. But his was a consuming fire.
This of the West, in spite of occasional black puffs of evil, was a
constructive fire that enlightened men's minds and warmed their souls.
On a Paris hill burned its brightest beacon, gleams from which
illumined far-off dark corners of the world.

Nine men of the century did much to feed this fire of the West.
One, Giotto, was of Italy. Saint Francis, through his ancestry, was
of the blood of France. Saint Louis was wholly her child. The other
six were foster sons of Paris. Thomas Aquinas, Albert the Great,

Roger Bacon, Bonaventura drank knowledge from her perennial breast. Dominic set up colleges and chapter-houses within her walls. And though no ancient hostel has handed down to us the signed registry of Dante in Paris it is implicitly recorded in his immortal verse. Before a long-gowned licentiate, with shivering bursars, the exiled, soon-to-be-laurelled Dante once sat, with curious, ranging eyes, somewhere on the Street of Straw.

Elsewhere others now and then did add faggots to the fire. The English barons wrested from dark John their charter. Into the House of Commons De Montfort put steel. De Mandeville travelled in Cathay. The Hansa cities formed their league. But everywhere men were looking at Paris over their shoulders.

In nine centuries the city had quadrupled Emperor Julian's twenty-eight thousand. Before the century was out, it would boast a hundred and fifty thousand souls in three hundred and twenty-nine streets— most of them short—within the bursting, pent-up compass of its city walls. And a commanding capital, a magnificent metropolis that meant, for the times. But not for its size alone did those throngs of pilgrims come up to Paris. "This noble and renowned city," said His Holiness of that day—and he meant not the Eternal City, but Paris—"is the day-spring of learning. The light it sheds over the entire world is the foretaste of the celestial splendour to come!" This hunger for the culture of the City by the Seine was expressed time after time by men of high estate, in letters in which they curiously reverse the heart's usual process. For them to be at home, but away from Paris, was exile!

Now others from time immemorial, Roman emperors and all, had rhapsodized about Paris. But chiefly they had extolled her entrancing air, sweet waters, wine, love, mighty churches and towers. Now in this thirteenth century they struck a new note—her ideas! In art, learning, science, religion, Crusades, cuisine, fashion, what you will, they have for ages enriched the world. Up to to-day, whatever may happen to her to-day, to-morrow, more ideas have been grown to the paved acre in Paris than in any other city. It was because of this magnificent, this profoundly moving magnetism, rather than her lighter if so very agreeable charms, that at varying intervals the good and the great have, like the seven we have just listed, taken their places in that immortal parade, that immemorial moving frieze over Sainte Geneviève's Hill.

Until well on in the twelfth century distinguished visitors had usually stayed on the Island, the original city and still, as it would always be, the sacred heart of Paris. But now most of the famous scholars passed over the Little Bridge to lodge on the Left Bank hill.

In that twelfth century an exodus of teachers and scholars had begun, and it had continued spasmodically through the early years of Saint Louis' reign. Gradually the University was deserting the ancient mother, Notre Dame, in whose porch—or in the porches of the two churches that had preceded the Cathedral—it had been born. It had been a fitting birthplace. On the Island's up-stream end, prehistoric men, Druids, Romans, the Christians of the early Church and of the Middle Ages, had by turns built their altars, at first to the Unknown, then to a more personal God. Stones of all the shrines had gone into their successors, the glorious climax of which was the Cathedral.

Here, then, where there had been such a continuity of worship and sequence of brotherhood, the University of Paris had first seen the light. Ahead even of ancient Bologna it had been, the very first of the long line of institutions which would nourish and spread the culture of the West in Oxford, Cambridge, Salerno, Toulouse, Orléans, Aberdeen, Heidelberg, Vienna, Palencia, and all the great cities of Europe. Though those exciting years of the birth of this alma mater of alma maters were relived so fully in that earlier story of the Cathedral, we must recall just these few salient facts for a proper understanding of the reason the University was now about to leave the maternal nest:

There had, of course, always been teaching going on in Paris. The Palace had a school. We saw Charlemagne himself gallop down from Aix to give prizes to his Notre Dame school-boys who wrote, spelled, chanted, rolled out the Latin, and did all the things at which he, the great conqueror, was so clumsy. Saint Germain-des-Près, Sainte Geneviève, Saint Victoire, all the abbeys kept nobles' sons from being downright illiterate, and gave much more to the promising sons of the poor. They taught to the novices and younger priests the Scriptures, the philosophers, the early Christian Fathers, manuscript work, illuminating, and the new part music discovered in the abbeys in the Dark Ages. And they instructed the lay brethren in masonry, wood-carving, stained-glass-making, and many crafts, and the peasants in horticulture, fighting plant diseases, and cattle-breeding.

In the tenth and eleventh centuries, many of the leading teachers of the bishops' and the abbey schools were not only brainy but big vital men. We love to speak of a torch of learning that is forever being handed on. There were then many little torches in combination. Gerbert of Rheims, Fulbert of Chartres, Lanfranc of Bec, Beranger of Tours, others of the great from their cloisters, their hill towns, signalled with their torches through the night of the then prevailing ignorance, flashing encouragement to one another. With them they ignited great beacons. These warmed the ever-increasing bands of watchers in the night in every capital by a river, in every great city on a hill. We who now carry on the burdens of the race should, in our hearts, be ever grateful to them.

So was lighted the greatest beacon of them all in the Cloister of Notre Dame, by the two old churches that had preceded, in fact were the parents of, the Cathedral. They had lain side by side, with the first Notre Dame built in the 500's, a little ahead of Saint Etienne. Saint Etienne was older. It was a picturesque, long, grey, belfried enlargement of a church, first dedicated to another saint and set up in this upper end of the Island of Paris in the 300's. Now Notre Dame, which was a little shorter but had greater glory of decoration within, now Saint Etienne acted as pro-cathedral of the City, according to the condition in which the latest fire or siege had left them.

There was another characteristic of Saint Etienne which, even in this skimming over of those crowded years preceding the birth of the University, should be recalled. Saint Etienne was in more ways than one a part of the life of Paris. It had used for its own south, its fourth, wall a section of the Island city wall. It had appropriated this and in turn had let its own round sanctuary apse serve as a fort on the city wall. Thus significantly, auspiciously, had ancient city and church been joined together.

Saint Etienne had stayed there longer—nine hundred years all told. First the original Notre Dame, then Saint Etienne had come down to give up their historic ground to the magnificent, uprising Cathedral. The older church had kept its lights burning, its bells going, through most of the construction. Saint Louis himself, as a boy, had heard Saint Etienne's bells. They had been stilled but a little while.

The cloister around the two churches, where had burned that beacon (much of it remained around the Cathedral in Louis' day) had not been the conventional cloister of lawns and arcades. Notre Dame Cloister had an herb or rose garden or two, but they were almost hidden; and the fountains were simply drinking ones niched in ancient walls. It was an immemorially old settlement of arched halls and ecclesiastical annexes remaining from Romanesque and early Roman times that had accrued around the two old churches, with winding little streets. Later there had been shoe-horned in, somehow, six-story mediaeval dwellings, thin and pinched and high up and set at all angles, but adding their carvings and bright colours to the prevailing greys of the tumbling-roofed sea.

In this separate, picturesque, but cramped little ecclesiastical city within the crowded capital dwelt and worked bishop, chancellor, canons, priests, and the large church service of supply. The activity had a proper seemliness, of course, but it was often almost tumultuous and very vocal, with stone-cutters clinking away in the work-yard back of a chapel, roofers working on church spires or attic slopes, masons replacing worn stones aloft, students droningly inflecting and cæsuring their Latin, ample canons dining on grapes, bread, cheese, in the world of dormers, sloughing shingles, and curled chimney-pots up there.

Below, in cramped quarters in the thin alley-threaded maze, tailors sewed on vestments, seamstresses on altar-cloths, church chandlers poured out the pure bees-wax required for holy candles. There too youths argued innocently enough amidst the clattering platters, splashing spigots, revolving spits of rosy just-around-the-corner little inns. And not so innocently—since he who wanders up and down the earth seeking whom he may devour loves to forage in sacred environs—crimps, card-sharps, and harlots shrilly laughed and snarled in dubious hostels in the bridge purlieus on the outskirts of the Cloister.

But ever above these earthly discords a Notre Dame bell would sound or in Saint Etienne the solemn-freighted resonance of a requiem chant to show that one was very near holy ground. And when one got lost in the confusion and came up bewildered against a blank wall, a dead-end buttress, or an unknown dripping moss-green drinking fountain, the candles suddenly going on behind a stained-glass window would show a radiant way out of the shut-in tortuous, grey world.

This was the Cloister of Notre Dame when the great Schoolmen lectured there and Abelard walked out, in the night, with Heloise. Such it was too, with a few more of the new mediaeval carved and gilded-up tenements, when Our Lady's lofty towers were raised against the sky. And much of this atmosphere it retained when Villon, after some prank at the Fircone or more dangerous misdemeanour, used to lose himself in its meandering ways.

One cannot tell in exactly what hour or in what square rod of all those grey acres the University was conceived or even in which of the two church porches it was born. What had literally happened was this: here, inspired by the abbeys and bishops' schools and the great teachers in them, to whom all who love the higher things of life owe a tremendous debt, the late eleventh- and twelfth-century priests, canons, students, native and visiting teachers had suddenly come together in search of knowledge in that Cloister, and behold, the University was! There was no incorporating or formal organization for a long time. Only their desire for the Truth and the bequeathed spirit of the Island brought them there. They had no class-rooms, dormitories, libraries of their own. They used the property of Mother

Church who had been the guardian of learning through the first Christian centuries and the Dark Ages, was giving it new life then, and who, in our modern times, would take in her wise stride the very science which the short-sighted thought would utterly destroy her.

All the work of these eager, gathering groups was done in those two church porches; in the arched ante-rooms where once the baptismal candidates, the catechumens, for whom the first part of the mass had been named, had been instructed; in canons' houses in the Cloister where devoted men both taught and lodged their charges; in the little stone campus of the budding University—the open space between the Hôtel Dieu and the two churches; and even around the very holy water font itself.

In that earlier story we saw the students, in their everyday routine, at their logic, mathematics, philosophy, the science of the day, and the eternal Latin. We lived through their higher, exciting hours when, in pursuit of the main objectives, the shining stars, Anselm, Roscellin, William, Abelard, wrestled, and Heloise with high heart and colour watched from the outskirts of the crowd, and her uncle, the canon, gazed malevolently from the great Last Judgment Door. And they wrestled as eagerly, as violently too, over invisible, intangible things, essences, concepts, "universals," as modern students over a visible and tangible ball. And the young people, the average citizens of Paris too, cheered them for it. For their prowess at abstractions they were acclaimed as heroes throughout the civilized world. It was one of the wonders of the age—indeed, of any age.

A modern one, engrossed though it may be in its own particular pursuit of the Truth, should pay homage to the influential periods of the past. Those troubled fighting Abbey days, and the glowing, resurgent ones of the budding University in the Cloister of Notre Dame were champion eras. And we boastful, ebullient moderns may well salute them and the heroes, the vivid personalities that moved in them. Those bright adventurous spirits, coming on the scene not long after the Dark Ages had gone out, dug deeper even than our own seekers after nuclear energy, final as that search may now, for the moment, seem. Things even more causal, of the spirit, the mighty minds of the Middle Ages were after. For hundreds of years their universal theme was those "universals," that is, what are left to the earth and its objects, to you and to me, after the "accidents," or qualifying characteristics, are sloughed off. Through three centuries, on into the thirteenth, they strove to find the Source, to lay fingers on the very composition of God.

So through Anselm and Abelard, and his pupil, the soberer Bishop Peter Lombard of Paris, and Saint Thomas Aquinas the magnificent quest continued. And for most of the time they were content to pursue it down there on the Island in the shadow and under the mantle of Mother Church. It was about the middle of the twelfth century that the real uneasiness had come, that the fledglings, the so very mature fledglings, showed signs of wanting to flee from that ancient mother nest by Notre Dame.

The first exodus, only a fractional one then, came with the expulsion of Abelard from the University and the Cloister. As we saw at the time, this had come about because of others' jealousy of his brilliance, for Abelard was far more than great lover and scandal-maker for the ages. His was a magnificently endowed, exploring mind. But a touch of heresy and a little inclination he had to show off, helped on that expulsion. The old abbey school of Sainte Gene-viève had been a good conservative abbey school. Now, through his oratory and drawing power, Abelard spectacularly expanded it.

About that time there appeared on the Seine a tiny building that was a physical symbol of the trend away from the Island and up the Left Bank hill. It was almost a literal bridging between them. A certain Father Adam, in love with learning and penniless ambitious youth, rented one of the half-timbered, out-of-plumb, projecting-storied houses lined up in two fairy-tale rows on the ancient Little Bridge. In a leaning upper story over the stream he set up a new little college.

It was the first little college chick to stray from Mother Notre Dame's side. But small as it was, this little half-way house, half-way college on the bridge, was a popular place. Housewives airing their bedding over the down-stream sills, often paused to listen. It was agreeable, when the sun sloped west, to hear the continual rhythms of the Latin, the learned murmur from the upper room flowing on in harmony with the currents of the Seine and the water lapping against the piles.

A second devoted father started another little half-way school on the Grand Pont, on whose wooden planks Charlemagne made such a clatter when he came down from Aix to visit his Notre Dame school. (The *Pont au Change*, Moneychangers' Bridge, its successor is called today.) But somehow the trend of learning was not north but south. The trek of teachers and students was over the Little Bridge.

After Abelard's day an acute housing shortage on the Island increased the migration. The influx of pilgrims in search of knowledge into the Island and Cloister was comparatively as great as the in-rush of tourists would be in the days of the later world fairs in Paris. Canons were doubling, students tripling, up. Landlords were turning country students into sardines. Rents of attics were climbing as high as their quaint peaked gables. Homeless students staked out claims to alley slits near revolving spits and to bakers' gratings through which the aroma of good things and warmth came up. An Englishman in pious mood on returning from the Holy Land, one named Joce—some say, more happily, Joyous—endowed eighteen beds in a Hôtel Dieu corner, not for invalids but for penniless students.

When these conditions were at their worst, a bishop of Paris, not Peter Lombard or the great founder of the Cathedral, Maurice de Sulli, but a narrow-minded prelate, made a tactical mistake. The University had hitherto known little organization, but it had a compensating democratic way of life. This bishop now insisted on the teaching body swearing a new and rigid oath of obedience to the chapter of Notre Dame, and, in especial, to himself. Restless for some time, several of the faculty rebelled against it as too strict. Then more packed up to go. And most of them did not need any huge-wheeled tumbril moving vans. Their belongings were few, and it was such a short journey over the Little Bridge and up the hill.

Now if it had been a common thirst for knowledge that had brought the first University body together around the two old churches, they had been kept together by the bonds that were Notre Dame's. Not only those of her properties and moral power, but her licensing power. Her chancellor it was who granted all the degrees. And since these meant not only prestige but also the licenses to teach others what they had themselves learned in the Cloister, the very livelihood of many was involved.

Then suddenly the hill school of Sainte Geneviève, which Abelard had so grandly expanded, and the near-by strong Saint Victor's appointed chancellors and assumed this licensing power. If the heart of Paris was in the upper end of the Island, it was now a greatly-extended, crowded, overworked heart, and its present bishop was a martinet. Besides, this hill of Saint Geneviève, the patron saint of the city, was also a sacred place. One could now get there the degrees needed for existence. And if there was not much more open space up there, so congested in every direction was this many-spired and towered, multiple roof-waved Paris, at least there were old halls up there that could be rented by new colleges, cloisters that could be turned over, and a very few garden sites that might be bought for new buildings.

Though it was sad for the Notre Dame chapter and all the older men who had long dwelt in the Cloister, these were picturesque moving days. The richer walked ahead of orderlies or wagons carrying furniture, clothes and books. The poor had their belongings on their backs. But usually they sang: songs of Roland, Lisette, of the

Three Blind Men, or the Tale of the Burghers of Orléans. The last was highly appropriate:

> "Four little clerk scholars of Normandie
> Carry their great round bags hung round their necks,
> Filled with their books, clothes, and gear.
> Handsome are they as on they go,
> Happily and joyously singing."

Ave Marias, too, often sounded as they proceeded over the bridge and up the hill slopes. In the earlier days, these were poignant farewells to Our Lady, patron not only of the first Notre Dame but of Saint Etienne. They two were synonymous, both her homes, and for periods when Notre Dame was dark Saint Etienne had even taken over the name of Notre Dame, later resuming its own. In the last phases of this intermittent emigration, the *Regina Cœli* and *Stella Maris*, all the other lovely evening hymns, were farewell salutes to the spirit of Our Lady hovering over her beautiful new home, the Cathedral, which it was such a pity they had to leave.

For Paris often sang. By that bridge, on the edge of the river, one could hear a strange commingling of music. There were these songs of the marchers, the choir chants from Cathedral and chapel in the offices at so many hours of the day, and that continual melodious harmonizing of the river currents and the rhythmic Latin of Father Adam's over-the-water, upper-room bridge school. With the sunset and the evening star, appeared the minstrels, by day so lazy, so spirited at night, and their rotes and lutes, their flutes and harps.

Then there were the singing guild brothers. As we have seen, almost every worker in the city belonged to some guild. Even those entertainer cousins of the minstrels, the Passion players, were later to have one. Only the minstrels' guilds seemed to peter out. Perhaps this was because they could not afford or else were too careless to pay their dues. And all the men of these mediaeval unions, at one time or another, broke into song, even those who but croaked their notes. Fortunately, most had an ear for music. Often, as the students packed their books over the river, members of the bridge-builders' guild repairing the piles of the Little Bridge, which in some form or other had been there since long before Christ, would pause between their sledge-hammer blows to send deep trolling notes up to the hill.

Of course, there were silent times in the city. Bad and bloody reports sometimes came back from the Crusades. There were days of mourning when famous people, their own beloved White Queen, for example, died. And the guild centres were very quiet when they held examinations of apprentices which were as serious as those of the students in the colleges on the hill above. But so often in the thirteenth century life was bright and gay. Paris might have its pest spots, its insanitation. But these could not blight her any more than the borers in a great oak, though they add some blemishes, can destroy the noble trunk or the gracious spreading foliage. Paris, those days, was a thriving, a happy, and a singing city.

It was well for the students going carolling or puffing from the uphill journey under their packs, and for the illustrious foreign scholars who now were moving up too, that Paris was not only a happy and a singing city but one prosperous and well ruled. In times of persecution religion thrusts its roots down deep. But it is in the sunshine of a prosperous peace that it sends up and out its branches of churches, colleges, libraries, hospitals, and the many leaves of the ministering services performed in them that through the centuries whisper a constant hymn of benediction.

Some schools still continued in the shadow of the ancient mother, but more went over. The majority of students and teachers set up their stone tents on the opposite shore. These, however, were not wholly to get out from under the mantle of the Church. The abbeys of the hill which had assumed the licensing power belonged to her. And later the Pope had a representative dwelling in the college precincts, he often taking the side of the University against the bishop below.

The "colleges" that formed links in the at first loosely connected, but later strongly organized, University chain on the hill were of three kinds. Some lodged or fed the students or did both, in addition perhaps providing places for study, but giving no instruction. Others offered that, but no home. Still others both lodged and taught them. But on migrating to the hill and its slopes, the teachers and students soon looked out for their bodies. The old Cloister had been hospitable. Its democratic way of life had been attractive. But they wanted to get away from the helter-skelter manner of lodging students in odd corners. What they needed was union and organization. Some tutors and instructors still tried to attract young countrymen and foreigners to their own residences or apartments where they hoped to make an income two ways, through tutoring and boarding. But the beds they advertised as so "comfortable" too often turned out insufferable from lice and old straw. Their rooms, with nothing but tattered arras against the wind, brought on phthisis. And it was hard for students with lumps in their throats from home-sickness and other lumps in their stomachs from bad food to learn their Lucan or

constellations. They could not make the best demonstrations of Euclid
with fingers blue with the cold.

So many unions that took in both teachers and students were
formed. These would have delighted Woodrow Wilson. They hired
houses, shared expenses, and elected managers. Later, instruction too
was very often added.

The "Colleges of the Four Nations," so celebrated in song and
story, had been founded to take care of their own nationals. For
many of their undergraduates in their early 'teens had been set loose
in a city which might be very intellectual yet had its temptations of
the flesh. One of the Four Nations, the "College of the Normans,"
continued to look out only for its own. The others became more
hospitable. The "College of the Picards" took in Flemish and Dutch
as well as the sons of Picardy. The "College of the English" finally
accepted, too, Germans, Irish, and Scotch. The "College of the
French" admitted with their own youth aliens from Spain, Italy, and
far-off Greece. There was more reason than one for calling that century "glorious."

Another reason besides that courteous hospitality was the charity of
Paris and her University. Poor boys now did not go shelterless and
hungry. A French widow used up her legacy establishing on the
Right Bank the College of Saint Honoré for the poor. The eighteen
beds in the corner of the Hôtel Dieu expanded to many cots in a
full-fledged college in a house of its own, appropriately called the
"College of Eighteen." The religious orders abounded with penniless scholars; and there were many burses, the mediaeval scholarships.
The new Sorbonne was the poor students' sanctuary.

While some of these institutions took over old hostels and halls,
many were new from foundation stones to ridge-pole. In 1217, as
we have seen, an envoy of Saint Dominic hurried up the hill to see
about a chapter-house for the great new order. Saint Dominic had
great good fortune then. A faculty member had purchased with his
life's savings the truck garden plot on the summit of the hill for a
college of his own. This the generous M. de la Barastre—all honour
to his name—turned over to the new order. Half-way down, the Franciscans started a convent and college. And nowhere did the students
fare better than in the schools of the Orders. Here they were sure of
shelter, sustenance, and security. Cells might be reasonably austere,
but refectories were not chill. And the new cloister would not be the
tangled grew world of the old Cloister below around Notre Dame.
It would be according to convention, with arcades, green lawns, and
sparkling fountains, very pleasant places indeed for study.

If the old University site below had been sacred and filled with associations, this new one on the hill abounded in history. On the hill-crest near that garden the picturesque Gauls with the bright helmets on their still brighter hair had gone down before Caesar's General Labienus.

Later a Roman theatre had stood on the hill-top, and the barracks of Julian's favourite legion. Across the way from the garden was the Abbey of Sainte Geneviève where she rested and where Abelard had made such a sensation. The very rows of peas over which they looked were descendants of those brought ages before by the Phocian Greeks. Roman generals were very fond of turnips. They had first set them out there. The grapes were from stock of the Emperor Constantine Chlorus. The shadows of two towers fell across the green rows. Through these in 1436 the French guarding the Gate of Saint Jacques, would ride to retake the city and justify the spirit of the dead girl from Domrémy. The very wall which would soon border the abbey grounds would run from a point in front of where the giant Pantheon pillars are now, down almost to Richelieu's white marble Sorbonne Tomb, turn near where Villon's uncle would chide and always forgive his brilliant, erring nephew, to round the old site of the D'Harcourt school and café, and the tavern where Verlaine would show the best and the worst of himself before he perished in that attic on the Rue Descartes, back of the hill-top. And in that abbey, when it was up, Saint Thomas Aquinas would write one of the world's six most influential books.

All this, of course, is what is the chief fascination of Paris. Everywhere they have lived, the men of ideas. Not always in her cloisters and colleges have these ideas sprung up but, like flowers out of the mire, up obscure alleys, in dark attics. The thrills of Paris should come not only in the newly-discovered recipe or gown, or even at Napoleon's gilded Tomb, but from faring where Saint Thomas so long ago wrote that book; from seeing on the Rue d'Ulm the place where Pasteur made his explorations into physics, the room in the Hôtel Dieu where he sucked the poisoned saliva from the mad dog's throat; on looking on Laennec's stethoscope, the first in the world; or the little chapel, once without the walls, where Jeanne d'Arc, who never got inside Paris, made her Communion. Wherever you go in Paris ten chances to one you are walking the paths of the famous, and half of the time in the footprints of the good and the great.

So through the next generations, famous schools sprang up on the hill to breed just such men, among them:

Constantinople, where Crusaders, staying on in the Holy Land, sent their sons;

Bayeux, for the young folk of Tapestry Town;
  Picardy, where Dante, on his tour, sat in the straw;
    Montaigu, where Calvin studied, Sainte Barbe, Loyola's alma mater;
      The Bernadins, which prepared boys for Bernard's Clairvaux;
        This Saint Jacques of Saint Dominic in the old truck garden;
          De Beauvais, where the *real* Cyrano de Bergerac went;
            The Franciscans "Cordeliers";

Navarre, which Villon burglarized;
  The Good Children, which Saint Vincent de Paul later took over for
    his lost sheep;
      The "Jacobins" Right Bank House and college;
        Tiny Mignon with its exquisite chapel;
          Lordly D'Harcourt, Lombard, Liseux;
            Cardinal Lemoine, d'Autun, de Presle;
              Breton Cornouailles, Chalac, the Cholets;
                The Joyous (or Joce) "Eighteen";
                  Saint Honoré, and the Sorbonne, college of colleges.

And dozens more added their new Gothic links to the heavy chain
of learning winding in and out of ancient Paris, and chiefly around
the slopes of Sainte Geneviève's fair breasts.
  Still many of the ancient names leap out at you from old charts,
books, the very street names chiselled in old house-walls at Paris corners. Several of the ancient buildings are still there. Across from Notre
Dame stands the university church of the Middle Ages, Saint Julian-le-
Pauvre. The Bernadins refectory is by the river, farther east. The Parisians nicknamed the Dominicans the "Jacobins" because of that great
Saint Jacques convent. They built a second, with a college, near Saint
Honoré Gate. And so are ages remote from each other linked in
Paris; Robespierre's Jacobins, borrowing house and name, defamed
both. That has disappeared in the building of the Rue Rivoli, but
the refectory of the Franciscans, whom Paris called "Cordeliers,"
because of their cord girdles, is still on the medical school grounds.
This too was pre-empted by a Revolutionary club. And plastered up
against the École Polytechnique you will find Navarre Chapel, the
scene of Villon's crime.
  Carmelites and Augustinians too had colleges in their abbey clusters. It was in the Augustinian Church (near where now is the *quai*
of that name) that Villon, seeing his mother at her humble devotions,
wrote his exquisite prayer-poem for her—and the ages.
  Gradually all these colleges formed a stronger chain and the

incorporation of the University became fact. In 1200 Pope Innocent the Third and Philippe Auguste had granted it something very like a charter. The faculties, in 1209, drew up statutes governing their body. In 1211 the Pope asked the University to send an ambassador to the Vatican, thus strengthening the bond to the Church. This automatically brought civil rights, among them the one to sue in court. And Gregory the Ninth granted the full charter in 1231.

Implicit in it was the curious right of striking. When one of their body was injured by an outsider and redress was not at once forthcoming, they suspended lectures; and at times famous men had to cool their heels in the halls, waiting for their doctor degrees. Students and teachers were exempted from taxes, from mediaeval subpœnaing by courts, and from military service. A special papal delegate was appointed to advise the University authorities and help defend them against encroachments by the officials of the town.

So a University republic, not quite a protectorate of the Vatican but a beloved protégé of it, grew up between the city walls of the royal capital. Many were the struggles during the next two centuries, between the college students and the city watch, the faculty and the provost. Sometimes when there was a riot or a killing, in the Latin Quarter, they would not let the provost arrest the culprit. They insisted on trying their student malefactors themselves. And Paris was frequently upset by bloody fracases between the mediaeval town men and gown men, in which the students fought with bare hands against steel, and with that amazing spirit with which future students in colleges of the hill would face the invaders from the Rhine. At the end of the fourteenth century the students forced the provost who, after a fray, hanged two students, to cut them down, kneel before them, and kiss their cold lips.

The "Colleges of the Four Nations" were the first to elect deans. These chose a rector for the Four. The University, as a whole, followed suit early in the fourteenth century, electing a rector over all. About this time too the custom of letting each student pay what he wished was abandoned and uniform fees were demanded of all but the scholarship bursars.

Students entered the "inferior," or secondary, schools, the colleges of liberal arts, very early, most at fifteen, the precocious often at twelve. In the "superior," the professional, schools of medicine, theology, civil and canon law, the students were older. Graduating B.A.'s were admitted into those higher schools in their twenties. More were thirty or over. And there were many grave and reverend men, even ordained priests among them. The liberal arts youngsters made if not a heavy at least a lively majority in the winding-alleyed campus of the hill, as in their all-too-long gowns they chattered their Latin, hurried from lecture to lecture, ate in their lodging-houses, refectories, or unions, ruffled it in the streets, plagued the Paris girls, or skylarked on the city walls in defiance of the *échevins* and city watch.

Blaspheming or free-thinking students were not welcome. Every undergraduate, whether he was going into theology or not, had to have at least a nominal religious background. And whether they honoured this in breach or observance, almost everyone accepted it. There were few if any mediaeval students to declare self-sufficiently, like the moderns, that there is no such thing as sin, only customs and *mores*. The backsliding bachelor of arts of Paris would have admitted that in his backsliding he was sinning and that merrily as he committed the more venial offences, or tragically the mortal ones, he must repent one day or pay. Their prize students, those flaming geniuses, Abelard and Villon, in line after line of tragic sermon and letter, or poignant lyric, vividly, unforgettably testify to this. In studying past history sin, at least the prevailing attitude of the age toward it, as much as economics, must be taken into account.

For many decades in the earlier life of the University the authorities had tried to inquire into the character of all entering it. For many more years all, students and teachers, had to be celibate. Later this was restricted to candidates for holy orders. But only the "seminarians" had to be tonsured, although all wore the long soutanes or cassocks, the uniforms which stamped them as students or "clerks" entitled to all the charter privileges.

When at work, the arts student spent much time in his union, draughty lodging-house or cloister, at solitary study. An even greater part of his waking hours was given over to tutoring or being tutored. In class the professor read the assigned book, analysed it, and dictated his conclusions. The first liberal arts course covered grammar, which included the Latin language; rhetoric, which took in oratory, all written and oral expression; and the dialectics, logic, and ethics which made up the mediaeval philosophy. Strangely, it was not until later when half-way through his course that he started, after all those profound studies, the easier ones of mathematics—advanced arithmetic and geometry—astronomy, with a little more of the natural science of the time, and music, which had shown some development in both harmony and counterpoint and boasted two fine poet-composers in France, Adam de la Halle and William of Michaut. The mediaeval scholar was an abler philosopher than scientist. But the modern undergraduate or graduate who might scorn such a curriculum would find himself, could the two meet, routed by many a mediaeval and younger man in dialectics, metaphysics, and debating.

The young guild apprentice, who had to pass relatively as stiff examinations in the lore of his craft, had given his name to the student on the hill, *bachelier,* in the old French. It was fitting. If he was an apprentice at weaving or fine saddle-making, or goldwork, the student above was an apprentice at teaching. From the name of the apprentice who worked with his hands—*and* his intelligence—by the Seine, and elsewhere, the bachelor of arts of Paris and, for that matter, of Oxford or Muskingum, has derived his name. This parallel of college above and guild by the river is typical of Paris and its eternal union of the hand's and the eye's skill with the mind's and the soul's fervour.

In his 'teens, the student won his baccalaureate. As he went on for his mastership, he had to teach, to tutor the scholars lower down. As before he had become an apprentice in learning, now, as a bachelor of arts, he was an apprentice in teaching. Midway in this course, he was given the privilege of sitting with the faculty, also a handsome biretta at an imposing ceremony. Then with his master's degree, he became a full-fledged teacher, a young professor in the University of Paris at the advanced age of, say, twenty-one!

Since in Paris that master's degree was equal to a doctor's elsewhere, the hill was full of these highly literate, youngish doctors. And now these mediaeval Boris Sidises had to read, absorb, and then expound such subtle books as—the catalogues are still extant—Aristotle's *Meteors, Physics, Ethics,* the eighteen of the *Institutions* of Priscian, Barbarissmus, Boethius' *Divisions* and *Topics,* and Porphory, whose name meant king and who was punningly rechristened "Purple."

The student in the "superior" school of medicine had to exhaust the great Latin doctor of eleven centuries earlier, Galen, and gifted Arab doctors like Avacinna. The faculties were wise enough not only to lecture to their students but to send them out to watch the graduated physician at work. With his master the tiro visited the sick and learned his methods, his best bedside manner, also that technical jargon which, through the very astonishment it provoked, eased the patient of half his pain.

Salerno, Montpellier, leaned rather heavily those years on dissection, and corpses were now worthily, again questionably come by. With the day's sanitation, there were enough of them. And they had added to the old Gallo-Roman knowledge of Caesareans, trepanning, bladder and kidney knifings, and similar pioneer operations, new and improved methods of treating neck wounds, venereal diseases, and smallpox. Pus and suppuration conditions were constant objects of study. They anticipated modern infra-red lighting by putting up red curtains around the patient's bedside. And their hospitals were better than students often imagine. The handsome up-to-date hospital at

Tampierre, for example, had beautiful carvings and arras and stained glass to delight the sick. The great ward was well ventilated, had partitions, and above, a gallery ran all around so that all patients might be under constant observation. Paris, which was to give so many illustrious doctors to the world, a large number of whom would work on this hill, in 1290 gave a home and post to a foster son, the celebrated Lanfranchi. Before Doctor Harvey, he distinguished between venous and arterial surgery and refused to separate the study of surgery from that of medicine.

The candidate of the school of law (also "superior") droned through his codes, digests, and decretals. And the teaching of canon law was carried on in a separate institution. But in neither law nor medicine did the University of Paris set quite as high standards or attain such fame as she did in the arts, above all in theology, in which lay her chief glory.

Important as were the solitary study, the classroom instruction, and the endless tutoring, the backbone of the University courses for the arts men, the superior "postgraduates," was the lecture. At the "ordinary lectures," the students merely listened, at the "extraordinary," they could ask questions. They went to lectures not only in their own but in neighbouring colleges.

The educational system then revolved around books, not laboratories—the great source books and others almost as great which interpreted these. At the opening of the semester, the books for the courses and the lectures were distributed among the teaching staffs, with the schedules of the appointed hours and halls for the lectures. And once again were the needy considered. The professors set aside hours at which those too poor to purchase books could have the texts read to them in advance of the classes and lectures.

The grand climax lectures were the "disputations." At the "ordinary disputations," held once a week, the masters chosen would defend the theses against opponents. Once a year there was held, with great oratorical pomp and rhetorical circumstance, the *quodlibet,* or "extraordinary disputation." As in the Notre Dame Cloister, the debaters in these hill contests were often celebrated men. Frequently Saint Thomas Aquinas, Saint Bonaventura, or a Roger Bacon would appear. They too were acclaimed like champions and their arguments were published in permanent form for posterity.

Such celebrated scholars lectured under the auspices of the third "superior" school, that of theology, in which supreme subject of the Middle Ages Paris was supreme. But, for a moment before we get on to those luminaries, lest it be thought that in Paris University, in every lodging-house and college, purity and piety prevailed, let us see what these arts undergraduates did in their off-hours. Current chronicles of them are graphic. Letters young hot-bloods left behind tell many tales. Though Mother Church tried hard to protect her youth, there were many beckoning girls and welcoming inns. If Solomon warned against looking on the wine when it was red, why, there was plenty of good white. For further thrills, they had the frays when they took on the townsmen and the *sergents de ville*. If the green Saint-Germain-des-Près meadows outside the walls, where they often made love, were sometimes smeared too red, that may have been a needed antidote against too much Priscian, Porphory, or Barbarissmus.

Now though only one or two of the colleges, like that of Picardy which Dante visited, actually was on the Rue de Fouarre, the "Street of Straw," straw was used in very many to prevent the cold of ancient stone floors, often above dungeons, from chilling too much the buttocks of the students sitting on the floors as they listened to the masters. Some decades later on, straw too was strewn on the street of its name to muffle late returning footsteps so that these would not disturb the students working by their candles, or little spout oil lamps, or only the hearth fire, over Lucan, De la Halle, or Galen.

A fair proportion of the students came from well-to-do families. Coxcomb youths actually hired orderlies to wait on them, carry their drinks and also their books ahead of them to the lectures. Such as these did not shine in philosophy or Plotinus, Rhazes or rhetoric, or the Bible, or anything except in bibulosity and boasting at the inns.

It was such parasites who wrote those wheedling letters that have come down to us. When they were cleaned out by the girls, the inns, or the snail-shell games of the minstrels, they would ask to have the next month's allowance sent ahead. Again one would demand money to pay debts or for banquets "to keep up his station." In other missives, the very phrases bleed with the sore feet, chapped hands, the mythical hemorrhages they describe. Their rooms are always cold— sometimes they overlook the fact that it is summer. Prices are forever going up. Clothes are all tatters. Hose are so full of holes that the hose have become zeros, all the little holes having finally merged into one big one. Many are the pathetic words designed to melt the hardest bourgeois heart.

But often a shrewd parent replies that the rooks have eaten all the grain, the pigs have sickened and died. So what is there to send? Another season the birds have pecked all the grapes, the old wine has soured in the casks. So what can loving father do for his very dear son? Again, brigands have rifled all father's packs on the trade-routes, and all his ships in the deep seas have foundered.

But there are other ruses. How the favourite son has now triumphed in the disputations! All the masters have gone down before him in defeat. Even the famous doctors, the coming saints, have stood aghast at dear son's brilliance. So, dear family, come, fling out your banners! Call out your musicians! Cull out a holiday! And play, play, play, to honour my triumphs! Of course, to match the celebration at home there had to be one in Paris—and the wherewithal for it. Such appeals to paternal pride more often than those to pity were profitable for the prodigals.

If merchant or farmer father was adamant, the distaff side might be more pliant. One tries a little sister. Could she not, now, sound out her rich husband on the trifle of a loan? Surely she would not have the heart to refuse her brother slowly coughing his life away. "I ask you, sweet little sister, to get your rich husband to deliver me."

And sweet little sister obliges, not without humour: "I send you the enclosed by messenger, but—for the sake of the dear God!—do not let anyone know. If my husband hears of it, you will have not a dear, but a dead, sister!"

Luckily, the number of these young long-gowned treaders of the primrose path was less than the number of the industrious student-poor. When there were not burses, or scholarships, to go round, boys without funds tried a variety of occupations. With ink-pot and feathered quill, they transcribed glosses and texts for the rich boys. Stationing themselves, with little stools, by the bridges, they wrote love-letters for the illiterate and loving. Some carried pails of water up many flights or emptied slops in the Rue Saint-Jacques, Fouarre, or Des Carmes gutters, or down the stone-seated privies which in winter were so cold that the students got severe constipation from putting off their visits.

How many were there of these students working their hearts out at such tasks, studying the heavens, searching for profound abstractions or for new wine-shops and girls? The number for the day was truly astonishing. For this the open-hearted Church was again in a considerable measure responsible. So many of these young people travelled practically free from town to town through the liberal hospitality offered by the monasteries and bishops and the poor rural priests. Truly that was a happy century in so many ways. The estimate by some contemporary chroniclers of thirty thousand, most on that Left Bank hill, is probably much too enthusiastic. The soberer figure, nine thousand, is nearer the truth. But nine thousand, all eager for life—high or low—with thousands of landlords, servitors, clergy, shop-keepers, bakers, washerwomen, fishermen, cooks, grave-diggers, cooped up within the less than one square mile of the Latin Quarter, its high-looming city walls, guarded by the thirty-five Left Bank wall towers, why, it was enough! Even the noses of the Island landlords were no longer out of joint. Their houses began to fill up from the overflow.

France had three other great universities—Montpellier for medicine, Orléans for law, Toulouse with a fine general reputation. So they would multiply through the succeeding generations until there were fine ones too in Dijon, Lille, Strasbourg, Grenoble, and all the provincial centres of France. Paris would serve as model for Oxford, Cambridge, Prague, Heidelberg, Vienna, Aberdeen, many others. But in the thirteenth century that same powerful trinity still dominated Europe: Bologna, almost as old as Paris, was pre-eminent in law, and Salerno in medicine. Paris, while maintaining her prestige for a truly magnificent all-around culture, was first in the great specialty of the Middle Ages, theology. She was famous, too, even in those days, for many lovely things: for her gold, stained glass, and bookbinding, for her good rule, upright judges, and beneficent labour laws, for the beauty of her abbeys, and churches, and her river, for her courtly chivalry, resplendent Crusaders, and great exemplar Cathedral. But strange as it may seem now to tourists seeking her more superficial attractions, this City of manifold aspects was then first among cities because she had on her hill not the religious capital, which was eternally in Rome, but the theological capital of the world.

If the University of Paris was the world's theological centre, the little Sorbonne was very core of that centre. No college ever had a more perfect founder. Robert de Sorbon was a man of considerable learning, even greater love of it, and of pure life and exalted ideals. From his little village near Rheims he had come up to Paris to study educational conditions. He had determined to set up a new college with a devoted and gifted staff to train boys of exceptional ability but no funds. The last request Saint Louis had made of his mother was that she execute promptly the deed to the little plot for it, half way up the hill. In 1252 Queen Blanche turned over the parchment deed to Robert while Saint Louis was chafing—and praying—in an Oriental prison.

Never at Oxford, Göttingen, Saint Andrews, Freiberg, Salamanca, Princeton, Grenoble, Jena, here at Paris, or in any university, would a Hume, Hegel, Balfour, Bergson, Jung, Charléty, Churchill, or any lord rector or distinguished guest make address more memorable than Robert Sorbon's on this thirteenth-century occasion that was so literally a "commencement" for this tiny cradle of a college which he would rock and nurse into a true and shining greatness.

These were a few of the simple directions which the founder urged on the students in his quiet but impressive, even noble, way, as a sun ray, coming over the roof of the neighboring Saint Benoît's, laid its bright finger on the scholarly face, seeming to pick out these words and illuminate them for all educational institutions for eternity:

"Devote, young gentlemen, a certain hour each day to the study of a special chosen subject.

"Concentrate on what you read. Never read superficially, skimmingly.

"Extract from the reading one salient thought and etch it deeply on your mind.

"Also write a digest of it. Thoughts not set down and so chained in words fly like chaff before the wind.

"Discuss, too, this thought and your digest with your fellows in all conversations. Nothing is thoroughly known until it is tested by argument."

In summing up, he gave this final suggestion which, unhappily, would amaze most modern student bodies, but which, could they by some revolution take them to their hearts, would galvanize all our modern education and society. For men cannot, as Robert knew, live by the bread of science, of facts, alone.

"My young friends, prayer is one of the best ways of learning. Elevate the heart to God, but at the same time go on—go on—with your studies."

So Robert Sorbon quietly laid down for them this all-powerful mystical law which today's teachers would stamp as merely psychological, and let the subconscious work for them. Robert, Thomas, Albert, the mediaeval thinkers all, thought of it as something else again: the opening up of the deeper layers of the mind for irrigation into fertility by the Holy Spirit.

The seventeen generous, devoted charter priests Robert had gathered together and the gifted poor boys started their work with joy. At once the Sorbonne attached to itself the little arts Collège de Calvi, to give the foundation training to the younger students; but its main objective, those first few centuries, was theology. Soon after the little building had gone up students from all over the hill began to drop in, in the free, hospitable university way, to hear William of Saint Amour from Saint Victor's and others of the great. They seemed to like to lecture in this new college which might be small but from the beginning held a certain tone and atmosphere.

Later there would occur two theological tragedies, one when the University saw to it that Jean Sans Peur was absolved of political assassination, the second when some Sorbonne doctors could not see the pure flame that was Jeanne d'Arc. But in a long and fruitful life, these were not ultimate Judas but temporary Peter lapses. The Golden Age of Greece had been reborn and given a Christian christening at the very doors of Notre Dame. It now burned with a no more intense but ever-widening circle of glory on the Acropolis of Paris, Sainte Geneviève's Hill.

If the places most sacred in the earlier days had been the church porches and the Cloister holy water fonts, the hill University's heart was the Sorbonne. Today you can see in one of its open courts, traced out with stones, the outlines of that mighty mustard seed, the first tiny Sorbonne. Those markers are like small gravestones bordering the last resting-place of something that has vanished and yet is marvelously alive. Like Thermopylae Pass, Runymede Isle, Lexington Bridge, the Jeanne d'Arc slab at Rouen, the lighted few feet under the Arc de Triomphe, the little plot outlined by those stone rows is holy ground.

Later the Sorbonne, grown mighty, would change from its theological specializing to a more general culture. The term now is not applied to all the University buildings scattered about Paris, but only to those above Cluny around the Rue Saint-Jacques in which the arts and sciences are taught, also the hilltop school of law and, of course, the Lemercier Sorbonne Chapel where Richelieu lies in that splendid marble tomb, with his red cap hanging above it like some antediluvian spider, symbolic of his statecraft.

So they came in, by up-river or down-river road or over the hill, by the thousands, to this fair city of Paris and its thriving University. They came in so fast that a little popular ditty went the European rounds: "No student has been a student who has not studied in Paris."

This referred, too, to the quality of learning's merchandise to be had there. And all the publicity was the more effective because it was unsolicited and spontaneous. Even in the nostalgia of plaintive letters there was a certain rich advertising value.

A bemoaning Milanese doctor of renown writes: "As soon as God permits, I shall hurry back to you. Heavy are the lost years spent away from Paris and its most holy and venerable studies."

In 1211, the year when the faculties drew up their first statutes in defense of themselves, William le Breton set this down: "In Paris Letters are brilliant. Never before in the history of the world has such a continuous stream of students poured through a city's gates. The causes are the privileges the kings have granted the students and the wonderful beauty of the city itself."

Saint Louis himself, in his little dedicatory speech at the opening of the Carthusians' convent and the college that went with it, reflected the general feeling about his fair capital: "Paris, the city in which bubble up the healing and abundant waters of pure and wholesome doctrine. This stream passes through the city, refreshing it, and then flows on, a universal doctrine, irrigating Mother Church and the whole world."

And Pope Clement the Fourth completed the letter quoted a few pages back with this sentence: "Those that have been taught in Paris shine gloriously wherever they fare. Those that teach in Paris will shine with the stars for all eternity."

Splendid are all these tributes and deserved of Paris and her University. But quite as affecting in its touching understatement is the name by which Robert de Sorbon always knew the cradle college named for him: "The Poorest Home of the Masters of Arts."

It is for such "trifles" as this, a thousand of them, that, no matter how she may—which God forbid!—decline, we should ever venerate Paris and the country of which she is the beating heart.

Not long after most of the teachers and students had come thronging over the Little Bridge to set up their new colleges on the hill, they were, we are glad to say, still mindful enough of their great original debt to Notre Dame, of their origin in the Cloister, to place on the new university seal, in the thirteenth century, the seal of the Bishop of Paris and with that the figure of Our Lady, of Notre Dame, of whom the University had been born.

Distances in Paris are still reckoned from that Last Judgment Portal of Notre Dame. There are so many other things around the world that can be traced to her door. Students in the far-off New World, on solemn academic occasions, raise their hats and with brimming eyes sing their alma mater songs. The very title they use came from an ancient hymn often sung on the Island of Paris, in the vaulted ranges under the rose-windows, by the lighted candles of the altar of the most venerable of alma maters, the Cathedral of Notre Dame— *Alma Redemptoris Mater.*

VII

*"The Little French One" who never saw France or Paris yet
changed them profoundly.*

N ONE OF THESE SEVEN GREAT SONS AND FOSTER SONS OF PARIS
had greater influence on the university, the whole city,
than one who never reached the capital or crossed over into
France at all. This was ironical, for his father, out of his great admiration for things French, as much as because of a reputed French ancestor along the line, had named the boy "Francesco," which is as
much as to say "the French One," "the little French One," or maybe
simply "Frenchy."

This amazing Schubert-Jonathan-Stephen rolled into one gave to
his indoor chants and outdoor lyrics, lovelier than any of Solomon's—
yes—and as beautiful as David's, something of the feeling, delicacy,
and grace, of the minstrels of Provence beyond the borders of his
Italy, elevated with the spiritual he added. His sermons, his ways, his
whole life had, with its Eden, its Galilee tones, a French Gothic
accent.

Francesco, Little Frenchy, who became the great Saint Francis,
never saw his Cordeliers convent. He never reached Paris on his
extensive poundings of the roads, God-bent and Good-Samaritan inclined. Yet he was ever there in Paris, not only in this convent half-
way up Sainte Geneviève's Hill. Everywhere in Paris, as in the rest of
Europe and England and the Near East too, he was present, and all the
time. In fact, as near as mortal soul may have, he had an omnipresence
of the spirit. You cannot know Paris of the thirteenth century, you
cannot know that century, you cannot know the whole miraculously
active and productive age, without taking Saint Francis into the
picture, into every picture, all the time. Leaving him out of Paris
would be worse than leaving Hamlet out of his play. It would be
equivalent to blotting out a very different Napoleon from the nineteenth century, a frighteningly different Marx out of the twentieth,
or omitting Moses from the Exodus, David from the time of the
Psalms. He and Saint Dominic, whom we did meet coming up that
Paris Hill, were co-progenitors of the armies of the friars. And theirs
was as mighty a movement, a forward march, a scouting of the hedge-
rows, the city slums, the over-seas jungles, as ever accomplished

results—for the body, though chiefly for the soul—in this hard-driven world. They added to the great central current of spiritual endeavour of the Church, which was ever going on steadily, quietly, powerfully, an eager, fresh companion current, a new influx of vigour and vitality. This would unite with the Church, the friars jointly with the priesthood, to carry on the work of the spirit, at an increased pace with a deepened conviction, and a new drive forward.

So Saint Francis was ever present here in Paris, through his regiment of friars, industriously reading their offices, singing their chants, pulling their bells, hurrying here, hurrying there, in the darkest streets, in the forests outside, by the charcoal burners' huts, in their swift, tender, multiple, and varied demonstrations of the love of God applied to the daily needs of the humblest of folk, glorious in the most inglorious of tasks. But his life was even more evident in the whole moulding and directing given to life in Paris and everywhere else, by him in his joyous, healing, and incorrigibly charitable way, and in the fiery, intense, incessantly missioneering and militantly exhorting way of Dominic. Dominic gave sermons and fire that never failed to burn deep. Francis shed a light and love that were contagious—a joy that was the unfailing infection of the spirit of God.

It is a pity that some of these truly great friars then living in Paris, the Dominicans, Thomas Aquinas and Albert the Great; the Franciscans, Bonaventura, Roger Bacon, and Alexander of Hales could not have known the beloved saint. That is, in the flesh. Intimately enough they knew him through his works and his influence. But he had died about two years before the greatest of these, Thomas Aquinas, had been born, down in Italy. Before his passing, Saint Francis had given up the commandership-in-chief of his army which had so changed history's whole course. Like Washington he resigned it with a farewell, but one that is even more beautiful:

"I give Thee back, sweet Jesus, this my family, all my faithful friars which Thou didst graciously entrust to my care. For Thou knowest that I no longer have the strength and wisdom to lead them. I return them to Thee. So take them, dear Lord, to Thy loving heart."

This little man, when from his eyes the brightness, from his lips the songs and kindling words, were fading, had received after a vision, what he considered the crowning decoration of his life, the nail-prints of Christ. The material accountings for these by some rationalizing physicians strangely accord with the supernatural explanations. If the processes of the soul, through the mind, have been rarely expressed outwardly in the flesh, if such images and symbols of the crucified Christ, long dwelt upon by the selfless leader, can by some teleophotography of the brain and sensitive nerves and skin, appear so vividly on the body of Francis, there was more than the purely physical in it.

A great poet warned his Horatio about discounting these signals from another world. Many a contemporary doubting Thomas saw these signs at Assisi, put his fingers in the worn palms of Francis, and felt there the marks so closely resembling the nail-prints in the hands of His King.

Saint Francis never climbed the hill. Still whenever you walk in Paris or through the Middle Ages, you must keep looking out of the corner of your eye for the little man, the invisible but influential citizen, who never lived in the capital by the Seine but on her left his shining and indelible mark.

Many books have been written about him. He is worth them all. For he was the loveliest character of the Middle Ages, the living theme song of the multiple and varied life of the time, the living smile that made Charity gracious, joyous the hard way of the Church.

Most exquisite poet of the age, too, he turned out, and its finest gentleman in his coarse gown and bit of cord. He was both at the same time in his salutation to Brother Fire, when, in his age, they were about to cauterize his eyes, hoping to save his dimming sight: "Brother Fire, God made you beautiful and strong and useful. I pray you now to be courteous with me."

The perfect lover he showed himself in a thousand ways, Lover of all the winged and four-footed creatures of God's nature. Of the sick and the poor. Of all who had need. Perfect lover too, with nothing of the flesh in the affection for her who was his immortal sister in Christ, and was worthy of him in sweetness and purity—Poor Clare.

So you could find him present, in many places at once. In the happy persons of ten thousand proxies, the gowned and corded Franciscan friars, the married and serving Third Order folk, among them our Louis and Blanche—all, all myriad little shards and gleams of heavenly light. So were the times filled with the actuality of his presence even after he was gone. Echoes of him then you could hear everywhere. Echoes of his blessing in his hedge-row wayside and leper charities. In the most moving songs ever composed by the heart. In the most fetching and telling (after the one on the Mount) sermons ever preached. Before the most heterogeneous audiences ever—street crowds, beggars, cardinals, sultans, and little birds.

Christ, had He come to earth, would have loved this little brown, sparkling-eyed, happy indefatigable, with the song on his lips, the love for all in his heart, and the flame in the whole life of him—loved him as He had Saint John. Unseen by us, He must have so loved him anyway.

This little man had by chance picked up one day an old piece of cord to tie his coarse gown. It became one of the great signs and insignia of the world. With this little piece of cord, he tied up the hearts of millions to him—to Christ and into His Kingdom of Heaven.

VIII

The Passing Throng on Saint-Jacques and De la Harpe. . . . The Great Men go to buy the New Rag Paper for their Books. . . . The Rough Paris Crowds are not so Bawdy as Twentieth-century Lady Novelists. . . . The Fields of South France are Blue with Flax for the Books of Paris. . . . The Bookseller-Stationers scour the Country-side for Fine Skins and Extra-quality Womb Parchment. . . . Saint Séverin of the Fishermen, River Sailors, and Frog-hunters. . . . Writers', Illuminators', Parchment-making, Eremboux-de-Brie, Sack-of-Lees, Lilacs, Three Candlesticks, and Little-Tax-on-the-Fishstall Streets. . . . Isaiah shows through Luke's Bethlehem on the Palimpsest. . . . As the Cathedral nurtured the University, now it sets up the Bookseller. . . . The Whole Quarter turns out to gather Ivy for its Carmine, Cornflowers for their Blue, to paint their Little Books.

The Mid-Thirteenth

SCHOLARS WITH RESOUNDING NAMES, ALEXANDER OF HALES, Albert the Great, Thomas d'Aquin, crusty Roger Bacon from over the Channel, Bonaventura, the "Seraphic Doctor," often in these middle years descended the gentle slope of the Left Bank Hill to Writers' Street and the Way of Parchment-making, the centre of the Paris book quarter.

Some of them big and very personable men under their birettas, most of them virile in their asceticism, they walked, usually in pairs to the bookseller-stationer's, to buy parchment and to inspect and perhaps lay in a little store—for trying out—of the new linen and rag paper then just beginning to come into vogue. Pack-trains would every now and then come up from the flax fields of the south. When, after inspection by the tax collectors, usually elected from the ranks of the Merchants' Guild, they had passed through the massive city gates, thence over the Little Bridge, and had clinked, with weary hoofs, into the dense-packed world of the men who made the books of Paris, the news was quickly carried up the Hill to the men who wrote them. It seemed almost as if they could smell from afar off the new virgin sheets waiting the impress of their great thoughts. They would not, of course, scant their reverence, but they might imperceptibly increase by a breath or so the pace of the chanted office, and hurry even more the lecture or the weekly *quodlibet*. Then, pausing only to don their birettas, they hurried down the Hill. They would go by either of the Hill's two "main streets," running north and south, and very near together in that compact walled University area. One was the old Roman highway that came up over the hill from Orleans southwest, Saint-Jacques, still with the Before Christ cobbles, which would remain there until about the year when a thin young Napoleon would look for cheap meals in that book quarter. The other was the Rue de la Harpe, whose lower part is still there but whose upper half vanished when Boul' Miche' was cut through on the hill.

It was a picturesque press through which the great men passed. All the way down, students poured in and out of college courts and cloister archways. Some sauntered along the street, reading digests of the lectures, long brown batons of bread under their arms. Others studied on high by attic windows under quaint gables, munching Oise country cheese and cherries, and throwing the pits down on the crowd. And clusters were always to be found lounging in the church porches, their eyes on very lively ankles passing as their elbows rested on the shoulders of dead saints.

Here the rather stately great scholars saw the sick being borne into hospitals; there the dead were carried out. Not only were children born every hour, but it seemed as though people were always dying in this very alive Paris. The baker by his oven, the groom currying Tour de Nesle horses, the Saint Benoît sacristan, hanging up amice and alb, would be stricken. The *blanchisseuse* beating clothes white by the river would be seized with the birth pangs. A housewife walking the city walls for a breath of air would come into her time and warders would suddenly drop their halberds to deliver her in the tower of the Saint Victor gate.

In this bridge-house one would weave a christening robe, her neighbour a shroud, for the Cathedral. Everywhere, in the room above, next door, across the court, midwife, priest with Viaticum—Life and Death—would cross the threshold. On this side of a wall a child would be oiled at his entrance into the world, on the other side a man would be anointed with oil for his passage from it. The citizens of Paris were born vigorously, to a yell, lived vigorously to a lusty clatter. And if they did not exactly die with vigour, they were accompanied by a great show of force, with book, chant, censing, candle, and a mighty pulling on toll ropes and tumbling of tongues in church bells.

And there were earthier cries on the street as Albert the Great, the Seraphic Doctor, Thomas d'Aquin, all the cerebral celebrities, passed down De la Harpe and Saint-Jacques—of 'prentices' calls, students jeering one another, of hawkers with fish or lavender. Shopkeepers spread out mediaeval hats, wood sabots, red and black shoes, on counters which by day were let down from, by night folded up into, the residence walls. Clerks draped maroon and purple textiles from shoulder to ankles on plump patrons' persons. From butchers' hooks hung rabbits, thorn-hedge sparrows, with spattered garnets in their white throats. Archers bore Chantilly deer hung from poles by their quarters, their eyes mute but still darkly eloquent. Servants convoyed smoking pasties and wine pitchers to lordly lodgers. In the inns bowls, spits, pans agreeably clattered, or sizzled and sputtered.

Friars went, in ones or twos, bare-ankled, gaunt, silent but so burningly absorbed in their calling that they seemed to strike fire as they passed by. Nuns walked with a little click of rosary beads and a soft susurrus of voluminous skirts that was like the constant whispering of a prayer. There one, with coif like snow, soul unspotted from the world, moved like a still benediction through the crowd. In an apprehension in marked contrast with the nun's peace, a girl, red-eyed, hollow-cheeked, desperate, would sneak past her to ask at the store with the ranged retorts, probes, catheters, the containers of animal organs and powdered unicorn horn and other ingredients of love charms, for an aphrodisiac for her reluctant swain. A woman against whom the apothecary had a grudge burst from the store because of the too powerful purge he had vengefully mixed for her, and hurried with great looping strides and hands clasped below her belly, up the alley. Ribald students watched, grinning, to see if she could make it.

Nearer the river smiths cradled horses' hooves in their blackened aprons and applied the hot iron in a great smell of scorched horn and hiss of white-hot iron plunged in water. Armourers clinked their chain-mail links, and wielded newly forged swords, and riveted silver ornaments on head-stalls for the royal stables.

The Paris speech the scholars heard, though picturesque, did not have the roughness one might expect from a vital mediaeval crowd. Louis the Ninth had decreed, not a clean-up week, but a moral as well as physical clean-up century. Under this spell, there had come to the Ile de France, and particularly to Paris, one of those interludes rare in this world, of chastity of speech. Quite different from the prudery of a Victoria, wielding parasols, riding in pony phaetons, sitting on cushions in church, this moraity of Louis, who rode chargers, wielded battle-axes, and, clad in hair shirt, wrestled all night in prayer on the cold stones, was a stronger thing. Under his militant decency, one did not hear in public in Paris half so often as now in the books, plays, talk of the West, the immemorial earthy figures of speech which men use to prove themselves men. These then did not explode out of every other sentence in the modern way. The Holy Name was then more than a mere name. And Saint Louis' weapons of last resort, the red hot awls for incorrigible, blasphemous tongues were not the only holds on mediaeval men. Louis' character, his justice, Church respect were stronger restraints.

Rabelais, to be sure, was to come on Fig-tree Street, to mulch with much of that earth his fine philosophy. In Saint Germain, Proust would emulate the pains and love which the illuminators below gave to their holy books—in trying with his precious words to illumine perversion. Even in Louis' time there were publishing, just as there were speaking, exceptions with those earthy figures of speech. False "goliard" minstrels hawked under-cover ribald verse. Southern titled troubadours tried to make license lovely on decorated pages. But the great mass of the books of Paris had this quality of innocence.

A great archbishop and cardinal of Paris seven centuries on would tell a crowd of union men in the city that reprehensible as was the use of soiling language, to use God's name lightly was infinitely worse. Cardinal Verdier would have welcomed something out of this thirteenth century in his own twentieth.

The scholars walking down De la Harpe and Saint-Jacques did not need these strictures of Louis. They had etched in their hearts one of Saint Paul's about things "honest, pure, lovely, of good report." But even the lay writers of amorous tales would never have set down on the clean vellum or the new paper they were going down to buy the brief body words with which twentieth-century novelists—so many of them women—speckle their sheets.

Now these scholars were not sour. Some of them were very robust saints. They would have admitted that procreation, with its purpose of God, might have, with all of life's serious matters, its comic aspects. And they did not dodge evil. Much about it had gone down in their books, but they had had a viewpoint and a goal. And whether one believes that evil should be lugged in or depicted only when germane to the subject, and then portrayed through the projection of an atmosphere rather than with a piled-on explicitness (the little painter people below would have said that the artist should suggest—he never threw the whole forest in), this much is true of that time which was surely a golden, and what is better, a captivating and refreshing age: Whatever went down in the day's exquisite calligraphy in their books, whether theological abstraction, lovely legend, happy lyric, they kept their pages as clean and fresh and fair as the delicate miniatures that illustrated their untainted text. Their heroes and saints, the little playful animals moved among idyllic groves and bright borders of flowers. They could only have trooped in such a colourful procession, such a gay and holy abandon, from the pens and brushes of artists who had taste with their skill, and devotion and a sense of responsibility to their art and its God.

So the scholars came among these valiant little people, scraping elbows against others, on shelves and street corners all along the queer contours of the mediaeval street. Their long gowns did not so much set them apart, for even the lay students wore these, though gradually theirs were to go up against the day when Villon, his poachers, poets, pimps, pickpockets would need more leg-play for flight. Cords and tonsures, of course, distinguished those in religious orders or in holy orders. But what marked them most was their fine dignity and serenity—and their birettas. A century before, the biretta had been but a skull cap like those of Oxford cricketers or Princeton football players of the 1870's. Once they had had tassels. Recently too they were assuming a little more style, and gradually they would be puffed up, and poked in here and there, as are modern fedoras, for a little more ecclesiastical chic. At last they would evolve into the three-ridged birettas with borders falling around the neck as you see them in portraits of Luther and the martyr Thomas More.

The shopkeepers here bowed respectfully enough, though these eminent scholars did not bring them much trade. For many of them were vowed to poverty, others had their modest needs supplied by the abbeys; and even those who were not in an order and had no thought of entering the priesthood had their thoughts on intellectual rather than on material things. Still, even the mercantile men had something of the traditional Parisian respect for learning and culture. Besides, though these great men were poor spenders at their shops, they brought fame to their city, and that brought hosts of visitors and lodgers, and custom to them.

Farther down Saint-Jacques, however, the bookshops began to appear, clustering around the outskirts of the little capital of the book world then, the eight or ten streets down by the river. By that riverside, right-hand corner of the quarter, the Petit Pont started its span of the Seine. The bridge was ages old, but this present self of it had been built in 1165 by Bishop Maurice de Sulli, Notre Dame's founder, to afford firm footing for the hosts of pilgrims his dream saw coming from the regions roundabout to gaze up at, and sing and pray and exult in, his magnificent Cathedral, Our Lady's beautiful new house. His dream had come true. But over the bridge and the roofs of the book quarter, which looked from above like shoals of fish, loomed something that had no beauty at all and no grace, the grim bulk of the Petit Châtelet. Almost entirely unrelieved by pierced-through windows, and with dungeon cells deep in the eartn—which were scarcely used, except for blasphemers under Louis' good rule and Etienne Boileau's provostship, but which were to multiply frighteningly their torture chambers in the following two centuries—this stronghold not only guarded this important river passage, but served as police headquarters and jail.

The other stronghold of the quarter, on Saint-Jacques, was a spiritual fortress, the Church of Saint Séverin. On their book shopping errands, the scholars would always stop in here, to utter a little petition and sign themseves with a few drops of water from the holy well in the ambulatory. But they did not see it as we do now, or as Camille Saint-Saëns, its famous organist, knew it, with its ring of fifteenth-century charnel-houses for the priests by the side, the porch with its Gothic petition, "Good folk passing by, pray for your sins," or the lovely palm-grove-like vaulting back of the sanctuary. There was then, when the scholars came, only the embryo of the church, the sixth-century oratory with the walls and arches for the new edition beginning to rise around it.

It was very old, this church, and it was one of the few, if not the only one in the world to have two saints of the very same name for patrons—Abbot Séverin and the hermit Saint Séverin, both of the five hundreds. Why, way back, hermit Saint Séverin had built a little osier hut by a spring he had found, and when it seemed to develop holy properties he built the little oratory around it. He could have served the privileged folk of the old Roman palace (whose ruins are now attached to Cluny) a little way up the hill. However, this attractive hermit Saint Séverin preferred to heal and to attend to the spiritual needs of the poor fishermen, river sailors, poachers, and frog-hunters there by the Seine. This grand old tradition of service the larger Church of Saint Séverin was carrying on now for the poor painters, scribes, and binders of the neighbourhood.

The little settlement in which the scholars (even poor Roger Bacon when he could lay his hands on any money) were good spenders had a pleasant all-pervading odor of ink, the nutgalls and vitriol for it, of leather and oil, and also of the flowers they were always crushing for the painter's pigments. It had, too, an equally enticing aroma of history. And the very nomenclature is redolent with history, melodious with music. On De la Harpe, bounding it, a music-seller had a beautiful daughter. Since his sign showed a robust King David playing a bright gold harp, and swarms of students assembled under it, it was the land-mark of the street—whence the Rue de la Harpe.

The street parallel with the river and next it, on which Napoleon would one day almost starve, was the Street of Lilacs and then the Street of the Little Tax on the Fishstall—De la Huchette. A little later it was awhirl with rôtisseries, and goodly brown worlds of roast and fowl turning on their axes. The starving who came here for sustenance from the very smell—the poor too of Paris are so very, very French—often turned giddy from the revolutions. Those with crusts of bread brought them here to dip them into the savour as into a rich gravy!

And there were Three Candlesticks, the narrow one with the tiny circle opening today out of its middle where once stood the neighbourhood well—Sac-à-lie (from the brandy made there), Sack-of-Lees—it was shortened with time into our Zacharie. The Street of the Priests of Saint Séverin—a single block's length too—was to become quite Bohemian for the Grand Dukes. It was then very orderly, as was Saint Séverin Street, along the Church's north side.

Writers' Street (Des Ecrivains) was the earlier name of Parchemi-nerie (Parchment-making). And Illuminators' Street (Des Enlumi-neurs)—it was thick with them—was to be Embroux-de-Brie (for a later resident), then Bourg-de-Brie, which in turn was lazily liaisoned into the Boutebrie we see now on its ancient corners.

To the music of these still surviving street names, and with the help of the considerable skeleton left of the quarter, in walls, dormers, corbels, gables, portals, you can make to live again the little spider-web of streets so short, narrow and dark, but which cared for a traffic more precious than the stateliest boulevard ever bore. All one has to do is to peel off a little encrusting stucco from the truly ancient buildings we see there now, paint up the timbers thus revealed, re-store some bas-reliefs, a few statues and fonts. Then turn on a stream of mediaeval book folk, to pour in from the two main highways into this settlement (which was far from being a backwater but rather the very active book capital within the greater city) with their antique hats, 'prentices' shock heads, birettas, their bundles of skins and paper, casks of liquid, and, also for the trade, sacks of nuts and harvests of flowers and vines on their backs, all eddying in and out of passage and lane, on the human tide.

This picturesquely congested quarter was not only the current but the pioneer capital of the booksellers' world. There had, of course, been libraries before, the magnificent one of Alexandria, for example. In imperial Rome, Homer, Virgil, Cicero's orations, Sappho's poems, had been sold, but not so much in shops as by the amanuenses who set them down. The sales had been individual, usually the fulfilling of outright orders. Occasionally a Roman stationer would exhibit outside his shop, as restaurateurs now post up their menus, lists of the few titles sold, with papyrus and tablets, within. But until the twelfth century there had been no very extensive, active, going book trade. The first real group of booksellers came in with Anselm, Abelard, Roscellin, all the old wrestlers of the Cloister; and were followed a little later by their trade brothers in the University of Bologna.

In both of these universities we have evidence again of the Church's eternal nurturing of knowledge. Since the older of the two sprang out of the Cloister of Notre Dame, we can see afresh what a very particular rôle Notre Dame played in the advance of learning, how the strands of all the activities of learning have been tied up with the creation of the noble pile itself. It almost seems as though the rich colours of the panes, the flowers and growing things carved on the Cathedral walls were symbols of all the lovely things that flower out of life and civilization through the Church.

This trade, art, profession, industry of bookmaking and selling, which gave body, swift wings, carriers, transports to the harvest of intelligence, was therefore, if child of the Church, the little sister of the University. And the University often came—in the persons of its leading lights, these great writers—to visit its little sister of the book world.

As soon as they had signed themselves with drops of water from Saint Séverin's holy well, groups of them, Bishop Peter Lombard in his time, before him the stormy petrel Abelard, and sometimes his eloquent-eyed Heloise, latterly Alexander of Hales, William Saint Amour, Thomas Aquinas, Albert the Great, or the troubled Roger Bacon, and the Seraphic Doctor, Bonaventura, would emerge happily on the street to indulge in the one dissipation of their orderly lives, fishing for books, hunting for paper. It always was like a homecoming week for them. Not only would the proprietors, foremen, and workers recognize and warmly welcome them because they were good spenders here, more because of their common interest and the bond between them: their loyalty to learning, and, in most cases, to God. But they were forever running across a friend from Saint Denis, Orleans, or Chartres or meeting some brother celebrity from Oxford or Dijon, sometimes even from the far-off Arno. The tiny streets were lined with the birettas, mixed in with the smocks, examining at stalls, the tall script of a Boethius or Plotinus, the binding and clasps of a Book of Hours, rubbing their spectacles—even the new ones Roger

Bacon had designed gave them headaches—and holding up to the light a sheet of vellum to catch the hue or any possible hairs in it, or rubbing it with the sensitive balls of their thick red or tapering ivory-white fingers to see if it was smooth enough for their books.

It is a question whether ever again there would be so harmonious a getting together of tradesmen and clients as there was then in this dense-packed little mediaeval Mecca. Certainly not in our world fairs. Probably not in Nijni Novgorod or in Leipzig, or ever—though the entertainment there was more bohemianly lively—at the fifteenth century Lendit fairs at Saint Denis for which the Paris students set out from Saint-Julien-le-Pauvre (hard by the book quarter) with *vielles,* whistling pipes, quips, jugs, songs, flowers, to purchase parchment.

Into this tenth of a square mile all the quarter's shops, courts, craft factories, painters' attics, and the *épiceries* and eating places, were jammed and wedged in. Shoppers, horses and wagons moved slowly. The visitors sidewised their persons between the human and vehicular traffic. They shoehorned themselves between shafts, wheel-hubs and the scraping stone walls. They had to, in this maze of short, thin streets cliffed between tall, peaked houses. Into it, scanted a little by the sun, candles, the jeweled binding of books, illuminated texts brought little gleams of light.

And all there, so busy at all the allied book tasks, proprietors, masters, foremen, *bacheliers* ('prentices), salesmen, binders, sewers, pumicers, dehairers, die-makers, amanuenses, copyists, drovers, painters, miniaturists, formed a confraternity that was not without its holiness of devotion to a cause. And they all spoke, if not the same theological and philosophical, at least a common book and art language.

A dozen and a half booksellers (two dozen by the end of the century) operated in this quarter. Between the stationer, whose name came from the Latin *statio,* for store, and the bookseller there was little distinction. Several bookseller-stationers sold writing materials, also books on commission. Where a proprietor confined himself to one branch of the business, he was always in touch with all the allied activities. The bookseller on Saint-Jacques or Writers' Street could get paper or parchment next door, vellum in the court behind, binding leather just around the corner. He could send downstairs to a wain whose drover had just rumbled in with his purchases from the stock farms around Paris for a sample skin, send a manuscript to be copied in his attic, and have it bound opposite the churchyard. And, of course, all the little painter people were near by, in their dazzling world, on Illuminators' Street.

Up until the twelfth century, the conception of the thoughts that went down on the parchment, the inscribing of them there, and their illumination and illustrating were chiefly abbey pursuits. And abbeys still had their *scriptoria,* or copying rooms, and their brother scribes. But in the dispersal of knowledge that came with the Gothic, the lay copyists, illuminators and miniaturists came into their own. Great nobles then, from love of culture—or vanity—had staffs of copyists at work in their castles. It was another instance of the way in which the rich sometimes make up—though never wholly, never wholly—with their nurturing of culture and of beautiful things to see, for their tremendous advantage over the poor.

If we owe a debt to the more enlightened among the nobility, in-finitely greater is the one we owe the monks. If the fine arts had been a monopoly of the monastery, the world is the richer for it. They were the valiant—this cannot too often be stressed—who through the Dark Ages kept burning enough of learning's light for any thoughts to be conceived and written down at all. Not only the churches all over the world, the college faculties, all who, atheist or believer, love learning, but the fraternity of booksellers should be eternally grateful to the abbeys and their monks. If the University was born of Notre Dame and the Cathedral, therefore, through the University nourished this bookselling little city, it was the monks who kept the bookseller's product alive through the ages, and saw to it that there were such things as books to sell.

The faithful monks still kept alive the thought, the word itself. But they had now passed much of the attendant service of the torch of knowledge on into the booksellers' trade quarters, into this little city of a dozen short, thin streets, cliffed between the high peaked houses by the Seine. And the book had come a long way by the time it got into Writers' Street. Indeed, it was now at the next-to-last step. The last would come in the fifteenth century when two enterprising faculty members would set up the first printing press in Paris at the Sorbonne. That printing press was to do both good and evil things. It would multiply the thoughts of the great men and spread knowledge, but it would in the end crush much of these lovely arts and crafts there by the Seine. The photo-engraver would give the final *coup de grâce.*

The book had started out from the ground up, literally, with the first baked earth or clay tablets and their cuneiform scripts. So had come, in turn, the papyrus of the Nile, the Roman waxed-over tablet, the parchment of Pergamos which gave it its name. This was made from the skins of sheep, asses, calves, goats. The vellum—a finer grade—was a womb parchment and came from stillborn calves.

Writers' Street still sold a lot of it, though the new linen and rag paper was beginning to come in. After the day of the cumbersome and inconvenient libraries, all the weight of those clay tablets, the first canned books, the papyrus rolls in containers, the evolution of the format we know today was simple. In the fourth century the Emperor Julian had received one of the very first samples of the book of sewn quires, under his Roman elms by his baths on the Cluny site, just a few hundred feet up the Hill from this quarter. The parchment sheet had been folded; eight or ten had been gathered together; these assemblings had been pierced on the inner edges and sewn with cord, thread, or thick twine, for the first signature; on the back of a set of these a leather strip was attached. It was all very simple, though no one had thought of it through all the ages before. Then, since the outer sheets of the sewn but as yet unbound book tended to curl or show dog-ears, boards were added to the sides, the leather backstrip being pasted on these. Soon the leather of the backstrip, increasing in quality, was extended down to cover the sides completely. Machines and reproductive processes have since come in to change the mode and fashion of the book, but for seventeen centuries its form has not changed.

Almost as much of a revolution as the introduction of the printing press was the introduction of paper, the product of flax, rags, or hemp, loads of which were coming, though at very long intervals, into the book capital by the Seine. Before many generations had passed it was to turn out a very practical medium. Also less expensive than the old, which was quite important. Even in enlightened Greece a little writing material had cost many drachmas. Before the coming of the abbeys, writers had either to be rich men or their *protégés*. Now it was soon found that it was easier to plant many acres of flax than to raise herds for the parchment skins.

As the clever Chinese were the first to invent the gunpowder for the dispersal of men into little pieces, as though to make up, they found the paper for the scattering of the thoughts of men all over. One Tsai Louen deserves the most credit. And it was about the year of Christian chronicler Tertullian's birth—100 A.D., or perhaps five years later. Appropriately, this was in the days when the early Church Fathers were writing half of their time, though not they, but their far-off heirs were to profit by the new process. A nineteenth-century proverb says that the French conceived most of the inventions which not they, but the rest of Europe, chiefly Germany, applied in those times. If the Chinese philosophers, poets, artists, used their paper, and to good advantage, they did not employ their gunpowder so much. Thirteen centuries later, the West did that at Civitale, also when at Crécy they blew French chivalry off the map, for the time.

It was the Arabs, however, who did most to nourish the paper industry. Now their code did stress a little more oriental revenge than the Christians' prescribed love. Their theology might not have been so subtle as that of the abbeys, being the crystallization of the rather melodramatic, highly coloured dreams of a gifted exotic genius. But it had its poetry, its music, and its own morals, its points. Their education had even more. In spite of Her Most Christian Majesty, the determined and really not so gentle Isabella, and her Ferdinand, who drove out the Moors—oh, that men could be fair!—the Arabs, through their cousins in Moslemism, these Moors, made a great contribution to the abbeys in algebra, astronomy, horticulture, architectural ideas, and to the castles of Spain and France and of all the Crusaders, in colour, weaving, so many beautiful things—and in manners!

Here was another of those paradoxes of history which make the study of it so fresh and fascinating. The Romans had officially executed Christianity's Founder. Then they built the superb roads over which His message was borne to all the world. Now the Moslems, who had tried on the fields of France to replace the Cross with the Crescent, by their culture of the new paper scattered that message even farther.

Damascus had been celebrated for many things. It had been the caravan cross-roads city through which had been cleared for the West those perfumes we call "of Araby," but which really came from the islands of the far-off East. For a long time the world's most beautiful weapons had been forged in this world's oldest city, of its steel. Now it became the great eastern paper headquarters. From there, in the early twelfth century, the new paper found its way into Greece and around the Mediterranean. We can see it still (without watermarks; these did not come in for another hundred years): in documents of Sicilian kings, a letter written by Raymond, the unbreeched count of Toulouse, to Harry of England, also one from a Visigoth king now in the Bibliothèque Nationale which multiplied Louis' "Little Twelve" books a half million times.

It was curious, too, that when the Moors advanced into Spain, Toledo, which, like Damascus, had been celebrated for its swords, now too, like Damascus, became a great paper centre. Her linen and rag sheets were as renowned as Toledo steel. So the industry crossed the Pyrenees into France, with the first paper (handmade, of course) factory set up about 1220 in Hérault. Seed of that exquisite flower which lasts but from dawn to sunset, winged its way over south France. Soon acres were blue there with flax for the books of Paris up north. It is interesting to note that in this land of books, France, there would be invented the first machines for the manufacture of paper and pencils.

But that was yet to come—with Napoleon—and at first this paper revolution was slow-paced. Not until the days of Jeanne d'Arc would paper be extensively used. Thereafter the practice of the southern kings who ordered paper for their documents would be reversed. That would go into the vast majority of books. Parchment and vellum would be used in a few special volumes perhaps, but chiefly for charters, citations, the modern "sheepskins," and certificates of doctors' degrees like those for which the Paris scholars climbed so high into the intellectual empyrean.

Except, then, for a curious examining of this paper brought by pack-train from the hand factories and flax fields of the south, and a little purchase of it for lecture notes, the men from the Hill whenever they shopped among the nineteen booksellers of Writers' Street and the adjacent lanes, looked for the material used by Jerome, Gregory, Alcuin, Alfred the Great. And it sometimes happened that scholars actually wrote on pieces of parchment and vellum that had been used by great men centuries before. Whenever, through all the ages, there had been scarcity of material, tablets had been given fresh coatings of wax over their former inscribed surfaces, papyri rolls had been erased and sponged, and vellum and parchment sheets had been sponged, pumiced or treated with gall tincture, so that they might be used again, even if a little the worse for the cleaning and the centuries' wear.

Such a renewed tablet, papyrus roll, or skin sheet was known as a palimpsest, from the Greek "I scrape again." Since the erasure was not always effective, the first writing would often show up through the new, sometimes in a startling way. An execution order for Peter might be used later by a scribe for a page of his Epistle. A still faintly showing Isaiahan prophecy of the coming of the Prince of Peace would be overwritten centuries after with Matthew's telling of His actual arrival. So in the wax, the fibre, the thoughts of different ages were interlaced. So great men walked in each other's footsteps on the palimpsest. The old ever shadowed the new. Though the writers themselves were not often conscious of this, it was as though the elder authorities were always looking over the shoulders of the new men as they wrote. Like visible overtones the recordings of the past hovered over those of the present. Sometimes they were in harmony. The old seemed to approve and endorse. Again the old messages were like old love affairs which haunt and challenge the latest comers in the heart.

The waste of original and priceless manuscripts was deplorable. For economy's sake, copyists would erase manuscripts to write down trifling things. Forever they were burying old authors under the new, covering the thought of a former century under a thought layer of a later one. But when they seemed completely interred, suddenly thought or author would come back. The old ghosts of the past would show up, in the fragments of the older writing, through the last script.

Delvers in the caverns of the past among the old sheets strewn and blown about like so many forest leaves, have so far been unable to rescue a single long manuscript entire from under its palimpsest layers. One complete book only has been assembled, and that by patching together many fragments written in different eras by various hands.

Yet still it remains a grand sort of archæology. It tempts one to think of discovering a centurion's account of John's beheading under the account of Pope Calixtus being struck down in the catacombs, or to scrape away or work with chemicals and find that it was a wild-oats confession of Saint Augustine that was topped by that remorseful love letter of Abelard. Once started, the explorer can rarely leave this prying of the layers of the centuries apart, the exhuming of the illustrious dead down in that palimpsest underworld.

This book and paper shopping, for Franciscan Master-General Alexander of Hales, Roger Bacon with his giant intellect and uneasy disposition, Albert the Great, and the Angelic and Seraphic Doctors, Thomas d'Aquin and Bonaventura respectively—never all together, of course—was a sort of lark. It was good for them to get away for an hour from their cloister duties, to descend from their mystical ladders into a practical, pragmatic world. The brainworker's labour of the hand cannot affect the quality of his product. He can write, almost illegibly, the world's most beautiful poem. He does not enjoy the artist's wholesome balancing of the hand's work, so indispensable in his creating, and the guiding brain's. Down here by the Seine, however, the scholar could vicariously have this tactile relaxation in watching the mediaeval artisans at the various processes of making a book; and all on so short a tour, a few turns of the street, a few crossings over, and one or two climbings of stairs. There were always some books at the different stages from the skin to the jeweled whole.

What the conscientious writer might fear was not so wholesome (though with all his celibacy, fasts, vigils, he should not have worried about this little human satisfaction) was the author's pride in his new-born book. A lay romancer like Jehan de Meung up on Saint-Jacques Street, the collaborator on the day's secular best-seller, *La Romaunt de la Rose,* could mentally strut a little in this vanity. But these powerful, attractively childlike wise men, on their return, would pray to be delivered from this vainglory. Inevitably they would pray the glory out of themselves and up to God.

Meantime, the author could watch, on his several little tours of this small but bright and active world around Saint Séverin, the brain thoughts he had conceived up on the hill being given birth, emerging in the flesh and blood of the sturdy Gothic script, and laid out on fresh linen sheets. Gradually he could see his brain child equipped with handsome leather jerkin, given a belt of bright metal clasps, and even decorated with flowers for the confirming.

In this court behind an archway, men would examine and sort the skins from the wagons of the countryside, the pelts of goats, asses, sheep, kids, for the parchment, the still-born lots for the vellum, grading all according to quality, the finest uterine bits being reserved for the new Book of Hours for the king. In an adjoining room, men would dehair and scrape the skins. In huge vats the *bacheliers* or 'prentices would wash and again and again rewash them. Always they took great pains, and on near-by tables there would be further scrapings, pumicings, chalkings, and the final smoothings-out.

In a corner where there was favourable light, a master could always be found leafing over folios of sheets to see if the pages all matched in tint, for the dehaired side usually differed in hue from the side next the flesh. It was not that meticulous scholars would complain of the uneven colouring or roughnesses and point out tiny hairs that had not been removed. The guildsmen's own pride in their craft made their own selves very exacting. Once, near the Golden Horn, in Byzantine times, they had dyed parchment purple for the inscribing with silver ink or gold. Effective as this might have been in the days of the grandiose Sancta Sophia domes, later scholars found it too florid, and the quarter parchment-makers left their pages cream, ivory, or white.

At desks or tables, in rooms above, next door, women would fold the smoothed and finished sheets. Numbers would be given to the signatures, or assemblings of sheets, but none to the individual sheets. There would be no paging for two hundred years. On an annex midfloor, the folios would be pierced and another group of workers would then draw the strong ox sinews or tendons through the holes to bind all the folios of the book together. Between these trips, upstairs and down, and all around the spider-web neighbourhood, the visitors could dimly discern at the end of some long passage tunnel the die men at work in a leaning house shored up by their neighbours, the makers of ornamental clasps. On the floor overhead the birettas would come into another of those bright provinces of this realm of books, where binders inset semi-precious stones in books for the nobles' new libraries, and rare gems in rich psalters for the king. Trays of these bright adornments sent darts and splinters of colour through the ancient mediaeval room.

And forever, between trips to this craft floor or that, as they emerged on the street, they would pause at the ground-floor shops or open stalls where the finished books were on sale—on commission. Here spectacles—usually the ones Roger Bacon recommended, since he had invented their convex style—were put on; and hours were spent, fingering, leafing, poring over, and excitedly commenting on some newly translated Bede, the dark, blind-stamped compendium of Hugo of Saint Victor, a gaily illuminated Dagulf psalter, an Abbot Grimaldus of Saint Gall, an Origen, Isadore of Seville, a Tours Horace, a German Ulphilas, an ancient Tertullian, Priscian, a very fine Deacon Bernon perhaps, a *quodlibet* set of Bishop Peter, a high-coloured book of the sinning monk of Saint Evroult, the latest commentary on a commentary on a great commentary, or some freshly-oiled child of the browser himself.

And, where the light was good, in upper rooms and attics of the crazily leaning, high-up houses looking down on the pigeons of Saint Séverin, down by the quai rookeries, and all around on Ecrivains, Des Prêtres, Lilacs, and Sac-a-lie, was to be found the little army of those who, after all, meant most to these scholars: the indefatigable, toiling, thin, bent men and women copyists, leaned over their sloping desks in their threadbare long gowns. Here was the ground army, though it was up so high, the infantry, the ones that dug in, the arm more basic than any.

They always worked in a fall of quill shavings, like nail parings all around on the floor. Sometimes the sun's rays came over the ridge-poles of adjoining houses into the loft. Feather fluffs from the quills, like thistledown, floated on the stream of dancing dust-motes revealed in the sudden light flashes diagonalling through the room. Spider-webs gossamered with their circular thread rungs the black beams overhead. When the ink was not made in another story, huge flacons of vitriol and sacks of nuts and containers for the mixing of these into the *incaustum,* or black ink, stood in the corners, with the carmine for the plainer titling.

In this characteristic craft clutter, the lay successors of the old monastic pen army, only a few survivors of which still worked in the cloisters, toiled with as great devotion as that of the old monks themselves. They would bend over their sloping desks, at very small pay, for an incredible number of hours at a stretch, only glancing up once in a while, pausing to wipe Roger Bacon spectacles which gave them headaches too, or straightening up from their curved pose, to circle their arms in their sockets, or to flex their wrists for relief.

Here one could see what was meant when it was said, a little while back, that the dwellers of the quarter, all that had to do with the making of books, made up (with some exceptions naturally) a holy confraternity. With great pains, concentration, and consecration, too, they made their up and down strokes of Gothic, the thick, full-bodied ones, the thin accenting and outflaring ones, with the *incaustum* on the fresh sheets brought up by the parchment-makers from below.

Very often they knew too, what they were putting down on those sheets. Deeply they respected the words they inscribed so beautifully on the pages. As the copyist made his strokes he seemed sometimes to be etching into his heart the very words, even when he might not grasp the mighty import of the whole paragraph about the Trinity or Divine Grace. The love messages and ringing *chansons de geste* were always clear enough even for a child. And when they wrote these down sometimes you could hear the old men or the young women humming them to old tunes or little ones they made up.

Often too the skilled copyist comprehended the profound sentences. If he didn't, he accepted them at their full and exalted face value anyway. And theirs was, they all felt, an important, a consecrated task. As scribes, they were the conductors, the conduits through which great matters were transmitted to the sons of men. And the artists would illuminate and glorify their meanings.

So the words they worked on, the completed manuscripts, came to be their children—their foster children at least. They acted, in a way, as wet nurses for these prodigy children of the brain. They had midwifed them, too, and they dressed them up, made them neat and beautiful. Again, when these humble workers, so drably dressed, held their pages up to get the whole effect, they were holding a grand review, with themselves in the bannered pavilions! Those impressive battalions of letters drawn up on the parade ground of the pages were their own soldiers, and when the artists gazed, entranced, at the capitals they would add, they were watching their own officers—all marching out to conquer the world of thought for Paris, the Church, and God.

Often the illuminators, the miniaturists, to whose shops the sheets when inscribed with the copyists' impressive letters were to go, held a fête day. It had both a feast-day and an everyday practical purpose. They went to gather the materials for their trade—not the metals they used for their pigments (they did not dig for these), but the equally indispensable ivy for their carmines, the cornflowers for their blue.

Early the streets were chatteringly noisy with the illuminators' assemblings by Saint Séverin. They crossed in a band over the Petit Pont, to roam the fields around Saint Denis and Chantilly or passed out of the west Saint Germain gate for the Saint Cloud woods. They went like a company of Canterbury pilgrims, quite as picturesque in the variance of forms and costumes, but not so colourful as Chaucer's flamboyant cast. These little painter people, so devotedly earnest of purpose, were often as serious of mien and sober of clothes as their pictures were bright and gay.

Before we enter their lofts and shops to see them at their fascinating work on another day, let us follow them for a moment on one of these fêtes, these floral parades. Men and women of all ages, some happy young matrons with babes in their arms, walked along slowly at first, in their ancient round-toed leather shoes or wood sabots, chattering quietly in shop talk of vellum and vermilions until the fresh air and general loveliness stimulated them into a real chattering excitement and laughter. Little children were drawn along with them, in small carts like modern toy express wagons but with solid one-piece wheels and thick tongues. Well their parents remembered when they themselves had used them a generation before. They had loaded them with pebbles and dirt, in imitation of conquerors, peasants, nobles, beggars, light-o'-loves, kings and queens who, scattered in a great line all over the plain, had together pulled the loads of stone in the great pageant help-day to shove up higher towards the sky Our Lady's beautiful house.

Sometimes, if their rendezvous lay north, they would stop on the way, and some with the children would paddle in the little Brook Ménilmontant, which has since been lost under the city's massing stone and which gave its name to the quarter of the gamin Maurice Chevalier who later carried on the old traditions of the minstrels of the Little Bridge. If their path went south, they lingered by the Brook Bièvre, which then too ran an unpolluted silver and green through the meadows. And they would lunch somewhere among the flowers, as their children rolled on the mead, plucking the petals or grasping futilely at miniature insects dancing in the sun. Then they would nap by some haystack cone or up against the silver-grey bole of a beech until it was time to gather the raw materials of their pigments for which they had come.

When at sundown they returned, these little painters, so sober of costume and mien, would often break into song, the old roundelays of the ancient people of France. When they reached the Square in front of Notre Dame, they would strike up the songs of the Blessed Virgin, for her whose lovely colour they wore so profusely in the cornflowers in their arms. All would join in, and even the little children would raise their drowsing heads and lisp out the beautiful words. The minstrels, congregating by the bridge-head for their evening performance, would welcome the miniaturists as fellow artists, which assuredly they were. And as the floral procession stopped, all doffing their hats, and crossing themselves, and looking up at Our Lady so lovely there aloft by the rim of the west rose window, the minstrels doffed their faded hats too and played their *vielles* and twanging harps and outflare horns in a great harmony of spirit if not invariably and unerringly of note.

> "Show thyself a mother,
>   May the Word Divine
> Born for us thine infant,
>   Hear our prayers through thine.
>
> "Virgin all excelling,
>   Mildest of the mild,
> Free from guilt preserve us,
>   Meek and undefiled.
>
> "Keep our lives all spotless,
>   Make our way secure,
> Till we find in Jesus
>   Joy forever more."

This hymn of Fortunatus written seven centuries before their day, was for them. For singing minstrel, painstaking miniaturist, as well as for a saintly king. For sinners, for all of them, they knew, they were sure, she cared.

This twentieth century of ours hasn't everything, after all.

We will follow them, in the morning, after they have rested from their festivities, to see them at their sloping desks deep in their lovely work. But so, in the primrose and serpentine afterglow, the little painters, with the trailing ivy, the cornflowers of her hue in their arms, the minstrels in their patched clothes, saluted Our Lady of Love before her gorgeous house, by the Little Bridge over the Seine.

IX

The Illuminators' Loft on Boutebrie. . . . Monk Miniaturists of Charlemagne, and the Art from the Golden Horn to Paris. . . . One Painter tries to make Enough Carmine Capitals to match his Scarlet Sins. . . . Red Lead, White Lead, White-of-Egg, Boars' Teeth, Butterflies, Nutgalls, and Whole-page Capitals. . . . The Great Gallery of Exquisite Paintings in Little Books. . . . Poor Men, Toiling Women of the Middle Ages enrich their Pages for the Libraries of Future Millionaires. . . . The False Illuminator of Fish-Storage-Boat Lane. . . . A Revolutionary Return to Nature, and a Gothic By-product. . . . They bring the Fields of France into their Pages. . . . The Little Books reflect the Cathedral's Glory.

In the Book's Golden Age

IT WAS NEVER MORE THAN A STEP FROM THE COPYISTS' ROOMS to the miniaturists' where the sheets with their word battalions would go to have their gay officers, the striding, prancing capitals, put in at their head, or to be given borders of flowers through which their columns could go proudly marching. Copyists' boys had been delivering bundles from this book quarter (or from the one or two earlier booksellers on the Isle) for a hundred and fifty years since the handsome nervous Abelard had fumed at the messengers for roughnesses or uneven tones in the vellum or for delay on the bridge. Heloise—his legitimate scholar for the while, or did she so early get clear beyond that?—would pull at the master's sleeves and with a little amused smile at the impatience of men, even when they were great, and her eyes on the messenger in such a contagiously mirthful and friendly way, would tell Maître Abelard that there were, oh, so many things to delay a boy in Paris.

Mademoiselle Heloise was right. There was continuous drama on street and bridge. Eight hundred years before the cinema came in, Paris was a grand one herself, a constant unrolling of vivid scenes, of sounds, ejaculations, street cries, songs, and love notes. And the

124

boys, after these so natural delays, would saunter up and down stairs of these streets where, like Napoleon, Trilby would look for cheap lunches after the reaction from the strain of having Svengali putting perfect pitch into her white throat, and where Rabelais, Ronsard, Anatole France would come to smell the rôtisseries.

The messengers, with their precious cargoes of thought under their arms or roped over their shoulders, would enter one or another of the doors in the blocks of those houses which, because of their inclinations and saggings, often resembled rows of staggering drunkards who by their very leaning against each other hold each other up. So supporting each other, these houses achieved a wrinkled but rock-like solidity and strength above the narrow cliff-like streets. And the lads would clop, clop up stairs that were out of plumb too, but which through the centuries would never give way. So they would come into the upper stories or the lofts with tables and desks crowded near large windows and corbels and pulleys outside, or trios of smaller windows with wood shutters thrown open to Paris summer sun or to winter pearl grey. Even when these skies loured low the little painters' bee-hive kingdoms were brightened with the gleaming and colourful materials with which the little bent-over folk of the squirrel brushes brought beauty and joy into the world of their day, as well as that of modern millionaires with libraries richer than those of the old-time kings—also for you and for me.

Now these painters of the small page scenes and the little medallions, and the illuminators who often worked symbols and tiny scenes around and into the impressive curves of their capitals, gradually were grouped as miniaturists, that term and illuminator becoming almost interchangeable. They did not, like the miniaturists of today, make lockets or put high roses in the cheeks of lovely ladies on little ivory ovals. Such artists would not come in until the gifted Clouet of the fifteenth century. These artists of Eremboux-de-Brie, or Illuminators' Street (Boutebrie today) worked in the small. But they were not known as miniaturists because of that. The name came from the *minium*, or red lead, which they were forever using. "Red-leadist" was what the term miniaturist meant in the Middle Ages.

This delicate art did not, of course, come in with the Gothic. It reached the height of its richness and subtlety then, curiously, too, when it was many ages old, its greatest freshness. The school of every age had its distinguishing characteristics giving it its own especial and individual charm. By the Golden Horn they often delighted in purple parchment inscribed with gold. Very early the Gaelic abbeys wove delicate silver script on violet vellum, all as lovely to look at as the later Irish lace.

Under Charlemagne, the monk miniaturists still rather slavishly followed the ancient perspectiveless fashions of Byzantium. The figures had the conventionality and awkwardness of pose, the almost macabre flesh-tints of the early days. Over and over these models were reproduced with small change and to what would have been a deathly boredom had not these toilers in the abbey *scriptoria* been such patient, painstaking, and pious men. But the very *naïveté* and quaintness of these Carolingian pictures gave them an engaging quality. As the breezy emperor had brought life into every activity, into the small one of this delicate art came something of a brightening up. The artists put a little more into their scenes. As though to make up for the stiltedness that still remained, the miniaturists lavished much more gold on their pictures—it was a distinction of the Charlemagne school. Some of their pages look as heavily encrusted with gold as embroidered coronation robes. A little of the sunshine which the great Emperor brought to break for a little space the clouds which in the Dark Ages darkened his Europe, crept through these new shining backgrounds into and around the angels and saints and heroes of the holy pictures.

When with Robert the Strong the butcher's son, and with Hugh and his famous little round cape the Capetians came in, the monastery miniaturists became even more engrossed with the illumination of the great initials than with any other decoration or complete pictures. Right royally then did those gorgeous great capitals stand out on the parchment pages. And as they came within sight and sound of the Gothic there was an increasing joy in colour. All the monks now intensified their hues, except the worthy but austere brothers of Bernard's monastery of Cîteaux, who had always been at odds with the Cluniac monks in regard to what the Cistercians called an excess of decoration.

With the 1160's, our Bishop of Paris Maurice de Sulli, that grand old builder, began to mark with his crook the outlines of his dreamed-of cathedral, to cut through the clutter of the Cloister a new road for the bringing in of the material for Notre Dame, and to rebuild for the flood of pilgrims a new Petit Pont. Then the old saint and angel figures which had been stereotyped copies of those of the Golden Horn, were superseded by much more natural ones. While many of the monks had engaged in horticulture and were therefore often out in the fields, too many of the painting celibates had been too long immured at their desks in the Cloister copying rooms. Now, with the coming of the Gothic and its proudest beacon, Notre Dame, artists for the first time in centuries forgot their ingrowing stylization and began to look outdoors.

Something mightier now than the personality and presence of any

Charlemagne, galvanizing as that had been, was arousing men. Though too many readers have never thought of this truth—the Renaissance begun in Italy being the only, the great rebirth for them— the Gothic brought a farther-reaching, a profounder change to men. It seemed to be a veritable overflowing into these western lands, headed by France, of the Fountain of God. And it led them not only to His altars, but into His fields.

Under this impulse, the painters left their desks for the open meadow, the green heart of the forest. They made journeys with the rest of the aroused folk of the Middle Ages into the sanctuaries of God's own nature. They returned with the spoils of fields and wood, not for beauty's sake alone, but to use as models, to distil from them some of the very pigments they used. The artist had at last become concerned with his here and now, aware of the world all around him. He saw that his France, his Paris, his Saint Cloud had themes as good as—nay, better than—those of any faded and vanished Byzantium. Hounds, hawks, oaks, beeches, fishermen with gudgeons, peasants with bill-hooks, harvesters with flails, lovers with their lasses, their own city spires and towers, went down on their pages. On Notre Dame walls across the river, carvers and stonecutters mixed wood flowers, garden legumes, orchard fruit, and fallow deer in with their monsters, which even in the prevailing Gothic joyousness had to go in to point a moral and show the offsetting shadows of life. Now the miniaturists transplanted the growing things, the folk around them, into the vivified scenes of their books.

In the swing of the times the heroes of the sacred stories, which for ages had been cumbersome if quaint and picturesque and gilded up, now, with the twelfth century, turned almost lissome. Gone were the old awkward chin-lifts, the twisted-around necks. The Peters, Rochs, Denises, Christophers began to be human.

In the history of France there are several periods of a general return to nature; in the days, for example, when Rousseau preached the idea and Marie Antoinette played with it by making her little toy dairy hamlet, and when Lamarck, in the plains of France, on the Alpine heights, conceived the theory of Evolution which Darwin, after him, reputedly fathered. But this going back to the good earth in the twelfth and thirteenth centuries was the most refreshing period of all.

In the thirteen hundreds the naturalization would reach its acme with the gifted Jehan de Pucelle. His little brush depicted, with astonishingly precise and captivating graphic mimicry, birds in flight, lambs gambolling, horses at a gallop, men chopping down trees in an almost contagious rhythmic swing. And trees were no longer stylized. In his priceless miniatures they were not just any trees but recognizable beeches, oaks, firs, with the leaf outlines as you would find them in the Chantilly or Saint Cloud forests. There was humour too in his peasants jigging, shepherds playing pipes, his dragon-flies and monkeys. And lifelike butterflies fluttered charmingly through the flowers in his borders.

Nebuchadnezzar proclaimed his walls and hanging gardens which glorified his name, the Ptolemys their pyramids. One would have thought that in the great flow of books in their time, the builders of the cathedrals would have seen that somewhere their names were recorded. But they did not. There are no autographed cathedrals. Only a fraction of one, Saint Stephen's porch, has been signed by its maker, Jean de Chelles. These masterpieces of art were composite, the greatest corporate and co-operative affairs ever engineered by man. And the guiding architects had no desire to be signalled out from the rest of the building army. Their piety subordinated everything to the great objective, the worship of God. Their sense of proportion left them humble before the might and majesty, the unity in tremendous complexity, and the climactic beauty of what they and their helpers had reared.

The makers of these dainty little masterpieces, so many of which paid tribute to the God, the Son, and His Mother, and all the saints and heroes of the Cathedral, were almost, but not quite so impartially and nobly anonymous. In the cloisters, occasionally an old monk who had not a rood of land or a silver piece to leave, thought it no sin to let his name unobtrusively creep into the floral foliation of a memorial as his memorial. That genius of a miniaturist, Messire Jehan de Pucelle, left a number of signed little beauties. In the Bibliothèque Nationale on the Rue Richelieu, that great spreading book mustard-tree that grew from the seed of Saint Louis' dozen little books, is an illuminated manuscript of the thirteenth century into which the artist ventured to put a little personal couplet—a charming link with the vanished past.

And one Honoré, a master miniaturist and employer of others of the guildsmen, is down in the Paris chronicles as working on this same Boutebrie, and keeping his whole family, from the oldest to the youngest, busy with the pigments, white-of-egg, and gold leaf. All helping, they put together a master psalter for Philip the Fair who rode his horse down Notre Dame nave, and which can also be seen in that great library. And we must not forget the little monk artist who (observing the letter at least) made as many carmine capitals as he had committed scarlet sins.

In this thirteenth century, the miniaturists, in the general Gothic exuberance, saw their little art so large that they wanted to illustrate everything. Bibles were issued in many volumes with pictures for almost every verse. They began to make inroads on the actual text, quite like the western folk of the 1940's and '50's who would engulf the reading area of their magazines with photographs. Sometimes an initial would be as tall as the page itself and furnish a thin frame for a complicated illustration. So did the mediaeval miniaturists encroach on the word. It was, of course, only a phase. The word remained paramount; the painting adding a glory to the word.

Often the pigments were prepared in another room; but frequently on the floor on which the miniaturists worked. When the visiting birettas entered such an illuminators' loft, they found people picturesquely busy with the raw materials of their colours. Minerals were compounded in mortar bowls. Gold leaf was thinned out at another table. Lapis lazuli was transformed into charming ultramarine, a distinguishing French hue. And the room was abloom with cornflowers from which they extracted a deeper and lovely shade of blue, and with ivy clusters from which they distilled a rich crimson.

At tables or sloping desks near the windows were men and women with more of those Roger Bacon spectacles, some of them well, if soberly clad, others with threadbare gowns with shiny elbows, all dipping pens in black or carmine ink, or brushes in the pigments, thinning the brushes to better points, applying white-of-egg or gold leaf, or spreading out the beautiful colours on the vellum's cream or ivory. Under the old smocks, the better tunics, the spines showed varying degrees of rectilinear rectitude. Some, after years of toil, had jack-in-the-pulpit curves. Seeking crumbs from the bread-and-cheese lunches of the poorer folk, mice had made little track patterns in the gold and pigment siftings on the floor. Bits of the light gold leaf had lodged in the fine-spun trellises of the spider-webs on black beams overhead. Powderings from the little pots of colour, the gold leaf trays, brightened and glorified the sober and the threadbare clothes as the Notre Dame torches had the patched clothes of the minstrels by the bridge. Fugitive gold leaves were caught like glinting feathers behind the ears of withered old women, in the grey locks of serious men, giving them a fantastic carnival look like that which confetti brings to wearied laubourers returning home among the revelers.

But these old men and women did not seem to be weary, though bent over their desks for so many hours a day. Their eyes had caught some of the brightness, the cheer from their own little creations. Sometimes, from consecration to their work and sheer delight in it, they had a look almost holy. Not only did the little figure of the artist seem to be drinking up joy from the rich hues he was laying on with his little miniver hair-points, but the tinier figures he was limning seemed to glow, to come alive, to leap into life, through the very vitality, the vividness of the colours that composed them.

It was the great good fortune of these Paris miniaturists who grew up in the art even as Notre Dame was rising, that there had been added recently to the old repertoire of singing colours, the azures, vermilions, crimsons, judicious yellows and golds, as still another of the innumerable by-products of the Gothic—a green of an unparalleled freshness and beauty. As, in modern times, the technicolour film at first needed a true blue to make its screen palette complete, they had long wanted a green. At last it was here—by the Seine. It was as heartening as the fair meadows they painted as an exquisite carpet for Our Lady and the Child, and which they compounded from this new lovely colour. It gave, in the thirteenth century, new life to the whole art.

Another novelty, a fashion, at the same time inspired these little people for whom Our Lady, they were sure, looked out. Not long before, these mediaeval miniaturists, unconsciously paving the way for the myriad Raphaels, had begun to take the Christ Child away from the old settings, and His dear friends the oxen and sheep, and little donkeys, and had put Him up in the all-embracing arms of Our Lady herself, as you see her across the river with the two angels, and just edging up, so pure and white, over the lower rim of the great western rose. They did not always so represent her, of course. Some of the little painter people, like Barye who would one day have a studio across the river, loved animals and would continue to give captivating expressions to the celebrated four-footed company of Bethlehem. But for others it was refreshing to seek new, effective, ever-reverent designs for the new Our Lady style. Many of them were no mean designers. Great Italian painters in the large later borrowed, for their canvases, ideas from these tiny masterpieces.

As the little gold and colour powderings and smears on shoulders and sleeves gave to these painters of sacred scenes in the life of Christ that carnival touch (which could not have displeased Him Who chose a wedding feast as scene for His first miracle) so the bright pictures on the sheets, the containers of pigments and gold leaf brought a many-refracted glory into the loft. Azure ovals, silver bars, crimson lozenges, flashed here and there. Above the river of dust-motes revealed by a sun ray diagonalling through the room, hovered gold sparkles like fire-flies, as though on this picture of an ordinary black-beamed, cobwebbed workshop had been superimposed a double exposure of a Saint John's Eve or Midsummer Night's Dream.

The *propriétaire* always took from the boy the quires of the unbound, loose sheets inscribed by the copyists and rapidly and with appraising look leafed through the folios. In the solid black text had been left many indentations for chapter or verse heads, and for those gay officer capitals. In some places the marching word columns had been narrowed for the flower borders. Other sheets had been left completely blank for whole-page illustrations. In many of these blank spaces the abler copyists or their foremen had faintly pencilled in, with black lead, suggestions for the pictures. In one or two surviving manuscripts these lines still show through the crimsons and golds, as the old writing sometimes does in the palimpsest or the cartoon lines on a canvas masterpiece. Where there had been no notations or where he rejected those turned in, the master often sketched in an outline himself. Sometimes he consulted the veterans of his staff and frequently accepted their ideas for the designs. When decided on, the illustration or miniature was explained to the artist who was to execute it, though he too was left with some freedom.

Often some very great man, Saint Thomas perhaps, Dante later, would look over the miniaturist's shoulder, with the awe the mightiest intellect sometimes curiously feels before one otherwise quite ordinary, but who can, with his nimble fingers, make things grow on paper or canvas. And he would watch with the pleased interest of a child, as the figure bent over the desk caused miracles to be performed on the page, in a full illustration, or depicted a colourful sequence of scenes with figures harvesting, hunting, or making love, Saint Sebastien being pierced with arrows, Saint Julien ferrying Christ over the Seine, cherries blooming for Our Lady, all in little medallions like those of the windows of Notre Dame choir. These settings in the medallions in the mediaeval books (which were now getting to be smaller than the old heavy quartos) were like the sets of Shakespeare in the old Globe by the Thames. A couple of gables, a tower or two did for a city; three trees and a thorn spray for a wood; a pavilion for an encampment, a squad of spearmen for a conquering army. But almost every "prop" and every figure—apostle, king, devil, horse, flower, boat, butterfly, dragonfly, or crown—was exquisitely done, no matter how simple was the scene.

The Eremboux-de-Brie, Parchment-making, Priests-of-Saint-Séverin, Saint-Jacques, and Sac-à-lie painters of the twelfth and thirteenth centuries were helped not only by that new and so-alive green, but with the gold leaf which had taken the place of the old liquid gold. With it they were surpassing the old Charlemagne background sheen. And Alexander of Hales or Thomas would stand amazed at the deftness with which the miniaturist on his stool would take just the right amount of white-of-egg with the miniver hair-point, place it on the page before him, then take, with the same brush, a corner of the tiny gold leaflet and lifting it quickly apply it to the white-of-egg just deposited on the page, finally smoothing it out with another, a dry, brush. And then everyone near the little artist, curdled Roger Bacon, saintly Bonaventura, or the Florentine poet with the aquiline saturnine nose—in their respective times, of course—had to hold his or her breath. The slightest sniff and away would fly that little gold leaflet tip like an angel feather. A gentle breeze through the windows now on a level with the arches rising around the old oratory with the holy well, and another gold leaf would float up to lodge by the black beams, in a spider web.

And one and all took such pains. Leaf after leaf they would apply until they had laid as many layers of the bright gold as Cézanne would of colour to give density to his rocks and to use colour functionally for perspective. Of course, these miniaturists did not attain these nuances. The gold was effective but superficial. But their colours were heavenly, their figures enchanting. And they worked as hard, those ancient miniaturists, male and female, as any modern experimenter with stippling or vibrating of colour. Indeed, the term "master hand" came down to us from the heads of such studio-lofts as these. They put the finishing touches of the masters' hands on the more elaborate sketches.

When all the layers of gold (sometimes as many as eight) had been applied and dried, there was the burnishing to be done. An old monk, Theophilus, whom we met in the earlier story of the Cathedral, was still the great authority in the quarter. You could find his handbook on art in every shop around Saint Séverin's. On the pages of one surviving copy we can still see the black leaded lines drawn to keep the copyist's sentences straight. "Start the burnishing of the little gold leaves very gently," cautions Monk Theophilus. "Then rub a little harder and so increase the pace until the sweat stands out on your forehead."

At noon the workers would stop to gossip, over their *déjeuners,* about trade, fashions and follies. People were actually beginning to wear pointed toe shoes! (The extreme would not be reached until the toes of fop footwear curled up like old Holland skates and were tied by ribbons to the knees, in Villon's day—in Louis' most people both spoke and dressed discreetly.) Parchment and the new paper would be advanced by a tenth in the springtime. Taffeta and wool were going up too; it was hard for a poor body to protect itself from the cold— but the king would see to it! The old housekeeper of the curé of Saint André-des-Arts had only three teeth now, sticking up in the cavern of her mouth like black gibbets. Old Roofer Radigat had been cupped

and bled to death in the shop behind that red and white barber's pole
across the way. And girls were having their troubles too. Isabeau of
the bridge when her time which (since her seducer had gone off to
the Crusades) should not have come had come, had climbed down
somehow to the piles under the bridge and had delivered her baby
into the water. They could still see her ash-grey face as they led her,
all hunched up, to the Petit Châtelet. That chit red-head from the
Street of the Little-Tax-on-the-Fishstall had deposited her baby by
night in the arms of the saint in front of Jean le Rond, the little chapel
that for a long time stood by the northwest corner of Notre Dame like
a tiny child church at the feet of its majestic Cathedral mother.

Often, too, they would retell the tale of the Lustful Illuminator
whom the Devil took. And no wonder, they said. He had begun all
wrong. Setting up in business where no proper guildsman should!
Two blocks from Enlumineurs, way off from the proper trade and guild
centre! If he had wanted to work down by the river, why had he not
rented a place on the Street of Lilacs (as De la Huchette was known
when the incident occurred), instead of on shadowy and smelly Fish-
Storage-Boat Lane.

Still, for a while he had prospered. Then one night, when he was
working unnecessarily and mercenarily late, a stranger came in—and
through all the bolted doors. He was one who traveled much, going
up and down the world. He had a visage, sardonic, saturnine, satanic,
but handsome, and he wore a cloak like a giant bat's wings. And an
offer he made to which no honest guildsman should have listened, no,
not for the time it takes to make the tiniest brush stroke. He promised
the Lustful Illuminator gold—a great deal. And for what this lean,
cloaked one said was but a trifling bit of work. He pointed to a book
with newly-painted pages open.

"For whom is that?"

"The Church of Saint Catherine of the Valley of the Scholars."

The great bat's wings cloak shook with the laughter of the stranger.
"Very appropriate."

This Right Bank Church, near the ground where Charles the Wise
kept his lions, was to be a much troubled church and to see much
bloodshed in the later Middle Ages. For an especially blasphemous
insult to this Saint Catherine of the Vale of Scholars, one day a soldier
(some said he was an emissary of this very stranger; but the incident
itself is actual history, not legend) would shoot an arrow into the heart
of its altar.

The cloaked one turned the pages: "Now just transform those
seven cardinal virtues into vices. Just change all those fine azure and
vermilion hues, all those gold haloes, the smirking faces into black or

dark crimson, with suggestions of fire here and there." He made a curious forking of his fingers, also a little skipping, mocking bow, odd in one so tall and stately, "In short, with all the skill you as a master can muster, turn—*if you want that gold*—all those heavenly colours into hideousness, foulness, horror. Men will love it."

In the bargain the tall cloaked tempter then assured the Lustful Illuminator he would enjoy such a drinking, wallowing, pleasuring in the said vices—particularly those that had to do with bibbling and chambering—such as no man had ever known.

For seven months (one each for his especial enjoyment of the various vices) the *propriétaire,* having dismissed all his force, for secrecy's sake and that of the gold, worked alone. Each night unholy howls were heard, lurid, sulphurous lights seen behind the barred attic doors on Fish-Storage-Boat Lane. It was part of the bargain too that the illuminator was to deliver the finished, defaced book himself. Then, suddenly realizing in terror what he had done, he hurried back to the loft and locked himself in. But the word of the holy book made unholy passed through the city. In a few hours there came a pounding on the doors and a siege by the enraged populace, and as wild and thunderous an excommunication by a shocked clergy as was ever heard in Rome itself. But before the guards with battering rams broke down the doors, someone, looking up, cried, *"Regardez! En haut!"*

The Lustful Illuminator had escaped, but to what avail? There was scarcely a worker, male or female, in the quarter, who had not heard a grandfather tell how he had flown, in the stranger's clutches, and a puffing of great sulphurous clouds, with fire and lightning lined, up over all the house-tops, the ramparts of the Petit Châtelet and the Notre Dame towers, to be lost, two smouldering specks, in the blue over Montmartre.

Then, just before the noon relief time ended, they might turn to gentler themes. Jeanneton, sweet child, was to be married in Saint Michael's Church on the Isle, hard by the Palace. The king often gave out gold for weddings there. The child might get some. The poor Widow Maquestre had launched on the river, according to the old, old custom, her little wood bowl boat with the candle in it, and had uttered the proper prayer to Saint Nicholas—not him of "the Thistle-down," but Le Tontenin, the patron of the river sailors. The little bowl boat was to sail to the spot where her boy had drowned. But, alas, poor woman, the wind had blown the candle out before ever the lad's body had been located. The Ascension music—had you heard it at Saint André's from the new water organ?—was beautiful. The *groseilles,* the little round, green-white gooseberries, this spring had been wonderful. So had the lilies of the valley and the frogs' legs—

extra plump this year—and the rich greens of their palettes. Their
grandparents had been on the point of retiring when that lovely green
came in. They might themselves now, were it not for its heart-refreshing hue, their shining gold, and all their dear colours bringing joy to
those that worked with them and the hosts who through the ages
would, marveling, look into their books.

So, when the sun was directly over all their crooked ridge-poles and
Saint Séverin's rising arches and the high towers of Notre Dame,
these little artisans gathered on their benches and stools. Though their
lives had been so orderly, they gossiped away quite like Villon's
Helmet-maker and, all "seated on their hunkers," hugging the fire,
her cronies, the old crones who had once been light but oh, such
young and pretty girls. So these little people with their bent backs,
shoes or sabots dangling as they talked, their old patched hose, and
their clothes turned by accident into Joseph's coats of many hues,
turned from their work with saints and sacred scenes and, if we can
borrow a bit of argot from a later time, let down their mediaeval hair.

Then they would return once more from their unbending to their
work stools and desks, and lock themselves up in those little jack-in-
the-pulpit poses, though with hands limber and drawing-free for their
inimitable painting. On the gossiping world, only agreeable for the
moment, since their absorbing interest was their work, they would
turn their backs, to re-enter a holy realm. It was that on two counts.
For surely devotion to one's task, the giving of one's all, can be, in a
sense, holy. And with their miniver brushes and gold leaf and varied
pigments, they were not only laying up treasure for countless contemporaries and future generations. They were compiling records that
would be immortal, often individually in many a little masterpiece,
and ever in total mass effect—vivid, adorned chronicles of their own
stirring, highly emotional, energetically acting, grandly producing,
and deeply believing epoch. For our everlasting benefit, they were
leaving behind a tremendous output of lovely legends and songs, true
sacred stories and historic martyrdoms, in pictures exquisitely unrolled
which, in spite of their naïveté at times, made up, because of their
beauty which but reflected an inner truth, an eye-delighting, soul-
refreshing, transcendent testimony to faith.

The link of these little people of the brushes, the bent backs, and
the long gowns to Our Lady, to her who made the name of Mary forever memorable and beloved, and whom they were delighting to
depict in the new fashion with the Child in her arms, as she was across
the river, on her tall, shining, beautiful new house, was both a practical and mystical bond. When the windows of an illuminator's upper
story or loft commanded a view between or over the twisting roofs

to the Cathedral at the end, you could often notice the workers gazing at Notre Dame not only in affection, but as though they were looking to her for cues. She gave them. And even when she was hidden from them by intervening gables, they carried in their minds her every lovely feature. Each day the miniaturists were getting those cues, themes, ideas, designs, from the wonderful shrine that overtopped even that tall aspiring mediaeval capital by the Seine. It is one of the loveliest, the most delightful characteristics of this Gothic time which never ceases to surprise us with its novelties, in every one of which there is something that goes far beyond the attractive and intriguing into the compelling, the inspiring, the awing. Three great treasuries these loft workers had. With their childlike propelling faith, their happily adventuring minds, their newly kindled imaginations, they drew on these three great storehouses: the Church lore of the past, God's own nature, as vividly embodied in the heart's own green forests and the fair fields of France, and this Heaven-approaching up-shooting noble pile called Notre Dame.

It was astonishing to see how these miniaturists, illuminators, did in the small so much that the Cathedral builders were simultaneously doing in the big. Almost, in their colourful attics, the painters of the books were like little children looking over to where their parents were and copying, in their tiny ways, what those parents were inscribing and carving and depicting so large. You saw the same flowers of the field, fruits of the orchards, leaves of the woods when you looked up at the great Cathedral façade and when you looked down on the little books.

And sometimes the little painter people went farther than the big. The chiseled scenes of the seasons on the Virgin's portal were expanded on the vellum sheets until you had a year's gloriously painted round: the flowers and amourous swains and planting in the spring. The sickles and the gleaners like Ruth. The harvesters with flails that were so much better for mediaeval folk than our belted, puffing engines, since they did not destroy but preserved the straw for the roofing of their homes. The hunting and the hounds. The women treading grapes. At last the winter months, with old men warming their hands at tongues of flame that were grey on the Cathedral but bright red in the little books. Not that there was not warm colour enough on Notre Dame besides that of the glorious glass. In that happy age, they kept their portals and their whole casts of saints and heroes, all their Stephens, Josephs, Marcels, Denises, and Our Lady, gaily painted. Great round haloes adorned the saints and kings on Notre Dame, little haloes their counterparts on the ivory-white vellum. Giant apostles and the half-inch ones had the same blue and crimson robes. The famous Last Judgment Portal's heaven and hell had their miniature reproductions on the parchment, the little miniver hairs achieving a dantier delineation of graceful robe-folds than even a master chisel. The shining gold of the tympan backgrounds of the Notre Dame niches and doors was reflected everywhere like a pervading sunshine in scene after scene of the miniature masterpieces. The men on scaffolds, the long gowns on their stools, worked with the same zeal, the same feeling and felicity of expression, on heroic-sized saint or angel up aloft on the Cathedral ramparts, and the tinier ones in the delicate hues of the old quarter folios.

It was fascinating to watch. There was the great father swing of action with hammer and chisel on Notre Dame, and the offspring motion with the little brush on the parchment or paper book. Both hammer and chisel stroke and that of the dainty brush kept pace with each other, with a startling similarity and simultaneousness, on Island, Left Bank, in the Ile de France, all to that great spiritual metronome that was the Gothic.

The University may have come over from the Cloister to the Left Bank and its hill, but the Cathedral on the Island still reigned supreme over Paris, the Ile de France, and, in a not too exaggerated manner of speaking, over the world. And the stained glass held the same sway as the magnificent sculpture over Parchment-making, Illuminators', Saint-Jacques, Priests-of-Saint-Séverin, Sack-of-Lees, and Little-Tax-on-the-Fishtall or Lilac Streets. Superb models were the great violet-and-crimson western rose window, the rose with the lighter blue tones south—when the lights were on. When they were out, the miniaturists well remembered their radiant colours from many a mass and canonical hour, or others simply spent on tours of the aisles, ever looking up—ever looking up. Always they were trying to transfer to their pages, if not some detail, design, or exact treatment, at least the inspiring feeling of the great glass. And for detail, the men with the squirrel brushes got their ideas for the divisional markings in their own designs from the black lead lines in the windows which united the separate fragments of the glass and at the same time used them, in the superb functionaling way of the Cathedral, as straight or curved lines for robe, sail, tree, cross, in the picture made by the assembled panes. And sometimes the miniaturists would imitate in their designs the tracery bars that spider-webbed into shimmering planes the great Notre Dame rose windows and wheels.

On a whole sheet they would draw a combination of medallions like those of the choir windows, each little round panel with something of the same colour which, through refractions, seemed fairly to leap and throb in the glass, and was now fixed in a lovely serenity on the vellum. The circumferences of these medallions framed the same celebrities, the same miracles and towns, Nazareth, Capernaum, Galilee, little children, sheep, fish, loaves, wells, lilies you saw in the entrancing colour in the panes. And again it seemed as though these miniaturists were children indeed, making little toy play-house sets in imitation of the majestic professional ones in the gorgeous theatre of God there by the Seine.

So this flood tide of the Gothic which threw up Notre Dame had its side eddies and currents which reproduced other beautiful things like these books whose little picture pools reflected the Cathedral's shining glory. All this is another of the many reasons why, no matter how great has been our advance with machine, device, process, the Gothic Age, with its interweavings of the physical and mystical, has never been matched. When those hammer and chisel strokes ceased on the Cathedral and the brush strokes began to fall short of their uncanny perfection, something passed out of the world. It will not come again until some millennium when science and secularism are no longer paramount, and art, nature, and religion are once more a life-giving three-in-one.

X

A "Quarter" Concierge, a Cathedral Charwoman, and Our Lady of Paris.

One Summer Night

HREE, AT THE QUITTING TIME, LINGERED BEHIND IN THE bright little world of pictures and pigments among the black beams and cobwebs of the illuminators' loft. Let us linger with them, now the mighty have gone; one gets the feel of a time better from the little people. One, the *propriétaire,* a man in dark clothes, with a fine presence, was putting away valuable psalters and the Books of Hours, for three queens—of Bohemia, Portugal, and Spain —and the Abbey of Men in Caen, and glowing Sainte-Chapelle here in Paris. Their glory was to be hidden for the night in the dark depths of coffer-like containers with locks as cunningly contrived as the bolts on the house.

The second, a woman in widow's weeds and of dark silences, was giving one almost unnecessary last rub to the Blessed Virgin's halo, as though she were loath to leave this bright world for her lonely home and were trying to bury the gloom in her heart under the bright layers of gold leaf adorning Our Lady of Sorrows.

The other, the concierge who cleaned up the miniaturists' colourful leavings had, while she worked, deposited her baby on her worn folded mantle. He was a livelier specimen of infanthood than the still little babes in the books left open to dry. There was a sweet company of them, in miniature mangers or perched on all the many Marys' arms in the medallions or in full page. Some had even been inter-twined in scenes occupying the decorated initials extending almost from the tops to the bottoms of the pages. Also he was much dirtier than those neat pink-and-white little holy children. Indeed, he had crawled away from the mantle cushion among the as yet unswept-up paint and gold leaf powderings on the floor and had daubed himself so that, with colour streaks and gold glisters, he looked like a harlequin child.

The mother stopped, leaned on her broom, and looked at the little vellum gallery of all the tiny Christs on the tables and desks. She pointed with her duster at a *crèche* with brown animals captivatingly depicted with the Holy Family, and all the vermilions, blues, and golds.

"Old Jehan did that one well now," she naïvely observed to the older woman of the dark silences and grief. "The horse has the patient look of the *charbon* carter's next door."

She walked to another. "Here the oxen seem almost to be chewing in the sidewise way they always do. And *voila!* the little donkey! His ears almost twitch at you and he is *très joli*. Also the little foxes by the trellis with the vines and the grapes. They're just like the ones you see up on Montmartre. But they never seem to get the Child!"

"I suppose you are right," said the older woman.

"Men never do get the Child right. Those saints there are very handsome. Their tresses, even their little fingernails are fine. But never, never the Child."

"So they don't, eh?" The *propriétaire* had returned from his locking up on the floor below.

The little concierge-mother took up her broom. *"Pardonnez-moi,* Messire Probert."

"No, no. It's all right. You may have an idea. Real ones, like great men, often come from humble sources. How would *you* paint the Christ Child, then?"

With the sudden courage of the shy, the little concierge whirled on her broom:

"Why, like all the babies in the quarter." She gave a little waving gesture with her arm. "Like all of them in Paris. . . . Like mine there now."

"You would have the Son of God like a child of earth?"

"To be sure. What else? He would come like all the other babies of the earth and yet unlike them. 'Tis the great secret of the good God and the Blessed Virgin. . . . Now take these here. They are pretty and plump, but they just sit. They don't do any of the things babies do every day and which make them babies—here on Writers' Street— and"—she seemed a little flushed and defiant—"and in Rome where reigns the Holy Father—right under his windows."

"Par exemple?"

She was in for it; and she plunged on, not without fire: "Well, I'd have him do just the things my baby does every day."

"But what?"

She thought, her head on one side reflectively.

"Well, first I'd have him patting things. They always do. That table. The arm of a chair. You know how their little hands go out—to the mother's cheek, her breast. . . . Yes, I'd put the Christ Child in, patting the Blessed Virgin's cheek and breast. . . . She wouldn't mind. She'd look down and like it."

In a reminiscent glow, the older woman in the widow's weeds nodded.

"And I'd paint in His gurgle."

"Come now! How can you paint a sound?"

"You can see his eyes shutting with laughter. You can see his little throat and lips working—it is so cunning. And I'd put in His little lips and throat as though they were *just about* to do that. That way you'd have it."

"And there, my daughter, you would have the height of art."

"I don't know about that. . . . And He must throw back His head too. The brush there ought to show that. When he's about to laugh. At a little dog crossing the Nazareth yard, a kitten, little chick, the wind, the trees blowing this way and that. He'd look up and laugh. And when He's full of milk, and as he gets it, the little Jesus must swing His little foot, to show he's pleased, the way a dog wags its tail. Babies do that, Messire Probert."

"And look there,"—her own baby was crawling across the floor—"He'd crawl like that, slap, slap, with his little hands. But oh"—her hand went to her lips, as she saw the bright powderings and débris through which the gypsy infant was paddling—"I've not cleared up yet!" And she took up her broom.

"Never mind," said the *propriétaire*, in part chuckling, in part baiting her. "It's life. And even a 'master hand' can learn. But tell me, would you have Him dirty like that?"

"Babies are, you know," she said sagely, "though not always so pretty as he with those colours and the gold caught in his hair." Head on one side proudly, she looked after him, then hurried to catch him up. "And, of course, the Christ Child was the prettiest of all. But the Blessed Virgin had to look out for Him. She was a mother, wasn't she?" A pause. "The Mother of all of us mothers too."

"You mean the Lord of us all was dirty too."

She looked a little frantic or frustrated as though she felt she were being rallied or deliberately misunderstood. "Yes, you have a great mind, Messire Probert, and a cunning hand to make all those beautiful pictures. But you have no hand with a child. And you don't know mothers and children. Though she was so great and her Son greater than all, she was a mother like us, He a child like ours. And that is a beautiful and a strange thing to know. She had to wipe the milk off the cheek of the little Jesus when it ran down, because He played with the nipple or thrust His hand too hard into her breast, or when He looked around at the bang of a door when Joseph came in, and when the bread crumbs, all soaky too, got in His little neck. And she would love it. She'd kiss the places too when she had cleaned them. And do you know?"

"What next?"

"Sometimes he'd crawl and play in the dirt in Nazareth Road. He'd even eat it!"

"*Mon Dieu!*"

"Was it not the Holy Land he'd be eating?"

"When," asked the older woman, "do you think He first crawled?"

"Oh, at eight or nine months."

"Mine," said the other—"he was born just before his father went off to leave him fatherless in the Crusades—crawled at seven months, three weeks."

"Would not the Christ Child be smarter than that?"

"No, no, messire," said the little concierge. "It's a great truth. In the big things when He grew up, the healing of the sick, the making of the blind to see, the casting out of the devils"—she made the sign of the cross—"the Judgment Day, and His sorrowful death on the Cross for us, He was the greatest of all. He knew more than anyone in the world. But in the little things, all the crawling and patting and all that, when He was a baby, in the taking of little children on His knee, when He was old, He was like all the rest. . . . Messire, I am glad that it was so."

She paused, then eagerly went on. "And in another book I'd have Him with one little foot flat perhaps—out that way." She pointed to the crawling harlequin child. "In another I'd make Him pulling at her skirts, then straightening out His little thighs as He tries to climb to her knee. Then He'd throw His head back, when He got to her knee; they're always so proud when they do a new trick. And it's there, Messire Master Artist, that your painter people might fail. You'd never catch that twinkle in His eyes, the chuckle."

"Mine," said the reminiscent older woman, "stood up at eight months."

"And He'd pick up a shaving from the Nazareth home floor, and curl it through His fat little hand, with the five fingers out like a one-sided star. You know how they like to put their fingers into little holes and chinks. Always He'd be trying to put them through the loops of Joseph's latchets. Or into the holes of the planes. And the Blessed Virgin would cry, 'No, no,' when she saw those fingers curl around the teeth of the saw, and pick Him up and kiss Him all over. Now Saint Joseph would be doing things for Him too as a proper father should. He'd dandle Him horse-back on his knee, pig-a-back on his shoulder. He'd make little galleys to sail on the brook from little bits of wood in his shop, with splinters for masts and sycamore leaves for sails. And often the Holy Child would be grave in a baby's way. But often He would laugh. Like a little bell it would sound. Laugh at things He saw and things He heard. When He banged a spoon on a bowl. When His mother struck her wedding ring against a pan or some pebbles."

"Did the Blessed Virgin have a wedding ring?"

"Certainement!" The little concierge was very sure. "Did she not," she asked irrelevantly, "go to the wedding at Cana?"

"He'd laugh when she made funny sounds with her blessed lips, little nonsense things run together. And when He'd reach out for a butterfly or dragon-fly like those in the pictures there. *Alors,* I'd even put in one of your books for Him a little monkey like those the minstrels get to do tricks by the Petit Pont for a supper."

"But they could not have had monkeys in Nazareth."

"Yes, they did. In Nazareth and Capernaum, all over the world. He'd pick up His little skirts"—all the costumes she saw in the book were of her own time—"and dance on Jerusalem streets."

"He first went to Jerusalem when He was twelve."

"No, messire, every year—to their Passover *fête.* And he'd dance on the Jerusalem streets the way the children do now on the Petit Pont. His little face would fairly split open with laughter. But the wicked Pontius Pilate and dark Judas, passing by, would scowl."

She sat down to diaper her own child now. "In some of your pictures, you must get the dimples. Not only in the cheeks, but here in the knees, there in the thighs, all over. If you took a fine brush you could get the hair curling at the neck line." With her finger tips she tenderly fluffed up the hair of her own child. "But for the Holy Child, you'd have to beat your gold leaf out pretty thin or just take the tiniest tip of yellow. It should look as though someone had spun out very fine the Bethlehem Star for His hair.

"And you'd have to get out your very best brush, Messire Master Hand, to catch Him with His head thrown back and laughing when He's done a new thing, learned something new to do with His precious body, and is so proud! The laugh of a baby drives out the gloom from a troubled mother's heart. The laughter of the little Baby Jesus in Nazareth would drive out the gloom from all the troubled hearts in the world."

"But," said the older woman, now relapsed into one of her dark silences, "they did not listen."

"No more than most do now. God forgive them! God forgive us! But see what he did then—my baby. Paint the Baby from Heaven, in Bethlehem, just like that. You saw? First he nuzzled me just like a little colt. Have the Christ Child do that to the Blessed Virgin. And then have Him put His tiny fingers—just as mine did now, into my throat, laughing at the red cave he saw, and touching my teeth and tongue with mirth in his eyes. Have Him do that—put His precious fingers down the Blessed Virgin's throat and then curve out His little mouth in a smile at what He sees."

"Are you not, my daughter, just a little irreverent? After all, the Babe you speak of was the Son of God."

"I've thought over that too. No offence was meant and I'm sure no offence would be taken by the Mother of us all. You see, she understands all mothers and their children."

She stood up, with one arm held her child, with the other threw her mantle over her shoulder, preparing to go.

"There's one thing more I'd have you paint in your books. Now you'll be shocked, but they, the two, wouldn't be. I'd have her do what all mothers do. I'd show her, yes, messire, in your best books, your very best, mind you, doing the most common duty of all women in the world. I'd paint her changing Him as I do mine, as all the mothers theirs, changing Him in her blessed lap. As it was with all the babies that ever were, so it was with Him. She would wash Him carefully with water from the brook or village well. She'd oil Him with oil from the trees of Gethsemane where, when it came His time, He would bleed in His prayer."

"You forget again. It was in Galilee that He grew up."

"Well, they had olive oil there too. There was much in the Holy Land. So the father read us in the lesson. Then she would swaddle Him so clean with linen she had washed with her own pure hands and beaten white by the brook, even as we women of Paris beat clothes white by the Seine. Always she would keep the little Christ Child clean and neat.

"And that, Messire Master Hand, is the way we women would have it. Like life." And then she repeated that magnificent paradox of religion which she, an unlettered concierge, understood, though the mighty were blind to it. "He and His mother were greater than all and over all, and yet in the little things they were just like us. Perhaps we love them the more for that."

Music now came up through the windows, from beyond Saint Séverin. Almost all the miniaturists in the quarter except the three had gone on the outing in the woods, the meadows, and by the river to lunch al fresco and gather the flowers for the books. And they could hear them singing their high song to the Virgin now. So the two women, with the child, left the little kingdom of the white sheets, the gay colours, the gold, and the books, and in their clumsy shoes clattered down the twisting stairs, and passed over the Little Bridge to the Cathedral. The little concierge wanted very much to talk with the Blessed Virgin, to tell her she had meant no offence by the familiar, the common, everyday ways she had suggested to the painter, and about which, though she had been so bold in talking to him, somehow now, she felt a little misgiving. The Virgin Mary stood, and in lovely replica very often, awaiting troubled souls, in every parish church of Paris. It is the reasonable way of the clergy to ask their flocks to maintain allegiance to the churches of the parishes in which they reside; otherwise the fickle might constantly be deserting to others whose music or decorations please their fancies, or going to hear this new preacher or that whose delivery captivates them, to the attrition of many an unfortunate church. Still, there was only one Notre Dame de Paris, before whose gracious presence the whole world came to kneel.

The singing miniaturists were filling the Cathedral Square with their vernal booty and the Virgin's own colour, the blue of the massed cornflowers, pausing there for a moment, just as the two women and the child entered the Square, to look at the lovely white figure which, with the Child, stood out, much as does today the beautiful restored one which Viollet-le-Duc placed there before the lower arc of the western rose window.

So, standing, looking up, with their colours, Our Lady's favours, over their shoulders, they sang the hymn so often sung between Trinity and Advent, the one written by Bishop de Moueteil of Le Puy in the volcanic south two centuries before:

"Salve, regina, mater misericordiae,	"Hail, holy Queen, Mother of
Vita, dulcedo, et spes nostra,	Mercy.
salve!"	Our life, our sweetness, and our
	hope, all hail!"

There was a gentleness in their singing as they came to the touching closing phrases:

"Turn thou on us, those merciful eyes of thine.
And after this our exile, show us Jesus, the blessed fruit of thy Womb,
   Oh merciful, oh kind, oh sweet Virgin Mary."

Out of the six open doors of the three portals now came little floods of water. Cathedral scrub-women were working within, even at this late afternoon hour just before the starting of Vespers. They were very poor, chiefly old women. Even in Louis' beneficent time, as in that of Louis the Fourteenth of the little heart rattling around in a vast empty rococo magnificence, or in the days of Daumier's toiling laundresses of the Ile Saint Louis, of Bernanos' consecrated country curé, or of the humble soldiers of the Résistance enduring the invaders' fiendish tortures, much of the importance, the dignity, and the solid contribution of France has come from her mining, digging, fishing, endlessly sewing and charring poor. Her shabby and splendid poor! Greatly as Saint Louis had, for the times, improved their general condition, even the Cathedral had its appointed "hewers of wood and drawers of water." In the long, tall, beautiful body of Notre Dame were hidden cells, dark recesses, in some of which down in the crypt with the dead, the Cathedral scrub-women kept their buckets and brooms.

Pilgrims from afar, worn, travel-stained, many of them downright dirty from their long journey to pay homage to Our Lady, had that morning made a pilgrimage around nave, aisles, and curving ambulatory. For the cleaning-up of Our Lady's house after them, these Cathedral scrub-women and men were carrying buckets of water up the nine steps from the little postern and wharf alongside Notre Dame, or lifting buckets from the Seine over the parapet by the Bishop's Palace, to empty them into huge barrels mounted on solid coaster wheels. The water heavily slopping against the green sides was then wheeled around to the transept and sacristy doors, and buckets-full were sloshed over the Cathedral paving. It was easier for the scrub-people then, for the Cathedral provided no chairs. The bishop had a throne, the canons their stalls; but the ninety-nine hundred the place held on sacred feast-days stood when the ritual did not call for kneeling, and there was not much room for that on such occasions. So the older people usually sought places by the pillars and walls where they could lean against base or moulding just as the canons sometimes did on the *misericordiae* or *misereres*—the little boards under the turned-up stalls—during the long chanting. Through this vast open space of the noble pile, then, the old men and women, whose round question-mark backs seemed to ask life an eternal "Why?", propelled the flood forward. Their big fagot brooms seemed to move in unison with the miniaturists' and minstrels' chanting of the Virgin's hymn outdoors. They swept the swishing freshet, extending along the width of the Cathedral, over the *Requiescats* of the horizontal headstones of the illustrious dead under the ambulatory paving, past the rood screen, around the feet of Our Lady, by the great pillar bases and chapels, and out of the three great now opened portals, scattering the flower-laden singers.

To avoid this, the little concierge, with her babe rounded the north tower corner, singing herself now, as the chanting stopped, a little Poitou *berceuse,* or lullaby, which, since she could not read, an old miniaturist had taught to her as he illuminated it for a book and she played with the child:

"Oh, there came long ago
   With the Star to the earth,
And song of angels on high,
   Christ in miraculous birth.

"Mary sweet washed Him clean,
   And swaddled Him white,
And looked on Him there,
   The Little Lord in the night.

"His eyes like a babe's
   Yet like the sea deep,
Their long fringes mingling,
   As He sinks into sleep.

"Hair like gold of the Star,
   On His little round head;
Perfect miniature man,
   On sweet-smelling hay bed.

"Little hands reaching up,
   In curve like a shell,
To Mary's dear lips,
   Who loved Him so well.

"Since you washed Him, dear Lady,
   As each of us her dear child,
And suckled and cared for Him,
   His mother so mild.

"As you hold Him up there,
   So safe on your arm,
Care for our own little ones,
   And protect them from harm."

She passed through the north door, dipped her fingers in the holy water stoup and made the most familiar sign in all the world on her forehead and the chest with the breasts which were very full for one so small, and from which, as soon as she had made her petitions, like the Virgin of the Pointevin *berceuse* she would suckle her child. Then stepping carefully, so that she would not slip with him on the still wet paving, she crossed in front of the great high pierced mediaeval rood screen (which since has been taken down), genuflected toward the

high altar near which Saint Louis' grandmother Isabeau and the English boy prince were buried, and knelt before the candle-ringed statue
of Notre Dame. It was not the Our Lady of Paris we see today just
off the epistle side of the sanctuary, with her little flare of robe and
almost coquettish fourteenth-century grace. She was not to be born
under the sculptor's chisel for another hundred years. But there was a
nobility about the Our Lady of those days as she reigned within the
Cathedral, with her crown, blue-and-white draperies, her stars and
golden lilies, and the banner with the Ship that Never Sinks upon it,
of the City of Paris.

Now she knew she must not think (for so the parish priest had told
her) that she was praying to that particular Our Lady before her,
beautiful as she might be. Holy statues had no virtue in or of themselves, he had said (according, though she could not know this, to
ecumenical pronouncement ages before). They were representatives
only, piously made. Of very great people, the heroes who had suffered
and died for Christ and had gone on ahead to join the blessed Communion of Saints. Or of Our Lady ever carrying with her the Child,
as the incarnation of Motherhood, though she had been Mother too,
bleeding in her heart, when He had grown up to die for us. These holy
and often painted statues then were like the bright figures in the little
books in the illuminators' loft she saw every day. Her baby reached out
and grasped for them and talked in gurgles to them too. Even she
would have liked to dream about and talk to them, as though they
were real.

The little concierge would have liked to own a picture of her dead
mother. But though there were some paintings in oil on wood in the
loft, they did not go in much for portraits or what we call miniatures
then. When we who are blessed with such souvenirs of our loved ones,
gaze upon them, we do not delude ourselves by thinking the pigments
or film show actual flesh and blood. We do not pour out our hearts'
voices to the flat representations before us, but to what is above,
behind them, to the spirits and personalities the likenesses recall, as
Cowper wrote his very soul out in his moving lines to his mother's
picture: "Oh, that those lips had language!" So the understanding
ones among the mediaeval faithful talked with the prototypes of the
symbol statues and paintings, with the lovely spirits, the saints, the
Mother, the Son whom the simulacra evoked.

We frail ones on this pilgrimage need so many aids, crutches, signals, cues, explainings, illustrations. Let the self-reliant proud behind
their pillars scoff; there will come one day when they will not. Signs
and symbols, then, these statues and sacred paintings were. Links with
Heaven. Links with the holy originals of the statues up there, with

whom, rather than with the replicas themselves, erring men and women communed—ever, it must be remembered, in the name of the paramount Trinity, with the over-all acknowledgment of the Father, the Son, and the Spirit, and by their grace.

They were spring-boards, then, these statues of the Cathedral and its many shrines to which the mediaeval craftsmen had given their all. Spring-boards for the leap, the soaring in prayer to where these originals dwelt, and where they watched out, in their individual and aggregate concern and the awe-inspiring corporate love of the Communion of Saints, for those who might grope and stagger and fall but who kept on trying and believing below.

Some, of course, of the more childlike souls in Paris were so stricken by guilt or grief, were of so naïvely literal minds, or dazed by shock, or dazzled by the lights, incense, music all around, that they sometimes forgot the ancient warning and mistook symbol for substance. But if they believed the holy statue—in this case, that of Our Lady—was indeed possessed by a presence, that she had descended, and from within the crowned, painted stone, was smiling at and taking pity on a poor parishioner, that was far from being "something else again." Surely Our Lady, the Mother Incarnate, that Babe, now tremendously grown-up and sublimated into the all-compassionate Son, and the Father who "like as a father pityeth His children," would understand.

Whether or not the little concierge was of the enlightened or the trusting unenlightened, she poured out her simple heart there, first in a set petition of the Church, "Hail, Mary, full of grace," and then in her own impassioned improvisatory plea, "Forgive me, oh Mother of God, if I have offended in telling them to paint thee in the ways of us common women. You know the hearts of us women. And oh, Blessed Virgin, I meant no offence, I meant no offence."

While she knelt there, the old men and women, trailing their brooms or carrying them over their shoulders, others with mop clouts and feather dusters and pails in their hands, had been clumping along over the Cathedral's drying paving to the little sally port door that opened into a small curving staircase leading to the crypt, there to lay their buckets, brushes, and brooms with the bishopric dead. But three old scrub crones, their faces all patterned with wrinkles as are snow-drifts in the morning with last night's birds and feathered creatures, paused near Our Lady, caught by the appealing spectacle of the mortal mother and child looking up at the immortal pair above.

Three more they were of the Paris poor. And yet, in spite of their aches, they often felt themselves rich. Christ, after all, was the most famous poor man that had ever lived. No hole had He where to lay His head. Even His tunic and cloak had not always been "fuller" clean; more frequently it was stained from travel with the dust and sweat, camel chips, and sometimes with charred black from fires He had made in the wilderness near Caparnaum or by the Galilee shore, to cook the fish. They did not know that mediaeval artists followed a contemporary realism or they would have realized that His mantle was not like that of the panes, but shepherd's blue- or brown-striped tent colour, crimson only when they crowned Him with thorns, white, perhaps, only on sublimely especial occasions like those of Transfiguration Mount, with the Easter lilies at the Resurrection, or the Ascension.

Our Lady of the heavenly coronation, with the fine crown, had used brooms like those on which the old folk now leaned, buckets too for water from the well, to clean the Nazareth house-floor and the street cobbles in front of her door. Everywhere, in the Cathedral, in our Notre Dame, as in life, was stressed this magnificent paradox which the humble concierge had sensed and which ancient Pharisee, Middle Ages politician, modern rationalist and hedonist would not—ever.

He had had no roof. And these scrub-women, the poor of Notre Dame, had one nobly vaulted, held up by majestic pillars. Under it they spent most of their waking hours. It was their house as much as the nobles' or the king's. Their own forefathers' pennies and backs too had gone into its building. Constantly they were warmed by the innumerable circles of shrine lights. On each side, all around, ran the chapels like little mansions of Heaven. The whole Cathedral was a many-tongued palpitation of light and warmth and glory. Whenever they bent their backs, rinsed out their mop clouts, as they scrubbed clean Our Lady's house, their shabby clothes, their stiff, cramped motions in their humble tasks, were given a high glory by the many-rayed lights streaming down from the choir and clerestory stained glass and the three great radiant roses of Our Lady. It was almost as if the rays were illuminating, in the centre of the Cathedral floor, a parable more active and vivid than any in the panes, about servants and ministers to men, and they who were last and would be first— as though, too, Christ was transfiguring, on the pavement there, the poor He loved.

And then as the mother knelt, her eyes adoringly, pleadingly on this lovely crowned hostess of the Cathedral, the baby's hands went up toward her lips.

Three old scrub crones leaned on their brooms in that streaming glory as Father Time leans on his scythe (indeed, they might have been old wives of his) and in their wearied eyes came a new light beautiful, for those that had eyes to see it, as that which bathed them.

"See," said one, "how his little hands go out!"

"Yes," said the second, "they always go out. Well I remember. Well I remember."

"But it's been a long time since."

The second sighed. "Yes, a long time since."

The baby's fingers in their pink shell curve were now going out and up to the moving lips of his mother in an exploratory way, as though he would catch and hold in those tiny fingers the sounds that issued from his mother's lips or he were caressing the prayer that came from them.

Suddenly the little earth mother stopped, looked down out of her praying and smiled.

"There, like that—that's it! That's how I'd have them paint the Christ Child. I must get there early in the morning and tell Messire Master Hand. The little Jesus with his hands like all the rest going out to, and just touching with their tiny tips, His mother's—the Blessed Virgin's lips!"

She rose, made the old sign once more and passed out from the Cathedral's glory into the night. For one going that way the glory never fades entirely.

XI

King and Conqueror, Assassin and Saint in the Hill Parade. . . .
On come the Great Men carrying their Big Books. . . . From Vin-
cent of Beauvais to the Britannica. . . . One Little Man succeeds
where the Forty Immortals of the French Academy later fail. . . .
Blind Spots and Achievements of the Mediaeval Scientists. . . .
Roger Bacon applies the Scientific Spirit, sends a Burning Glass
and a Pathetic Letter to the Pope, and is locked up by the Friars.
. . . Albert the Great builds an Entrance for the Great Citadel of
Thought of Thomas Aquinas. . . . Doctors "Wonderful," "Uni-
versal," "Subtle," "Irrefragable." "Angelic," and "Seraphic."
The Vast, moving Power of Mediaeval Belief. . . . The Trinity of
Chivalry.

The Heart of the Thirteenth

ILLUSTRIOUS MEN AS WELL AS THE HUMBLE WERE FOREVER
ascending Sainte Geneviève's Hill. That endless parade had
started before Christ and would probably continue until He
came again. Kings, conquerors, assassins, saints, celibates and fops,
cardinals and courtesans, gin-setters and layers of traps, college rectors,
poachers, *sergents de ville,* barmaids, magicians, papal nuncios, skin-
flayers, verminors, canons, minstrels, friars, sausage-makers, drain-
cleaners, plenipotentiaries, counts, castrated sopranos, midwives bringing folks into the world, the Saint Innocent grave-diggers taking them
out of it, they came from all the wards and suburbs of Paris, and from
almost every city overseas. Whenever we stand on that Hill today, we
are crowded, jostled by the illustrious ghosts. Wherever we walk there
or in any other stone acre of Paris, we stand in the footsteps of the
great. On every side we are challenged by the voices of the invisible
immortal.

In the thirteenth century in that colourful endless parade pre-
eminently the scholars stood out, soberly clad, but impressive of mien.
And every celebrated man carried a great big book of his own writing

under his arm, or outlined in his great brain. Scholars were daring then. As a rule their tremendous tomes covered everything. They traveled thoroughly from Alpha to Omega. They tried to scale heavenly heights and sometimes succeeded. And they almost filled the world with their holy encyclopedias.

The word "encyclopedia," in the original Greek, means "learning's whole round." Pliny started the encyclopedia procession on papyrus. Capella of Africa in the 400's did one in verse. In the 600's Bishop Isidore of Seville got together a large one that was used for centuries. Dante's tutor, Latini of Florence, turned out a *"French* Treasury"— so pre-eminent then was France as a land of culture. Ma-Twa-Lin made up fifty-two hundred volumes of information in Chinese. In Westminster in the fifteenth century, Wynken de Worde issued Friar de Glanville's. Diderot, D'Alembert of our Hill and their clique turned encyclopedia-making into a modish business. And these are but a few of the legion of editors of many tongues down to 1771. Then some Edinburghers brought glory to England—the Scotch are forever doing that—by publishing the first *Britannica* in three volumes!

This thirteenth century was the golden age for encyclopedias. *Summae* they were dubbed then. Since their main concern was with the two master subjects of the day, theology and philosophy, which were sometimes so closely intertwined as to appear almost identical, they seemed to bring practically every entry under one of these two heads. As for science, that, for the mediaeval man, stemmed straight back to the Source of All Things—God. So, although there were exceptions, and in these a great mass of secular material was included, most of the giant works which they carried up the Hill were, in very truth, holy encyclopedias.

They did not have our knowledge of natural phenomena to help them out, and had not enlarged very much on the old Greek idea of the body's being governed by the classic "four humours"—blood, phlegm, black and yellow bile. There was that vital essence too, *"pneuma."* This had been ingeniously conceived as being sucked in by the lungs, thence distributed by the blood to give life to our internal processes. Even here the mediaeval doctors had drawn in theology. In the mood of the time the temptation could not be resisted. And they had added to the *pneuma* conception certain mystical connotations and complications.

Of drugs, which were often rather soundly used, they had abundant stores in hospitals and abbeys, also a great deal of information about them obtained from their smart foes, the Arabs and the "Moors," who had taught them a not inconsiderable part of all that they knew. Pharmacopoeiae, really excellent considering the times, had been compiled;

and the pharmacy course in the University of Montpellier, France, was now as fine as that at Salerno. Down by the river the "Superior School of Medicine" was increasing in its registration. We have noted the hospital of Louis' sister at Tampierre, beautiful with stained glass and holy statues, and very practical with its excellent ventilation and supervising gallery from which the nursing sisters could see all that was going on in the beds and wards without making endless trips to each one. Doctors now had to dissect and study theory for five years in the medical school and spend one in assisting in actual practice before they could start their own probing and prescribing. Their advance had been great, as we saw too, in venereal troubles, venal and arterial surgery, pus. They knew the value of alcohol. But they did not know the exact composition of bone and tissue, of glandular processes, the cellular kingdoms, and the interrelation of most of the organs. Their knowledge was, in short, rather disconnected. These blind spots later Frenchmen to experiment on that hill, Bernard, Pasteur, Laënnec, a host of great doctors, would magnificently heal.

As for the stars and the surrounding universe, they had had no lecturers like the Ampères, Cuviers, Curies, Lamarcks, or any of that extraordinary band of French physicists and discoverers to bring them up to date on the universe's make-up. Temporarily up to date, that is, since all the fashions in theories sooner or later are outmoded. Astronomers still got too much from Hipparchus and Ptolemy. They did not, however, think of the earth as flat. No mediaeval wise man believed, with the limited man-in-the-street, that if he got too near the edge of the world he would fall off. Five hundred years before Christ, the Greeks had talked of revolving spheres, though Aristotle had rated his earth a little too high, too near the centre of things. Ancient Aristarchus had suggested the startling vice versa: that instead of our so highly valued and boasted earth, the sun might be the centre after all.

One special handicap these otherwise learned men of Paris had. They had not isolated our chemicals, our elements in nature. They experimented with fire, lead, iron, salt, sulphur, mercury, aided by their forges, crucibles, and retorts. They observed that iron in water turned to rust, that fabrics faded in the sun, casked grapes fermented, leaves in autumn turned to gold. Why? Nature, for them, kept her beautiful, enigmatic lips sealed. How happy they would have been with our chemical repertoire! With what joy they would have made all the combinations possible! But they could not analyze processes, break down objects into their constituents. To us, working in a multiple-tooled and infinitely processed laboratory world, they with their crucibles and retorts were like children playing with kits of magic toys.

The swift oxidation, that common phenomenon fire, was for them a bright, leaping, lovely mystery that both destroyed and increased property. It would be ages before the Da Vinci of France, Lavoissier, would show the sons of men what fire really is.

The mediaeval scholars sought Truth, chiefly in sound but occasionally in bizarre ways. Then their very respectable chemistry went wild, indulged in pyrotechnics under the alias of alchemy. Yet this pursuit was sufficiently dignified by them to go down in their encyclopedias too. It was not, of course, the alchemy of Hugo's and Scott's wierdly-set necromancers; but it was not held in great repute. The very greatest scholars, like Aquinas and Albertus Magnus, never strayed up this scientist's primrose path. But a few—good men too, like Roger Bacon—dabbled with alchemy for diversion, much as our presidents try crossword puzzles or mystery stories. And a few affected to see in this rather unworthy pursuit a worthy objective. At least economically. For they strove to find in nature—no, never, they said, would they distort her—a natural formula for transforming base things, lead and tin, into the precious silver and gold. At the same time they sought the basic essence, the old, old, forever elusive "elixir of life."

The modern man should not scorn his forerunners for their sometimes narrower range when his superior view is obtained from the mountain top of the accrued knowledge which they have built up for him. With that they might have done even better than he. And if in this realm of science they were ages behind us, in philosophy and understanding of the soul, of Man's relation to God and God's to him, they were often aeons ahead. Besides, one should never discount the old champion. Consider his tools. Barefoot, having lost his shoes, on a gravelly and pitted track, an 1890 runner's 4:20 in the one mile is really faster than the later champion's approach to four minutes, with spiked shoes on the latest word in tracks. What scholar of the twentieth century can hope to influence human philosophy seven centuries hence as Thomas Aquinas does today? Those mediaeval fellows will still continue actually in the van, if to some things we do not get back. If we do not learn once more to relate things to the Source.

If these mediaeval men did not know the chemical composition of all the things they took out of the earth, they wrought them into marvelous entities like that Cathedral below the Hill, whose magnificent blending of height, strength, elasticity, endurance, perfect functioning and harmony, beauty, and grace, we with all our machines and science cannot match. As for our higher (mechanical and convenience) standards, they had more standards concerned with inner states, man's relationship to the life after life, his union with God, and also justice for maker and buyer alike. Though there were warped exceptions, there was a general feeling of content with one's work, of functioning happily in field, forge, hospital, at the desk, of being a carpenter, mason, bookbinder, reaper, stone-cutter, vine-tender, seamstress, clerk of God as well as of the man whose name might happen to be on the sign above.

There were many famous names in that striking division of the scholars, of the big men with the big brains and the big books, in the immemorial hill parade: Alcuin, Adelard of Bath, Abelard of Brittany, Albert the Great, Roger Bacon, Bonaventura, Duns Scotus, Fulbert of Chartres, Hugo of Saint Victor, John of Salisbury, Raimon Lulli, Roscellin, Thomas Aquinas, Vincent of Beauvais, the Williams of Champeaux, Saint Amour, Occam and Auxerre.

Perhaps there is little need in giving the scores more (though all left their mark on their own times and many alone, and all in combination, on the times coming after them), except for the strange rhythms and music of their mediaeval names—how a stage manager would have loved them!—Golden Peter, Alain de Lille, Bernard of Trillia, Davy of Dinant, Raoul of Britanny, Robert of Melun, Remi of Auxerre, and one could go on. (Also Plato, pale ghost, and Aristotle wandering in and out among those philosopher platoons.) It should be proof to cynics who, overmindful of occasional ebb tides in the forward sweep of the Church, question her guardianship of knowledge, that quite as her famous doctors had been the intellectual leaders of the world in the early Christian centuries, and the little monks in the Dark Ages had conserved all branches of learning for a later completely flowering life, all these celebrated *Summa* men in those marching columns were priests, friars, or monks ordained to the work of God and His Church.

One of the first of the Big Book men to come up the Hill, though he lodged in the old Cloister, Peter Lombard, was a very poor boy. Born of obscure parents in north Italy, he migrated to Paris before the middle 1100's where he studied under the day's idol, Peter Abelard. Not through any brilliance like that stormy petrel's, but rather through soundness of teaching, he was considered Peter's successor after that great man died.

Peter Lombard's *Summa,* called *The Book of Sentences,* was a grand digest of doctrine based on the Scriptures, the writings of the early Fathers, and the important ecumenical pronouncements since. For generations it was the Blackstone of theology, the most widely read book in all Europe. To be sure, most of the reading men were in the colleges and cloisters teaching or studying, but they were legion and they made the best-sellers. In a short time they had a flock of commentaries on Lombard's *Book of Sentences,* of source books about his source book about the great Source Book, the Bible itself. And others of these *Summae,* though often very theologico-technical, often too, in range and style were sublime. In actual historical importance, many of these writers should rank ahead of the picturesque men in mail. The great lay populace might not be able to read their books, but they moulded the mindedness out of which the deeds of the men of action sprang.

In the long line of Bishops of Paris, dating from Denis of the 250's, Peter Lombard was the prelate preceding another poor boy, Maurice de Sulli from a French farm, who rose to be the builder of Notre Dame. When De Sulli was a young priest dreaming of raising a great Cathedral to Our Lady in the lovely new exalted style, Peter Lombard occupied the ancient Bishop's Palace which we must picture as lying until the seventeenth century alongside the Cathedral, east of the Hôtel Dieu. When Peter lived there, this Gothic episcopal pile was just back of the then eight-hundred-year-old Saint Etienne. Its buttresses at their bases were Nile-green from the river; blue-backed swallows constantly flew in and out of the round arched windows; and wall flowers cascaded out of the timeless grey walls. Even while young Archdeacon de Sulli, with his great Cathedral plans in his head, was threading the old Cloister maze deciding where the lines of the new great shrine should run, Peter Lombard, oblivious of the coming glory, made the last emendation of his best-seller in the noble old Gothic Bishop's Palace. He did not live there long but he was to be quoted for centuries.

The next Hill-climbing encyclopedist, little Dominican Fra Vincent of Beauvais, who stayed in Saint Jacques from 1215 to 1220 or thereabouts, and was often in the royal palace chumming with that great booklover, Saint Louis, did decidedly have a mass of secular information in his mighty work. Here are some of its headings:

History of the Jews, the Byzantines, the Moslems. The Oceans and the Great Waters. Dew, Precipitation, the Mists. The Stars, Plants and Horticulture in General. Trees, their Saps, Fertilization, Pruning and Grafting. Zoology. Fish. Man's Organs and Faculties. Medicine for him. The Education of a Prince (much more wholesome than Machiavelli's). Wine Presses. How to be a Just Judge. Commerce, the Spices of the Indies. The Great Trade Routes. The Church Doctors. How to make a Good Helmet. Legends, Miracles. Light. Colours. The Angels. Creation. God. These are just a few. Incidentally he put in to spice his considerable body of fact a pinch of fantasy. Charlemagne was eight feet tall! He could take a fully armed knight and hold him out in his extended palm!

Brother Vincent of Beauvais was a prince of understatement. He called this work—eighty volumes, ten thousand chapters, millions of words—his "little book"! He, the little friar, had really done the work of forty men. Vincent finished his cover-all encyclopedia, the best all-around informative one of the Middle Ages, where the Forty Immortals of the French Academy never finished theirs. A one-man mediaeval *Britannica* was this little indefatigable Dominican.

It was in these years too that a famous Englishman took up his quarters in Paris. Many a scholar today would rather be called the Roger Bacon of his era than to receive the Nobel prize. This Bacon, greater than Elizabeth's bright but devious Nathaniel, came over from Daughter Oxford to Mother Paris. He stayed there quite a while, creating a stir. A Franciscan, he did not possess the lovable spirit of our Francis. He was a crusty curmudgeon of a scholar, ever with a debating chip on his shoulder. The Franciscans could always make good use of difficult men. Later they took in by the Rhine a gangling unhappy boy named Ludwig, taught him the organ, and he became the troublesome Beethoven who wrote a most glorious mass. Roger Bacon's father had lost his fortune in fighting for his king. Perhaps the poverty that followed accounted in part for Roger's churlishness. However, the old man also transmitted a dogged fighting loyalty. This Roger yielded not to any king, but to Truth.

Now the logic of the great doctors of the Church had been sublime, that of Saint Paul supernal. But often, too, they had moved up toward Truth by a galvanic mysticism and emotion. In the third century, the great Origen wrote, some say, six thousand books, though these may have been like Methusaleh's years, sections of books as the years were seasons. And thus early Origen tried to introduce into theology a trifle more of the scientific spirit. With him, all the sacred, revealed writings were more painstakingly investigated, all versions were examined and compared, and translations and interpretations of texts became accurate, even meticulous. Roger, in the thirteenth century, was the first to introduce this scientific spirit with which Origen had helped theology, into the study of the natural world. Not the day's foremost theologian, though an excellent moralist, he was its first empiricist. It might be all right to arrive at a theory through argument. The true test lay in seeing *if it worked*. In a mysticism-complexioned era, this was rather a new thing.

So Roger Bacon was forever opening Nature's concealed doors. Occasionally this mental curiosity got him into trouble, and he strayed down that alchemy-astrology road. Once an abbot, fearing that Roger's serious work might be tainted by the dubious experiments he had seen him making, had locked him up, leaving him without ink-pot or paper. It took the Pope to free him. Roger too seemed to be trying, with his many interests and his speculations with flying machines, explosives and such, to qualify for the title of champion all-around man which Leonardo da Vinci never won so completely over Roger and Lavoissier as the uninformed sometimes seem to think.

The three tall volumes of his *Summa* were serious enough. Within their ornamental clasps Roger tried to clasp the universe. Besides the alchemy shoved in with metaphysics and Moses, he had other pet subjects: amalgams, lodestones, magnetism, optics, perspective, transmission of force. A cardinal theory with him was that the forces in Nature by their actions on matter produced all the phenomena, and these could be geometrically expressed in straight lines.

His ideas on education got him into almost as much trouble as his magic. Professors and teaching priests, he announced orally and in writing, were uniformly ignorant. As linguists, they were lazy and incompetent. Their very text-books were couched in bad Latin, worse Greek. It was not to be wondered at that he was not popular in University circles on the Hill.

All clerics, he averred, spent too much time on Peter Lombard's *Sentences* and on the source books about this source book about the Source Book rather than on the latter itself. The trouble with this cross-grained if noble scholar was that he went about it without tact, with too many blanket indictments, too little allowance for human frailty. Often it seemed as if he refused to see anything right in the world outside his own mind.

Roger did not, however, get out with the Pope, the Bible, or God. Science, even mathematics, he maintained, lay in, *was* God. And he cast no aspersions on the early Fathers. To contend with the men of the past would be like struggling with ghosts. A rugged fighter, he took on the alive ones of the present. Particularly his brothers of the Paris Faculties.

Naturally the Pope heard the repercussions. He was a friend of this stormy scholar, who was forever tinkering with embryo-telescopes and all optical instruments, as well as with metals, crucibles, retorts, and fires. Indeed, Roger had once sent him a burning glass—appropriate souvenir. When the friars had sequestered his stationery, because Roger had edged a little too near the necromancy border—and the friars were more interested in Christ than in Zoroaster—this Clement the Fourth was the Pope who had ordered him freed and supplied with materials. A narrower prelate, conscience all too rigid grown, might with the dam of conservatism hold back a new stream of Truth breaking refreshingly out of tradition's ancient rock. Most pontiffs like this Clement, however, were ever ready to let in on the fat extended Church acreage of souls the refreshing new waters with their fertilizing alluvial vigour. All they asked was that the quality of the water first be tested, given a little analysis. One must not on the instant welcome every innovation. Investigators must keep minds open and yet truly probe. Of all institutions, the Church can least afford to go off half-cocked. Patience accords with its majesty, its sacred history, the ancient trust it holds. Besides, Truth never objects to a little time.

So Clement the Fourth asked to see something of Roger's manuscript, and with his quick grasp at once detected the abundant wheat and separated it from the chaff. Sitting in his palace near the old Gothic (not the present domed) Saint Peter's, he nodded his head in especial approval of the clauses Roger had cited for that alleged pedagogical ignorance. Though the wholesale nature of the attack was absurd, the shoe fitted too many, as it would fit all too many in college circles ever since. For look at his Six Causes of Teaching Ignorance:

> Reliance on Unsound Authority;
> The Over-Academic or Reactionary Attitude;
> Lack of a Willingness to say "I do not know";
> Saying "I know" when one does not;
> Pretence to Wisdom not Possessed;
> Fear of, and Catering to, the Crowd.

Pope Clement the Fourth was able to put into effect some of Roger's suggestions, particularly those relating to the more rounded education of the teaching clergy and the relative time given to source books and Source Book before he was gathered to his holy fathers.

Roger Bacon spent a little too much time swinging between true astronomy and seductive astrology and the like, in carrying that debating chip on his shoulder, and in being miffed, to rank as high as he might have on Fame's not always too well-checked and balanced roster. But when we survey the achievements of this truly gallant, if hardbitten, scholar, we must remember him not so much for concrete results, though these were considerable, as for the stimulus he gave to the minds of men. Roger was later supplanted as were Newton, Copernicus, Galileo, as Einstein one day will be and all the rest, at least in a measure. They are not to be honoured for arriving at finality—they never reach that—only the temporarily or relatively true. What matters are all the doors they unlock for their successors to pass through to other temporary but very helpful discoveries.

In his injection of the scientific spirit into the mediaeval curricula, which were rather heavily overweighted in the metaphysical direction; by his eternal stressing of proof, proof, proof, he was handing others a mind compass, starting them in the right direction, passing on a new wave of energy or adding to the tide started by other great men before him that would go on forever. This is the charm of history and biography—the observing of the changeless changing of the composite current ever being driven forward by these linked, shouldering waves of the energy of men.

Churlish Roger might be attractively remembered by a letter he wrote to the understanding Pope when copyists were so expensive, parchment and vellum and paper so hard to come by for a poor writing friar:

"As a friar, I have no money. I cannot borrow, for I have no expectation of that with which I might repay. My father, once rich, lost his all in fighting for his king. Friends who might have lent me money looked the other way. I even went to the length of asking other friends who were of limited means to expend their all in my learning emprise. I could not, therefore, refrain from assuring these good people that I would approach Your Holiness, appealing to you to send me enough to recompense them."

Though Bacon thought himself much abused, and sometimes was, his foster-mother Paris treated him in some ways rather handsomely. A good and unique title she granted him; and it was all the more flattering because it was informally yet unanimously conferred: Roger Bacon, "the Wonderful Doctor." It sounded well, and only a few scholars through the next century and a half were similarly distinguished: Albertus Magnus, "the Universal Doctor"; Duns Scotus, "the Subtle Doctor"; Alexander of Hales, "the Irrefutable Doctor"; Thomas Aquinas and Bonaventura "the Angelic" and "the Seraphic Doctors" respectively. No stipends, cups, or gold were thrown in. Like the Golden Age of Greece, when champions asked no cash prizes or athletic scholarships and were delighted with laurel or bay, the thirteenth century was, for scholar, artist, craftsman, even when they worked for a wage, in spirit a simon pure amateur age.

All this is proof in itself that there was an intrinsic merit about that century that went beyond a wistful writer's romantic pen, that was more than any nostalgic charm of the *temps perdu*. If you could plunge yourself right into that struggling, creative, hammering, building, painting, writing, digging, praying, colourful time, you would be galvanized into action yourself, on the market, city wall, shop, forge, orchard, or Notre Dame spot, and go bustling and shouting and singing and working away with these sometimes soiled, more often splendid, emotional, holy and hilarious mediaeval folk.

The Golden Age of Greece gave to mankind a balanced, sane, intellectual light; the first century the transcendent illumination of the soul; the so-called Renaissance the warm summer glow of the humanities. The thirteenth century of the great Gothic Era prismed something of all these into its immortal ray.

Which is why we must watch, as these scholars pass, just one or two more of the oddly, beatifically named "Angelic" and "Seraphic" and so-on doctors.

Saint Bonaventura (with the final "e" instead of the "a," if you prefer the anglicization)—the "Seraphic" one—was another Italian who became a devoted foster-son of the great Mother Paris, another of those poor boys who rose to great glory in the Church, for the greater glory of God. At thirty-five he was chosen master-general of the Franciscan order, the youngest ever to receive so high an honour. Many of these great leaders known for the might of their reasoning powers were marked by a serenity of countenance which often comes to those who think long and well and who have lived pure lives. Even among such, Bonaventura was notable for benignity and beauty of expression. As in certain pictures the Beloved Disciple stands out from the others of the Twelve, through a handling of light, so Bonaventura stood out among the scholars. It was in part because of this sound and shining sweetness that he was called "the Seraphic Doctor."

Saint Bonaventura spent many years in Paris continuously, Thomas quite a number on his four different stays. But for some time the University authorities held up both from their higher degrees. In these years before the maturing of the Sorbonne as the leading school of theology in the University, the Dominicans (Thomas', Vincent's, Albert's order) and the Franciscans (Roger Bacon's, Alexander of Hales', and Bonaventura's institution) had dominated the Hill teaching staffs not through any politics, only through their mental power and eloquence. Suddenly the long-smouldering jealousy some of the lay professors and teaching secular priests had felt toward the gifted and self-sacrificing friars broke into flame. William Saint Amour of Saint Victor's touched it off with a book which fairly scorched the friars. The University exercised a charter right and staged a University strike, the reverse of the ones we know, for not the underbody but authority struck, closing all the University halls. Bonaventura and Thomas Aquinas were left awaiting their doctorates, cooling their heels.

Then as William Saint Amour had written his acrimonious little plaintiff book, Bonaventura wrote a nobler one for the defendants. It was the famous *Poverty of Christ*; and it not only pleaded the cause of the mendicant teaching friars, but it emphasized afresh for the world the principles of the founder, Francis, and before him, of Jesus. Though small in size this little masterpiece, *The Poverty of Christ,* was as important as Bonaventura's *Summa* in four great volumes. The civil war was appealed to the Pope. Albert the Great went to Rome. His brilliant oral defense, Bonaventura's written one in *The Poverty of Christ,* won. Not long after, in 1257, Bonaventura and Thomas were given the doctorates which they should long ago have had.

A remark of Alexander of Hales about Bonaventura sums up the quality of "the Seraphic Doctor." To comprehend its significance, we must remember that the age was full of notably holy lives. And all these scholars, in their lectures and *Summae,* had made much of what Adam had brought into the world, "original sin." This theological explanation that Adam, who through morbid curiosity risked and lost his birthright of innocence and Eden, had handed on his perverse curiosity to all his heirs might annoy bio-chemists, but not the historians who have seen their history drenched with man's bloody repetitions of his failures.

Realizing this mindedness of the time, one can see what a beautiful tribute it was that the "Irrefutable Doctor," Alexander of Hales, paid to the "Seraphic Doctor" when he said, "It would almost seem as though the noble Bonaventura had escaped this common curse of Adam." It would serve as epitaph for Bonaventura as beautiful as that paid by De Joinville to Saint Louis.

Albert the Great, in the immortal Hill procession, was the last one before—and the grand approach to—the great champion of the Schoolmen, Thomas Aquinas. Born in Swabia, Germany, Albert wore the Dominican black-over-white. He did not make as many stays in Paris as Thomas, but he was there with him in Saint Jacques Convent from 1245 through 1248. Thomas was thirteen years younger. Albert served as his great friend and adviser and, indeed his John the Baptist.

Both of their fathers were counts. They joined the long line of those who tried to make up to Christ for the young man in the Gospel whom He loved and who so disappointed Him. John, Paul, Barnabas, Ambrose, Augustine, Gregory, Benedict, Dominic, Francis, Quintivalle, Albert, Aquinas, Xavier, De Sales, Leo the Thirteenth, the women, too, Catherine of Alexandria, all the Catherines, Monica, Dorothea, the Margarets, Clare, Teresa of Avila, one could go on indefinitely. It is heartening to know that those who gave up their all for His sake, like those who rose from obscurity to glory in His service, are so very, very many.

Paris not only gave to this foster-son of three years, Albert the Great, one of her grand honorary titles, "Doctor Universal," to indicate the sweep of his knowledge. She left her name for him, Albert le Maître, on a street which still winds down near Maubert Square with clifflike, upsloping walls and deep cavernous windows and doorways opening into mediaeval twilit vistas.

Albert was as all-around in gifts as Roger Bacon, Da Vinci, or the French Prometheus, Lavoissier. In actual published words he surpassed all these Big Book men except Vincent of Beauvais. Ten and a half million was his score. Since he was, too, a constant lecturer in many cities, an indefatigable traveler as bishop, also as general officer of the Dominicans, and even preached a Crusade, his contemporaries constantly searched for new adjectives for him. Always they fell back on "Stupendous," or "Stupefying." It must have been rather a burden for a simple man to bear.

Albert the Great was so in his own right. And he was great through others. Through his own teachings and books. Through that masterpiece of his pupil, Thomas Aquinas, one of the half-dozen most influential books of the world, which still, this very hour, sways men. He paved the way for Thomas and his thinking and theology. He baptized him with the living water of his spirit. Lighted him with the illumination of his own surpassing intelligence. Also he served as architect for Thomas. A few thoughtful souls before Albert had dimly glimpsed three truths which Albert first established as working principles in philosophy:

Science was in harmony with religion;

There were two roads by which one arrived at Divine Truth: Revelation and enlightened human reason;

The great pre-Christian "pagan" philosophers, Aristotle chief among them, were in harmony with Christian beliefs.

After Aristotle had inspired and been fought over by the Abelards, Williams, Roscellins, all the old wrestlers of the Cloister around ancient Saint Etienne's and the first Notre Dame, it was Albert who brought him from the Notre Dame porch up the hill to the University in its new halls. Or perhaps it was that Albert called attention to the fact that Aristotle himself had ascended and was operating among them. In the end he left it to his pupil, Thomas Aquinas, to make the great pre-Christ thinker an ally of Christ. And these three great principles we have just mentioned Albert le Maître laid down as broad steps up to the mighty citadel of thought Thomas would build.

However, before we take the last step up to that conclusion of centuries of Church and University and Schoolmen's development, the very climax and apogee of the Middle Ages' composite thinking, Thomas Aquinas himself and his citadel, we should pause to ask ourselves this: how was it that religion and the philosophy that doubled for it, could—so astonishingly for us of this materialistic and rationalistic age—completely dominate and sway and mould the men of one of the greatest of all ages. Why it was that whole communities, the black of heart, the red with blood, the white of spirit, crowded into Notre Dame.

We must not think that all was harmony within the Church. Jealous faculty members tried to cool the fire of the friars. A bishop of Paris said Thomas Aquinas was all wrong. Almaric of Bena said that God occupied the bodies of others besides that of Christ. A bishop had Almaric's bones exhumed, consigned to unhallowed ground. Though Paris in the Middle Ages was never smitten with any chronic *auto-da-fé* fever, she had a touch enough of it once for her king to burn ten who thought there were innumerable Christs. University cliques aped the brilliant, but unsound Moor Averrhoës, in denying individual immortality—strange doctrine on that sacred Hill!

There was, too, much debate over the Immaculate Conception, the belief concerning the birth not of Christ, but of His Mother. This (none contested it) had come in the old human way. Mary had been conceived by Joachim; she was not incarnate like Our Lord. But with the birth of the rest of us there has always come that legacy handed on by Adam's, man's, mishandling of his magnificent birthright—the inclination to experiment with evil, called Original Sin. It is common to all and is only eradicated with a very great fight and God's grace. The early Fathers pondered its connection with Mary. She who had been chosen out of all the race to be the human instrument for the entry into the world of God descending through boundless love to save it, must, they were sure, have escaped that taint. The idea appealed to many as not only beautiful but inherently right. The difficulty was to rationalize their intuition, to reconcile a perfectly natural human birth and her immunity from the common legacy.

Despite occasional exceptions, Mother Church has been on Nature's, on Science's side. Logic, with her, is not alien to faith. Nature is a manifestation of God on this plane. The Church does not want the processes of Nature interfered with except when God sees fit to override a set of natural laws with a higher whose workings we on another plane will understand. Mary's was a human, not a supernatural conception like her Son's. In her birth God stepped in only so far as to secure that stainlessness which would seem so logical for the human Mother who was to bear the Divine.

It was to take many centuries after Thomas and the Middle Ages arguers to arrive at the true solution. Conception was not the answer. There is the time when the embryo in the womb receives its personalizing, is animated with its soul. In that moment there enters with the soul the ancient weakness. And then only had God mystically intervened. In the union of the soul with the embryo, there had not been the infusion of the age-old tendency to evil, for Mary of Nazareth who was to be the Mother of God. It was in the nineteenth century that Pope Pius the Ninth thought it high time for the beautiful intuition of the holy men of past ages, for this long unofficially held theory to be confirmed. He made it one more of the infinite number of little pebbles of tenets that form the great conglomerate that is the doctrine of Mother Church.

Certainly all did not go off holily to the Crusades. The Cross often covered a longing for lust and loot. Merchants mulcted the pilgrims coming in. So, even in this magical thirteenth century, which is always written of as though it were one phenomenal harmonious pageant, there was considerable contention; and those Albigensian cities were still smoking. But in spite of all these cross-currents, the main one, the dominating trend was distinguishable, and it was more markedly religious than any other age can show. The tiny barks that were men's souls then clearly revealed the hand, the piloting of God.

And the main distinctions between that age and our own more mechanically-favoured one were two: the tremendous gusto with which they pursued their every activity, religious and secular, and the well-nigh universal belief that laymen as well as clerics—the bad with the good—had in God, however they might obey or disobey His commandments. They did not, like us now, hawk atheistic newspapers on the streets, start atheistic museums and parades, or defile as they have in eastern Europe, sacred symbols. Such a procession would not have gotten more than a hundred feet before it would have gone down under a storm of stones, besom brooms, candlesticks and chamber-pots. Even to the blasphemer—we have seen how rare in Saint Louis' time were open offenders—the deities he swore by were real. He used sacred names in vain, only to give edge to his curses. Unlike an American Nobel novelist melodramatically shaking his fist up at God, daring Him to strike him dead to show that He was not, the mediaeval blasphemer defied an actual Him. Above all, when a man sinned those days it was not with any modern idea that sin was but the violating of some inconsequential custom of a country. He sinned weakly or wildly, but knowingly. Heaven and Hell were as real to the mediaeval malefactors and the upright as they appeared in the vivid Cathedral panes.

When Saint Louis from his palace ramparts, or the student from his attic eyrie under a sway-backed, crooked-tile roof, looked out upon the stars, they were not gazing in modern fashion at illuminated mathematics, but on the glory of God's handiwork. If ever in that age there was any mass sinning anywhere—even as now, though never so great—there was no mass doubt, which is not at all as now.

Quite as when on coming into a land one sees stakes out at sea,

dories upturned and being calked, nets being mended, and sails of
tacking fleets disappearing over the horizon, one knows he is coming
into a fishing country, with all the signs you saw in Paris and Saint
Louis' Ile de France you knew that the main industry of this amazing
capital and the fair region roundabout was, actually, religion.

Spires dominated every city sky-line, where today they have either
disappeared or have been humiliatingly dwarfed. Holy books were
constant school text-books; in public schools today the very Scriptures
are banned. Indeed, half the books issued then were on religious
subjects, half the songs sung were of God, His Son, Our Lady.
Crucifixes, calvarys, confessionals, cassocks, parables in stone and in
glass, church spires gave the background; chants, requiems, bells for
holy offices, sacred names and phrases in royal edict, law pronouncement, and daily greetings added an overtone to this crowded, colourful
age in which Parisians thrillingly lived and moved. This constant
ecclesiastical characterizing of life would have made it oppressive,
perhaps, had not most of these properties and symbols been so moving and beautiful. Every moment almost in Paris, you looked on some
delicate flèche pointing up and signalling that the House of Many
Mansions was still there. As you turned a corner, a sudden going on
of candles in a church brought a bright Saul vision into the dark
Damascus of a narrow Paris street. Or on surrounding grey walls a
great stained glass expanse broke into a transport of glory.

These high towers and shining windows some now would preserve
as merely antiquarian. Where, they ask, did all this church-building
and church-going get them? Did it get much beyond habit or fear?
Did it all strike through the pageantry to the heart?

There was then a vast externality to religion. Hypocrites, dull con-
formists, religious opportunists practised it. Frequently the sincerely
devout laid too much store by symbol and sign, though the Church
for ages had pointed out that in rite, holy pictures and statues there
is no absolute, only a suggestive quality. The gold circlet recalls the
bridal troth. A picture summons up a loved one far away. So these
holy pictures and heroic statues revivify thoughts of God, His Son,
Our Lady, and the whole protecting company of Heaven. As reminders
they nourish the faith for the simple, also for the intellectual who
knows it is the wise part of intellectuality to become as a little child.

Worshipping words and motions took up then a staggering total
of the hours of the lives of the people of France. Not only the mass
piety, but the very hypocrisy and opportunism was telling evidence
of the religious centring of life. That vast externality could only
have grown up around a tremendous internality of the spirit.

And a very great number of those gathered around the pillars in nave and aisles, chapels, and galleries, accepted in a truly happy and single-minded way this omnipresent phenomenon of sign and symbol and rite. All these made up the beautiful and stirring mechanics that helped here below to carry religion forward. They were but the fitting, the profoundly moving outer projection of the inner life.

The extraordinary last half of the twelfth century, and three-quarters of the thirteenth combined in the Gothic age that was characterized by a practice, sincere or motivated, of religion wider-spread than in any other era. When we shall have religion enough to do away with our wars, then we shall have an age that is even greater. Only then.

For consider the amazing total of religious activities. Hundreds of thousands in the various uniforms of the Church baptized, confirmed, wived, shrived, and buried men, and educated them with lecture, book and quill. They instructed them too in making stone arches—always good ones—brick drains, sound live stock, embroidery, sewers, carved angels. Hosts of unordained men and women in the friar third orders tended to jobs, homes, yet laid aside many hours each week for religious work. As Franciscan auxiliaries, corollary Dominicans, they attended to their devotions, and scrubbed floors, whitewashed walls, peeled vegetables, beat mattresses, patched clothes, removed pus, washed dirty bodies, healed wounds, in abbey wards, church asylums, in which the latch-string was always out for God and His poor. Now such institutions are dedicated in so many cities to the community. Then, not occasionally as now, but always they were avowed carryings-out of the will of the Christ Who gave the words "Charity" and "Brotherhood" new warmth and meaning. The current of this chronicle itself, like that of Paris life, is forever running between shores lined with these going concerns of God.

Behind, Notre Dame on the north, was a great many-gabled camp of stucco, timber, brick, and stone, of another, an ecclesiastically industrial, army. Spinning, stitching, forging, appliquéing, annealing, beating, hammering out, processing innumerable items for the Cathedral:—Cinctures, slippers, felt shoes. Bishops' canopies, silver-threaded altar-cloths, gold chains for suspended coronas. Flower garden-backed chasubles, fonts, sanctus bells, chased chalices, embroidered paten and burse. Black neum notes on two-foot choir sheets, vitrified parable and hero and holy scene in the deep-dyed glass. Heroes from the chisel. And Holy Bread.

So around Notre Dame, men and women swarmed like busy bees in their close-packed, painted, timbered hives, in their cloister cells around the great golden lighted honeycomb of the Cathedral.

If, as observed before, it sometimes seemed as though the city walls were about to burst out, those house roofs go up and off with all the ebullient energy of the Parisians, fully half of that remarkable activity was generated by folks engaged in service, direct or indirect, to God.

For there were always the by-product movements. In all the colleges that took up so much of the life circulation of the city. In all those guild members who walked uprightly, in the sight not only of their chiefs, but of their God. They invoked Him at their meetings, and what union or management conference—or even council of nations—now opens its assemblies with prayer? Those guilds were another striking evidence of the day's very general acceptance of God, in their everyday work, in their honest pride in the various crafts, their high standards, their seeking for justice and fair dealing for all sides.

People poured out their earnings for laces, carvings, gems, ivory, gold, to make God's cathedrals beautiful, and in sums out of all proportion to those given today. Into the making they threw all the strength and skill and grace and heart they could muster. All these lovely objects, the floods of paintings and illuminated books gave a delight to God, not only because they were tributes to Him, and gave adornment to His lovely house, but because they too gave delight to His poor who otherwise wouldn't have had so much warmth and colour in their lives.

The chivalry of the times which, like the Gothic, the Crusades, the troubadour minstrelsy, was a wholly French idea, or at least drew a particular splendour from the French, had been moulded by religion. Chivalry too had its trinity. "Love, Charity, God, are all in one," was one of its slogans, observed too by quite a fine number of knights, however some titled profligates might pervert it.

One of the true knight's objectives, celebrated in story and song, and in injunctions to the new knight at the receiving of the accolade, was to give to the poor clothes, "even those out of his own wardrobe, where necessary, and food and money when his neighbours had none."

Chivalry had another lovely motto:—"Be of open heart. Learn to endure pain. Above all, love one another with all your souls." There was, after all, quite a period when knighthood was truly in flower.

And there was in western Europe a grand religious hospitality. For greedy bazaar people who overcharged at the gates of pilgrim cities, abbeys and castles abundantly made up. With fire, water, food, wine, fresh straw, towels, new sandals, they kept open house for the dust-stained travelers all along the way.

The religious spirit was not nourished at all by the loot-lust-minded in the Crusader trains, but Godfrey of Boulogne and hosts more endured fever and death and all things for Christ's sake. They had put on that Red Cross as they believed He had taken on His. You cannot discount it or wave it aside. For all the flaws and the waste, the great over-all motive of the Crusades was to save the Tomb of One Who was very precious to millions, One Whom they loved. It is one of the amazing phenomena of history.

It is significant that the ablest leadership of the period went into the Church direct or into vital association with her. And there is another evidence of the devotion of the times, in the prevalence of prayers, some wasted, empty, as we have seen, more fervent, passionately pleading. Tremendous was their power. Only God could devise a system for measuring in some mystic energy units, their combined galvanic strength. In that era prayer ascended to Heaven in a vast volume that swept over the country-side far and near, and not only for the benefit of the multitude of petitioners themselves, but so often for others, all the sons of men.

With saints *and* sinners, which when one comes to think of it clinches the point, their cathedrals and churches were filled to the overflowing. Religion then was so live a thing. Now the churches in many a city of many a creed draw each scarcely a corporal's guard.

As for these children of Notre Dame, some still insist that it was mass fear and superstition that by their slave necks haled them in. Some fear—not wholly unwholesome, either, for why should not one be concerned for his soul's as well as his body's welfare—there undoubtedly was, also a measure of superstition. But among so many of those legion unlettered in tattered *tyreteinne* or patched wool, kneeling on the Notre Dame stones, there was a sincere, if sometimes humanly complicated allegiance, and often a pure and single-minded devotion to the Man of Sorrows elevated on His Cross among them, and a childlike confidence in Our Lady and the maternal love so beautifully expressed by the cradling of the Child in her arms.

Even when there was not quite that single love, there were so many piteous things calling: sores, groaning backs, hobbled feet, empty stomachs, bruises, wounds, deep human needs, yearning, despair. Such have been calling out, of course, down the centuries since. There was a difference, however, then. The hearts of great hosts of mediaeval worshippers, crossing themselves, looking up at His pendant figure, all melted together by the love in their hearts and the origin Love in His, and by their burning need of Him, believed, not a few here, a few there as today, but *en masse*, when their voices went up in the ancient petition of Temple and Cathedral, *Christe eleison!* Christ have mercy! *Miserere nobis!* Have pity on us! And the kind of religion that cries out for help, that casts one in despair upon Him, is a kind of religion that is very dear to Him.

The Gothic tide washed all these generations with its gold. It is a question whether, just as in Paris philosophy and theology were almost interchangeable, this Gothic tide was not actually a tide of religion. If it did not bear all men in harmony on its bosom, it carried them forward. It touched them all, if it did not wash all of them quite clean. Currents from it eddied around every street corner, swirled into every court, seeped under every door. Spray from it caught men challengingly in the face, gladdened them with a new and eternal freshness.

These men of the Middle Ages sinned even as we—but—this must be repeated—they believed—they believed! Some with the grip of the letter. More with the profound conviction of the spirit. Only by understanding this can we enter into the feast prepared for us by these shabby and splendid mediaeval hordes with their bundles of inconsistencies all bound up by the one priceless consistency, a belief in the One Eternal Fact. So only can we know the wry taste of that banquet, its sweet flavour, bite deep into its flesh, drink of its wine which, despite all their errors, had a touch of the sacramental.

These rough, battered, sweating, sublime crowds, with their wages, muscles' might, and hearts' blood, shoved up the noble Cathedrals to the sky. Then, instead of throwing out their chests in pride as we would have done, they humbly knelt within their achievements.

XII

The Roof Sea of Paris. . . . The Family of Thomas Aquinas, not wanting him to be a Friar, lay Traps of the Flesh. . . . Ancient Battles on the Paris Left Bank Hill. . . . The Sorbonne Professor who let God teach for him. . . . The Guilds declare Saturday Half-Holidays. . . . The Mother Church denounces Usury as Persecution. . . . Mediaeval Librarians must know Everything, answer All Questions, and guard their Gorgeously Decorated Books. . . . The Beautiful Library of Sainte-Chapelle. . . . The Count-Cousin of the King and the Saint read a Great Romance and a Mediaeval Best-seller together.

1248 A. D.

A BIG MAN STOOD BY THE WINDOW OF THE HILL-TOP CONVENT of Saint Jacques, looking down on the Paris roofs. He was not only big in body but in brain and, although in his late twenties, was by way of becoming a great man like the king, though not through the battle-ax and the judge's bench, only through that brain and his books.

The name of this big man was Thomas Aquinas—in the French, d'Aquin. He had come to Paris from Italy to study for his doctorate. The records of his itinerary are unusually clear for the old days. Certain it is that he was here in Paris, at Saint Jacques for three years from 1245 to 1248, as well as on several long visits afterwards. Some say he came first to Paris from his homeland Italy, others that he came by way of Cologne. And sooner or later he did spend some time in study in the shadow of the Rhineland Cathedral. This was the old one. The lofty, massive, mechanically majestic Cathedral we know today would not be started until after the fire, when our own Notre Dame would be a hundred years old.

Notre Dame lay below him on the Isle; and the prospect of her and the whole city was very fair. The mighty belt of the city wall, with its stone like the Cathedral's still light and fresh of hue, gave a bright

172

and happy look to the capital which for all the recent painting-up might have seemed a dark old city.

The wall coiled, with its hundred capping towers and high city gates, around his abbey home and the crowded Left Bank dwellings down to the Seine. The huge river chains which, to guard the city, were stretched across the Seine at night, in the morning sunshine lay in rusting coils on the strand. The Isle had a circling wall all its own. Over the river the wall took up its sentry march again through the Right Bank meadows. Abbeys and farms lay between the wall and Montmartre. Mediaeval wind-mills, vineyards, and little stone Saint Pierre stood out across from the watcher on the summit.

Within the city wall's stone embrace surged an endless roof sea. Near at hand the watcher caught some of the detail: the gable peaks, the crooked ridge-poles that formed the curled-up ridges of that sea of housetops. But afar off it was just one mass, with the roof waves curling low or rising high, and many at such angles to each other it seemed a shambling, tumbling sea, stilled at its choppiest in an infinite variety of wave formations. Above it everywhere hovered little plumes of chimney smoke like white-caps. Palace, guild-hall, mansion, and round-sterned churches rose above the house-top waves, resembling ships and galleons there riding. All the fortress towers stood out like light-houses by the sea. From every quarter sounded the brazen tongues from innumerable belfries as from so many bell-buoys on the roof waves. And over all rose the great sanctuary-ark, Notre Dame, with its twin towers, beacons of Paris and the world.

Thomas had been born in the 1220's—the Middle Ages were as careless about their dates as they were about their spelling—near Naples, at Aquino which gave his father his title as count. High in a vaulted chamber of Roccasecca Castle (even the Count was never sure about the numbers of c's), the future saint was tumbled into the world on a five steps-up, arrased pavilion of a bed in a wild country and a still wilder time. The Languedoc flames still were rising. Holy Roman Emperor and Pope still were at odds. Far to the East, marauders of Tsschinghiss Khan (as the casual orthographers had it then) were taking great bites out of Asia's huge body and Europe's east flank.

It had been a stormy winter night when there had sounded above in the castle a sudden great bustle. Midwives and servants clop-clopped about on the bare stones of the vaulted bedchamber, or went more softly where rushes had been strewn or the new oriental rugs purchased for the *accouchement* of the Countess of Aquino. Cauldrons of boiling water, flacons of olive oil, sea sponges, swathings of linen they bore, with the anodyne mandrake for easing the pain, during the crescendo of child-birth screams which could be heard through the thick mediaeval walls which should have been sound-proof against even the shrieks of the tortured.

After gazing, at the summons upstairs, on the little red wizened sprite under the canopy, the Count announced to those assembled below, "The little calf has arrived." It was not so inapt, perhaps, for the one whom in Naples they would call an ox, and who, when he became a saint, was to have that animal for a symbol.

Often, on these winter nights, possibly on this very important one, travelers returning from the trade routes enjoyed the hospitality of Roccasecca Castle. After the hazards of the road, it was pleasant sitting in the great hall before the cavernous fire-place in which an ox was roasting whole. Often, as they watched the little blue flames spurting out and little trickles of suet bubbling and running down, they would tell of this same Tsschinghiss and what they had seen of him.

The whole vast Ural landscape, they said, was flooded with these hopping, skipping, skimming beetles, these comical, deadly fellows with the yellow-brown skins. The merchants need not have been so patronizing. For their own Christian men-at-arms and the knights of whom the troubadours sang appeared ludicrous enough with their kitchen pot helmets, their having with their weight of armour to be hoisted up in the saddle, down there in the Holy Land. Besides, Tsschinghiss had been irked into his atrocities when these highly-churched knights—not Godfrey or his kind, but others of a skin-deep Christianity—broke their treaties and assassinated his envoys. Furthermore, these *"parfait et gentil"* knights had done some tall butchering of their own in Jerusalem streets. It was fortunate that, to better balance the score, the truly *gentil* Saint Francis of Assisi had gone down there too. He had, as we have seen, those wonderful, animated eyes, those lovely songs and irresistible sermons, and a way with him for all—of every sort—a way like Christ's, with Francis' own adaptations. Not even excepting Godfrey or Saint Louis who with all his justice and pity still had that battle-ax, which was repelling, disaffecting and could never woo people, he was the only one in Christendom to show the Saracens there could be Christians that actually merited the name in full. Well the Moslems noted and never forgot it.

Meantime, to the north of him, the men from the Yellow Sea with the bias eyes, the heads like dried light brown cocoanuts, little black whiplash ends for eyebrows, and chin and upper lip whiskers, tumbling out from that great race cornucopia of the East, were rolling on. Tsschinghiss' chargers stretched from horizon to horizon in great traveling arcs. From farmsteads and villages all over the plains, flames and geysers of fire curled and shot up like waves and spume from some red-golden sunset sea.

But the really epic sight, the merchants told the castle crowd with the smacking gusto of those who have traveled wide and have seen many things when relating their adventures to the stay-at-homes, came on nights after some of Tsschinghiss' smashing victories. There was a magnificent display of booty. Before him on his throne under a pavilion of silk banners on spear points, they rolled out their gargantuan loot: acres of precious rugs and shawls of softest tones and sheen. Bushels of rubies, emeralds, diamonds, bracelets and armlets of bangles, silver, and gold. And, literally, barrels of cropped human ears. Then as the crowning evidence of his triumphs, they rolled out before him on the spread-out silks a bevy of bodies, this time whole and female. Over those festoons of breasts, rosy or almond-hued, tip-tilted or pear in shape, of hips brown-olive or impearled, the Tsschinghiss agate eyes glinted. As he glanced down the luscious prizes, the long-nailed index finger indicated those he wanted held for his copulating cavortings that night in his pleasure tent.

Thomas began his good works early. At ten he was studying in Saint Benedict's monastic capital on Mount Cassino. At sixteen, in the University of Naples he enlisted among the young men who had been fired by the living influence of the dead Dominic. Still, Thomas was not so fortunate as the founder, Dominic, whose family had helped him in his chosen career. The Count and Countess of Aquino were dead set against this last choice. They may have been conventionally religious. The priesthood, with the chances offered a fine mind of a prelacy and its accompanying prestige, might have pleased rather than have offended them. But it irritated them to see their boy in the habit of a poor friar.

Eventually the brothers, the rest of the family either conniving at, or not preventing it, abducted him from the monastery and locked him up in Roccasecca. There the whole family showed themselves desperately anxious to get him out of that coarse wool, at least into a secular priest's habit, if not the silks and gold of the young aristocrat.

All their attacks failing, they tried one last bitter ruse. When one night Thomas had gone for his daily prisoner's walk along the parapet, the brothers, while the sisters watched, ushered a handsome young woman into his room and placed her, stripped, on the bed. The end was not quite what they had expected. When he entered, all the desires which, to keep his vow, he had so far successfully routed, returned full force to plague him. Then, suddenly, with a resolution which must have cost him something, he whirled around, seized a torch from a wall bracket, and brandishing the flaming pine knot, drove her naked and screaming out amongst the startled family on the stairs.

The story was too good to keep. If the brothers were silent there were many servants in the house. The Naples smart set jeered at his conduct as "abnormal." Others roared at the scene as farcical. Even in those who have a boundless admiration for the saint, there might be humanly permitted, if not the cynical levity of the Neapolitans, at least a little of amusement at the picture. But it was a serious enough matter for a taut-strong adolescent with a noble purpose. It was actually one of the decisive battles of a great life. It left its mark upon his career as we shall presently see.

On his family, that is the women of it, the effect was immediate and remarkable. Mother and sisters all, they now listened to his talk of sacred things. Instead of violently trying to dissuade him from his career, they prayerfully urged him on into it. Saint Paul was his idol and the women now took a leaf from the Book of Acts. They let him down over the castle walls in a basket. So like Saint Paul—Mahomet, too—the youth escaped into the longed-for service.

In this struggle which some are inclined to sneer at or belittle, above and beyond the physical victory there had been inwardly born a determination not only temporarily to restrain the flesh, but to devote his every last ounce of energy to work for the Lord. When he re-counted it in later years to his amanuensis, it was always with something of remembered awe at the profound and unforgettable experi-ence that had succeeded the tawdry episode. He had fallen on his knees in the room, he said, a sixteen-year-old shaken by what he felt might have turned out badly for his career, to pour out his soul in petition that henceforth his vitality might be conserved for his King. Suddenly he was aware that there were by him in the room two angels; a great gladness, then a following great peace came upon him.

So it was not the immediate conquest for chastity that mattered. Even a saint might have fallen, only the stronger to rebound. History would seem to prove that chastity is not an ingredient necessary to attaining military or statesman's greatness. Witness Solomon, Caesar, Hamilton, Peter the Great, Henry of Navarre, a whole picturesque glamorous flock. Chastity, however, played a part in the history Thomas made up in Paris.

These saints were no weak ascetics, but dynamic men. They knew marriage as a divinely-ordained institution. They had no foolish idea that celibacy was indispensable for service to His Kingdom. The married too could perform that. To those who for completer service to Him had given up earthly ties, Christ's love went out in a special way. But He did not command celibacy for anyone, only commended it for the few. There were no orders. Without bonds, as Paul too emphasized, advance scouts, pioneers, could travel lighter, faster. House walls confine, hearths keep calling back. The soldier does not want to drag out wife and family with him to the arena or the crematory. Home, too, means property, wills, concern for the future about which Christ's advance guard, full-time soldiers, missioners, priests, must have a divine heedlessness.

This celibacy was simpler than it seems. The imagination can whip up the body. Where there is motive enough, the mind can take the body under its complete governance. These good men, great and obscure, had motive enough in the desire to hurry on His Kingdom and please Him. And here is where God's Science helps His Nature. The mind can spur or curb the body—yes, and more; it can act as transformer for the currents in the body. Through a miracle of science designed long ago, Nature can return then those urges of the body, the very seed potentials of them, back into the bloodstream, transforming them into a powerful energy to be spent in the Cause. These mighty galvanized men we call saints, whole armies of lesser men who equalled them if not in gifts, in devotion, simply channeled with prayer and science those troubling, traveling energies of the body elsewhere within themselves for Him.

Thomas Aquinas was more fortunate than most men in this. That one night of the brandished torch had been effective. He had no more struggles on the primrose battlefield where other great men, Saints Anthony and Augustine prominently among them, were a long, long time engaged in getting the upper hand of the flesh.

This youth already powerful in body, potentially so in mind, was not appreciated by some of the teachers in Cologne as later he would be elsewhere, say, in all the bookstores of the world that sell important books.

As a young man, he was meditative and sometimes appeared slow. A faculty member in the Cologne *studium,* blind to the gifts obscured by Thomas' manner, exclaimed in irritation one day, "Why, the fellow is as dumb as an ox!"

Another—no less a person than Albert the Great, discerning in this splenetic outburst one of the worst prophecies ever in this world, retorted: "You call him an ox? Fine! And some day the thunder of his bellowing of Church doctrine will astound the world!"

Because of this reply and the ox-like strength of him from sturdy neck to his great legs, writers and artists later allotted him, as saint's symbol, the ox.

So, some years after his early seminarian training, Thomas Aquinas was now here in his new home on the top of the Acropolis of the mediaeval world, the capital of the empire of intellectual light. The French use the word convent for both male and female cenobite institutions, the homes of both men and women religious. The Convent of Saint Jacques, the first Paris house of the Dominicans, was deep fertilized in history. Where Thomas looked down on the Paris roof sea, the old Gauls of Paris in the Battle of Montparnasse in 52 B.C., outnumbered, outweaponed, had made their last stand. From there the battle-line had run to the Seine. Brightly had shone their emblazoned war chariots, their coral-and-silver decorated shields. Bravely, in the last defiant gesture of Death, had waved their red cloaks above the shining helms on their bright hair, then had fallen to the ground. So they had plunged on into the Roman death. And into, it is to be hoped, their old dream of immortality for all who never flinched from the foe, protected their comrades with their own breasts, down by the sea in the old bright Gallic heaven of the West.

There were so many historic tie-ups to this site. Clovis and Geneviève lay, just across from Thomas, in her abbey with some eight-hundred-year-old towers, and some comparatively new Norman ones. Philippe Auguste had looked at the city gate being erected just back of the Convent cherries. In its environs on the Hill, Villon would loaf, make love, pilfer and write verses, Ronsard, Rabelais would chat in inns, Calvin and Loyola arrive at such different conclusions in the hill schools. Francis the First would near by put up his great college, Napoleon would strut, Josephine flirt, Ney be shot. In halls, haunts, pensions all around it, Pascal and Bergson would lecture, Verlaine drink and dream, Becquerel, the Curies discover radio activity, Claude Bernard explore the body, Bernhardt play, Massenet write his Saint Sulpice scene, César-Franck his benediction hymn, the "Panis Angelicus," Renoir, Cézanne mix paints, Zola drum up his Dreyfus defense, and Voltaire, Mirabeau, Rousseau be buried. And this is just a sample, a taste of that hill-top. A thousand more of the illustrious of France would here pursue their infinitely varied and illuminating activities. And most of the famous of the rest of the world would come to this summit, to drink in learning or inspiration or simply to wonder.

Only by thus weaving the warp of the present on the woof of the past, embroidering both with the scarlet of this era, the gold or purple or black of others, then appliquéing on them the lace and braid of still other and expansive periods, and adding a well-worked-in patch or two and the stains of the years, can you know the fascinating fabric that is Paris history, and so wear it like a coat, slipping your arms in it, your hands in its pockets, and getting to know its wonderful feel.

Those who would like to forefinger down its very seams can trace the line, for example, of that Convent, in fancy restore the cluster of yellow and grey buildings, with their orchard and garden closes of green. The old vanished St. Jacques wall began where the giant Pantheon pillars are now, crossed in front of the present School of Law, through the new library, down to the Sorbonne Chapel where Richelieu lies in his beautiful white tomb. Rounding the Café d'Harcourt and Marne martyr Péguy's bookshop, one must walk north on colourful Boul' Mich', past Verlaine's La Source, all the shops with stationery, books, or sweaters for the students, the zinc bars with their coffee and croissants and brioche, when wars are not on. Opposite the Edmond Rostand fountain, you turn back again by the Rue Soufflot to the giant Pantheon pillars. That walk would have circled then every last cloister pillar, altar, cell, domestic building, craft shop, candle, torch, chained book, hospital bed, fountain, beet, and pear within the Saint Jacques *enceinte*.

As he stood in one of the buildings, looking north, toward the Cathedral, it could be seen that Thomas Aquinas was truly a big man. His chest was deep and strong; his neck thick-set. His legs under the soutaine, on the ground were firmly planted. The broad planes of his serene face had the pleasant hue of the brown earth with a little of the yellow of the good earth's wheat in it. His eyes were kind for all the earth's children.

Curiously, in general sturdiness of frame he bore a resemblance to the Luther of three centuries on. Not in face, for Luther was gaucily ruddy, where Thomas had that good earth brown and the wheat yellow. But could they have been stood up together, they might have been taken at a little distance for twins. In temperament, point of view, they differed widely. We, maintaining that bird's-eye view of different epochs at one and the same time, the ability to live on several different levels of time—that historical perspective of which we spoke —might here compare them. We will, however, speak only of the divergence about that on which Thomas had been looking down:— The Cathedral! Luther did not think so much of Our Lady. Thomas loved her. Luther said everyone, even he himself, could be as good as she. "What!" Thomas would have thundered. "Erring man match her whom God has picked out of all the world, out of all time, to be the chalice of the Divine, the bridge of flesh by which the Divine entered the world!"

His life, with all its poise and serenity and reflective calm, its contemplations at midnight, noon, and in the early dawn, its visions of

God at unexpected moments, had many active facets and phases. On this morning, for example, when he came down from the convent and his survey of Paris to start his teaching rounds, on what was to be an exceedingly busy day, already he had put in many hours between the early office of Lauds and Prime in carefully making notes for his masterwork, which he did not know as that. For ever did humility mark him. What turned out one of the half-dozen truly great books of the world he started as a simple text-book.

He never knew how unusually impressive was his appearance in the Dominican halls or in other colleges of the seemingly endless chain on the hill. At the daily lectures in which the students only listened, at the "extraordinary" ones when they could ply the master with questions, at the ordinary disputations in which there was much argument back and forth between the doctors before good-sized audiences, at the "extraordinary disputations," the yearly big days when celebrated men foregathered to stage adroit and brilliant duels with words in the bare, cold rooms of the old-fashioned Romanesque places where students in winter squatted shiveringly in the straw, or in the newer Gothic and more splendid halls with carved benches and podium and coloured rays from great stained glass windows filtering down, he always stood out. Other fine-looking men too crowded the halls. Among his peers in this intellectual arena, Roger Bacon might look irritatingly acid or belligerent, but Alexander of Hales was stately, Albert had a fine dignity and air of power, and an aura of saintly light emanating from the beautiful soul that was Bonaventura's actually seemed to play about his face and person. Even among such mind-mountains of men, when he stood over against some Heaven's-blue-revealing window Thomas Aquinas towered like an Alp. As he grew older the more did he give that effect. With his height and great strength and the early snows of his hair on the fine dome of a head, he was like a Mont Blanc with the sunlight playing on it, and rising just a little above the rest of the towering scholars and saints.

In the faculty body and on some of the abbey teaching staffs were over-theologized technicians and maddening hair-splitters, as Thomas knew. Saint Bernard in the preceding century had fumed that, "Ignoramuses discuss the Virgin Birth and the sacred mysteries at the street corners." Stephen of Tournai complained that nincompoops "cut up the Trinity at every cross-roads." And not without truth. As Thomas came down from his eyrie investigation of that Paris roof-sea, his friend this morning walked with him. This was Albertus Magnus or, as the Parisians called him, Albert le Maître, whom we met when he was building that grand approach to the great Cathedral of thought Thomas was building now in the early morning and the late midnight hours. Thirteen years older than Thomas yet to live long after him, Albert ever played a magnificent Jonathan to the younger man's David. And Thomas told him of the Abbot of Corbeil who had such a debating din and dialectic dither raised about his, the Abbot's, ears that he had even set up a sign by the communal latrine. The friars could only go in singly, so fierce and stormy had been their disputations in those unsavoury quarters.

"How different now," observed Thomas, "had been Robert Sorbon and his heavenly college!" In the Sorbonne there had been no trivial dissecting, nor in Saint Jacques, nor in the Franciscans', the "Cordeliers." The great scholars had not been caught up, tripped, in any such ecclesiastical red-tape. He repeated what Robert Sorbon had once said to his scholars. "Pray, for this is one of the very best ways of learning. Elevate the heart to God, but at the same time go on with the studying."

Such team-work between mind and spirit was characteristic not only of this little ideal college, but many another teaching institution in the Middle Ages. Never before had the subconscious been so consecratedly used—and for that matter, never since has it been used with quite such understanding. Though these enlightened mediaeval teachers knew nothing of our modern jargon, they sometimes displayed more knowledge of the mind and its layers than our best psychiatric technicians. They had, to be sure, an explanation of the underlying mind quite different from today's glib charging of everything to human chemistry: their subconscious, they believed, was irrigated by the graces of the Holy Spirit into a richer blossoming and fruitage of teaching.

A Sorbonne teacher when asked by the king why he taught with such apparent effortlessness replied, "God teaches me." Saint Thomas understood. Another professor of the Hill did not. He burned olive oil or torch until long after midnight. So intensely he prayed it was almost frantically. He was furrowed and spare from his frenetic search for more erudition which he believed would better fit him for instruction. In short, he fairly battled for light instead of calmly opening himself up to it. And still his classes kept shrinking while those of the quiet Sorbonne teacher were always full. The unfortunate indefatigable and over-anxious tutor tried to extract the other's secret. And his brother in education and Christ replied, quite as he had to Saint Louis and Robert Sorbon: "It is simple. God studies for me. I attend mass and when I come back I know by heart all I have to teach."

Thomas loved the little teaching friar and thought him a beautiful example, with his great deep pool of inner calm, out of which came fortitude and light. Thomas and Albert and Bonaventura, though they were not aware of it, were quite like him.

This morning, he and Albert, between lectures, offices, and work on manuscripts, were going to visit libraries. There were several well-stocked ones in the city now. Saint Martin's Abbey, just outside the north city-gate, Saint Germain-des-Prés (the name meant "Saint-Germain-in-the-Fields"), Saint Victor's Abbey, south, the Cathedral and Sainte-Chapelle on the Isle, had each considerable numbers of well and some exquisitely bound books and precious manuscripts. At its start, our friend, that same little College of the Sorbonne, was content with bare cold rooms and meagre salaries, so that it might have a remarkable library for its size. If the booksellers' quarter on Writers', Illuminators' Streets, that of Parchment-making, Saint Séverin, of the Little Tax on the Fishstall, was in its hey-day, the librarians too were having their golden age.

Other matters besides those of religion came within the scope of the activities and interests of Saint Thomas' magnificently capacious mind. He had, for one thing, a very active social conscience and curiosity. As they walked downhill, they paused for a moment, as they always did, before the portal of a church on Saint Jacques. It always seemed to puzzle them into a shaking of heads. For it had been built a few years before as the one church in Paris, the only important one in France, that was turned the wrong way. "Saint Benoît Bientour-née," or "Saint-Benedict-Turned-Around" it was called. Very early in the Christian era, it became a sacred convention, if not an ecclesi-astically prescribed architectural rule, that all churches should have their altars facing the East where Our Lord had been born. Curiously did this church violate it, reversing the rule, and turned its altar to the west. In the last century it still stood just across from Cluny. But a modern wing of the Sorbonne is on its site now. And that dispenses much light. Still, it is a shame that they destroyed Saint Benoît. Not only was it the one unorientated church of any note in west Europe, but in its cloister, at a house called "The Red Door," once lived and studied, when he was not abroad on his wild misdemeanours and even felonies and murderous battles, François Villon whose life was sad and brilliant and as askew as "Twisted Saint Benedict's" itself.

Further down the Hill, the two friends passed a stucco and half-timbered building in which there were shops below and a guild chamber above. And Thomas remarked that it must be gratifying to everyone in the Church that the guild meetings of the city almost always voted some rule or ordinance that was helpful to the better life. All this labour legislation was not only highly liberalizing, but thoroughly Christian. Not so long before the guilds in general had reduced their mediaeval working hours to seven and a half daily. On Saturdays now they were closing at two!

"Think of it," said Thomas Aquinas, "and remember the long hours the serf worked in the Dark Ages. The world is far from being perfect, but if we are observing and watchful we can see an advance all the time, with a retrogression, of course, every now and then. But the rhythm is not two steps forward, then one back, but three steps forward, and two back. Which makes as much of a general gain as we can ever expect until His coming."

"Yes," returned Albert, with more dryness than optimism, "we're growing by spiritual inches, if not leagues."

"Further, to their general insurance provisions, they have just added one for theft insurance."

"No!"

"Yes, curious, but certainly practical."

"And all guildsmen must now take their families on all their picnics at Saint Cloud. Anyone who leaves his family behind is fined."

"He ought to be." Then Albert went on, "Our own guilds in France do very well by the Church. But a guild in Durham, England, requires candles to be lighted by members at *every* mass of the year. There's faithfulness for you. 'At every mass,' the bylaw reads, 'so that God and Our Blessed Virgin and the Venerated Cross may keep and guard all the brethren of the Guild!' This communal feeling, this movement for industrial brotherhood grows by leaps and bounds."

"For years," said Thomas, "you remember, the Guild of Prostitutes here gave a carved canon's stall or some adornment to Notre Dame. Saint Louis and his Etienne Boileau have stopped that—that is, forced the Cathedral chapter to stop it, and have dissolved their guild—poor frail souls! I'm not sure that the king and Boileau in their zeal were entirely right. 'Without sin—the first stone'! The chief fault of these women is the men themselves. The Church must be pure. Naturally. But so long as there was that little tie to the Church of their gifts and confession they were not wholly lost.

"That little sisterhood on the Rue Chanoinesse, at the bend, shows what ultimate material there is in the magdalens. Better material than a lot of orderly citizens I could name. Repentant now, they work for the Cathedral as seamstresses. 'The Seven who Sew for Our Lady' they rightly call themselves. Though we friars do not wear such glorious vestments even when we celebrate, you must know them."

Albert nodded. "But," Thomas went on, "though my own I prefer plain, the copes and chasubles they embroider for the Cathedral are truly beautiful. We might stop and visit them on the way back."

They were in the middle now of the Little Bridge crowd of fishwives gutturally, raucously arguing back and forth, shopwives and housewives, noisy and resonant, singing gypsy minstrels more musical, as carefree and motley a crowd as would delight your heart in any town.

Oblivious to all the excitement, Albert spoke now of the trading with the enemy. "It's a treacherous thing, love of money. These southern merchants—a not inconsiderable fraction of them—are shipping goods from Marseilles for the Saracens."

"Who in turn," said Thomas, "are killing their countrymen, the Crusaders, with their scimitars and deadlier Greek fire. It seems inconceivable."

"Especially," returned Albert, "when His Holiness and his predecessors, try as they have, cannot seem to put a stop to it."

So the two scholars and scientists and saints, who were in the bargain very human men, shook their heads over this dark spot on the glory that was their century's. Another dark exception, proving the exceptional glory of the age that was the rule, troubled them then.

"Now," said Albert, "that Louis has got himself off to the Crusades, the usurers are raising their heads again, trying to get their practices legalized."

"They stand little chance with Boileau."

"Not now, but before the century is over they will be plying their nefarious trade in full force."

Albert le Maître, of course, had a receptive audience in his friend. Of all the champions who took up the Church's quarrel against usury and its dislike and mistrust even of plain interest, Thomas Aquinas was perhaps the greatest.

Almost from the beginning the Church had fought against usury, with a great reduction of it though not a complete rooting out. Her dislike of ordinary interest would puzzle now many a business man. In the fourth century, Saint John Chrysostom of the Golden Tongue had used that tongue in fighting it. One should never charge a fellow man, he said, for helping him with money in distress.

Saint Thomas himself had written not long before that a man should make enough profit in his transactions to keep going. But more was sinful. And this had always been the feeling of the Church. Her priests preached what was called the "just price." The labourer was, of course, worthy his hire. But dormant money—so Thomas had recently set down in his big book up on the Hill—was worth no hire. Money should not earn anything unless the lender himself was active in the business. The only exception allowable, he wrote, was in a foreign venture when considerable risk was involved in expeditions abroad.

"I never could understand," he told Albert while they were on the subject as they crossed Jewry Street, on the way to Sainte-Chapelle, the first library to be visited, "how the abbeys once played bankers, even though honest ones. Saint Martin's here in Paris, as you know, once did a very large business in mortgages. And as much as a seventh of the loan sometimes, they got back each year in return, never less than a fifteenth. It didn't take long that way to double their money. It is true that they conducted their business honestly, that is, for a business that is not primarily or ideally honest. And they lent only to the rich —half the time to barons or counts for outfitting a little army to join in the Crusades. And it is sadly ironical to see an abbey, an institution of Christ, charging interest on money going to fight to save the Tomb of Christ. I am delighted that His Holiness has stopped this business, once conducted by some, though by no means all, of the abbeys. The clink of coin does not accord with *Kyries* and *Agnus Deis*."

Such ideas as this which Saint Thomas so strongly championed for the Church were, to be sure, not good for business. They were good for an ideal state in which the bias, the accent was more on Christ than Caesar. This no interest principle was a corollary of the Golden Rule. And the Church continued to hold it up as an ideal that might be at times, but was not always, impracticable. Even when later robust Protestant business men of England and Holland insisted on charging all they could, the Church in Rome denounced usury and wanted the interest principle modified. So this ancient and nourishing, if not quite business-like, Mother of us all has continued to live and set an example down to—well, this very week.

Quite different from the abbey libraries was that of Sainte-Chapelle, which Thomas and Albert entered now. Around the Gothic or more often Roman arched abbey library rooms, which sometimes included the *scriptorium,* or manuscript workshop, and the illuminating room, were shelves and desks and containers with books of all sizes, bindings, and hues, some of them secured by chains they were so precious. The abbeys never had the actual brilliance of Sainte-Chapelle, but there was always some colour even in the darkest halls. Not only did the little lights and the great one from the ceiling, a corona, flash patens of light into dark corners, but gleams from beautifully illuminated books suddenly opened by the librarian or the privileged readers added a little shifting radiance to the hall. But Sainte-Chapelle was just a blaze.

The librarians had each to take an intensive training. They had to know values without and within. They must intelligently gauge vellums, leathers, inlaid coral, ivory, gems of the books costuming, the illustration, the illumination, and all the thought content inside. And they must be prepared to answer any questions about their wares, whether by a great scholar or the poorest student. For any of worth could enjoy the library privileges. That is, of course, after he had handed in the best of references as to his need and seriousness from some professor or abbot. Even so, the librarian had to be vigilant. A reader, in his zeal, his excitement over some intellectual adventure, might crinkle a page corner, smudge virginal vellum, the azure and rose of a miniature, or with his sleeve fleck off a bit of gold leaf.

Sainte-Chapelle then housed valuable secular as well as sacred things. Saint Louis allotted a section of the lower floor of the beautiful place for the archives, also room there for fine books and manuscripts. Later a large space in the part of the rambling old palace near the chapel was turned over to archivist and librarian, and the lower story was used for mass for the retainers of the nobles and knights, who had mass celebrated for them upstairs before the sacred relics shrine. This adjoining palace annex then would house too the Knights of Saint Louis, an order created to guard the relics, and to stand watch by turns before the altar, with drawn swords.

For Vincent of Beauvais, Saint Louis had done rather a nice thing. This champion encyclopedist he employed to assemble the archives and books. The little friar, who for a time lodged up in Saint Jacques, had only to mention in the king's hearing that the library needed a book (a rare one it was like as not to be), and the king would send out and by hook or crook, at any expense, get it for him.

Even the lower floor was beautiful in itself and the glory of the upper came down. A privileged great scholar might take a script and read in that glory upstairs. So studying in this library of Sainte-Chapelle then was different from working in the darker Romanesque halls of the Cloister libraries. The hanging gardens of stained glass appeared to be suspended from the ceiling. It was like working in a hanging garden, doing one's toilsome research in a corner of Heaven. The most precious relics in the world, a fragment of the True Cross Saint Helena had found underneath Calvary, a bit of the bloodied Crown of Thorns, an authentic Holy Nail, were upstairs over the altar in a radiant reliquary. The slender pillars were painted in both stories a resplendent scarlet and gold. And the whole place seemed fairly to throb with the glow as though it trembled in the glory of a Pentecost made manifest and permanent.

After Albert and Thomas had crossed themselves and genuflected before the shrine, and in the library section had glanced over a volume or two, Thomas noticed a young man whom he recalled and who looked about seventeen. He was none of the palace princes; Louis' oldest, who would be Philippe the Third, was then but three years old. But he was one of the flock of royal cadets, blood of Louis, blood of Blanche, that were forever coming to the Palace.

Saint Louis' grandfather, Philippe Auguste, mighty in more ways than one, had married three times and had presented, indirectly, to Louis quite a crew of little royal first and second cousins. Clermont, Namur, Brabant, Auguste's daughters had married. The boy—Thomas took to his face—was a Count Namur, the librarian believed. Furthermore, he whispered, this young Count Namur was to undertake the long night vigil, in Sainte-Chapelle here, become a knight at dawn, and set out with his cousin by marriage, the king himself, for the Crusades in the morning.

Casually the young count noted the titles of the books the two scholars were looking at, and moved on. Thomas and Albert, two of those great celibates who understood human beings and loved young people, did not blame him. A gloss by Anselm! Adelard of Bath's *On Identity and Difference!* And so on. Down to a synodic by Zacharias, eighth-century pope and saint, the Gospel-Harmony of Zacharias Chrysopolitanus! Worthy, useful books for scholars, yes. But for a young handsome count and *cousin de la royauté* about to become a knight, and in love—the librarian had further informed them—with the big black-eyed Brabant girl visiting too in the palace? Well, hardly. And Thomas smiled happily to see the book in which the young count immediately became engrossed.

It was a very delicately painted and illuminated copy of an old Norman tale of two lovers who had been parted and of all their weal and woe and adventures until they came to the happy ending. Now despite the holy vigil he, as knighthood's candidate, must observe all night long and the devoir he must make in the Cathedral for Our Lady, love for a maid, purely felt, and the revering love for the Blessed Virgin could, in a young man's heart exist side by side in the days of chivalry. And that chivalry, since it nourished so much that was fine and true and beautiful, the Church blessed as one of its very own by-products.

Aucassin and Nicolette the old Norman story was named. And through trellised borders of leaves, vines, trefoils, and flowers, and by milestones in the story of full page pictures of the most admirable daintiness and deftness of line and of the most entrancing shades of azure and violet, crimson, and gold, vermeil, light yellow, and emerald or apple-green, the beckoning road of their fortunes blithely and brightly flowed. Lordly castles, high-stepping chargers, granthers and sages with daisy-white beards, knights so ready at insult and challenge to pull out the sword, twinkling-eared donkeys, bill-open, tail-up, cocky little birds carolling on fretted bough, lithe, supple maidens, with hand-size waists, in gay raiment making little moving rainbows over the dewy grass, with flower meads and heart-refreshing greenwoods for them and their lovers—all gave the mediaeval readers infinite delight.

So, in the stained glass glory of Sainte-Chapelle, the famous scholar saint and the young count about to be made a knight read on side by side.

It was a sprightly tale of a young knight of Beaucaire, Provence, Aucassin by name, and

> "Of the troubles he passed through
> And the great deeds he did do
> All for his fair, graceful may."

"The fair graceful may" or "fere," as she at other times was called, was, of course,

> "Nicolette, the white and slender,
> For whom he has a love most tender."

However,

> "Her his father had refused,
> Direful threats his mother used:
> 'Silly boy! The Devil take you!
> Wretched wife she would make you!' "

Her own godfather too now interfered and locked her up in a chamber near the castle top with an old crone. They needed no text verse now so vividly had the illuminator from the Street of the Priests of Saint Severin painted this "fair graceful may." The cornflower blue was deep in her eyes. Her hair was as yellow as that of the old Gauls. And he had put roses climbing up the castle's round to her window and he had picked two of these to put in her cheeks. From that window

> "Looked she o'er the flowers below,
> Saw the opening roses blow;
> Heard the birds' clear roundelay.
> Sorrow's orphan, loud she cried,
> By Mary's Son, Who for us died,
> Seigneur Dieu, I'll find a way."

Aucassin then goes to her godfather to ask her hand. But the count who has been frightened by the Count of Beaucaire swears she is but a slave girl, no fit bride for him. Fie out on him too! He but wants to make her his concubine after all. And for that he should burn in Hell!

There is a colourful little picture then of Aucassin's hands going out from under his sky-blue mantle in proud disdain. And as the two distinguished library borrowers read the first words then of his speech, the grave scholar and saint looked out of the corner of his eye at the young man and there was an amusing vice versa, the count so looking at him. For cries the knight:

"Paradise! That is no place for me! I'm not out to win Paradise, only the sweetest friend I know. Nicolette. Do you want me to tell you who go to Paradise. Why, none but"—he went on in his sudden choler, "Old priests and your old hobblers and cripples who are bent and on their knees, and those who wear scuffed and threadbare mantles, and have no shoes and show their sores for pity. Such are they who enter Paradise. I'm not in their company."

Prince and saint exchanged glances now with smiles almost breaking as he fumed on:

"Yes, Hell is the only place for me."

"After all," observed Thomas, "it's only a tale. And this blasphemy is but a play-acting blasphemy, the outraged cry of a hurt boy. I am sure the young knight, God assoilize his soul, will at last choose Heaven not Hell. He would have to, you see," he smiled, "for the happy ending. They must have that, mustn't they?"

On one side of the pages the text here had a flanking of angels in green groves, and a flowery mead with blossoms blue, crimson, yellow, and white standing up with nodding heads in a very beautiful design. Thomas bent over to see the leaves of the grove. Yes, assuredly, they were oaks. Very accurately and delicately limned were the leaf scallops and indentations.

The fires of Hell in the other border should have been frightening but they leaped with such a pretty flame colour and with snapping pennons that they made more merry and alive this sprightly tale.

But the young knight of derring do in it was rambling on in his young love's sulks: "No, it's the ones I like that go to Hell. All the brave knights killed as they fight gallantly in wars. The lovely ladies who have lovers three or four besides their husbands. And you'll find in Hell no tatters and rags but all the ermine, the silks and the silver and gold. Also the singers and minstrels and acrobats who make life happy and gay with their instruments and blithe melodies. With them to Hell I'll go!"

At this, the jaws of the young count were open as though he were about to snap at Aucassin for his blasphemy in his distinguished friend's presence, so actual and like life seemed this tale in the other world glory of Sainte-Chapelle. The saint's eyes twinkled.

"It will do no good to chide our hero," he observed. "The inimitable artists have given him everything that looks like life but not breath. And about this boastful blasphemy now, I have an idea that Aucassin, before the tale is done and he gets Nicolette, as the boy always does—doesn't he?—will confess and reverse his two after-kingdoms. In fact I'm sure of it."

Now Aucassin with lavender hose, and emeralds and garnets in his belt is changing his tune to (as Monsieur Bourdillon has it):

> "Nicolette, thou ever fair,
> In thy talk and in thy toying,
> · In thy jest and in thy joying,
> In thy kissing and in thy coying,
> I am sore distressed for thee,
> Sweet sister friend!"

Now the miniatures flash vividly forth an attack on the castle with a few symbolic shining spears, two or three soldiers in mail near the draw, a few fighting down from the turrets and hoardings. But Aucassin refuses to defend his own father's castle at Beaucaire unless his father give him "my sweet friend."

Adamant at first, they settle for "time for two words in her ear, one kiss only." Distressed looked the two readers. He had settled too cheap. And now Aucassin goes into action:

> "Helmet on his head he closed;
> Shining lance in rest disposed;
> Hauberk put on reinforced.
> On bold charger, nobly horsed,
> Gold hilt, gold shield shining wondrous
> Proud he rode into battle thundrous,
> But his sweet friend? He thought on her."

As he went into action. And there was now a fine lift to the horse's feet, a fine champ on the silver curb and bit; his fetlocks were well done; and the scarlet and purple of his caparisons and housings were dazzling.

Fine was the score now of the boy the poem calls "tall and strong" —seven knights injured—ten slain! Nonetheless did his father, Count of Beaucaire, return him to prison. As sad is his lament now as was Cœur de Lion's to his Blondel.

"Flower of the lily, Nicolette,
Sweet as ripe grapes on the vine,
Sweet as mead in maselyn."

So were the saint and the young knight about-to-be reading together
the best-seller, a leading romance of the day, in the refracted rays of
this beautiful house, when Thomas asked the librarian for the time.
He had to hurry if he wanted to attend None in the Cathedral and to
see the books there, also to visit "The Seven Sisters Who Sewed for
Our Lady" back of Notre Dame. Ever since the days of Ambrose and
Augustine and good Bishop Hilary the canonical Hours had been set;
and they must be observed though one could sometimes say the office
in private. And he wanted to hear the Notre Dame organ.

It was two and a half hours after noon, the librarian told him, by
the water clock in the court-yard and the great red and gold one on the
face of Charles the Bold's tower (whose successor is still there on the
very same tower today). He had just passed there on his way by the
Great Bridge. No, there were not many books more often called for
than that which they were reading. Of course, the glosses and *Sentences,* and several, *monsieur,* of your own are in great University
demand. And *Reynard the Fox* and *The Roumaunt de la Rose,* by
Jehan de Meung up on the Rue Saint-Jacques right near their convent,
with the help of William Lorris, had a great waiting list. But there
were many names waiting for a second copy—not this edition, it was
too valuable—of *Aucassin and Nicolette.* Thomas said he would stay
to see how it all came out in a very hurried reading, of course. But
the pictures helped so delightfully to delay them. Here was Nicolette
now, that bewitching heroine, in all innocence.

"Lifting skirts and letting show,
Pretty ermine dress below,
Under smock as white as snow,
Ankles two, dainty, trim.
When this sight flashed on him,
Lo! sick Aucassin was healed!"

In and out of jail they both seemed to be all the time in their series
of misadventures. And now once again Nicolette was in. A glance then
at the girl as she ties towels and sheets and pillow-cases and bolster
covers together with pretty tough knots for such dainty hands. In a
very graceful way she drops down from the arrow slit, past all the
climbing roses nodding at her in crimson courtesy as she descends,
milk-white hand over milk-white hand.

And the miniver brush seems in the artist's hand to become as enthusiastic as Aucassin over Nicolette now. It limns on her "two little breasts that swelled beneath her clothes like two nuts from a walnut tree, a waist that your two hands could circle with no space between, gold curls and a sweet little face," with just the suggestion of Queen Blanche's aristocratic aquilinity. This miniaturist from Rennes and the Cul de Sac Salembrière had well accompanied the text with his daisies to which he had actually given a personality and which, "as they flashed by her toes seemed black, so white was her skin!"

> "Darling dear, in all this life,
> I may never be your wife.
> Me your father can't abide;
> All your folks do with him side.
> For your sake I'll cross the sea,
> Hie me to some far countree."

So on her doleful but fascinating odyssey she starts out, "in one hand taking her dress before, in the other hand taking it behind." Such a charming dress it was too, with a pretty cherry red design in the border, a cincture of gold, and breast of blue.

And now she is lost in the woods, as Albert comes back to them from his perusal of a newly-bought *Evangeliary* of Monk Godescalc made originally for Charlemagne himself. However, Nicolette is now threatened by the wolves of the wild wood—so just a moment more. And she is meeting too in a grove of good beech trees some shepherd boys who have spread on a blue mantle laid on the green a loaf of bread of a tempting honey-brown hue. She enlists their aid in the search for Aucassin, this

> "Girl with hair of gold, lithe and slim,
> Eyes so blue with bloom for him.
> So she gave to each a penny,
> For to buy them presents many,
> Sheaf of leather, and hunting knife,
> Flute and viol, whistling fife."

And then they had to wait still another minute, the count and the saint, for this scion of Beaucaire, the love-lorn Aucassin, thinking again on his "most sweet friend" had fallen from his "big and high horse," and had put his shoulder or his collarbone out.

Sick as he was, he composes a neat little song for her as he lies on a big rock in the green wood all in a border frame of beech leaves and wood flowers cunningly intertwined. And the story took them the longer to encompass because each page, every adventure, was so beautifully and enticingly framed with designs of interlocked ivy or lettuce leaves and cabbage tops, or nimble little hopping animals, and city pinnacles and spires arranged in most pleasing if somewhat geometric designs. And each tempted not only the delighted eye but the tracing finger to follow. Like this went the song:

> "Little star I see on high,
> Bright moon up there in the sky,
> Nicolette is with you there,
> Sweetheart of the golden hair;
> God has taken her to Heaven,
> For His own lamp to light the even."

Then, Seigneur Dieu! she finds him at last and sets his shoulder in place and kisses him and caresses him, and the joy of both is most beautiful to see.

And now as this later phase begins they must leaf over the pages which are as lovely as if they had been embroidered, for young Count Namur, who would himself become a knight like the one in the book, must hurry on soon to try on his new suit of armour before the vigil.

They come by chance then to the shore and make a bargain with some blue and white sailors for passage on a mutton-sailed brown ship on a silver sea, with gold-tipped sunlit waves. There is a storm too with waves dashing and leaping as high as they might in a little miniature medallion.

It bore them over the seas to toss them on the shore of a land with the musical name of Tellelore. There, not the queen, as is usual, but the king has taken to bed of child in the quaint old custom of *couvade*. The artist introduces a note of humour in this royal bedside scene, and in that of a most unusual battle. Unique are the missiles: red-cheeked crab-apples, crêpe-fluted mushrooms, flesh-coloured eggs, yellow cheeses. Quite shattered and mussed-up are the casualties at Tellelore.

Thomas called the attention of the count to the adroit delicacy of the miniver brush that had worked on the mushrooms and then to the fine burnishing of the red copper gold in the next inset. Swart Saracens gay with plumes, yellow scarves, red rubies in their turbans, and scimitars agleam now separate the lovers.

The little heroine now rubs herself, in a little medallion, with an herb. Into a berry-brown she rubs herself all over, giving an extra depth of stain to the skin from the hair-line down under the smockline, so that if dress or smock slips it will not reveal the betraying white of the Christian. Later she makes a little coat all by herself and dons this, a man's shirt, also a cute little pair of breeches. Also she puts on a smile, flashing her teeth white as fresh udder-drawn milk to disarm all strangers. So she skips from bright rectangle to gay-coloured square between all the decorative trellises of the pages, play-ing her little lute with a cherry-coloured ribbon (whose folds too are sometimes intricately woven into the borders). And as a masked merry minstrel, with a male cod piece which her pretty white body could have no possible use for, she fools them all (all, that is, but one) on this search of the world for Aucassin her lover.

The one is a rich paynim with a white stream of a beard under a swathing, top-lofty turban all gemmed. A swordsman with a huge naked, brown torso stands by ready, in case she refuses to marry his lord. Then he will cut off the gold curls, also the dear little head under them. But at last—there must be an at last if young Namur is to be "dubbed," Thomas to visit Notre Dame, the Seven Sisters, and do his lecture—Nicolette escaped! After playing her lute and singing to it over hills and meadows in many lands, she reaches Provence and his Beaucaire. Her minstrel look admits her to the castle where amidst his barons Aucassin sits in the high hall still mourning his "sweet friend." Under the spell of the song and her unrecognized voice, the young knight lifts his head and she swings into a little love tale in verse of a girl she says was named "Nicolette." Head averted, in one of the last medallions that have in a lively way run on with the tale, she recounts aside as though she were relating it to her little lute with the cherry red ribbon that "all misfortunes Nicolette had en-dured, all suitors refused, for the sake of this Aucassin. Yes, dear my lord, she thought only of him."

> "By God's true name she swore,
> None she'd marry evermore,
> If she could not have her love,
> This Aucassin she was fain of."

Suddenly the skin-deep disguise of the dark stain and coat and trousers and lute was pierced. She takes a milk bath to rub off the berry-brown, clothes herself in Crusaders' silks of bright blue, circles her wrist with bracelet of gold, and sits on an emerald coverlet, still the virgin pure, maid demure, after all her male masquerading. There in a frame of lilies and roses from which cherubs are withdrawing green thorns with little silver pliers for wedded happiness—a brank-some border which would have done for the Beaucaire bridal boudoir itself—his "sweet friend and gladsome may" awaits the young knight Aucassin, healed now of all of his love's wounds.

Perhaps none has translated the ending with more flavoursome spirit than Monsieur Bourdillon:

"Now had Aucassin his joy,
Nicolette the same way.
Here endeth our song and say.
I know no further."

So the angelic Doctor and chivalry's acolyte, this candidate for knighthood, read together a popular novel, an exciting romance of the day, a mediaeval best-seller in the library of the Holy Chapel with the sacred relics near by. In among the mightier tomes this little volume was like a brief bright hour sandwiched in for relief among the leaden-footed ones.

On leaving Sainte-Chapelle, one always turned and stood for a moment looking back at the shrine. One could not help it, no matter how much he may have looked at it on coming in. When the poorest Parisians came in out of the everyday world to the court, at sight of it they immediately crossed themselves though they had not entered the sanctuary. When you entered the court it was a sunrise breaking in splendour upon your sight. When you looked at it before turning away it was like a sunset undying.

Even the two saints who were supposed to have great visions and high imaginings of Heaven were always amazed anew as though gazing at something that never could have been yet indubitably was there, and right before them. Something too that seemed as though it never had been constructed, but had arisen, full-blown, evoked by a miracle out of the earth, or had been let down from Heaven in all its glory for some illuminating and divinely proselytizing purpose of God.

This afternoon though they were but going from this Church splendour in the small to that in the large, Notre Dame, they stood there a little space; and we should stand with them, not only to take in more deeply than ever before the quintessence so beautifully preserved for the ages there, of the compounded mediaeval religion and the Gothic spirit, but also because we may never see it again. Thomas and Albert had written home about it after their first visit, Albert to Cologne, Thomas to Aquino and Naples. Neither had been moderate. But it was not overwriting. When one writes of Sainte-Chapelle superlatives just don't exist.

Still, even when one knows it so well, on looking back in his dazzled bewilderment over its surpassing beauty he almost overlooks the fact that there is stone there as well as glass. Then gradually he discerns the slender sections of the wall skeleton that hold together the great heavenly areas of the stained glass. But the proportion of these thin wall factors bordering and holding in the glass rainbows are so small in comparison with the proportions of the glazed expanse, and the adjoining colour seems so to overflow into the wall segments that it fairly overwhelms with glory the grey stone. When the sun strikes it direct or the candles go on in full sacramental power within, the whole narrow rising-up pile appears to be no fabricated shrine, but a vision of palpitating loveliness.

Thomas never had the poignant pang that comes to us at sight of it. Though it has stood there for eight hundred years, the sheer fragility of its beauty suggests that devil's atomic potion we have brewed that could so easily destroy it. Yet were it to go, it would never go. It would forever remain in picture and book and memory as one of the most exquisite achievements of the skilled hands and artistry and the guiding brain of man.

Thomas now gave the knight and crusader-to-be in the morning, the cousin once-removed of the king, young Namur's count, his blessing for the vigil of the night, and the youngster hurried over to the armoury to see if hauberk and helmet fitted; Thomas, meanwhile, passing over to Notre Dame.

XIII

The Oldest Going Hospital in the World. . . . Long ago People
began to leap into the Seine. . . . The House of the Musicians.
. . . The Seven Who Sewed for Our Lady. . . . Paris Magdalens.
. . . Holy Needlework matches the Illuminated Books and the
Stained Glass. . . . The Bright Path of the Embroiderers from the
Promised Land to Paris. . . . Arab Roses, Green Lions, Red and
White Leopards, the Miracles of Christ, Angels on Horseback. . . .
Origins of the Priest's Costume. . . . The Vestments blossom out.
. . . Bright Chasuble, Crimson Cope, Pure White Corporal. . . .
Sewing Art, Stitching Technique, and Needle Wizardry. . . . Our
Lady's Song.

1257 A.D.

THOMAS NOW WENT BY THE LITTLE COURT CHAPEL OF SAINT
Michel at the mid-Palace gates, and through the Street of the
Jews into the Place du Parvis de Notre Dame, the stone
campus of the University of Paris, the arena where the old Schoolmen
once had wrestled. The square had not changed since the departing
Saint Louis had clapped in delight at the gay minstrels and acrobats
and the little performing monkey on the Cathedral buttress. There
were the same ancient painted picturesquely out-of-plumb houses bordering the square west and north. And at right angles to the Cathedral
which towered over the east side, the Hôtel Dieu, the then thousand
year-old House of God, ran along the south, the riverside where open
green and the mounted Charlemagne are today.

The latest, but still very old phase of this sanctuary for the sick was
a thick-masonried, Roman-windowed sequence of adjoining buildings
with a long row of gable teeth indenting the blue over the Seine. An
annex of the hospital extended over the Little Bridge itself. Desperate,
deranged invalids had been known to reject the spiritual consolation
of the visiting Notre Dame priests and the House of God sisters and
to leap through the windows into the river. Recently the windows
therefore had been barred. But forever people have been leaping from

197

bridge or *quai* into the Seine here down the ages until yesterday afternoon.

In the light from the early summer northering sun the square was cluttered with clumps of crutch-clattering crusaders and civil cripples, carters, fishermen, frog-hunters, chimney-sweeps, *blanchisseuses,* scrubwomen, suffering with arthritis from too much march fever or Seine damp and all the ills the race is heir too, including that dread disease which the Spanish call French, the French English, the English Italian, every glass house race by the name of the one just over the border, none of them without sin yet casting the stones just the same.

Thomas, when they hailed him in his friar's corded soutane, or when he thought they were looking for it, raised his hand in the old, the most reassuring gesture in all the world, that of blessing and benediction. As he went by a heavy-arched window he heard a little sob, then the portentous death rattle in someone's throat. The sob was from a daughter burying her head in the clothes of the capacious, wardrobe-like bed with many compartments in it. The rattle came from her father, the pill-and-potion pharmacist from Paradise Street. A priest from Notre Dame had been hurriedly summoned and he was coming, his stole flapping around his neck in his speed. He clasped to his breast the Blessed Sacrament for the dying, the Viaticum. But before he could reach the side of the stricken man, Thomas had gone in. He hastily bent down to catch, if he could, the last confession, rapidly uttering the beautiful old formula and then intoning in a sad but impressive way the consoling words for those at the threshold of death. At the same time the great bells of the towers of Notre Dame above began to boom as though with a resonant anodyne for the passing for a humble soul in that fleeting moment equal to the greatest.

Crossing himself as the sister, ages-after successor of Geneviève in her old haunts, closed the eyes, crossed hands on the breast of the one who had spent his life fending off Death (perhaps sometimes hurrying it on with his drugs), Thomas left the House of God and came into the twisting lanes at the side of the Cathedral on the north. This Cloister quarter was not as tortuous as it would be in the melodramatic days of the fifteenth century. Then everything almost in Paris would seem to be at odds with everything else. Lanes, roofs, buildings would be twisted, warped, leaning this way and that in an intricate architectural hodge-podge—rich territory for elusive hot-foots like François Villon.

However, in the thirteenth century there was variety enough in the street and lane amblings and turns, in house alignment, and in the structural whimsicalities of sway-backed ridge-poles, witch-hat gables, sloughing tiles, painted beams, curved portals, carved images, jutting dormers, niches, fountains in walls, stout church portions with spires, pinnacles, and towers signaling, and sudden stained glass pools of light illuminating the way to Heaven.

Just as in the times of Robert the Strong, the Butcher's Son, and Fat Fighting Louis the Sixth, the sounds of active thrumming, throbbing church industry pleasantly counterpointed the main melody of the Gospel story. One heard here the click-clack of the ever-going needles, the day's dish-clatter, the snap of shaken sheets, thump of beaten mattresses. Now there broke on the ear the metallic sounds of repairing tools on stone, lead, copper, again the silver sounds of the sacring and Sanctus bells, and the brazen thunderous tumult of the tower bells above—also little phrase fragments of baptism, or requiem, the refrains of *Credo* and *Magnificat,* and of practising canon and chorister.

There was ever another accompaniment too prevading all these lanes and dead ends just as agreeable. Quite a nose-salad this was and it was quite a compounding of: Candles being freshly chandlered. Incense for the thuribles. Olive oil for the lamps and Extreme Unction. The baking of the Holy Bread when that was not done in Saint Denis. The scorched smell of heavy cloth vestments being pressed. The emulsified smell of soap and the laundering of the linen amices, maniples, and albs. The fragrance of sweet fresh berries and melons for the Bishop's kitchen and his guest the Nuncio. Tangier emanations from onions, garlic, mint, thyme. The marine smell of gudgeon and bream for the canons' quarters alongside the former home of the canon-uncle-by-marriage who made Abelard somewhat less the man and ultimately more of one. Spices too for sauces and pasties. Honey for sweetening. The freshening smell coming down from up Seine. The perfume of rose petals pressed in jars for comfits. The scent of roses, jasmine, mignonette in the few garden plots that could find soil, air, sun enough in this close-packed Cathedral settlement.

In a little company of seven half-timbered houses closely huddled together as though they were masonry kith and kin, two stood out because of their decoration. One house displayed at the corners of the frames, the doorheads, corbels, in the stuccoed panels in between the half-timbers, musical instruments in a great collection. There were life-like hautboys, lutes, fifes, whistling recorders, all gaily painted up. The horn shone with silver. The harp glistened with gold. A little suspended drum was blue and had a red band. Over the door was a water organ tempting the passer-by to thump on its black and white keys.

Music was continually being played in the rooms behind this fascinating façade. So the house front of the inimitable "House of Musicians" was like a great sounding board. As the live musicians within see-sawed and blew and tattated, it seemed (and the suspended instruments swinging to and fro heightened the illusion) that the music came from the mimic, playerless instruments up and down that façade. It was an eerie and charming effect.

Almost as many as stopped to examine this interesting "House of Musicians" paused to look up at the decorated front next door. Here in panels and at structural vantage points were shown carved and painted vestments in miniature. The inmates sewed on what appeared to be the larger originals within. On one side of the entrance door was an alb of white with painted imitations of the linen and lace; on the other a brown soutane with cord. Above in an arch was a celebrant's chasuble of green with the orphrey bars indicated in yellow. An amice, a maniple, cincture, sandal pair, scarlet biretta and yellow-and-white stole were carved in panels. Two croziers with little brush dots of colour to suggest ornamenting gems crossed in the middle of the façade. At the corners hung a prelate's spoonbill mitre and Saint Peter's golden keys. The officiating priest's entire wardrobe, the bishop's and the pope's were depicted in carving, paint and gold leaf on this quaint façade of the "House of the Seven Who Sewed for Our Lady."

This little holy order of midinettes tailored and embroidered vestments here. Both were crafts more delicate than, but quite as old as, Tubal Cain's. Early worshippers of all religions were not as self-conscious about music and the arts as John Knox and the pitch-pipe plain meeting-house Presbyterians of New England. In the sunrise of history they flamed out in colours. They praised their Deity with the dance. When the sun came up over the desert it shone on High Priest Aaron in gold thread decorated gowns. When it rose over Sion later, the priests were marvelous in purple, blue and scarlet with pomegranate designs.

The climate of the Nile is agreeable and favourable for tourists. Also for archaeologists. Its equability and dryness have preserved for years for us thirty-five-hundred-year-old linens, adorned in red, green, blue, black, and one king's robe all covered with lilies shaped like the French fleurs-de-lis, perhaps lilies like those among which in his tiny boat cradle the little Moses was found sleeping by the princess. In building their Temple with its profusion of adornments, Judah recruited an army of artisans over which the chronicler waxed orientally enthusiastic: they were all "filled with wisdom to work all manner of works of the engravers, of the cunning workmen, and of the embroiderers in blue, purple, scarlet, and on fine linen and of the weavers and of those who devise cunning work."

The Greeks wove and embroidered a great pavilion top for their Athena of the Parthenon. Early Christians in Egypt needled flora and fauna on purple and crimson wool. Some of the richer and not very popular early church members by the Nile adorned their robes with "needle paintings" until they looked like "walking houses" with frescoed walls turned inside out. For ages no one was bashful about colour and adornment. These "cunning workers" of all tribes made a broad path of pattern and colour girdling the world.

In the Middle Ages many extraordinary hangings went up on French church walls, among them these striking examples, many of which Saint Thomas would see on travels later:

Persian "tissues" of silk with beautifully woven undulating figures, in a Loire church;

The Auxerre cope with Arabian roses and spread eagles in silk;

A Saint Denis cope filled with gold stars on blue;

Green lions rampant with finely sewn red lines for muscles and ribs, on Saint Germain's burial robes;

The Thomas à Becket vestments with gold crosses in circles in Notre Dame's cousin-Cathedral at Sens;

The gorgeously-hued silk arras which Saint Louis would bring home from his first, the Seventh Crusade in 1254, and which Saint Thomas often would see hanging from the south triforium of Notre Dame;

The chained leopards at Chinon, some white with red spots, others yellow with green spots, and all bearing birds on their backs on a blue ground;

A chasuble at Laon, with parables in brocade, rich foliage around the neck;

The hanging made by Richard Cœur de Lion's consort, with stories of the Blessed Virgin and the Saints vividly pricked out, in Rouen's Cathedral, not far from Cœur de Lion's buried heart.

Vienna exhibited with pride a Holy Roman Empire cope with lions leaping on and clawing a camel, all on a blood-red satin ground.

On feast-days Bayeux Cathedral hung high the celebrated Conquest serial worked by Queen Matilda in eight coloured worsteds, with knights, galleys, chargers, all sorts of exciting history, stretching seventy-seven yards down the nave.

The world-girdling path of pattern and colour, once so straight and shining, soon began to run through tapestry jungles of thick needled and appliqued foliage, birds, and beasts. So much became encrusted, lush. Consider these specimens:

In a church south of Paris, a cope with angels on horseback, lions with curled tails, four fish on horseback, and four roses!

An English altar frontal, with an embroidered Trinity, four Evangelists, four angels, and an army of patriarchs, apostles, virgins, with Our Lady; and an accompanying frontlet of cloth of gold, with white silk embroidery on it portraying the Blessed Virgin again in a circle of eight angels, her Son in another circle of eight angels.

The prices sometimes were staggering. A Roman hanging had cost two hundred sesterces. The Bishop of Hereford's cope, three hundred and sixty pounds, or a hundred thousand dollars in the value of to-day. The English king had a velvet vestment embroidered for his confessor, costing over two thousand pounds—or several hundred thousand dollars as money goes to-day. A Fishmongers' Guild in an English county town extravagantly assessed its members for a Saint Peter enthroned in gold, carrying gold keys, and incensed by angels with faces made of light-coloured silk, hair of long yellow silk, and their wings of peacocks' feathers!

In spite of those angels and fish on horseback, and the roses, they did order such things better in France. Particularly in this House of the Seven. Simple great men like Thomas and Albert welcomed some pageantry in the Church. It was all right in the worship of the Lord. He showed pageantry too in the Heavens, forests, and fields. But to serve in peacock feathers, the Lord Who had not where to lay His head was a different matter. When confronted with these English fabric extravagances in such bad taste, later on they would look at each other in an almost amused askance and explode in a very earthly "Bah!"

The titled English ladies were forever stitching bright pictures on covers for their knight's shields. Many English women worked in what they called "Shee Schools." But embroidery was not all on the distaff side. Men did the Temple veil. Mediaeval monks worked with silver and gold thread. A guild for male embroiderers had long flourished in Cologne.

Saint Bonaventura, that morning, had been calling on the Bishop of Paris in the old Gothic episcopal palace between Notre Dame and the Seine. He had paused a moment to see De Chelles working on the Saint Stephen door and happened to round the apse and to come into the street where stood the "House of the Seven Who Sewed for Our Lady and Embroidered for Our Lord," as Thomas was at the door.

The friendship between the two was almost as great as that between Albert and Thomas. Just two years before, in 1255, the two had been kept cooling their heels for their doctorates due to that feud aroused by certain lay faculty members jealous of the great attainments of the teaching friars. When that had been settled by the defense of the friars in Rome by Albert and John of Parma, and also by the influence of

Bonaventura's own beautiful little book, *The Poverty of Christ,* the two in 1256 received their doctorates together.

And their paths were always crossing in their second and beloved home, this Paris. Thomas lived there from 1245 through 1248. In 1252 he had come there again to live on until 1259. One more visit he was to pay in 1268, and during these middle years he began to lay the groundwork for his *Summa,* the greatest book of a great book age.

Bonaventura, the youngest minister-general of the Franciscans ever to be accorded that honour, spent years in the Franciscan convent whose refectory (later the Cordeliers' Club) we still can see on the Rue de l'Ecole du Médecin, half-way up the Hill.

"This place," said Thomas, after they had affectionately greeted each other, "never offends with its wild fancies in vestment, altar frontal, and hanging. All the work is done in a wholesome manner. And yet despite all the occasional excesses and extravagances of embroidery in other places, the whole history of needlework is fascinating to follow. In following it too, you get the whole history of man in a bright digest. The mother superior—a remarkable woman—tells me something new about it every time I come."

Saint Bonaventura too was glad enough to go in. Here he might find a little relief from the vexations which, with all the exaltations, are mixed up in the holy life. For all his sweetness Bonaventura was a hard fighter when a principle was at stake. There had not only been that faculty feud, but there was not always evident among the Franciscans that brotherly harmony so dear to the heart of "The Little French One." They were very, very human. Some strove to be Franciscans entire, pure, in the lovely way of Assisi. Others wanted a bit more of the practicality of the world. This young minister-general had to be a veritable walking phial of oil for the troubled conventual waters.

So much paper and organizational work, too, there was for a man who might have served merely as idealist and living inspiration. In addition, so many books had to be written besides that famous *Poverty of Christ.* On His Passion. The Mystic Life. Dozens of commentaries on the books of the Bible. Guide books for the Third Order whose ranks Louis and Blanche had joined. To say nothing of the official life of the founder, the stigmatized saint of high-road and hedgerow.

When they came to offer Bonaventura the cardinal's hat, they found the minister-general of the order washing dishes in a convent dooryard. "Hang it up on that tree," he said, waving at the red hat, "until my hands are dry." And he went on washing his dishes, then refused the red hat, after all.

It was characteristic of Bonaventura too that it was he who in 1263 would start the angelus at nightfall for the Annunciation in all his convents. About 1266 they started ringing it in Paris.

Both were now in mature middle age. Fra Angelico should have done the serene reliability of Bonaventura, Giotto the more solidly hewn reliability of Thomas, who had his rare sweetness too. Indeed very simply, all unaware, they appeared to distribute a twin benediction as under the crossed bishop's crooks they entered the door.

"No, it does not disturb us," the mother superior said, referring, of course, to the music which so quaintly came to them through the sounding board façade of the gay "House of Musicians" next door. "We even find it pleasant to stitch to sometimes. That is, when they all play the same air."

She offered them chairs and a dish of light golden pears, descendants of those which had been growing in Armorica, or Brittany, for thousands of years and of the somewhat later crimson lake plums then a great favourite in Paris.

A countess of a famous Chevreuse family, she now devoted her time to charitable works, chief among them this institution. She had not calculated much on any such ornamental front to this building she had endowed. But the builders had renovated the place when she had been ill. They were so proud of their handiwork that she did not have the heart to order the well-carved and embellished devices removed. There were seven, usually, besides herself, although sometimes the number was augmented because of the increase of orders from beyond the parish when visiting clerics, seeing the fineness of her work, ordered vestments sent overseas, or when she heard of another unfortunate girl whose circumstances fitted all too perfectly the purpose for which the little order of holy midinettes had been founded. Though much smaller the place was quite like Queen Blanche's refuge for lost girls. All here had at one time or another plied an old, old trade on the streets or surreptitiously from the dark doorways of Paris. But some years before this, Saint Louis with Boileau's help had begun that thorough cleaning up of the capital, the Ile de France, and as much as possibly could be covered of his realm. This economic condition resulting from their being closed up and out was not the main cause of the regeneration of these women. It was rather a matter of the love of God and the countess' work.

When at Thomas' request, she had quietly related their story to Bonaventura, Thomas as quietly returned:

"I often think that those who have touched bottom only to rise again, have a quality which the noblest of the innocent cannot know. The once lost have gained the mettle that comes to some from pro-

foundly tragic experience; and it is enduring. The fabric of their transformed souls, because it has been stained that deep black, attains a
richer hue of happiness with the redying by redemption. Because of
the remembered darkness of despair, the more splendidly shines the
Light. The rare souls who start out with what approaches complete
integrity, that is, as far as major transgressing goes, have not an easy
innocence of the sheltered, but a strong, fortified innocence that
matches the transformed strength of the once lost and saved. But there
is no question of the superiority of the one quality or the other. Both
are needed in the Kingdom of God. In the beautiful Parable of the
Vineyard, those who come late are rewarded even as those who were
very early on hand. They receive the same coin of the realm of God,
the same proportion of the imperishable treasure that is laid up in
Heaven for all who believe."

Then he added, looking around at the women with the new light on
their faces, some of them humming softly with the music that filtered
in from next door: "After all, your children have not come so very
late. They all can remember how tenderly Christ dealt with her whom
the corrupt self-righteous would have stoned. And, of all His company
it was to the Magdalen that He first appeared after He rose."

Thomas could be ruthless with the incorrigibly impenitent sinner.
Already he was gathering material for his great work, beginning to
erect out of the tenets of all the theologians of the past the irrefragable
steel framework of the constitution of the Church. But since God is
not only One of Justice, but of Love, he had trained on that framework the roses of mercy and love. Just now he had plucked one of
those roses of God and handed it to her on behalf of these onetime
magdalens of Paris, holy midinettes of Paris.

An immaculate chastity characterized both the mother superior's
habit and features. Under the dark folds and the white of the linen,
her frame was tall and spare but very graceful. She moved with a
natural dignity, one motion flowing smoothly into another. As the
little musicians next door behind that quaint façade, who had been
silent for a while, now played a nostalgic Poitevin love air plaintively
from the wind instruments, tinklingly from the strings, she moved
quietly like a lovely air herself, from table to table, giving her directions rather like courteous suggestions or requests.

Grace and a refined personableness had, of course, been hers from
her noble birth. But features of such classic perfection might have
been sharpened by age into a repellent severity. They had, rather,
been modulated by love into a beautiful warmth and light. Strangely,
there was a similar look on the faces of these seven quite plebeian girls.
Here was an aristocracy not of birth but of rebirth. The same sort of

look you will often see on the faces of the sisters vowed to the service of God—the gentlewomen of Christ. Not out of the ranks of chivalry, the courts of love, but out of the old, old Church came then, as it still comes, the truest courtesy in all the world.

This "House of the Seven Who Sewed for Our Lady and Embroidered for Our Lord" was as picturesque as any theatrical wardrobe and dressing room. At one side, on tables and in coffers, were piles of cinctures, stockings, all the priestly accessories of wool or silk, or linen. On the other side, on hangers or in armoires were draped the heavier vestments. Around the room the sisters were busy at tables, patterning the fabrics, cutting out slighter pieces of linen, or great semi-circular sections of purple, scarlet, brown, blue, crimson wool or satin, sorting gems, semi-precious stones, sewing little crosses on linen vestments, stitching on appliqués in tapestry frames, cutting out metal sequins and sparkling disks, or embroidering orphrey bars, gold mixed with colour, up and down or across the coloured chasuble backs. The room was all aglint and ablaze, filled with darting and sparkling motions, happy glances, bright intermittent chatter, and snatches of song to the airs from next door.

In our earlier story we noted the development of the vestments that made up the priestly wardrobe, rich specimens of which lay in various states of completeness around the room. Still, the chief items should in their order be briefly listed here.

The *amice* was the first garment donned for the mass. It was the foundation cloth over the sub-foundation, the drab soutane or cassock. This amice was the descendant of the ancient neckcloth used in hot oriental countries to keep the perspiration from soaking into the scrupulously clean white of the first sacrificial or eucharistic garments. It is made of linen and on feast days can have a lace border. There is always a little cross embroidered or plain-needleworked in the centre, which the priest must kiss. In the countess' time a beautiful strip of embroidery too was allowed on the amice.

The next, the *alb,* from *alba* or white, was an over-all garment, reaching to the ankle. Until the laying by the Pope of the Notre Dame cornerstone, the alb was worn by the clergy on every religious occasion. Gradually the white surplice began to take its place and the alb was reserved principally for the celebration of the mass. In the early centuries of the Dark Ages they added to the pure white linen, to which the alb has reverted again in our time, richly decorated borders and cuffs. In the youth of the countess they were starting to sew rectangles of handsome brocade on the breast and back of the alb and on its cuffs. All during the Dark and Middle Ages one finds exceptions in this garment, different localities displaying albs of silk and velvet, blue and purple and crimson, even black in hue, and one or two woven entirely of cloth of gold. Colourful as these were, they were far from correct. The alb in the authentic tradition went from white linen through that decorated border and cuff period, then the mediaeval phase of the bright "apparels," those patches of rich brocade always on the white linen, and back to the original snow, occasionally with a lace border, and its giving way for most occasions to the surplice, and its restriction to the mass of our times.

The great sacrificial garment, the eucharistic indispensable part of the costume was the *chasuble,* so-called, from *casa* or cottage, because of its wall of cloth around the priest and the chimney hole for the emergence of his head. It was sewn together, leaving two armholes; and it was vibrant and warm and alive with colours and designs in those times. And on front and back of the chasuble much of the mediaeval decoration still appears. Most prominent are the distinguishing bars. It was from the chasuble decoration chiefly that the word orphrey, which originally meant the thick beautiful embroidery as a kind of needlework, was transferred to the bar itself. But the orphreys differed in Rome and France. A cross was always formed by two or three of these blazing, colourful, golden, and silken colour-accented marks. Sometimes that cross took the form of a Y. But in the Roman rite this tall cross was on the chasuble front, two bright orphrey pillars on the back. In those tailored in our shop near Notre Dame, the pillar was on the front, the cross on the back. Since for so many moments during the mass the priest addresses himself to the altar, that emblem of emblems, the cross, shines out much of the time on his back for all to see.

Deacon and subdeacon wear, respectively, dalmatic and tunicle. These are about the same, and in form like the chasuble. But their bright orphreys do not form a cross. Two decorated stripes running vertically down the back are crossed by two others at the bottom (in all sanctuaries, it might be added for the liturgical precisionist, where the Roman rite is observed; elsewhere the horizontal orphrey cross the vertical ones at the top). The Bishop celebrating pontifical mass adds, under his chasuble, the deacon's dalmatic with its two up-and-down shining bars and the one—or two—across them.

The descendant of the classic cloak is the *cope*. Though longer than a poncho, it is a poncho-like, almost all-enveloping mantle open in front with its edges joined by a great clasp, and a hood in back. This hood, like the human vermiform, has since deteriorated. Into chapels improvised out of catacombs, deserted theatres or upper rooms, for the first service, embryo of the later richly developed mass, the Apostles used to come wearing these out-door mantles, dripping with the rain or dusty from the wind, over their tunics which had to be kept scrupulously white for the altar.

This mantle had of course, no sacerdotal, only a sartorial significance then. Since, it has known many changes in fashion and in use. Through the Dark Ages, it was worn during certain parts of the mass. In the ninth century, however, the chasuble became officially the primary and distinguishing vestment for the sacrifice of the mass. The cope thereafter dropped as a costume out of this heart of the high drama. But it continued to be very prominent in certain offices and particularly at feasts and in processionals.

Meantime, it had continued too to be used as it had been in the beginning for many secular purposes by all branches of the clergy, especially for weather protection when abroad. You couldn't keep track of them. It turned up as the Roman *cappa* all over Europe and as the *pluviale* (so-called because of the protection it afforded against rain) on canon, deacon, and priest. In the eleven hundreds the cantors, choristers, all the worshippers of the voice, appropriated a form of it serviceable and dark in hue, so that it became a sort of singing mantle. Later, in red it became the "great cape" of the pope. His investiture with it on election developed into a picturesque and important rite. From 831 we have a record of a cope of a seldom mentioned hue—chestnut, bordered with gold. Then began the rich blossoming out of the cope, so many instances of which we have just seen.

Meantime, it had kept its basic shape. When spread out on the table like these being worked on that day in the house near the Cathedral, the mantle was an absolutely perfect semi-circle. But the onetime very useful hood had in that very century become a little upright, stiffish, much-adorned board, shooting up behind the neck. Later it would be more greatly diminished still.

So the cope had lost its place as an intimate participant in the holiest of rites. That it had is curiously and not wholly happily evidenced by the fifteenth and sixteenth century reformers in England not throwing the cope out altogether. The earliest of the zealots in some shires had once sung a song:

> "Whatever popish hands have built,
>   Our hammers shall undo;
> We'll break their pipes and burn their copes;
>   And pull down churches too."

The less unrestrained reformers later, however, who were rigid enough when it came to stamping out the pure form of the mass and hunting out confirmed continuers in it, and in destroying so many rites, did not protest the cope, since they thought it had no eucharistic significance.

But the cope was left a very important and a striking place in the offices of the Church. It is worn at Benediction, major consecrations and blessings, at absolutions and burials of the dead, and during the *Asperges,* "Oh, sprinkle me," before mass. For many centuries not a sacrificial garment, it had become a striking processional vestment. With the sheen of rings and crooks and all the corollaries, the sparkle of its great clasping brooch in front, and the rich needlework pageantry on the robe folds, it glorified the regular high mass processional from the sacristy to the sanctuary of Notre Dame. For Corpus Christi, Assumption, all the great feasts, multiply all this magnificence by the number of prelates who then join in. The countess mother superior seemed to have here a shining assortment sufficient to outfit all.

In the priest's wardrobe there are four more but smaller vestments, which should be at least sketchily noticed: so that we may know them when the mother superior shows, as she will directly, her choicest specimens to Bonaventura and Thomas and to us.

The *cincture,* which today is a silk cord, was then an ornamental sash of silk. In its humbler style beloved of tradition and association, the cord of the friars, particularly that of the followers of Francis, it received a very special blessing.

In early Christian history the celebrant at the altar wore a long handkerchief over his arm, called from the Latin for "bundle," a *maniple,* since it was often folded. Used, as the amice over the shoulders, to prevent the perspiration from soaking the white predecessors of the vestments, it was formalized into a liturgical vestment. Originally of linen or some other material, in the Middle Ages it was, as it still is, made of silk. Under the sisters' hands it received its due meed of decoration.

The *pallium* had once been reserved for the Pope. However, it became a custom for him to bestow it on prelates as an honour. A band of fine wool with two tippets hanging, it gave the wearer, they thought, the appearance of the Good Shepherd carrying a lost lamb.

Last and very important was the *stole.* Properly this is seven and a half feet of silk, two to four inches wide, in those days with considerable decoration and always with a sewn cross in the centre. As a matter of fact, it was the third of the vestments donned—first amice, then alb, and then stole, before the all-important chasuble, and the enveloping cloak, the cope. Once it was worn at almost all Church functions. Now its use is restricted principally to the mass, the administration of the other sacraments, and for all the moments when the Host is touched. The strict limitations of the use of the stole are not well recognized by many. It is never good practice to wear the stole in the pulpit though sometimes an unorthodox local custom permits it. The reverse of the cope, it is never a processional vestment. If the cope was the most spectacularly handsome of the priestly garments, the sacrificial chasuble was the most truly beautiful and the most sacred, the stole was often exquisitely embroidered, was indispensable for the mass, and always especially significant for the priest of God.

The French priests have worn the stole since or just before Sainte Geneviève's time. In Charlemagne's reign and for some time afterwards, they decorated the ends with tassels, fringes, and little bells which, fortunately, quaint as they may have been, have been banished to limbo. As the pennon, banner, or gonfanon was the sign of the knight, the stole was the insignium, badge, and device of the priest. The conferring of it on the priest at ordination of the Knighthood of Christ, the Chivalry of God, was even more sacred and impressive than the "dubbing," the bestowal of the accolade, on the aspirant to knighthood in the secular feudal ceremonies of royal France.

The ordained deacon too received his stole. He wore his stretched from the left shoulder across the breast and returning like a sash to the right side. The priest's stole circles around the shoulders and falls over the shoulders, straight down these days if the priest happens to wear the more modern surplice; crossed over his breast if he has put on the old alb.

Like the knights of the natural world, these of the supernatural received their injunctions in the words of impressive, even awesome formulae.

"Receive from the hand of God the white garment and fulfil thy duty, for God is mighty to give thee His graces in rich measure," the officiating prelate says to the kneeling deacon. Crossing the ends of the stole over the breast of the new priest, he says, above his bowed head: "Receive the yoke of thy God, for His yoke is sweet and His burden light."

Saint Thomas was said to know by heart the entire New Testament. The story does not need to be heavily discounted. He had the most apprehending, comprehending, analyzing, synthesizing, filing, coordinating, and interpreting mind of the Middle Ages. He never missed sequence or parallel. Christ in a parable had spoken of the great spreading tree that had sprung from a tiny mustard seed. And Thomas was happy in tracing these giant multifolial trees of the Church back to their tiny seed sources. To the highly civilized mother superior he pointed out the seedling of the old Roman meeting house or guild lodge and what had grown out of it. It was just around the bend in their street. That superb Cathedral tree with its lofty leaders of towers and the wide-spreading vaulting foliage.

Then there were those seed sentences of Christ instinct with such tremendous potentialities. Out of them had grown the infinite number of sacred writings, all the theologians' books whose leaves were as infinite in number as the leaves of the forest. Indefinitely he could have gone on, but he had time for but one more great tree. The midinettes, these "Seven Who Sewed for Our Lady and Embroidered for Our Lord" might not have taken all the others in. But they could understand and looked delightedly at one another when he spoke directly to them about the great mustard tree in whose shade and with whose many-coloured foliage they themselves worked. It was nice to know that these white lace and wool creations, all the gorgeous vestments which they had helped to make, had grown out of the very simple and plain old coats and cloaks and gowns the disciples had worn when they walked the streets of Jerusalem and the roads of Galilee with Christ.

Bonaventura had been remarking to them that there had been a great many innovations since the Cathedral had been started. From the Notre Dame pulpit had been read the decree that every communicant to remain in good standing must make his confession and communion at least once a year. Secularly, the flat shields and sugar-loaf helmets had come in. Coins were being dated for the first time. Incorruptible *baillis,* upright judges had been set up by the king throughout his realm. Bishop Eudes de Sulli, following though no kin of Maurice the founder, had started the sacred and lovely custom of the elevation of the Blessed Sacrament. Before it had been raised just a little at the proper point in the ritual. Bishop Eudes had made it a signal action by raising it triumphantly so that all could see the transformed Body and essence of Our Lord in the farthest reaches of the Cathedral.

"And in this lovely field of the vestments," he said, addressing the mother superior, "you reign over a very important little province."

"Not reign, Brother Bonaventura, if you will, only humbly guide."

"Which is all the more effective," the other replied. "In this field then has come the organization of colour. This demanded rules. It was easy for the early Fathers, when everything was the purest white, and even up to Gregory's time, when the only addition had been stripes of red on the borders of the white. Then bishops of imagination fancying colour began, each in his own way, to relieve the old white or red-and-white uniformity with the colours of the sunbeam when it is refracted into several hues or those of the rainbow, if you prefer. In 1215, by Pope Innocent's order, the varying colours were made to accord throughout Christendom."

"And think," said the mother superior, "of the infinite variety and all the combinations his decree has made officially allowable. We have much leeway still; but now it is an ordered freedom. It must have been lovely when the saints, Peter, James, John, Cyprian, Cyril, all the rest, in early times gathered around their altars, and at the agapes or love-feasts, all in the purest white. But God must love colour too, for 'consider the lilies of the field.' "

The Seven looked up from their needles, scissors, and fabrics, and smiled.

"The glory of the lilies," said Bonaventura, looking around, "seems to have been transferred to your rooms."

In the sacristy of Notre Dame there must hang a complete colour set for every priest. For all the major vestments, except the ever-white alb, were involved. The mother superior had registered the measurements of the bishop, the priests, archdeacons, and deacons in the Cathedral chapter, and of all of the clergy in the two dozen churches on the Isle.

The sanctuary drapings too had to match and conform to the ordered colours of the seasons: Altar frontal. The burse in which the Blessed Sacrament is conveyed to and from the altar. The corporal on which the Blessed Sacrament and the chalice are placed at the beginning of the Sacrifice. The veil of the chalice. The veil of the tabernacle which houses the Host. The dominating colour of the fabrics of all of these (not necessarily the ornamentation) had to be the one prescribed by Innocent for the season of the particular mass or office.

Very much like today's colour calendar (which follows) was Innocent's system of liturgical colours which, by way of this holy tailoring shop, made a garden of Notre Dame sanctuary:

Violet (some people's purple): For Advent, the season of the coming of Our Lord. And from Septuagesima Sunday (third before Lent) to Easter, on the fast-day vigils, the fast days at the beginning of the various seasons, called ember days (excepting the vigil of Pentecost and ember days of the Pentecost octave). For rogation (petition) days, votive masses of the Passion, of penitence. At all blessings of candles and holy water. In the administration of the Sacraments of Penance and Extreme Unction and in the first part of the baptismal ceremonies the stole must be violet.

Green: Between the Octave of the Epiphany (January sixth,

"Twelfth Night," "Holy Kings' Night") and Septuagesima (third Sunday before Lent). Also between Trinity Sunday and Advent excepting vigils and ember days, and on Sundays within an octave.

Red: For Pentecost Week. (Pentecost is the fiftieth day after Easter; its name in the Greek means "fiftieth." It is known, too, as Whitsunday because of the white once worn by baptismal candidates.) Also for the feasts of the Passion of Christ and His Precious Blood; Saint Helena's finding and the elevation of the Cross; the feasts of the Apostles and of martyrs; and in the votive masses thereof; also on the feast of Holy Innocents, if it comes on a Sunday, and in its octave.

White: Trinity Sunday (the first Sunday after Pentecost). For the feasts of Christ, excepting those of His Passion. The feasts of the Blessed Virgin and of confessors, virgins, angels, and women who are not martyrs. Also the feasts of Saint John of Patmos, the Evangelist, of the birthday of the Saint John called the Baptist; of the conversion of Saint Paul; of the Chair and Chains of Saint Peter; and All Saints. For the burial of children and nuptial masses. The anniversaries of the elections and coronation of the Pope. Of the election and consecration of bishops. The consecration of churches and altars. At services in connection with the Blessed Sacrament, at the administration of Baptism, of Extreme Unction, and Holy Matrimony.

Black: For Good Friday and offices for the dead.

Later there was added a

Rose: For Gaudete, or "Rejoice" Sunday (from the Introit)—the third Sunday in Advent ,and for Laetere, or "Rejoice, Oh Jerusalem" Sunday—the fourth one in Lent.

Of course, these vestments scattered around the room were not veritable vestments yet. They had not that reality that comes from their having been worn, becoming fitted to the body of the wearer and accompanying him during high service after high service down the years. And they had not, according to ancient custom, been blessed.

By pack-train or boat the richest materials for them found their way into this room: gems from the mines; silks and satins of an exquisite sheen and suavity from Arabia, the Golden Horn country, and Sicily; linen from the blue flax fields of south France. For example, one of the sisters was working on a *pallium* for the Bishop of Paris. The wool for this pallium for the Bishop had come from a carefully selected and pastured yearling from Gascony. In Rome for the pallium of the Pope they took the chosen lambs, before putting them out to pasture, to church to be blessed on Saint Agnes Day while nuns from the Church of Saint Agnes sang the *Agnus Dei*.

Here, as Thomas Aquinas had told Bonaventura outside, there were to be seen no too ornate designs, naive conceits, or fanciful excesses. In what might have been a confusion of many bright things, balance, order, and good taste prevailed.

The countess mother superior courteously demurred when Thomas again referred, as he had outside, to the extent of her knowledge about the craft.

"With your knowledge of all things, *chers messires mes frères,* you can tell more than I. The vestment history is, after all, so simple. You remember: The apostolic white in the beginning. The first red stripes not long before Gregory, the more venturesome bishops then trying out a little colour—and why not?

"And in Charlemagne's time came the gold and embroidery. The first alb all of gold cloth. Their way was different from ours though sometimes here we use their way too. They sewed the embroidery direct into the fabric. Vines, flowers, figures, were stitched into the garment with such beautiful accuracy—long and short stitch, chain stitch, satin stitch, all, straight, zigzag, or diagonal—that the designs seemed to have been gone in, to have been woven in warp and woof, at the making of the fabric. The embroidery appeared to be one with the vestment, as the gold threads were one with the vestment in that cloth of gold alb. The embroidery was thus an integral part of the raiment as the colour and design are part of the Cathedral's stained glass."

The twelfth and thirteenth century stained glass in all its glory, she meant, not the "new" of much later ages when colour and scene were but *painted on.* The difference in analogy was that while the old glass is infinitely superior to the new, the old embroidery of Charlemagne days was not superior to her "new" embroidery, though that was applied like the painted-on glass.

"Though we still do some embroidery in the old way, sew it directly into the fabric, our principal work is with appliqués. Our decoration is turned out in those little frames." She indicated several held by midinettes around the room. The little wood and wire panels were similar to those the castle ladies of the day used in their boudoirs and housewives of later times for samplers. "They make their little pictures on linen, satin, silk, wool, secured in those little frames, then apply them later to the main ground of the garment and sew them on. There is one other difference between the work of the last few centuries and our own besides that between the direct and appliqué methods. They used to cover almost the entire cloth. We leave spaces between the designs—which makes the designs stand out more strikingly, don't you think?—thus covering the vestment only partially with the embroidery. Would you like to see our work a little more closely, *messires, mes chers frères?*"

She passed around the room, they following, as she gave to the workers her corrections with so pleasant a manner and in such agreeable tones that criticism was almost as welcome as downright approval to the members of this unique order.

At the first table she paused to suggest to a worker that she substitute "gold passing" or metal thread instead of the silken floss.

"Most people do not know it," she explained, "but the metal embroidery does not tarnish so badly as they think; anyway, it does not tarnish half so fast as the floss fades." She held up two specimens for comparison. "Another thing, yellow silk never represents gold as well as the metal thread."

In a corner one sat cutting with dies out of metal sparkling sequins, lozenges, diamonds, shining discs. She rectified the position of the fingers of the sister working the die.

A seamstress was threading in on a violet Advent cope a rich border of gold thread, coral, and metal sparklers.

"Not quite so thickly there," the mother superior cautioned.

She turned to the visitors. "If you encrust the fabric too much, the garment will be too heavy and uncomfortable and not set right. It will look stiff, even stuffy. To get the richness of effect and at the same time avoid stiffness is an art." She turned now to the girl. "And you're getting it quite well, my dear."

A little design for a miracle of Christ stood out on the table next. A sister was indicating the outlines of the drawing on a piece of silk in her frame so that she might copy it in threads of different colours. Then she would transfer the whole to the vestment. Such indicating marks, which give these ancient pieces reality, you can still trace faintly on the Thomas à Becket vestments at Sens.

The mother superior mentioned the name—a well-known one in the Illuminators' Quarter—of the artist of the sketch. "We always get the finest they have on *Enlumineurs,*" she said. "The love and pains these sisters give to their work deserves nothing less than the best. In fact, they may be almost too good. The tile-makers in the Tuilleries are copying our designs—and his. 'Tis stealing. We'll have to get the guilds to make a law against the theft of ideas as well as any worldly goods."

The linen patch at an adjoining table had already been marked with the lines of the model sketch. The Cana miracle was the subject. The midinette had already worked in with her needle a white satin face of Christ and had given him waved chestnut hair. (No, the effect if quaint was not macabre, but rather agreeable.) From out of a good earth-brown jug her needle had sent spurting into mediaeval, not Palestinian, bowls (artists always expressed themseves in completely contemporary terms) a stream of good Beaune. She had given a pretty good Burgundian red to the wine.

"Notice the stitches," she said, indicating two examples. "This chain stitch is apt to get rough after it is sewn on the main ground. The old long and short stitch always leaves a smooth surface. Here, just as in the old way, we are making a design with heavy gold cord, then stitching it down.

"Your frame, my dear, is a little uneven and too tight. The picture when applied will scrunch up or buckle."

"This appliqué is ready to come out." It was a Flight into Egypt, with a cherub-like Child and a personable donkey in silk thread and worsted worked. "All ready, my dear." The girl loosened the wires and burrs and took out the embroidered scene, and applied it to the specified section of a white Trinity chasuble. It was to go in the broad golden orphrey path down the back.

"There, that is exact. Sometimes we gum appliqués on the cloth, but this is to be stitched. She cuts it close around the edges, you see. After it is stitched down, she will add a little diagonal stitching with silk twists or combined silk and gold thread to conceal the rough edges of the appliqué."

There was such an infinite variety of work going on in that colourful room. Bright horizontal bars were going across a deacon's red Pentecost dalmatic back. A sister was at the top of an H in the silver IHN on a black requiem hanging.

Banners too were coming into bright being around the room. Some were for illustrious crusaders of Saint Louis, and some for draping on the façades of the Paris houses when royalty came home from their won battles. We do not find so many of these surviving from mediaeval times as we do of the vestments. But then, the vestments were kept indoors as a rule and carefully cherished. The banners waved exposed to all weathers. These were not as beautifully done, with as much skill or as rich materials, as the garments for the clergy; and that, after all, was the main business of the "House of the Seven Who Sewed for Our Lady and Embroidered for Our Lord." One banner still exists showing the naïve fancies which often composed them, down at Orleans in the banner of Jeanne d'Arc with the angel and the little Jesus. But, then it suited Jeanne. Supremely endowed as she was with personality, military gifts, and mystical vision, she was after all but a country girl. She loved that which we would laugh at—when we might be doing something decidedly better.

The mother superior now had two of the girls hold up a silver and blue altar frontal of the Annunciation. This did not have to be in any seasonal colour for it was to hang in the transept just opposite the Blessed Virgin.

The most striking piece, perhaps, in the place was a God the Father enthroned in the clouds with angels and seraphs and the heavenly host arrayed on both sides of the throne. One would not have thought that a plain needle and silk could have wrought such dominion and power and glory.

As technical achievements she pointed to two Crucifixion scenes. In one the linen of the ground had been used to form the shaded parts of the faces, silk thread supplying the outlines of the features. The light parts of the same countenances were made by white silk thread solidly sewn.

"And in this," she said, "is as fine artistry as I have ever seen. Notice the drapery of the robes of the figures at the foot of the Cross. The high lights are, of course, on the breast and face of Christ on the Cross above. But there is an especially fine shading in the robes of the watchers. They are made of gold passing. But the lines made by this run parallel with the robe folds and they are stitched down with green silk of varying shades all graduated to give the shadows in those robe folds. It is a very subtle effect to be gained by needlework."

But there were other things there that she and the sisters loved best—smaller things too than these great frontals and banners. For this busy season they had taken in others and one worked a Saint Veronica on a maniple. Another embroidered on a stole the cross which, before he donned it, the priest must kiss. This stole had already been marvelously adorned with a cunningly interwoven strip of silk, real pearls, and coral.

On the green ground of an after Epiphany chasuble, a sister worked a Tree of Jesse. This pedigree Tree in green and red went very well in the bright shining broad path of the orphrey down the back. It would have matched beautifully the great Tree of Jesse window down at Chartres Cathedral.

Always there seemed to be for the working sisters, a special fascination in making the orphreys whose splendour appeared, as their needles shuttled back and forth, to be reflected in their happy shining faces. Who could blame them? Those broad bright stripes, forming pillars and cross on the chasubles, whether on the seasonal violet, red, green, or white ground, were strikingly beautiful. Sometimes they looked like moonlit paths on the sea, with rainbow mirages in them. Again, with their gold and silver encrustings and the colourful accents of the variegated embroidery composing them, they were like long strips of meadow strewn with flowers set in sunlight gold.

An annex opened out of the large front room of the shop, and its ceiling was very high. From it were suspended vestments in various states, with quite a few finished and waiting the messengers of the out-of-town prelates who had ordered them to come and take them away. Usually cloth covers enveloped them, protecting them from the chisel and mortar dust blowing in from the last ring of chapels which were going around the stern of the great ship that was the Cathedral. But these covers that morning had been sent for laundering to the Seine, so that there was nothing to dim the radiance of their bright array high up over the heads of the willing workers in the rooms.

Another vestment, a gorgeous piece, elevated by an old male helper pulling on a rope, was going up to join them. The magnificent semi-circle of cloth, fashioned to fit the shoulders of the Bishop of Paris, was headlighted as it rose with a great ruby set in flower petals, clasping the open edges in front. Sweeping circlings and convolutions of gold flowers and vines and foliage, with grace and finesse in every stitch, covered the midde sections of the great crimson satin expanse. "Apparels," or embroidered panel pictures extended up and down the open edges in front and around the hem. A life of Jesus in little richly-brocaded pictures ran outside of and beyond this amazingly gold-figured crimson satin field. The embroidered serial extended down the borders of this open-in-front cope, then horizontally around the hem. Even the darkly tragic scenes were all a splendour.

It began up near the collar with a metallic-thread silver Star in a violet sky over sheep and Bethlehem roofs formed by leaving patches of the undyed linen unworked, and bordering them in green thread. Succeeding were inimitable coloured figures in a score of scenes: On the Egypt Flight. The preaching of the youthful sermon before the crimson and purple Temple doctors. The stilling of the blue waves by a figure in a white-satin robe in an undyed linen boat. The letting down by ropes, through a removed roof open to the sky, of a cripple into the emerald cool of the Bethsaida Pool. Five fish and the mir-acle baskets—one could not understand how fingers could get all those miniature silver scales. An exultant once-blind, flush-cheeked Bartimeus. The waving of the palms with delicately worked fronds on the entry into a shining pearl-like Jerusalem with needle-pricked pinnacles on a day for which this magnificent cope would have been just the thing.

Very bright was this garment pageant. The Seven Sisters Who Sewed for Our Lady and Embroidered for Our Lord and their full season helpers had worked well with their first quality Nuremberg needles, their wool, linen, satin, silk, their threads, cords, twist, and metals, and all the materials and hues of their midinette palettes. Even where the subject happened to be sorrowful, each picture was a delightful exhibit of skill.

In and around all of these panels and inset pictures there ran like a river and shining little brooks attending, a border shining with all the bright encrustings and colour accents. Most adroit, perhaps, had been the skill of the oldest sister in working in tiny red thorn pricks and welt stripes on the white satin Body of Our Lord. And never had embroiderer used gold more lavishly or more tellingly than on the Resurrection Light coming up over the Garden. Gold represented triumph. And here was the place for it.

The whole garment was headlighted by that great ruby in the clasp brooch in front. As the House of the Seven hired the best illuminators and artists, so it engaged the most skilled lapidaries; and the ablest of them in Paris had worked on this gem. This great crimson stone was indeed the highlight, the cynosure as the gown ascended, of all in that room. It was the summation and symbol too of all those pictures on the vestment, having gathered into its heart the blood of Christ.

The youngest and most vivacious sister in the room looked up. "Regardez! Elijah ascending!" She waved at the array of vestments overhead up near the ceiling. "Voilà! In their bright robes, they come to receive him, all the army of the blessed."

She had not meant to be flippant, she was only very thoroughly in the spirit of the thing, of all their work. This magnificent garment which at last was complete and on which at one time or another all had laboured, would go with the Bishop of Paris in the processional of the mass on all the feast days in the holy calendar of the year. It was a vivid, moving history in needlework, a biography in embroidery of the most important Hero in the world—in the Universe. The Cathedral which used every signal, every pointing arrow to drive home the central truth of the altar and its sacrifice thought it completely fitting that these scenes of the Divine Drama should mov with that mantle in these sacred feasts, and should go with the high priest as he came to the altar, quite as the Cross was set up there, not only above the high altar but bright and shining and standing out on the chasuble back for all to see as the priest celebrated and relived that sacrifice.

There would be those who would not like all this efflorescence of love in the making and adorning of these costumes and of the altar and its appointments, indeed of the whole Cathedral. We had, for example, that ribald ditty about pulling the churches down, quoted a few pages back. And Saint Bernard's dour but doughty Cistercians of the century before had not been for it. They could not see that in all this beauty, nothing had been superimposed, poured in from the outside, that it was just a natural flowering-out of people's worship of and devotion to Our Lord. Lock and bolt they would have put on this sacerdotal costuming place, the gorgeous garments all committed to the flames.

For Thomas and Bonaventura and all the rest of that grand company, the life blood of the heart of God flowed through His body, the Church, in a quickening fertilization, a blossoming-out into a thousand things, among them these lovely robes and rites. They gave bright accents to the message of God. They warmed the hearts of hosts, opened them up to the Word.

It would have puzzled them to have any one question the propriety of thus glorifying Him with the best things of His own earth. Metals, gems dug out of His footstool. Wool of the green pastures. Silks and satins of worm and mulberry tree. Scent from the East. The bee's hivings. Leaf and flower forms of forest and fields. "Sapphire" in the bright glass. Wind in the organ. Tone in the throat. All were not only earthly symbols of the life above, in the Cathedral. They were God gifts, and realities with the validity of God. The return of these, His own gifts, with the added beauty of the art of man in tribute to Him, was the rounding out, the completing of a sacred circle. So the wise minds, the beautiful spirits of the Church had combined His earthly things with the heavenly, in a most impressive, appealing, tender, beautiful and majestic program to draw all men to Him.

To throw up toward Heaven those Cathedral towers in a humble yet grand reaching out after Him, was no hollow service. In with the hammer's ring went the heart's ring and that of the blood-and-sweat-earned coin they so freely poured out. Nor was it artifice to fill that Cathedral then with incense and soaring song, the flowers of the glass, and candle flames ascending like so many souls to Him, nor to robe His priests who revive the ancient sacrifice, who play out over and over again the divine, the greatest of dramas in the most beautiful vestments loving hands could weave. They gave Him of their best. One does such things when one loves. For a bride. For the Church and her God. There is no stint. One pours out in abundance. As one brings flowers and music to a wedding. Banners and pavilions and song to the celebration of the independence of one's native land.

The children of the Church would dig and scrub and die for Him. They too would deck out His altars and His House. In unassuming grey, earth-brown or drab, His priests would go on their swift errands of mercy in city street or dark wood. When they attended on Him, they put on white and purple and crimson and gold. Nothing could be too fine, no garment too carefully prepared or richly adorned for Him. To those who have given themselves completely to Him, there comes a kindling of fire within, a holy joy that streams out in an endless spiritual largess that overflows in every kind of spontaneous and beautiful gesture and service, menial and self-sacrificing, or merry and festal.

Further, Thomas and Bonaventura would have said that God Himself had something to do with majesty and splendour. He moves in it. His halls are garlanded with His stars. His footstool is illuminated with the sunrise for break of day, the sunset for the going out of it. His earth mantle is magnificently embroidered. He speaks for Himself in the voice of the thunder *fortissimo,* again in the soft chorals of the birds. Is there not for all our altars a precedent here?

Nor (they would have added to those who protest that the open air services of Christ were in plain places, that He delivered His magical words in the cornfields, among the mountain rocks, as they hauled in their nets, in the storms of the sea) did He denounce the beautifying of His altars and His Church. In Jerusalem He went into the Cathedral every day. The ancient Cathedral of the Hebrews, the Temple. He did not order out, as He did the money-changers, those gold-from-Ophir corners on this Cathedral, the sweet-smelling cedar, the horns of the great altar, the gems on the high priest's breastplate, the embroidered Temple veil. He watched without any feeling that they were not fit the genuflections of the priests, the incense go up; listened, always moved, to the ancient chants. The only repulsion He ever felt was when He thought that they had subordinated an end to a means, that the heart had gone. Then down came the scourge, the even more excoriating, the magnificently biting lash of His tongue. The conscientious but warped Huguenots—they who brought their hammers down on the heads of the Virgin—the pitch-pipe Auld Licht men of Scotland, who banned all melody and the bright glass, might not always have found comfort in being in Jerusalem with Christ.

Thomas and Bonaventura and all the faithful conceived of the Church as the Blessed Body of Christ. He had not rebuked the Magdalen who paid her tribute at the feast. All this beauty was their spikenard which they poured out on His Body every day in the year.

There were seven magdalens in this room; in a corner, one in whose eyes there were traces of the dark ashes of spent passion and yet the light of a new steadily glowing fire. She was embroidering a corporal, the cloth on which Blessed Sacrament and chalice stand before the consecration in the mass. In those dark eyes there was too a deep awareness of her task, preparing the cloth almost as had the Three Marys after the Crucifixion for the sanctified Body of Our Lord.

The mother superior murmured, as the splendid cope was secured above—"How happy it would make us to prepare for both you brothers beautiful vestments like that!"

"They are fine," returned Thomas, "for the Bishop and the secular priests. We ordained ones of the orders celebrate mass, but always in plain vestments. The rest of the time it is the gown and cord for the friar."

"Yes," put in Bonaventura, with the little tentative smile that won all, "in the service of the Church, there are the varying seasons, the harvest of beauty, the austerity of winter. For us friars it is usually that."

"But, my dear brothers, you have your sun!"

"Yes, we have our sun always," they both as one replied. Then Thomas added, fearing lest he might seem to have deprecated her lovely work and so to have hurt her, "There are all kinds of services, and yours is a very beautiful one here."

They stood up now to go. Bonaventura had a lovely presence. Thomas, whose big body loomed large in that room had size and dignity and presence too as he glanced once more around at the bright mixture of both order and picturesque disarray. There were so many elements of beauty there. The pieces of all sorts, of all colours, the glinting sequins and discs, the glittering gold and silver threads, the twists and floss of all hues, the sheen of the shuttling needles, the splendid shining of the bright orphreys, and the "waste," the odd pieces of coloured cloth, twists and floss, were all raw material for a kaleidoscope.

And there were constant movements of the Countess passing from worker to worker, of the pieces and semi-circles of fabric being held up, pressed, or folded, of scissors, thimbles, and needles, of the sifting of gems and bright metal things in the trays, or the setting them in the cloth, that sent more sparkles and glitter and all sorts of refractions through the room. The westering sun that shot down alongside the Cathedral and came through the front windows was now like the proverbial lily gilding all the glitter and dazzling splendour in this "House of the Seven Who Sewed for Our Lady and Embroidered for Our Lord."

"What a round it all is!" Thomas said to her. "All the bright scenes on the vestments here, in all the libraries, the little illuminated books over the river, and up in the shining panes of the Cathedral!

Each art, medium, phase, shines out, reflecting and signalling to the others. That is how it is in the Kingdom of Christ. Everything is connected, ties up, helps to carry out the whole Divine Scheme, is part of a great net mesh, an arc of a universal round and circle."

"If you could come to see the cope blessed by the Bishop, it would give us great pleasure," she said. Then as the mediaeval music sounded once more through the room from the House of Musicians next door, "There it is again, their song. They must sing it for you before you go."

It was another Poitevin air. The strains they heard did not have the full-bodied tonality of our songs to-day, or that this plaintive air might have had in a modern, full-orchestred arrangement. But if the music was a little thin and fine, it had an old-world, an other-world quality, a nostalgia for Heaven that went straight to the heart and shook it but shook it very sweetly.

It is hard to get mediaeval French, its rhythm, rhyme, or assonance into a modern metrical frame. But here is the heart and the full intent of the song.

"Mary the Mother, bend low, bend low,
So that you may whisper to us,
The poor children of your Son,
As you whispered, when you carried Him
In your arms, in His little flower of an ear.
Whispered those baby nothings, those darling nothings,
That made the little Lord smile.
Whisper now, we pray to your tender heart,
In the ear of Him, almighty grown and up on high,
A little petition, a tender prayer for us,
That all our sins may be lifted from our hurt souls,
As the great stone was rolled away
By the angels at the Tomb.

"Mary the Mother, bend low, bend low.
Hear the prayer we whisper to you.
Take it into your heart;
It will be your prayer then.
And our prayer, your prayer now,
Whisper up to Him, your Son up on high.
That we may fall asleep in life,
Peacefully as a sea bird, folding its wings,
Sinks to rest on the wave.
That we may fall asleep in His Death,

Peacefully as the leaf of the wood
Falls to its last sleep on the earth;
Peacefully we because of sin removed, sin absolved,
Through the merits of His cruel, His sweet death.

"Mary the Mother, bend low, bend low.
And hearing this little rest of our prayer,
Whisper it back up to Him,
In His ear as you used lovingly to whisper to Him
In your arms, your enfolding arms:
That we, the humblest of His sheep,
The once lost of His sheep,
May find a little croft,
In a corner far off,
Of the least starry field of His Heaven.
Mary the Mother, bend low, bend low,
And breathe on us
A breath as soft and sweet
As you breathed on Him
Le petit bon Dieu,
The little Lord,
As He lay in your lap.

"Mary the Mother, bend low, bend low.
Mary the Mother whose soft hands
Strayed softly once over the little head
Of the Little Lord.
For one fleeting, healing moment
Let those hands stray
Over us, over us.
So shall we on earth below
Sink sweetly to sleep,
Sink softly in Death.

"Oh, Mary the Mother, bend low, bend low.
As once under your heart
You cherished le petit bon Dieu,
For one fleeting, healing moment, cherish us too,
Under your heart.

"Oh, Mary the Mother, bend low, bend low."

The echoes of the joined voices of the "Seven Who Sewed for Our

Lady and Embroidered for Our Lord" carried out over the Seine lapping and enfolding the Isle, and up to the Paris hills.

"And now," said Saint Thomas, "I must get back to a do a little work." So he turned from all these extracurricular activities "to do his little stint of work" on one of the half-dozen of the truly great books of the world, up on the Hill.

XIV

The Prince takes his Farewell of Paris. . . . A Pious Woman burns down the Little Bridge. . . . The Beautiful Spider Queens of the Tour de Nesle. . . . Blue Mantle and Red Mantle. . . . Some Very Fine Mediaeval Plumbing. . . . Tournament Scores and Bashed-in Skulls, Knocked-out Teeth, Hernias, and Other Casualties of the Gay Jousts. . . . Fifty-two killed in one Grand Pageant. . . . Barnstorming Knights like Modern Tennis Professional "Amateurs." . . . They hang their Tourney "Captives" to Gargoyles, City Gates, and Church Steeples. . . . Saint Louis cleans up these Practices for the True Knights. . . . Wild Boar, Bream, Venison, Roast Rainbow-Peacocks, Pepper Sauce, Spiced Drinks at the Tourney Banquet.

1266 A.D.

PRINCE PHILIPPE ASCENDED BY THE STONE STAIRCASE AT THE Island end of the Petit Pont to the broad way on the top of the city wall. He was to stand vigil before the Virgin in the Cathedral all night; in the morning he would be dubbed knight. Then he would start out of the east gate. He did not particularly like his goal, Naples. There, as the prince head of a squadron of knights, he would help out his uncle, Count of Anjou and Provence. Uncle Charles was consolidating his new position conferred upon him by the Pope as King of the Two Sicilies, which included Naples. As a matter of fact, his father's, King Louis the Ninth's, concurrence in this "crusade" to overcome the Neapolitans who did not want any foreign head, was one of the saint king's two mistakes. The other would be his second crusade. From the wall, Philippe looked reflectively on the Seine, ever with waves, craft, and men in motion. He would have preferred a *bona fide* crusade to the East in the Holy Land. He would have liked to have gone there with a great sword and battle-axe like his father's. These, when a lad of three, he had seen forged for the king, in the ancient armoury of the Palace Yard,

226

alongside the Seine. He had even dreamed of having shining weapons like them and riding in the steel saddle up and down the Holy Land, under frowning mountain fortresses, before fiercely-defended cities, at his father's side. But there were no real crusades on. He must go in the dawn to Naples. Still it would be a fine thing to have come of soldier age, and to be a knight as well as a prince. By no means were all princes and kings knights. He must try to be worthy of the honour. For on his father's death, he would be King Philippe the Third.

It was gay and stimulating up on the city wall where the king's son walked above his Paris and the Seine. The sun wrote a foreign-looking script in leaping fire upon the stream. Below him, in the shops, people pierced leather with awls, felt between thumb and forefinger bolts of bright coloured wool, over in the *charbonnier* of Notre Dame made a cheerful chorus with their chisels.

Like a backdrop upstream over the Seine stretched what seemed like a cut-out of the high, squeezed-up houses of the Petit Pont, whose roofs seemed to have copied the wave forms of the river. To loaf, as the prince did, on the parapet of the Island wall and gaze over at this bridge was like leaning against a theatre gallery rail. Through the windows of the bridge-houses human scenes were forever being enacted. Housewives set dough to rise, darned husband's short medi-aeval drawers, smacked twig brooms against the outer wall, threw pans of dust into the Seine. Maids boxed the ears of men trying to kiss them or let them. Little boys swam on pigs' bladders near the piles. Old women washed and shrouded those who had just passed beyond that river. Students sing-sang their Latin in a little upper-room over-flow bridge school.

That Little Bridge, which was working in Roman times and, long before that, was not always the same bridge though it stayed in the same place. The structure there then had been built by Bishop Maurice de Sulli while he was putting up his Cathedral, to give wider access to it. In the next centuries it would be burned eleven times. People were forever doing such foolish, if sometimes such pious things. On one of the last conflagration occasions, the mother of a drowned boy had taken, according to tradition, a loaf of bread to Saint Augustin's Church (that of Villon's mother) to be blessed. Then, still following popular custom, she had placed the loaf with a large lighted candle in a great bowl and set it afloat on the Seine. This rite and an urgent prayer to Saint Nicholas was to discover the body of the drowned boy, for the bowl was supposed to stop its voyage above it. This time, however, it did not, but floated upstream, under the bridge arches, to land by what is now the Quai des Tournelles, and set ablaze some barges moored there and loaded with hay. Frantic owners cut the boat ropes and set the fiery craft downstream to touch off the Petit Pont. It burned in a skyscraping blaze, lighting up the Cathedral and the city for three days before the final charred remains hissed down into the water. So a mother's pious little candle for her dead boy wrought great devastation in a mighty city.

But the bridge-houses were up there this morning of the prince's farewell in all their triangular-gabled and painted picturesqueness. Of course, not every unit along the water front was agreeable-looking. Right next the Left Bank Petit Pont bridge-head, the Petit Châtelet stronghold was just an ugly uncapped round tower with a grim shape-less storehouse-like annex. It was an affront to the bright setting and the shining Cathedral across the river. Street gamins guyed a chained felon being led into this prison. Being boys, one could hardly blame them. They had so little chance in the sunny moral climate of Saint Louis' reign.

Downstream and across the Seine was a horrid pile, the Tour de Nesle. In it, later queens of his family, the chronicles say, would sit at their arrow-slit windows like beautiful spiders, without hairy bodies, but worse, very seductive ones, and invite in male passers-by, peasants, poachers, or potentates—rank did not matter so long as they were personable—to share their beds. Warm was the welcome in the night. With dawn it was colder. These princesses had these anonymous lover-lodgers for the night sewn up in sacks and dumped into the river.

Philippe's favourite squire who had been looking for his gypsying prince now joined him up on the wall. Now squires were very busy people. Though princes might dream as suited their whim, the squires had to be about their business. They had to polish their masters' armour, make sure their horses received the best care, often even curry them with their own hands. The wardrobes too of their lords came under their supervision. At banquets they must see to it that the servers brought fresh linen towels and a due meed of wines and honeyed drinks. In battle as well as in tournament, they led their chiefs' steeds to them, saw them mounted and off, lances couched, maces raised, or swords up, into the ferocious enough *mêlée* of the joust or the more deadly one of the battle. And with Philippe's vigil ahead, all the knighting ceremonies, and the departure, this squire was well-nigh frantic; yet before his prince, the heir to the kingdom, he had to maintain his composure and a certain good cheer.

So he leaned over the parapet with his prince making his silent farewells of his Paris with a sort of pre-nostalgia. And there is no better place to see Paris than from the Island wall or the city wall and the riverside. Back of them and below, near the Hôtel Dieu and in the very shadow of the Cathedral that held up a constant and beautiful invitation to them to return to the Man of Nazareth Who had come out of them, was the Street of the Jews, La Rue de la Juiverie. One could guess that from the quaintly capped, kindly-faced Hebrew matrons at the doors. One was quite sure of it when he saw the little children scrambling in the gutter, their single garments, little shirts, hiked up above their middles.

The residents on the river were quite as industrious and varied as the shopkeepers and all the residents within the walls. Craft propelled by little figures rowing in rhythmic unison carried passengers or freight. Interesting cargoes lay on the decks in the waists of boats with sails. Coming from Rouen and down the river they were trying to catch a capful of wind. The sails were dyed ox-blood, mocha, burgundy-red, and plum, and these hues were quiveringly reflected in the current ever sliding past.

To assist the passage of these craft the piles and arches of the Petit Pont had been set high, so that the bridge-houses above had the appearance of having been built on stilts. The skippers lowered their masts to go under, quite as modern barges jackknife their funnels. Once the cargoes had been landed on the Island strand; but the prince's grandfathers had built new docks upstream on the Right Bank near where the Arsenal Library would stand and, in Victorian times, Barye's studio in which he would carve his leopards and lordly lions.

As the prince and his squire leaned over the parapet near the gate, arch waggons passed under that made their mouths water. There were four streams of goods forever going into this city which one day would be Philippe's capital—he hoped not too soon, for he admired and loved his father dearly. Two streams of craft came in by the north and south forks of the Seine encircling the Isle. Two currents of huge-wheeled, thick-tongued tumbrils rumbled over the bridges north and south, the waggoneers cracking their whips and whistling as they came under the gate arches and not infrequently cursing jocosely, in spite of Saint Louis, at the warders on top who returned their own racy resonant antiphons. Sometimes files of pack animals coming from the hinterland and the south up along the river roads joined in the provisioning.

So were continuously brought into the city by land and water tin ore, coils of wire, dyes, packages criss-crossed with diamond-hitched ropes, rolls of Persian rugs and hangings, Saracen silks, steel for swords, kegs of nails, casks of wine and olive oil, beeswax and tallow, loads of rushes for withes, plaits, strewing on floors, limestone from

Pontoise, plaster from the Paris valley, drugs and aphrodisiacs from
the Arabs, mercury and cobalt and bronze for the Paris church-bells.
Ever there were arriving loads of piled suet-white and red-meat
shoulders and quarters from Flayers Street on the Left Bank, the
beloved little green Paris cabbages, baskets of crisp-podded peas,
purple and bone-white turnips, fresh cheeses in straining cloths, red
rasps, crimson berries of the straw, crates of pigs with ears curled like
forelocks over their eyes, crates of cackling geese who seemed to
imagine they were saving Paris as once they had Rome. And on the
back of one load were curling-tailed monkeys and parrots whose
colours shrieked as loud as their voices. It seemed to the prince looking down as though his Paris must have a tremendous maw to be fed,
and thirst for novelties to require all these parades, all this pageantry
of provisions.

As he walked on with his squire downstream toward the armourer's
now, he gazed on queer assemblages of houses, in and around the
churches, palaces and public buildings, within the walls on both sides
of the river. He could see into the very hearts of these homes as he
had into the rooms of the bridge-houses upstream, for on the Island
wall he was on a level with their fourth stories. Here too there was
liveliness enough for a prince saying good-bye. And you who love
Paris in modern times would have loved its vitality and urgency and
picturesqueness in the Middle Ages.

Odd mobilizations of dwellings these might have been called. The
military term fitted. Each block or row of dwellings, on Right Bank or
Left, was always in fine parade front along its own little line. But
no two squads of dwellings were in alignment with each other. They
looked like many corporals' guards of tall, thin, pressed-in, "front
dressed" toy soldiers with gables for cocked hats and brightly painted
timbered façades for belted and gay strap-crossed uniforms. But all
these corporals' guards were at cross purposes with each other, without
battle plan or parade design. They all appeared to have been halted
while wheeling, manouevring, marching in different directions. One
thought what a *mêlée* would follow if they were given marching
orders again.

So, sad at the farewell, yet not escaping the mediaeval city's vivac-
ity, the two youths walked the wall, the one from the Capets descended, with reflective blue eyes in a serious face not unlike his
father's, and in a blue mantle going well with them and his blond
hair; the squire with quick glancing black eyes, eager movements, and
in a mantle of crimson. They walked past all the soldier house squadrons, the fortress towers, the grey-green roundings of the convents,
the fresh green of the little interpolated gardens, a little boatful of

gray friars singing a holy song to the movement of oars and waves, the singing skippers at their tiller sweeps going along with them, and the church-bells ringing out some one of the three-hour separated canonical offices, with a Notre Dame tower tongue booming and throbbing and echoing over all. And there, circling beyond this Island wall was the outer city wall, which his great-grandfather Philippe Auguste, had set up there, containing all, embracing all. Uphill, downdale, over river it stretched like a tremendous dragon with crenel coils and barbican joints, but a friendly dragon lying in the sun protecting his Paris.

No matter what the day's duties that lay ahead, and the delay in which the squire fumed, though very discreetly, they had not wasted their time. Nor have we in following Bluemantle and Redmantle. There has been no other grand view of this ebullient, colourful capital more memorable than this from the Island wall at the riverside. No city can be truly magnificent, no capital immortal unless it has the quicksilver pulse of a nourishing, world-connecting river flowing through its heart, a mighty many-towered wall impregnably belting it, the overtone of the voice of a great Cathedral and its accent dominating all the city's life. All who wandered from it, the Crusaders, even the dissolute, could never wholly forget it. The prince knew he would see his Cathedral towers miraged on the Naples sky, hear Our Lady's bells even in Rome—or Jerusalem, if he should ever get there.

There was no other place in the city that gave one such a feeling of the city's greatness, of security, as a seat in one of the crenels, those wall embrasures that cut jack-o'-lantern teeth out of the ramparts, especially when the sun fell warm and intimately upon one, with the mighty masonry under one's feet and seat and at one's back. When the Prince reached a point in the wall just above the armourer's he motioned the squire to stop and for a moment Bluemantle and Redmantle sat in warm adjoining crenels before going below.

This forge had been making royal weapons for Clovis and all the monarchs through Robert the Strong, the Butcher's Son, Hugh with his little cape, Fat Fighting Louis the Sixth, Weak-Lover Louis the Seventh, the strong and competent Philippe Auguste down to this later Saint-King. Poitrine de Carotte, the Armourer, was the present *chef de la Forge et le Grand Armurier du Roi.* He it was who was making the sword and battle-axe which the prince would take to the wars.

A little staircase ran down to the Seine for the fetching of the water needed for the forging of true weapons. Beyond the armourer's was the palace practising and tilting yard. There young knights and candidates for knighthood, with a master of fence and arms and a veteran warrior or two, were fencing mediaeval fashion, wrestling, hacking at oak posts, engaging in English "singlestick," couching lances and riding hard at dummies to upset them, so that they might be able to better their jousting scores in the tournament or the even bloodier counts of true battle. From the wall *garçons* and *types* who, even in a day of feudal caste, were no respecters of persons, made droll, satiric comments when any of the mediaeval young bloods missed the dummies or were unhorsed, rousing the easy risibilities of the crowd.

Prince Philippe's own knighting the next morning would be attended by the solemn and sacred ceremonies in recent years adopted by the Church, but not by the old-time splendour of secular festivities. It was then quite as it was in our own world wars. The Crusades had interrupted carnival athletic competitions. Too many tournament champions had been busy with the real thing. Saint Louis, who had returned from the East a few years before and was away in the South now, had never liked the old expensive knighting celebrations anyway. And the young prince, being, as we have seen, like his father in seriousness and sense of responsibility if not precisely in his gifts, was glad that he did not have to face the gorgeously arrayed chattering women spectators, all the bright agitation of the galleries. He could do very well with the impressive vigil, the petitions to Christ and Our Lady, the blessing of the sword.

Still, the warm sunshine in the crenel brought back to him exciting memories of more colourful days at the knightings. There had been, for a particularly shining example, the Castle d'Artois jousts when he was a lad. His mother, Queen Margaret, had taken him. His handsome grandmother, the "White Queen," had preferred the Sainte Chapelle chants and prayers to the romantic but sometimes deadly horseplay of the tournament, and had not come.

One tower of this chateau survives. You will find it rising unromantically out of a modern schoolyard near 20 Rue Etienne Marcel, called now the Tour de la Burgoyne, for Fearless John, Burgundy's dark murdering duke, who later acquired it. But when the queen took the little prince there it was the Château d'Artois and owned by the count of that name, brother of the king, and father of that day's knighthood candidate, the cousin of Philippe. This Château d'Artois stood, moated then, in the open farm fields, near Saint Martin's great abbey, and beyond the city wall. Especial lists, larger than those of the castle tilt-yard, had been laid out in the open beyond the moat, among the meadow flowers. The reviewing stand of the lists resembled a flower garden, with all the spectators' costumes and gems like dew upon them, and striped pavilion tops adding further colour. Down the sides of the tourney field, or lists, stood, trumpeting or at attention, heralds and pursuivants in tabards, their gay, playing-card-like tunics decorated in front and in back.

Little barricaded retreats had been cut out from the jousting area at the sides of the lists. Hurdles barred these enclosures; and they were surrounded with pennons, bannarets, shields displaying leopards, lions, dragons, swans, castles, suns, moons, stars, and all sorts of heraldic devices brightly painted on them. In these retreats, quite as in modern polo fields, the contestants' strings of horses could be blanketed by the little armies of retainers. From them litters, for stretchers, could be trotted out to the unfortunate armoured knights who had been unhorsed and badly damaged and dented. In them too, they could be unhelmeted, sponged of their blood and sweat, and soothed by balm, unguents, or the magic mandrake for the deadening of pain. If the warrior were too far gone, under the pavilion top the priest could administer the last rites.

The many-coloured decorations gave the enclosed retreats a mock carnival touch. But these bannered bays of this open-air hospital were no mockery. For such "games" were in bloody skull-cracking, limb-crushing earnest. The jousts were very like the modern sport of football in their practice with dummies, the manoeuvring in the limbering and warming-up, the grim spirit of competition, and the taking of triumph or defeat for issues as important as those which settled the fate of the world. But tough as that modern sport has been considered, its casualties should be written down in a comparative pale carmine, those of the mediaeval entertainments in a very deep and gory crimson.

Ladies in those days had a number of activities. As capable *chatelaines* they ran their households. They taught their children, helping out the tutors and priests, invented games and told ancient stories to them. They embroidered hangings and altar cloths, also sashes and covers for shields for their gallant knights. Some of them were excellent swimmers. They practised in the castle lake or pool, in chemise or dainty bare skin at twilight. The most expert could swim under water and had been known to rescue children and even submerged knights. They were deft too in making balms, unguents, splints, bandages, and in smoothing the unhelmeted, bashed-in heads of the just tumbled, steel-burdened warriors.

The Prince could remember the shattering headache he had endured at the Château d'Artois as the day wore on. He had liked it when they performed the first acts on the tournament bill, those games in which points counted and not the blood, displaced brains, and fractures. Not that these last were ever totalled up, but they thrilled the spectators.

In these earlier games of comparative gentleness, in which scores were kept, the knight leapt into the saddle without recourse to the stirrup. This was a real achievement with those many pounds of steel on his body. It would be worse when complete plate took the place of chain mail. Many saddles, like King Louis', had cantles, pommels, and seats of steel. It was quite a jar for both rider and horse when the stirrup-scorning, leaping, steel-encased knight came crashing over into the steel saddle. It was hard on knightly coccyx and thighs and on the horse's spine. More risk they ran of strangulations, fistulas, sprains, bowel displacements than our modern riders in their rodeos.

In these solo numbers, the knight often more expertly unhorsed the dummy than he did the knight in the later duel. They had shields, too, decorated with gay escutcheons and armorial bearings, set up in the lanes as targets for the competitors. One knight, Philippe could remember, riding hard, had pierced five of these shields with one thrust of his lance. Skill, good aiming and timing counted here, rather than force itself. That was needed in the final mass tilting. Pretty much too in the knightly duels that came next.

Nobles in full mail, with lances firmly set, each one of strong ash and eight feet long, rode at top speed toward each other. The shock was terrific when they came together. Sometimes one, often both, would be unhorsed. If not completely out, they would renew the battle with sword or axe on foot. It seemed to the prince that his own ribs cracked with theirs every time he saw one of these steel men go over in that accumulated weight. Once a horse rolled over on a prone rider. Sometimes horses and riders seemed clashingly, inextricably mixed. Very near where he had sat, one knight had lain horribly inert. Blood had gushed through the eyeholes and ventilation slits of the helmet. It had made him suddenly feel faint. Another's helmet had been removed; and he had seen red matting in the hair, and brain pulp running down a face. It was a very ordinary tourney, indeed, that could not show a large total of fractures, concussions, ruptures, and hernias. Also deaths. In the early eight hundreds, the first tournaments had been held in Barcelona and Strasbourg. They had not improved since.

If it be thought odd that a queen could subject a little boy to scenes of such violence perpetrated in the name of sport, it must be remembered that royalty and the nobility then were much stiffer than the peasants and burghers in discipline. The little mediaeval people of the thirteenth century were, in some ways, more fortunate than those higher up. They pampered and indulged their children. But the pedigreed youth had to learn to study, hunt, swim, pray, fight the hard way.

Spectator interest mounted as the afternoon wore on and the casqued warriors increased in numbers. Fives now made up the shining chain-mailed, lance-bristling squadrons that rode at each other in tumultuous and bloody delight. Then teams of ten could be seen trotting out from the retreats and to the ends of the lists. There they turned, aligned themselves. The grand marshal's gage was dropped; the trumpets sounded, and they were off. Each band became a gleaming of chain-mail above, a twinkle of galloping horses' legs below, a gathered sunburst of sharp lance points, in front, ever ahead and fast traveling down the course.

Suddenly there came the heads-on collision, with a crash such as would have been made by dropping metal and wood chariots over a cliff. The smooth flowing charge was ripped up into a horrible *mêlée* of frenzied men at sword-thrust, axe-crack, dagger upstroke, and all sorts of bloody and most direct of actions. To the nauseating of the then small boy prince's stomach, out of the horribly mixed anatomical pile, horses' forelegs rose thrashing in the air, other horses trumpeted with slashed throats, lances cruelly found crevices in armour, spurred heels with a ghastly ludicrousness appeared upside down on top, and human heads like waxen but bloodied heads in museums, with casques off, and the chain mail neck and head hoods, the *camaux,* horribly flapping. And there were all sorts of battle and débris details, terribly satirizing chivalry's splendour and nobility: grotesquely arched figures catapulted from steel saddles, to fall and thrash in agony about; horses' hoofs frantically trampling on a breast-plate to the sickening giving way of the human frame underneath; and a Death's junk-pile of tossed reddened shields, splintered lances, broken recently blessed swords, knights' plumes like white spume, and bubbles of horses' froth and of gore on the vortex of the maelstrom.

Those whole enough to proceed under their own power extricated themselves from the utterly still or thrashing figures, and thrust chains around the necks of the defeated and dragged or lance-pricked them before them as "captures" of the tournament. So they marched them down the field as from all the bannered bays the litters rather blithely were trotted out to salvage such smashed knights as might be patched up.

It was not, of course, a law that a knight could not shine unless he had killed a whole squadron. So long as he had manfully ridden in the preliminaries at those dummies or a live knight and bowled something over, he could score points and sometimes win prizes, money too. He was not actually disqualified because he had not killed his enemy outright or smashed every bone in his body. It was not the aim of the tournament marshals to have all the contestants like ancient gladiators destroyed. It was a great success if scores were rendered *hors de combat*.

Still, Death was hospitably admitted as guest and umpire. There had recently been as many as fifty-two killed in a Class A tourney. But, of course, there had been tournaments distinguished by less violence and a fine sort of honour when Louis was at home.

They were quite sanguinary, but loyal and brave, most of these mediaeval men in mail. Back in the palace the prince had always been hearing about them. Bits of his boyhood came back to him as he sat in the warmth of the crenel. To be sure, his grandmother, Queen Blanche, had more often chosen as subjects for her lessons the saints, but she always sweetened this drink of knowledge for the boy with a dash of chivalric adventure. His mother, Queen Margaret, and his tutor, who later became the Abbot of Saint Denis, regaled him with heroic tales in even greater measure. The very phrases stayed with him:

"Charlemagne, who rules sweet France, was seated on a golden throne outdoors under a pine tree. Very handsome he was of face and in body. One thousand knights of his beautiful France sit by him, around the gold throne, scattered on the sweet grass. The elders engage in chess, the youngsters in sword play." So, infectiously, ran one remembered song of Roland.

And even the peaceful sport of chess, the song reported, got out of hand. In a dispute over a queen's move, one player in the sunset of life got up and brained his adversary with a chess-board. The boy had laughed fit to kill when they read of the page who had taken his bread and meat knife and while his testy, grumpy master was asleep had sliced off a good portion of his beard. The seven years the page got for that the prince thought overlong just for a trick.

Often all this jousting, riding at dummies and at each other, and all such by-products of chivalry and knighthood got out of hand. There had been, for a curious instance, the day up at Coucy Castle. The knights, all the liege followers of the domain, young, middle-aged, old, had beaten off the raid of a too militant neighbour. But they had beaten him off too easily. The young gusty, ebullient knights had gotten a taste for the fighting. They hadn't had enough, but they couldn't fight men who ran. So they turned and fought their own side, defenders mixing in with other defenders of the castle. The crazy affair was not without its casualties. It can be seen why those days "uneasy lay the head that wears a crown." Especially when feudalism, an institution making for something of order in its first phase, had now left a legacy of constant bickering and battling among a contentious caste. All the liege lords were striving to be cocks of the national walk, kings of the monarchical mountain.

The body politic was a constant choppy, tumbling sea of waves of all the heads that longed to wear the crown. The one who did wear it had to compose that sea. Considerably more stormy had been the unrest in previous reigns. Yet, deserved as had been the golden acclaim won by Saint Louis' justice, he had no recipe for perfect peace. And it was immensely to his credit that he had poured the oil of his presence, his great calm and good will upon that shifting confused sea. He had so ordered it that he siphoned off the vast energy of the militant zeal of these mad milling knights from its own counter-currents and channels into a united and vast effort flooding over into the East, for the saving of Christ's tomb and capital on earth.

Still, chivalry and feudalism had troubles enough when Louis was off fighting sultans and Greek Fire and cholera. There occurred then at home more of these break-neck pilings-up, masking as knightly carnivals. And into what had once been a purely amateur, if danger-ous, sport, crept professional and semi-professional abuses. In this there was still another striking resemblance to modern sports, and the tennis players, for example, who debonairly go from tournament to tournament, posing as amateurs while they handily scoop up quite a livelihood. But perhaps it is fairer to liken the mediaeval tournament campaigners to the ex-army pilots who, after the First World War, used to tour the country in worn-out crates doing flying feats at county fairs and country circuses. They furnished nobler spectacles when as amateurs of amateurs, volunteers, they fought in France than when they flew in these shabby spectacles, though still they had courage enough.

Mercenary knights formed travelling circuses, with their *remudas,* and went from tournament to tournament, whether invited or not. Through constant practice, they became so skilled with horse, battle-axe, sword, and lance, that they were sure in whatever event they entered to win valuable souvenirs, prize money, and "captures" (the defeated knights whom they always held for ransom).

Some of them were Homeric jokesters too. Way down the lists you could hear, resounding like trumpets, their gargantuan guffaws. Out of their "captures" (the knights they had toppled or smashed up) they got both golden livres and a huge boyish delight. Their delight was almost as great when they were refused as when they were granted the ransom. For, denied, they had the extreme pleasure of dragging the dented knights, chained, though the main streets of their own home towns, and then suspending them from gate arches of their city walls, from corbels of their mansions, or from the church towers, ringing the bells above deafeningly so that all in the town might turn out to see. Then, like champion bull-fighters of Spain, these armoured pugilists of mediaeval times retired to the inns, smashed gauntlets on oak tables, roared for wine, ever more wine, pulled girls down on their still undoffed hauberk chain links, tickled them, and trolled out their jovially rascal, ribald songs.

Now all such practices, the tournament massacring, this tournament touring, would vastly disgust Saint Louis on his return in 1254, six years after the Artois affair. He knew the true knight—and such predominated—as a *parfait gentil knight,* and as no semi or full professional, only a simon-pure amateur, of the finest blend, for were they not loyally vowed to Christ and Our Lady and did they not serve them for love, not any earthly pay?

About this time there had been held in the South another spectacular tourney that proved the last straw for Saint Louis when he heard of it on his return. Two little armies, of a hundred mailed knights each, galloped at each other down the lists in a thunder of hoofs, and engaged in a murderous *mêlée.* Suddenly out of the bloody mess, the survivors of one army, cut in half, turned tail and galloped all over the landscape. The other little army, badly damaged too, but victorious, pursued the fugitives, cracking down hard, when they could get near them, with sharp battle-axes and maces. Also these winners cheated. They had stationed in ambush men-at-arms, in leather quilted jerkins, leather head-pieces, little else, but with deadly cross-bows. There was no carnival of chivalry here, but a sort of pole-axe and cattle slaughter.

Now Saint Louis and his knights might make in the East something very like this picture, without the ambuscades; but it was for what the times accepted as a very fine purpose. And the king on his return from the Crusades extended his justice and organization to the tournaments.

There was, in short, a grand cleaning-up of these sports—for the time. Gradually the jousts became more civilized and less robust. Mediaeval Marquess of Queensberry rules were arrived at. The tourneys became less like Donnybrook fairs. To be unhorsed was a knockout. You did not have to hold the knight for ransom, kill him, or drag him chained all over the field.

Lull set down the rules in a book of jousting protocol and mediaeval tourney etiquette. Later, as fencers would one day take the sting out of their rapiers by putting buttons on their foils, the men of the fourteenth century blunted both swords and lances, though Sir Walter Scott and the historical novelists have not let us in on this. These later knights looked grand parading past the beauties' boxes, with open visors, uplifted lance salutes, plumes streaming from towering baroque head-dresses on helmets, gold-inlaid armour, and gaudy devices on their surcoats and shields. In the 1400's it all turned into an ornate, overblown chivalry with a gilt gingerbread crust. Of true-hearted knights there had been, ever since Charlemagne, a devoted effective minority. But by that time the honour for such had been pretty well prettied out. What had been, in the early 1200's, a valiant, robust, if over-rough game and pursuit, turned, in the later 1300's and 1400's, into elaborately-rited, over-coded, splendiferous artifice. As the Renaissance approached, the once tough, sometimes unscrupulous, often heroic and vital heart of chivalry had a very feeble beat.

But before that, even in this renowned thirteenth century, three quarters of which was turned into a truly golden age by the sheer character and attainments of the White Queen Mother, Saint Louis, the great men, so many of whom we have already met climbing our hill, and the swinging into the godly line of the majority under the impulsion of this grand minority, we cannot (and this cannot too often be repeated in the face of the somewhat over-publicized goodness of the age) lay down a blanket godly rule for all of it. Even in this renowned Saint Louisan apogee, the Middle Ages, for all their unquestionable, unchallengeable and very genuine glory, had their corruptions that resembled, if they did not in quantity match, the public festerings of our own commercialized, down-to-earth time.

For there were not only the Holy Land lootings by the unworthy lords, these titled jousters, these professional and semi-professional tourney knights masking as amateurs, these lawless mediaeval barnstormers. The very sacred chants which made the city melodious were jangled by the lewd songs of the false minstrels, the goliards, whom we met before, who sang their ribaldries and impieties in dark corners, quite as Algerian peddlers buttonhole tourists now in the porch of Notre Dame and show them silly cheap concupiscent cards. Also there were foresworn and atheist dubbed knights who, if they ever made the sign of the cross on their unworthy chests, did it in much the way one thumbs one's nose.

An old curmudgeon of a chevalier has left us his advice given to his heirs: "Sure, hear mass every day, but build no more convents. Respect the humble and poor but give them no leeway."

Listen to a song surreptitiously current then. It is really so bad that one might suspect that the creator must have been having a sort of depraved satirical fun with people:

"Dash little children in pieces. . . . Bite them whenever you meet them. . . . Kick old people in the faces and if no one is looking, strangle them. . . . Burn down the convents. But first be sure you have raped all the nuns!"

Pretty! So all knights were not Rolands, Arthurs, Ivanhoes, or the *parfait gentil* ones beloved of Knights Philip Sidney and Walter Scott.

But we can deplore such things and, in a way, be amused at them, then place them in our memories' pigeon-holes to bring them out later to check for balance so that the fine integrity and the very real magnificence of this century won't overpower us and make us dissatisfied entirely, like clever Chesterton, gifted Belloc, with these days in which we live and move and have our being.

Prince Philippe wanted to become a fine knight. Again it should be noted that not all princes or kings, either, were knights. They had to want it and prove themselves worthy of it. A few precocious ones were dubbed at the age of sixteen, more at the age of twenty, and many later. And they were not always so confirmed in the order of chivalry in times of peace, as his cousin had been, or as he, Philippe, would be that night. Many a true knight—and they were so numerous in these high golden days—had been made on the battlefield itself for the valour he had displayed. Some were "dubbed" at the city gates of capitals they had led in storming, or for saving the oriflamme of Saint Denis from an attacking army. They even knighted the gallant dead on the battlefield, following up this ceremony with a solemn requiem.

As the blue-mantled prince dreamed in the sun on the wall by his red-mantled squire, other scenes of that heyday of his cousin and of his own boyhood came vividly back to him, for he spoke of them to his companion. Very well he had served his own apprenticeship for his knighting. The training of both the cousins had been very much alike. He had loved the periods out in the country, particularly at Montlhéry. As a small boy he had played see-saw, merry-go-round, marbles, in addition to learning his letters and listening to Books of Hours and tales of high adventure. In his early 'teens he had been introduced to the trivia of the scholars, to checkers and chess, hare-and-pheasant hunting, had become proficient in the hop-skip-and-jump, leaping over brooks, in riding horses and currying them down. He learned much about falcons, the rare white gerfalcons, the more delicate sacre-falcon, the *pélerin,* with the greenish-blue feet, and how to hood, call, and feed them, with cheese, beaten eggs, and meat cooked in milk. In his palace room he still kept his boy's record book of all the birds his falcons had killed. It was very neat. His royal father had insisted on that.

So he had graduated into the lists and the tilt-yard, the practice with dummies and trained knights, the English single-stick and fencing, the handling of battle-axe and lance. His culture had kept pace with this. As a matter of fact, there has been written much balderdash about the grand, gross illiteracy of the Middle Ages. Of course all of the charcoal burners, the *Jacquerie,* did not have college educations. Half of male and female Paris had to have their love-letters written for them, and there were some ferocious knight champions as bad at pot-hooks as, ages before, mighty Charlemagne had been. But many poor boys were being given a chance for bursarships, or scholarships, in the bishops' schools and up on the hill. They could not fix electric bells, take down motors; the elect among the scholars did not discuss the quantum theory or relativity. But there was a higher average of accomplishment in philosophical exploring and adventuring, of core thinking, of far-reaching ratiocination then in every college acre than most college acres today. The Prince did not go that far, of course; but he could read a little in the now dead, then alive, Latin, and had a bit of mathematics and logic and other worthy studies in his head. So, in the sound and assiduous training of mind, body, and soul, he went through the *enfant cadet,* or *damoiseau,* and squire stages on the way to knighthood and was knocking there at the threshold today.

His cousin, that spectacular day, had had a fine supper laid out for him. He would not have one so fine. In war times the Palace was on an economy basis. And he would not have so many ladies waiting on him. He was glad of that. Some had helped his cousin of Artois, after his bath and donning of the silk undershirt and pants, with his armour, had placed, these maidens, one left spur on, then one right spur—yes, in that order—also the chain mail hauberk around his torso and thighs, the long chain hose and gauntlets. Also they had given him a sash and shield cover they had with too many flowers embroidered. As for a whole bevy of women handling *him!* No! So he almost spat it out to his crimson mantled squire. In all this he was very like his father.

There had been some nice things about the old ways, after all. He had admired his cousin when he came out to do his *devoir.* The castles then, particularly those out of the city a ways, had within the inner ward, a broad staircase with a wide platform leading into the donjon keep. At the top the nobles and their guests sat, facing the retainers below, who were ringed around a cleared circle. In this the piebald tumblers and minstrels had already agreeably performed. Then his cousin had entered. Philippe could remember the thrill as his cousin nimbly leaped, in his armour, into the saddle, without the stirrup, as prescribed, and had beautifully caracolled, made figure eights, and leaped over bars in the circle.

The banquet following was even more memorable. It had been merely an extravagant and expensive enlargement of what was typical then. Even now it made the prince's mouth water, so he told his squire. All ablaze with costumes, jewels, and armour (although most of the latter they doffed on entering), the company had trooped into the hall.

The seneschal and squires were busy ordering the servants about the hall with its minstrel gallery, rich hangings, a dais with figured oriental carpets, loot or purchases from the Crusades, also benches and even ottomans. For some nobles, to Saint Louis' disgust (he wanted people ever erect and straight) had acquired the soft oriental way of reclining at meals. The staff had placed table tops and planks on trestles ranged all around the rush-strewn floor, for a huge banqueting table leading up to the dais where the duke and duchess and, of course, the queen and the prince would dine. Ewers and towels had been presented to guests in a retiring room near the entrance. Some, however, had retired to a lavatory and private privy with stone seats and stone or metal-rimmed fountains for ablutions. Since the lords were admitted here in order of rank it was hard sometimes on those lower down with aging or tourney-over-excited bladders. For the reader's olfactory reassurance, it should be mentioned that servants were constantly sweetening the hall against hounds wandering in, scarce-dried blood from lesser wounds that had not required dispatching to an infirmary, and under-arm perspiration from many leather and steel layered knights, by blowing on the rushes little bellows'-sprays of incense.

And the visual display was impressive. People ate in pairs, and there brightly shone silver, beautifully chased porringers or platters out of which they ate in doubles, with a gold-lined goblet at each place. The scintillating gleam from these, the copper plates, cups with lids like later tankards, great carven spice containers and golden-hulled, silver-sailed boats filled with salt in their waists, gilt knives (no forks) met and interwove with the scintillations of the jewels of the highest nobles of Paris, and colour patterns of all the priceless tapestries, arras, hangings around the room, the carpets on the dais, and the tall rich containers of flowers, roses, lilies, late golden-cup daffodils, and high-coloured gladioli down the long table.

Being forkless, they did eat with their fingers, but these were at intervals cleansed from perfumed ewers. And some of their manners might have been with profit copied by diners of today. Sharing with another the same platters of entrées, fish, game, meats, a dining partner would often pick out with his fingers an especially toothsome bit and hand it to his companion. Over their individual bright goblets they would bow, toast, or salute each other as they drank. And this dining in pairs on the more solid viands made the banquet a greater conversational success than many modern dinners. For dipping in the same dish, a pair had to carry on with each other; and a diner could not turn his back on the brunette baroness he had brought in for a blonde countess on the other side.

And this was the bill of fare, monstrous in quantity, but most delicately cooked and sauced and served: Venison, brown from the spit, on splendid platters, with a *sauce Poivrado,* or a peppered fluid poured over it. Platters of wild boar, peacocks roasted with tails and heads put back again in all their rainbow colours and many eyes. Capons of all sorts, and wild fowl. For fish, mullet, bream, shad, salmon, and trout. And herons, hares, rabbits, ducks, pigeons. The cooks put much pepper on. But the diners kept constantly shaking on more. The cooks with fine culinary proportion used spices. The guests were forever resorting to the dishes of cloves and ginger near their plates. And since, though some careful milords, who were chaffed for it, like Saint Louis watered their wine, many drank deep of the constantly circling honeyed wines, all the spiced drinks, particularly the one called *piment,* and the drugged one, *bouglerastre,* it seemed as though they were, with all the condiments on the side, deliberately egging their palates on to more liquor consumption. Tonques circled too, and increased in loquacity. The prince, so little then, had not cared for all the glitter and confusion; and his stomach was a little queasy still from all the tournament massacre. He leaned up against his queen mother's shoulder and asked why that lady down there had giggled so like a peacock; and she had said "Shush!" And there was a continuous parade of noble names to the private privy with the fountain, and a lot of knights that had not been unhorsed by the lance or spiked mace in the joust were now by the spiced juice. Not nearly so many, of course, as in English Guards' or Seventh Regiment, New York, banquets at the turn of the last century, when it was every soldier's sworn duty to be under the table or very near it, but far more than you would have seen when Louis was at home and Stephen Boileau was on hand.

There was one social custom that made as great a difference between dinners then and nowadays and which, in fact, made almost as much of change in life generally as the eighteenth-century-discovered electricity. The air was much sweeter then, not only through the bellows-scattered scent, the aroma of the heavily-spiced drinks and preserves, the fragrance of the flowers, but through the absence of volumes of curling, swirling, pirouetting, clouds of smoke. Knights and ladies did not have nicotine coughs. Ladies did not have fumbling hands, had poise, could sit still without lighting up. The beautiful table was not littered with a vast débris of butts. People weren't forever having frantically to run around to the corner store for smokes. Young men like this crimson-mantled squire did not have to see one tenth of their incomes every year go up in smoke.

There was one custom that Saint Louis could not get the people to change. At each place in the banquet, besides the shared utensils, there was not only an individual tall goblet, the beautiful bachelor knife needing a fork mate, but a loaf of white wheaten bread. To the vassals, the lesser fry in the court, villeins and vassals all, went the lower caste rye or black bread. When Saint Louis sat down to eat, he ate the rye or black bread himself in example and always had the white wheat distributed among the three hundred beggars he fed every night no matter where he was, even if his hosts had to gather the beggars in from the countryside. But usually they did not have to bother if the countryside knew Louis was coming.

The prince roused himself from his dreaming, and summoning his squire went below the wall into the armourer's shop. Poitrine de Carotte's rufous arm was frantically working the bellows. As the prince entered, the whole place suddenly lighted up as though with a suddenly ignited train of yellow sulphur. The Red Armourer, the sooted 'prentices, the blue-mantled and crimson-mantled youths in the burst of light vividly stood out.

XV

Armour Fashions Old and New. . . . Macled, Trellised, Horn War-Shirts. . . . The Kind of Armour Lohengrin and Launcelot really would have worn, but which you do not see on the Stage or in Picture Books. . . . Anachronistic Stage Designers and Artists. . . . The Red Armourer of Paris and the Ancient Forge. . . . The Great Chain-link Age. . . . Steel Mittens come in. . . . Lionheart and Louis. . . . The Revolution of Plate Armour. . . . Bright Banners, Shields, and Surcoats. . . . Chivalry Protocol. . . . The School of Heraldry grows up. . . . Armour and Chivalry turn Magnificent, also Outmoded and Useless.

1266 A.D.

THE FORGE FIRES LIGHTED THE ENTRANCE OF THE BLUE AND crimson-mantled youths. Hammering, lifting, straining workers, smutted with sweat on their chests like globules of oil, looked like refugees who have swum through a submarined tanker's spilled cargo. Poitrine de Carotte, "Red Chest the Armourer," was finishing a great blade. His rufous torso, covered with the coat of fine hairs that appeared like a henna plush broadloom carpet, seemed like the deepened shadow of his fires. New spear-heads, sword-blades, cross-bow springs sparkled among dulled weapons of bygone kings. Inter-weaving lights from flames suddenly aroused by bellows' puffs and from the rose-golden and polar-noon white of molten steel, shot up from the basic gloom of the forge and played among the high ceiling's grey-white cobweb mists on age-black beams. They revealed darkened and rusted steel with now and then the faded belt-gold or dimmed jewels of ancient swords and historic weapons. One of great Clovis', for example, with great bites taken by battle or time out of its blade. The good Dagobert's wicked dagger knife. A bruising knobbed, spiked mace of Lothair's.

Prince Philippe was far more interested in this display, in the armourer's craft and technique than ever he had been in the culinary art of the belly-and-bladder-filling banquets. And this industry and its guild, sanguinary as its objectives might be and less desirable than the beautiful crafts blossoming around the Cathedral, had a great living part in the history of the Middle Ages. The pomp and parade of the lists, the shining armour and golden crests of battle (which, incidentally, had many ugly accompanying things to dim a little of the glamour) did not give the real power and glory to the Middle Ages. These came from the little books and big, their illumination and gay verse and pictures, the exquisite needlework, the light-heart secret of the minstrels, the avid, burning culture of the colleges, the sages' midnight visions and ecstasies, the abbey prayers and scholarship and husbandry, the beautiful carvings on altar and house-front, the wonder of the glass, the soaring Cathedral towers, the Cathedral's amazing integrated unity in infinite mutiplicity, the incredible mass conscience in industry and artistry down to the last cunningly-wrought detail, the shoulder-to-shoulder mobilizings in the ways of the Church, in the raising of altars to God, the whole great galvanic mass surge of work and prayer and piety.

But since men are so Cain-minded, in at least a third of their moods, so bent on battering and breaking, smashing and crashing each other, the very organizing science they introduced into so disorganizing a pursuit is both historically and technically interesting. Absorbing is even the briefest survey of their evolution in technique, ingenious device, in the creating of beauty—the whole changing panorama of the Dark Ages and mediaeval military mailed fashions. Alterations in bustle, skirt, low bodice, have, like Cleopatra's famous nose, done things to history. Not nearly so much, however, as changes in steel neck nape, "nasal," chain-link, breastplate and visor.

Prince Philippe and his squire, rubbing their eyes smarting from the smoke, their noses because of the wry, acrid forged metal smells, could see a good deal of this development up among the age-old rafters, and all around in that puffingly lighted cavernous forge. They took for granted what most of us do not know, that the two main pieces in the knight's wardrobe were—actually—just a cap and a shirt. Through all the wars of the Dark and early Feudal Ages, even up until the fourteen hundreds. The styles, of course, changed, but cap and shirt (or helmet and hauberk) remained basically just those two things—reinforced cap and shirt.

Blue-Mantle and Crimson Mantle, prince and squire, saw a lot of ancient and historic knights' war shirts up among the blackened beams and cobweb tents, all hanging, dully, heavily, like great reinforced dresses or pinafores, though once they had protected, or failed to protect, the lives of great kings.

"All, all your ancestors', my Prince," said the Red Armourer.

"enough Louises to use up all the L's in the schoolbooks. But that thick one is Strong Robert's. The smaller one is Hugh Capet's; he even kept his famous little cape over it all the time. That dented one is Eudes' worn at the north bridge over there when he discharged on the thick Norman heads boulders from ruined Notre Dame and boiling lead from the roof of Saint Etienne."

These battle-shirts, or hauberks, all stretched from chin to knee, and were divided in the middle for striding the mount. For several hundred years the base was leather, a sail-cloth sort of linen, or thick lozenge-quilted cotton. These were completely covered with pieces of horn, leather, or metal. Toward the eleventh century when chain armour came in, these seemingly insufficient hauberks became really quite strong. Their leather or thick fabric bases were effectively and not undecoratingly encased in the macle design of overlapping metal rings, flattish oval ones, arranged in a trellis pattern with studding nail heads on the ring centres, or interlocked rings with strips of reinforcing leather running across.

For those who run to history glamour, the caps were rather more stylish. They were of iron, then steel, round and Juliet-cap-like at first, but developing into a pointed cone or acorn shape, with more steel down the nape of the neck.

The early Middle Ages foot-soldier, the mediaeval foot-slogger, was, of course, worse off, there being no mindedness as yet to make things fairer for the G.I. of the Middle Ages. He had little on over his overworn undershirt and drawers but a war shirt, or jerkin, of heavy quilted fabric or leather, a leather cap-piece, boots, and leggings.

The Early Middle Ages noble had this equipment: An incomplete helmet or casque, by no means covering as yet all the head. The iron- or horn-scaled long shirt, or the improved metal and leather-layered hauberk. Infantryman's leggings and boots on his legs. For weapons he had his shield, his long sword, knobbed mace, spear-lance to furnish the offence that inversely is defence; but his body was poorly protected.

So one can see how badly the opera costumers and fine illustrators have pictorially deceived us, while, of course, giving us a very good show and much fine drama. The old painters badly misrobed Christ. He wore their eternal white perhaps on Transfiguration Mount and in the triumphal entry, *but the shepherd's blue or brown striped dusty white* on His beautiful everyday missions. The Renaissance men did allow Him the scarlet of Pilate's Judgment Hall (and even there two of the gospels differ as to whether it was scarlet or purple; which, of course, is admissible, human eyes differing so about colour). And these great painters have given us, of course, deep beauty, high emotional drama; but there are those who would prefer to have presented less contemporaneity and anachronism, more of the true homely details of Holy Land daily life.

So too book illustrators and stage designers have badly miscostumed the old heroes of chivalry. King Arthur, Alfred, Roland lived during the Dark Ages, or just as there was beginning to be a trifle of light; storied Parsifal and Lohengrin about the time of Arthur's Table Round, long before early crusade and eleventh century chain-mail, centuries before armour made of plate. Jeanne d'Arc did come in time for that shining armour, in 1430; though the Domremy statue does not do fairly by her. It properly encases her in that shining plate, but with the many knight's over and under-things that had accumulated by the fifteenth century, it makes overstocky a girl who was a sturdy peasant yet lithe and elastic enough to lightly mount scaling ladders, to handle horses perfectly, and ride easily in the saddle from dawn to midnight. It was Francis the First who, in the early sixteenth century, came in the height of armour style, the glory of the plate, with all its intricate sliding riveted steel planes and units, the bright inlay of gold and magnificent crests, and long shining spurs which romancers and illustrators mistakenly give warriors who came almost a thousand years earlier.

And these are the things one should keep in mind, to recognize the ages of armour:

The very early reinforced hauberk shirt and round casque and un-protected limbs of the Dark Ages and through the nine hundreds.

The eleventh century chain-mail, with the old casque more pointed.

The chain-mail continuing through the twelfth and thirteenth, now frequently completely covering the body, with the great over-all pot-like helmets coming in. At the end, plate for some joints.

The late fourteenth century's locking the knight in complete plate.

The fifteenth's shining plate armour with cunning hinges, rivets of all sorts for the visored casque.

The sixteenth's beautiful, technically perfect, but decadent efflores-cence when armour was really on its way out.

We can still admire our real historic and story-book heroes of Avalon and Montserrat for courage and high heart and—some of them—for loyalty and purity. But we must strip off their costumes and much of that showman's glamour. Real Arthur, Charlemagne, Alfred, Roland, came in the Dark Ages; fictional Parsifal (or perhaps true Percivale the Pure) and Launcelot no later, possibly some of them back nearer that Twilight of the Gods. Lohengrin, even if you grant him the swan instead of a live horse on which a true king and knight would have entered, would never have come on in that blazing encasing of armour. No, not by almost a thousand years. Nor with that crest. He would have just had on that long shirt hauberk, gleaming perhaps just a little with metal scales, leggings, thick boots. The one rather splendid thing about him would have been his hefty, long, two-handed sword. Much as it may disappoint matinée-goers, the only accoutrement with any chic at all would have been his well-shaped steel casque. It was with such primitive protection, the long pinafore encrusted with horn and iron scales, Tommy Atkins leggings and boots, and the bright casque which salvaged a little of the novelist's glamour, that Parsifal and the Knights of the Table Round would have set out for the Holy Grail.

In the nine hundreds, they spoiled a little the good lines of that early casque by adding a metal "nasal" suggesting the nose-guard of the American football player of the 1890's. However, for the two centuries it was in fashion, it may have served to prevent the slicing off of the long noses which nature seems to have given so many of the able kings of France. Then too they placed under the casque a piece of quilted cloth to prevent chafing, running sores, shock and Caesarian baldness. Most knights of means, in the late nine hundreds, began to wear a meshed chain hood, or *camail,* extending from under the helmet over the necknape and ears.

Discovery and invention moved then at a slower pace than in our day. Little Hugh Capet, who came up almost to the round 1000 A.D., could not add many novelties to his crude armour. All he had over the limited protection of the hardy Roland and Oliver were these just-mentioned things—nasal, casque lining, chain hood, and the iron macles on his hauberk shirt.

A much surer outfit was prepared for William the Conqueror and his "French"—as he calls his 1066 invaders. Prince Philippe had seen William (we can too) in the greatest sampler ever made in this world: the seventy-seven yards of the worsted-worked history at Bayeux. Very early there is pictured the chain-mail which changed mediaeval life as the steam engine the modern. The lively worsted stitches show William as though with ash spear, sword, shield, he were about to execute a little dance.

For battle dress, William wears something very old—the leggings, for instance—and something new: his casque, still with projecting snout "nasal" and hood, is more conical. The hauberk is no longer a heavy cloth shirt with horn pieces or scales. It has completely sloughed off its cloth base. It is all one piece now, of integrated, interlocked links.

Through the early eleven hundreds, and the later ones while

Notre Dame was abuilding, further changes came, in helmet, crest, shoes, and hose. Richard Lionheart (he just scraped the thirteenth century, dying in 1199) more nearly lives up to the glamour artists' ideas. Beginning at the bottom—Richard had very good legs—he had, at very long last, these protected with chain hose, feet with steel shoes, hands with steel thumbed mittens. The hauberk is one seat-slitted and very smoothly working collection of wedded links. Over this is a surcoat to prevent rust of the mail; and on it is some fine escutcheon embroidery. On his helmet is the crest which was an anachronism on Lohengrin and Launcelot. And that helmet was heavier, while the *camail,* or link hood, had been extended beyond the neck to cover the ears and chin.

Though in chain link steel—none of the heavier plate as yet—he was fairly elastic and could vault easily into the steel saddle. Lest some tender soul feel here like calling in the mediaeval S.P.C.A., it should be explained that the squires set under the steel saddles blankets and cushions of sweet-smelling spruce boughs and plants. The fragrance of these was a godsend too, offsetting a little the smell of blood and sweat.

The helmets, in the early thirteenth, went two ways; there was a curious dividing of fashion opinions. In the very late twelfth and early thirteenth there came in the huge over-all helmet, shaped like an inverted truncated cone or a spoutless upside-down coffee pot. It sometimes was one piece with cut-out eye-holes and broad nasal; again a *ventail* (hinged visor) took care of sight and ventilation. The bodies of the early thirteenth-century knights were athletic enough and rather splendid-looking with fairly elastic chain-mail suits and bright surcoats and shields. They were not at all like modern divers below, but like them, a little topheavy-seeming in the heads. The new heavy *heaumes,* or helmets, looked somewhat awesome, ogreish and Hallowe'en-like when knights wearing them bore down on one on foot or unhorsed. But some stuck by the old though improved pointed acorn casque with nasal and hood—now wrapped around the chin. It was as though the armourer-designers split as modern milliners over large picture hats and more compact toques.

There were some who, like Godfrey of Bouillon and our Louis the Ninth, disdained not only the over-all helmet but even the nasal, and plunged regardless into the fray. Clear, under their unaccessoried shining casques, you could see their faces, a puzzling mixture of saintliness and deliberate, conscientious blood-letting. They would find moderns unsympathetic, these fighting God's Fools, but they had their courage and picturesqueness, and in that age their distinct use.

Men were hammering out swords, shaping helms all around the prince and the squire in the fitful, puffing light of the forge. But they were still working at that chief factor of warfare from the 1050's on through the Prince's time: the chain links. The Red Armourer showed them how they were made.

"First we wrap wire tightly around an iron core as that man is doing. The next is cutting this wired core into rings. We flatten out the overlapping ends, pierce them with a punch like that, and insert the rivets. These are hammered flat, as you observe, on that anvil, or finished in a steel vise. Lately we have been interlinking the one link with the surrounding four, as in your suit. Oh, there are lots of tricks to the trade. For instance, that smith there is working the cold chisel, as he should do, from the outside in. On breast-plate and helmet we can concentrate strength at any point we wish. The steel itself is always harder on the outside, that is, the anvil side. But here is your suit, as fine as this forge in its long history ever turned out for any of your royal ancestors."

Almost as lovingly as the armourer the prince examined the cunningly-intertwined links. One or two which the *chef de la forge* did not think shining enough he submitted again to the grinding wheel. With their own grinding wheels, the squires would keep their young chief's armour bright in the palace, even in the Crusades, where, after the conquest of a city, they would remove the blood and grime for the victory parade.

Now nothing would do but that the impatient young prince must try on his shining new suit. His civilian clothes he doffed and hung up on a peg. Instead of measuring their customers with tape for sizes as modern outfitters do, these metal tailors asked their clients to send in their cloth clothes and took from these measurements for the heavy war wardrobes. It made the armourer's forge more than ever a colourful history polyglot, with these gay-hued mantles, tunics, hose, scattered among the historic accoutrements of long-vanished battle-lords and kings.

Over Prince Philippe's skin clothes first went the heavy quilted *haubegon*. Like a shirt the linked hauberk now clanked over his head; they tried it for armpit and groin fit. The two schools of helmet fashion were now drifting into a sort of compromise. The heavy, ogre-eyed, pot helmet was reserved for the jousts by most knights, the pointed casque and hood for war. The squires—another of the Prince's retinue had come in—took in their arms the prince's everyday clothes and the heavy heaume. Now he stood forth armed cap-à-pie, a fine sample of the 1260 knight, of the great age of chain mail. Let us, for accuracy, look at him as he stands brightly outlined and gleaming by the forge.

For the late twelfth and early thirteenth century knight, who fought with blazing valour, if bloodily, through the Crusades, and who thought he was doing a very good thing in trying to win back Christ's Tomb, is about to vanish in the mists of history forever. Chain mail is about to disappear before steel plate as sail would before steam.

Prince Philippe, though his armour base was like his father's, was now more mail-modish and better protected than the king. In fourteenth century pictures, knights are mixed up in styles of the different ages, in casques, grimalkin helmets, chain-mail, plate, some old ones with faces and necks bare. But the main trend is always discernible. And from top down, Philippe ran this way:

Bright acorn casque, or basinet, still with the old nasal. A meshed chain mail hood, the *camail,* muffling now, not only neck-nape and ears, but the chin. A beautifully-wrought one piece, chain-link hauberk. Strips called *ailettes* projecting from the hauberk, for shoulder protection, and looking like decorated angels' or butterfly wings. Two new-style plates, invisible under the hauberk, fore and aft, for defence of back and breast. A surcoat, to prevent mail-rust and display royal arms, over the hauberk. Steel mittens with fairly flexible thumbs. Chain hose. Steel shoes, with revolving rowel spurs.

All this turnout was accented now by the beautifully decorated heraldic devices on the surcoat, ailette wings, and shield. The school of heraldry was still a kindergarten affair, but with Philippe they had done pretty well. He looked the sufficiently decorated, the sufficiently elastic Middle Ages warrior. And he had this advantage. That fine crested casque with its hood was much better-looking than the grotesque examples of mail millinery of the later fourteen hundreds.

Of course, individual knights very early proved ornate exceptions. A century and a half before this prince, Godfrey of Bouillon in the Holy Land had diamonds, topazes, emeralds set in his helmet, and embroidered white drapes put on his horse.

All these millenial mail military modes went on at a leisurely pace. As prince and squires gather up his outfit and his father's sword, and before they place them for his vigil near the tabernacle in Notre Dame, we must peer swiftly over their shoulders into the future to see the flamboyant armour climax. Towards the thirteenth century's end, all added knee-caps, plate greaves, like the old football shin-guards for the legs, and revolving eight-point rowel spurs. Before the fourteen hundreds came in, the knight was almost encased in plate. All that was left was improvement in fittings, the addition of plumes, gilding, decorations.

It would be even harder then for the knight when he was unhorsed. With all the added weight, he was like a submerged man, and couldn't come up for air. Sometimes, when they unharnessed him, it was difficult for the squires. There was all too acrid and pungent a smell of sweat, blood, of excrement exuded by fear in the armour.

The top of the knight had been changed most. In the old casque he had looked pretty well. In the middle period, heavy, ogre-eyed *heaume* he'd have scared Ichabod Crane. In the early thirteen hundreds, his helmet casque, now called a *basinet,* was cleverly equipped with a riveted sliding visor. The warrior looked all right when he rode by to salute the ladies, with lance and visor up. When the visor was down, it had been so snouted out that he looked like a penguin. But, of course they would pretty this visor up for the fifteen hundreds, Henry the Fifth, Henry the Eighth, and polished, urbane Francis the First, for the splendiferous, silken-tented, glittering knight-mane-quinned "Field of the Cloth of Gold."

There was one accessory avoided in the outfits of today. Like a big flower, the mediaeval metal jock-strap, the cod-piece, proclaimed the knight's sex in front. Conveniently it was hinged and latched for relief on the march. Luckily, for Jeanne, there was the bright surcoat to cover it up.

When the era of the over-all steel plate came in, the *camail* and nasal had long since gone. The helmet was too complete, and they had a gorget like a steel collar bone around the neck. They even began to do away with the shield. Almost the only remnant of the old armour was some chain-mail, showing like a slip in the seat, for the saddle. Even the mittens had given way to gauntlets of steel with exceedingly flexible fingers.

Hardly an inch of this man-knight, as the Middle Ages closed, was vulnerable. He was a flexible sheath of plates all over. These were admirably riveted and strong, giving free play all over for the body. And here and there were underplates beneath the strong outer ones. Critical parts, like shoulders, elbows, underarms were fitted with little pleated accordion-like plates—they were astonishing—and bosses, cops, rings guarded vulnerable joints outside. There seemed to be as many little static or movable units all over his body as there are pieces in the gear of a ship.

It was most amazing. Never had man—or woman—been a more beautifully turned-out or a more efficiently functioning thing. The question, of course, was whether the sport was worth so expensive a candle. And aside from that workableness and practicality and the sheer beauty of the mechanism, he added an external beauty of streaming plumes and remarkable gold in-lays (the Maximilians and Italian petty princes lavished fortunes on this, but the French showed the better taste).

And the heraldry school turned post-graduate. The intertwined designs and heraldic insignia were spread all over shields, surcoats, banners, pavilions. There developed a tourney protocol as elaborate as that of a modern congress. Lull wrote it all up in that big book.

Then, of course, just as the flamboyant phase inundated the true Gothic—remember the Rouen Palais de Justice which, unhappily, was bombed in the Second World War and parts of its Cathedral—an over-ornate trend inundated this admirable armour. Crécy, Civitale, to be sure, had something to do with it. Just as the great full-rigged ships shook out unheard-of pieces of top hamper and sky canvas, and became all too beautiful as they were about to be forever whisked away by the genie steam, the suits of armour became all too mechanically ingenious, and gorgeous just as they were about to vanish at a whiff of gunpowder. In an abortion of chivalry, a decay of pageant, the once robust knights would go down in an inextricable tangle of plumes, gay pennons and tabards and inlaid mail, to remain stock characters only for the period-mixing novelist and the romantic school-girl and not even for her when the aeroplane entered the sky lists. Still, it had been a gallant and fascinating, if bruising game.

As the three heavily-burdened young men came, heavily-clanking, under the pieces of armour up into the palace yard, the forge hammers, tools, and cold chisels sounded again in that clinking counterpoint to the harmonious booming resonance of the Cathedral bell, the voice of Paris. It was the *Ave Maria* bell now ringing out the Angelus. Nine strokes the great bell made in three-triplet, ancient Ave Maria rhythm.

The Angelus was never rung then at dawn or noon as it would be in some countries in later centuries. Theoretically it was supposed to sound after Compline, the last office of the evening. Actually it was rung, as now, just after Vespers. Well the prince knew that bell. He had climbed the towers to see its famous inscription. Like so many immemorial sentences that are soul reassurances of Mother Church, the "May his soul and the souls of all the faithful departed rest in peace," "Holy Mary, Mother of God, pray for us sinners now and in the hour of our death," the old words, *"Ave Maria, gratiae plena, Dominus tecum,"* carved in the rim of the great bell, always gave the prince, a thoughtful man like his father, a feeling of nostalgia for a far-off country.

As the great bell rang out, they made for the palace where Prince Philippe would go through the ceremonies of the bath, the donning of the required garments, vermilion robe, gold spurs, and all, as we shall see, and then place every piece of his armour on the high altar before Our Lady, near the tabernacle for consecration through nearness and association, while he prayed the long night through. His sword would be blessed by the bishop at dawn.

XVI

*The Colée, Accolade, Black Shoes, Gold Spurs, Vermilion Robe
of the New Knight. . . . Mediaeval Nihilism of Degraded Knights
and the Commandments of the True Ones. . . . The Midnight Vigil
before Christ and Our Lady and the Blessing of the Sword. . . . For
All its Faults, Chivalry protects the Weak, defends the Faith, gives
to the Poor with a Magnificent Munificence. . . . The Hounds of
Notre Dame. . . . The Pope bans Cross-bow and Arbaleste as Cruel;
the Armies do not heed him. . . . The First Attempt at a United
Nations.*

1266 A.D.

THE ABBOT OF SAINT DENIS, OVER FROM HIS ABBEY, WAS A
little disturbed. He sat opposite Prince Philippe in the Palace,
uprightly ensconced in a chair so high it rose even above his
snowy mountain peak of a head, his eyes, strangely for so old a man,
of the hue of violets. He was the spiritual adviser of the prince and
continued so when Philippe became the Third, the King. He had
come to talk with him on the eve of the sacred vigil which would
usher in the youth's entrance into knighthood which, truly under-
taken, should prove his spiritual coming of age. So did all true kings
and leaders take it.

Stopping at a bookstall for a wanted treatise, he had come on some
things that distressed him at such a moment. In the tourney chapter
we met some degenerate rhymsters who took a malicious delight in
composing ribald blasphemies to upset people. Many of these were
unworthy goliard minstrels, others degraded knights. Their heraldic
devices had been effaced, their heraldry trailed in the mud. Heralds
had thrown basins of dirty water on them, had ridden them on
hurdles covered with undertakers' cloths, and priests had recited over
them the offices for the dead, for dead they were to true knighthood.
They longed to get even with their quills.

On the bookseller's counter was Raoul de Cambrai's brutal, "Put my
tent in the Church, my bed on the altar, my hawks on the crucifix!"

255

A Mayecais piece, "Thou shalt not keep thy word, shalt betray honest men, uphold evil, abase God, ravish the poor, disinherit the orphans, and violate every one of thy oaths." Also another pretty one, "Don't believe in anything. If you meet a good man, beat him. Do wrong. Commit sin wherever you go." Then this awful one, "Be cannibals of priests. Their flesh is exquisite. Try it!"

These perverse blasphemies, usually kept under the bookshop counter, had been brought out for a very rich, libidinous student who spent all his time in potting and cuckolding tradesmen's wives, and was headed for expulsion. Unfortunately these hot specimens had been left out, when the bookseller's attention had been called away, for a high churchman to see.

Perhaps not too much attention should be paid to them, as we thought when we read the others. They were curiously obscene and exceptional phenomena, coming at the end of a reign so upright as Saint Louis', perhaps a tribute to its excellence, as vice and hypocrisy are really unconscious salutes to virtue. Perhaps, too, as we suspected before, the composers were just having fun with people, though rather reprehensibly. Possibly some of them were just sticking out tongues, making faces with words.

The Angelus of the Notre Dame Ave Maria bell, which the returning young prince had heard, scattered some of the abbot's troubled thoughts like incense with its sweetness. But the ghost, the evil spirit of them lingered slightly. And almost as though to make sure the prince had not been contaminated by any of this new thought of the day, he asked him to name the Commandments of Knighthood. The young man did. They were very impressive, and showed how religious a base had the true Chivalry of the Middle Ages:

> Believe all the Church teaches and obey its injunctions.
> Defend the Church.
> Respect weakness and protect it.
> Love thy native land.
> Do not fear the enemy.
> Fight against the foe continuously, mercilessly.
> Respect scrupulously thy feudal duties so long as they do not violate
>   the laws of God.
> Never lie; keep thy pledged word.
> Be generous. Give largesse to everyone.
> Be everywhere the champion of the right against evil.

"You have taken these commandments deep into your mind, my son, and with all your heart, as knight, will cleave to them?"

The prince bowed. "Yes, father."

The abbot looked at the boy with the strangely flower-like hue of his eyes under the noble Alp slope of brow and crown. So often one's work went for naught. Here, he felt in his heart, it hadn't.

So, as through the two narrow arrow slits of the palace apartment, two slanting shining spears of sunlight fell athwart the rushes and strip of gay carpet, the abbot gave a little review for the boy of all the fine things pertaining to knighthood, of its great literature which he had been studying through the preceding weeks. It was a final but a heartening cramming for the great soul examination of that night and at dawn.

It was a review which dissipated any recollections of the sub-rosa, under-counter, mediaevally bootlegged scurrilities and rhymed irreverences which had for the moment troubled the saintly old man. For the literature of knighthood was a noble literature. Fit answer it would be for the cynical synthesis of bad-livered chroniclers later. It was not a complete defence, the wise old man knew, for the system of feudalism, with which chivalry at times became entangled. Feudalism was like, he would have said could he have seen so far forward, the later capitalism. Neither would be the final answer. Both carried within them the proverbial seeds of their ultimate collapse, or, if not quite that, their sliding into something more enlightened. But for the times both, with all their faults, would buttress society. At least this feudalism was the only workable system at hand. The priest must support it to the moral extent of teaching respect for order, one's oaths and legal superiors. But he could try to elevate it.

And chivalry fortunately grew clear above it, knew an idealism feudalism could not know. Despite all the falsity, looting, and pretence of certain lords in mail, there was the never to be denied minority of true knights that served as the leaven of which Christ spoke, and which, on occasion, in crises could raise the mass of their fellows into mighty movements. At least there was always that possibility. And, anyway, what counted was the high standard, the ideal towards which some reached. And this whole literature of chivalry, of knighthood, breathed it, despite the amourous outpourings of Provençal Courts of Love. And they were not wholly untouched by it.

From the very beginning the priests had referred to knights as "men of God." And that is the way the sincere knight looked at it. In early mediaeval field and church masses the knights held their cross-hilts upright in making their vows to keep the faith of Christ.

"What a beautiful salute that is to Christ, my boy!" said the abbot, referring to this custom. Then he went on: "What was it that Pope Gregory the Ninth said?"

The prince could repeat it: "The Son of God whom the battalions of the celestial army obey has established here below as a sign of

His divine puissance, a certain number of knights. As the tribe of Judah received a special blessing from on high, so the knights of France and France herself had been endowed by the Hand of God with especial graces and privileges."

The white head nodded. "And Saint Bernard?"

This was in exculpation of the crusading knight: To submit to die for Christ or to cause His enemies to die is naught but glory. . . . The soldier who brings death to a malefactor is not a homicide but a malecide ("an evil-killer").

"And Charlemagne?"

"Well, Almeric of Narbonne remarked to him: 'Your true knights are both very poor and very proud.' And Charlemagne replied, 'Nothing is more true. Still does not God reign? The best prayer is that which heart puts in words!'"

"Nobly said and well repeated," said the abbot.

"Also Charlemagne remarked," said the prince: "'Frenchmen are good. They fight like mighty soldiers.'"

"That," corrected the abbot, "was his nephew."

"And the books are full of our France," went on the prince, his eyes, lighter blue than the old man's, lighting up impulsively. "That book *The Gay Knight* says of the French Crusader in the Holy Land, 'When the soft wind blows from the direction of my native land, I fancy I inhale the perfume of Paradise.' I wonder if I'll feel like that when I'm over there."

"That has little to do with your coming vigil."

"And this fine old poem goes on," continued the youth, unheeding in his patriotic enthusiasm: "'Death approaches. Let us, as becomes brave Frenchmen, die fighting!'" Doubtless the pieces of his new armour on which he gazed had something to do with his spirit now.

"Well, I suppose there is no doubt but that our dear land is the cradle of chivalry. However—"

"Take this now: 'The chief of all countries' crowns is that of France and the first King of France was crowned by the angels.'"

"I'm afraid you won't be, my boy, though your responsibilities, with the anointing will come direct from God. And we are straying, if only a little, from the humility that is the first step toward becoming a knight, a 'man of God.'"

He spoke then, as the Seine waves lapped softly against the cone towers which you too can see if you wish (both towers and Seine), of the constant injunctions in chivalry's literature, about higher things. Over and over the candidate was warned against drunkenness and treachery. Again and again he was told that he who aspired to Heaven must be pure in mind as well as in body.

These verbal sign posts found in so many mediaeval books reveal unmistakably the high standard set. Also there was a surprising number of knights who, under the impulsion of their vows and the warm feeling they had that they were doing a distinct service to God in fighting for the Tomb, did preserve abroad and at home a rigid chastity of mind and body.

And generosity was an ever-recurrent theme. Philippe could quote by the hour from his studies, from all the books he and his father had, and all he had read in the Sainte Chapelle Library. Back and forth from abbot to student prince went the quotations now: Robert of Blois: "What is learning after all, if cupidity goes with it? What is valour in covetous calculating knights?" From the *Chanson d'Aspremeont* in Charlemagne's time: "Do not be stingy in your expenditures, even though not a farthing may remain in your coffers."

An ancient missal read: "It is not enough to relieve the poor, the widows and orphans, you must go further, embrace in its widest scope the words largesse and charity. To disinherited good men and true, distribute your wealth, riches, furs, the vair and the grey. And do not make promises. Just give." From an old chronicler then: "The true knight gives. That is the real secret of the great and the powerful." And for the oath: "Keep your pledged word. The God who never lies keep you knights true."

It was like a confirmation or instruction class for admission to the Church. And here was an apt pupil, after his father's own heart, ready to graduate. And knighthood, the abbot impressed upon Prince Philippe, was an institution second only to the Church, indeed a branch of it.

For a breathing space the abbot and the prince tried the fruit on the table near—the boy was to fast the rest of the night. For relief, too, as he now leaned against the wall by the arrow-slit, he listened to the song of a minstrel who had strayed over from the usual haunts on the Little Bridge, hoping for some deniers from the palace. "Give, give, give!" the old missals had bidden the knights. He tossed a silver piece down. It made a clear ring on the pavement; and was a fortune to the poor singer of dying strings and fading patches.

The song was as out of tune with the lesson as the strings were out of tune with the true notes they tried to hit. But it was pretty and poignant:

> "As candle in the wind,
>   Snow-flake in the stream,
>   The dew on the grass,
>   So brief is life!

"So glow, candle, with life,
Dance merrily, snow,
Dew, throb with the dawn,
So brief is life!"

But lovely as the song was, such wistfulness was not for the true knight about to endure an austere vigil, have his sword blessed, and then depart for the wars.

So, the Compline bell sounding now, he went through the final principles long ago established for the *parfait* knight. Poverty, humility, generosity, purity, valour, truth, they had pretty well covered. Now they came to the loveliest qualities of all, tenderness, love:

From an ancient missal of the 1000's: "The bounded vowed duty of the knight is to sustain the weak and to see that none of the strong shall oppress them."

And from this same Saint Peter's missal: "Be the living protection of all weakness."

There was a passage from a poem, *Girars de Viane,* to which the abbot himself called attention, perhaps because of the very fact that he was a churchman. It was double-barrelled, stressing the obedience the Church felt must be paid to the superiors to whom one was bound by his feudal vows, and yet protecting against any persecution, by these superiors, of the weak:

"As soon as one holds a fief he is bound by law to come to the assistance of his liege lord, on every needful occasion, provided that same liege lord does not try to disturb the Church of God nor to harm poor folk, for no one can be bound by any fealty vow to wage war against God."

And, mind you, even the lofty liege lord had his responsibilities, not through this rather holy knighthood, we mean, but through that very same feudalism, which was not all one-sided. A noble swears right out of ancient literature—the noble himself: "By Saint Peter I will work and sweat and labour too, to protect us both, through the covenant of Holy Church, and so that you my vassals and freeholders may be spared from the wicked men that would destroy us. And I will keep off and hunt all hares, badgers, boars, that break your hedges, kill your fowl and crush your wheat."

As for that true knight, like Geoffrey de Bouillon and Louis the Ninth, who quite as much as the great Cathedral was the product of the Middle Ages and the Gothic, there were three more quotations in the instruction lesson:

William of Charroi had declared: "If any one injures these little

ones, here is the sword that shall cut off the heads of such traitors
and robbers." He was not boasting.

Again the Saint Peter's missal had this: "Be thou the defender
and the bold champion of the Church, the *widow, and the orphan.*"

William of Durand, who was as much of an authority on the
spiritual side of knighthood as Lull was on its physical, its tournament etiquette and protocol, gives as one "Knight's Benediction":
"Oh, God, Thou hast permitted the use of the sword to curb the malice
of the wicked and to defend the right. Grant therefore that Thy new
knight may never use the sword to injure unjustly anyone wherever
he may be, but that he always may use it in defence of all that is good
and right."

No, whatever of scandal you or we may rake up out of the Middle
Ages, we cannot discount this same knight.

The abbot raised his fingers in blessing, put on his mantle and
biretta and went down the narrow circling winding palace castle
stair. The violet eyes, so odd yet so beautiful in the old face, had dew
upon them. He loved the boy, but very likely he would not see him
again. "But he will be leal," he said, to himself but aloud, as he
descended, "he will be true."

Not that the Abbot of Saint Denis was not glad to see him go.
The Church had done what it could to mitigate the harshnesses of
war. The Pope had banned arbaleste and shaft, which he thought
(it was all a matter of degree) multiplied wounds greatly in massed
battles. It did not entirely negate the effort that the ban was little
heeded. The ideal of Pope and Church was what counted. On the
other hand, soften war as it might try to do, the Church was careful
not to soften the soldier. He was needed for righteous war and
robustness was needed for that. Violators of law. Breakers of treaties.
Those who refused to right wrong when admonished, to restore
expropriated properties and moneys. Oppressors of the weak. Enemies
of God. Anti-Christs. Wars against such the Church must sanction,
at least until a better way was found.

Poor knight, poorer Christian, the Church held, was he who would
not lend his body to the fight against evil. To be sure, mistakes,
misguesses, were made in the indictments of evil. There were times
when it was rather a case of aberration and unsoundness, negative
ills, rather than pronounced positive active evils. But in the majority
the instinct of Church and hierarchy was right. What they attacked
principally were flagrant offenses against law, injustices, tyrannies,
underminings of the Church, which was Christ's body, and attacks
on God Himself.

So the knight must ever be ready to place his body in holy jeopardy in a just war, just as the saints of old had given their bodies to the torch. Early this truth had been impressed on the well-inclined, devoutly-trained mind of Prince Philippe: there were two martyr-doms, that of the saint, and that of the knight. He was ready.

Even so, with holy warfare justified, as by Saint Bernard when he defined the killing of a truly evil man not as homicide but as malecide (which is at the opposite pole from today's miserable genocide), the Church continued with preaching might and excommunicating main to reduce the actual bloody physical contacts. Curiously, as most moderns do not know, she went forward toward her goal of peace, almost inch by inch, increasing here and then there the intermissions between fighting. There were the natural times when men got bored, went home for harvests or procreation. The Church added the "Truce of God." First, only one day was ruled out from fighting, from Saturday night until Monday dawn. Then with an admirable and conscientious diplomacy the prelates called attention to the fact that Ascension came on a Thursday. Thursday went out from the military calendars. And there was Good Friday. Again the impressionable nobles and knights were impressed. All Fridays went out. Saturday the mediaevalists reckoned as the time when Christ actually rose from the Tomb, though the Mary who loved Him did not discover it until the Sunday morning when she took him for the Gardener of Calvary. These quarrelsome, bellicose, but at times such amenable and devout children, ready for any interpretations from on high, assented. On Saturdays too they left off their mail and attended to hedges, hops, moats, forges and their estate *ménages*. Soon too they excluded Lent and Advent. There was left but one fourth of the time for what had been considered their main pursuit, and the Church was trying to make it even less. France, with a will, observed this "Truce of God." The English, not liking it, as a rule, demurred. This truce applied only to private wars. The Church decreed that the war in the East for the salvaging of the Saviour's Tomb must go on. Still, though it was but that inch-by-inch advance toward the Church's eternal goal, "the peace of God," it had its great effect on frail human beings.

Another valiant effort has been lost sight of now: this was the Church-inspired enlisting of a great host of knights called *"Paciari,"* which is to say, "peace-keepers." All were vowed to try to enforce the peace on all fronts in Christendom. Three quarters of a thousand years ago, here was an attempt at a United Nations' police force!

And well was the individual soul looked after in these far-off battles, at least before hostilities were joined. Every knight and soldier, except the renegades (and some of these) confessed on the eve or dawn before the conflict. Peter Lombard, the Paris bishop, compiler of that best-selling book, the *Sentences,* writes of a provision of the Church in his time—similar to that for baptism—for the confession of the soldier when no priest is at hand. Peter tells us: "One ought to confess first to God, to the priest afterwards, and if none is there, to some relative or friend." Following the innumerable confessions there were field masses, such as have never been since, at which whole armies with their armour shining in the rising sun flashed a new splendour on ancient sacred mount and plain, as they knelt as one man before the altar.

Philippe being, like his father, very often of serious vein was glad that his knighting was not to be attended, because of his father's absence and all the casualties caused by war, with all the old romantic colourful hullabaloo, but was to be very simple. This fitted in well too with the mood of the times. Once it had been more or less of a secular affair. Some well-known noble, the sponsor of the knight, attended to the actual dubbing, with the *colée,* a sort of rabbit blow on the neck. High-born ladies had attended to the fitting of the virgin armour; then there had been the caracolling and all the stomach stuffing afterwards.

To be sure, this secularity had been somewhat redeemed by the old actual vigil all night in the chapel of the castle or the nearest monastery. As a matter of fact, in character it was not unlike some modern weddings which are solemnized by the mass, but then, in *estaminet,* descend to much horseplay with a touch of vulgarity afterwards. But of late the Church, especially in this golden and propitious time, had taken over for its own the dubbing and most of the ceremonies. In reality the Church took over for its own the new knight (or as many as it could of him) as one who was sworn to serve the Church and whose vows and higher mission made him something more than a layman of the parish.

Servitors brought in ewers of water and poured them into the tub for the bath which preceded the vigil. Prince Philippe then put on the silk and linen under-things, and cast over this a tunic of white, then a robe of ermine. The squires now took up the pieces of his new armour, black shoes, gold spurs, and a vermilion robe, and carried these down the staircase to the bridge palace entrance. His queen mother was waiting and kissed him good-bye. With all the bright accoutrements, and little candles, the small procession passed through the streets—the little children clapping their hands—into the Cathedral Square. At the portal the bishop awaited them.

Philippe had made his confession in Sainte Chapelle after vespers, and now, according to custom, he passed down the nave, with his own sword held slantwise, the squires following with the armour and red robe. They came to the great rood screen which in the Middle Ages made a division between the audience space in nave and aisles and the holy place, the sanctuary, not wholly shutting out sight of the sacred mysteries there, but veiling them a little. Genuflecting, the squires gave the armour to the bishop, who, piece by piece, placed them on the high altar under which the prince's great-grandmother was buried, and right near the Presence in the tabernacle. Nearness to this, the sacred association, would sanctify, they believed, the prince's weapons and make him wage more valiantly the fight against evil. Over the kneeling boy, the bishop now preached a minute sermon whose burden was "Love God."

So he was left alone by the altar, spread with his armour, to spend the whole night in prayer, the sacred light burning red above his head. For long spells his lips moved in prayer with a fervour which this good prince truly felt. Sometimes he knelt; on occasion, as was allowed him, he stood, for relief. And since no young man's mind can be every minute filled with petitions or the holy emotions that should accompany them, sometimes it seemed to him eerie there, above the illustrious dead, with the Holy Presence to which in his humility he felt himself, as a very ordinary and human and frail young man, altogether too near. The muted chirps of birds, lost among the rafters and wandering like lost ghosts high up near the beautiful vaulting combings, came down to him. The mastiff dogs, like those which still protect the Cathedral by night, with strap and chain leashes in the hand of the patrolling night watchman, guarding against theft of sacred vessels such as the poor prodigal Villon committed in a church on the hill, padded all night around the aisles, the pillars, and in chapel corners.

A ghostly little procession of canons came silently through the side Red Door near midnight, solemnly to chant the grave melodious measures of matins. More palely than the sun by day, the moon now shone through the serried rows of windows, purple and golden emerald and gules, cast almost indiscernible traceries on the cold paving stones, the *requiescats* inscribed in old Gothic there, and played eerily athwart pillar and gallery, on giant crucifix and long gone saint. Ever it revealed the hanging figure above him. Sometimes in the feeling of the place and of his solemn obligations, there came an overwhelming longing to restore for the Christ His Tomb, in repa-ration for all His sorrows, the most vivid of which were so sadly depicted there. And in the feeling a sob caught in his throat. Then he thought of His peace of which the abbot had reassured him, and he saw His Mother, the Eternal Mother of us all, standing in blue, with the gold lilies beside her, her features still white in the night, but with, too, a holy joy and peace on her face. There was many an Ave Maria he said to her. And the peace of the Mother, above all of Her Son, came to him. He feared no more. In the spell of it, he almost fell asleep on his knees. His watching squire caught him. The long night over, the bishop, deacon, and subdeacon priests, in full vestments, came in for the knight's final vows and his confirmation into the ranks of Our Lady's, God's own knights.

There were many variations of the ceremonies since the Church had so very properly taken over, as the historian of chivalry, Lambert d'Ardre, and William Durand tell us, but this was the way the Notre Dame rite went then, beginning with that vested procession of the clergy. When the candidate donned the vermilion robe, the priest spoke of what it symbolized: "Remember the passion and death of Christ." He added, "Be ready to shed every drop of your blood in defence of Christ." At these solemn injunctions, the somewhat square-set features of the prince had much of the religious look of his father; in the light from the altar candles and the reflection of the sacred vessels, they appeared, for the moment, carved cameo-white.

All the pieces of armour the bishop had blessed. The girdle went on, then the heavy hauberk, which jingled like sacring bells. The squires helped him with gleaming casque, martial gauntlets, hose, shoes, the long gilded spurs; and the bishop admonished him: "Be obedient to the Divine as the charger is to your spur."

The bishop gave a special blessing to the sword. Once, even in the early limited religious rite, the old *colée,* or dubbing blow, had been accompanied by but a few words: "Awake from dull sleep and rise to the honour and faith of Christ." Now the Church had a more elaborate and truly beautiful knighthood office.

Just as the priest gives to the newly-confirmed light buffets on the cheek, he gave lightly on the neck the accolade.

At Saint Peter's in Rome (and all this shows how serious was the intent of the true knight) they had this in the office: "Take this sword and with it exercise justice and cut down injustice. Defend the Church of God and all faithful ones. With it disperse the enemies of Christ. Raise up what is saintly and what you have elevated preserve. Put down injustice and strengthen what is of good report. By these means, all radiant in the triumph of virtues, you will reach the Heavenly Kingdom where, with Christ, whose type you have become, you will reign eternally."

But just as the dawn coming up over the Seine seemed to be filling the Cathedral, from great pillar base to highest arch point, with a

new light like the blessing of God, the bishop used the two Notre
Dame prayers for the accolade and the blessing of the sword:

"Bless this sword so that Thy servant may in the future be in oppo-
sition to all cruelty of the pagan foes, and remain the defender of the
Church, of widows and orphans and all who fear God.

"Bless this sword, Holy Lord and all-powerful Father, eternal God;
bless it in the name of the coming of Christ, and by the descent of the
Holy Ghost. Grant that Thy young servant, always possessing love
as his armour"—there was more than one parallel in the knight's vesting to the priest's—"may tread down his enemies and, victorious, may
be sheltered from all harm."

The young knight took the sword, wiped it under his arm in token
of cleansing it of the blood of those enemies of God. Those on whom
this gesture does not set well should call to mind the times, the
universal acceptance of certain things by the purest and greatest
leaders of the age, the general absence of non-violence, and the
sturdy feeling of the grand majority that the knight worth his salt
must go out and not simply pray for the kingdom of God on this
earth, but physically fight for it.

It was, naturally, all rote to some, of meaning to some who later,
in the outside world, forgot it. There were many, like the young
prince, with whom the memories of the vigil and the consecration
remained always.

At the last the priest took the sword again and said to him, "Receive
it in the name of the Father and the Son and the Holy Ghost." Crossing himself, the young knight took the sword, thrust it in his scab-
bard and then as a final salute drew it and raised it on high pointing
toward Heaven.

He did not go home. With his little squadron of squires and men-
at-arms, he passed out of the east gate. As he went, the trumpets
sounded. He carried before him the sword, so like his father's, of
which he was so proud. In the palm's-breadth-high sun it glittered like
a long splinter from it. Somehow sun and trumpets and sword seemed
one and the same.

His old friends up in Saint Jacques on the Hill saw him go. They
raised their hands both in farewell and benediction.

XVII

*Thomas Aquinas starts a Little Text-book to help Struggling Boys,
but it turns out one of the Six Greatest Books in the World. . . . He
brings Home a Guest from Greece. . . . The Noblest B.C. Men too
have Light. . . . A Heaven-high Ladder. . . . Stout Shoes, Soap,
Abbey Budgets, Fertilizers, Angel Wings. . . . Dawn in the Mediaeval Gardens of Paris. . . . A Scientific Discovery in the Abbey
Garden. . . . Great Hymns of the Middle Ages and an Affirmation
for the Sons of Men.*

1269 A. D.

THOMAS AQUINAS SAT IN HIS CELL. HE HAD EATEN THE BREAD
and the fruit of the frugal meal in the refectory. Now he must
work far into the night. He had to hurry if with all his other
duties, some of which took him far away, he was to finish the great
book, which he did not take for great but something of a help for
poor students on the hill.

Meagre was the furniture in his cell compared with the magnificent
furnishing of his mind. For him simplicity sufficed: a pallet, tin ewer,
basin, slop-jar, pegs for clothes, a row of books by his friends in the
flesh, and the friends of the past, a sloping desk. At this he worked
after covering the space near it with manicure-like slivers from a
goose quill which he sharpened to a better point. A little candle
lighted him uncertainly with its swayings in the wind. There was
nothing uncertain about the strong torso, the great head, and the
calm face with its earthen hue that showed against the cell window.
About him was a sustained poise that could melt into a consecrated
humility when he knelt and prayed at the sound of a summoning
convent bell. But for most of the hours he wrote on pieces of paper
of a peculiar periwinkle blue--for the night's stint, and for the ages.
Above him, over all the room, in stark simplicity and grandeur
loomed a large crucifix.

He was now at Question Fifty-six (or was it Sixty-one?). He
would not finish all these Socratic building-up questions here in Paris.

He had worked away at them in Rome, Cologne, Naples, London, on all his trips. Very simple seemed his intention as he expressed it at the start. He was just going to write a little book, a text-book sort of affair that would make things easier for the students everywhere. clear up God and knowledge for them. This simplicity was not affected. He meant it. But the result turned out tremendous. The little help-and-answer book turned out the biggest book of all the great ones we saw the illustrious scholars lugging in that endless immortal parade up the hill. It would become, this *Summa Theologica* or Sum of Belief, one of the six greatest books ever, of those most lasting in influence. It would coordinate, as no work had ever done before, the doctrine of the Church, and prove a storehouse too for other creeds coming after. Seven centuries after he wrote on the blue paper at his little desk so certainly in the uncertainty of the candle flame, it would give not only seminarians but all thoughtful students their peerless example in logic, give depth to clever men like Chesterton and his crowd, and a life's labour to the most gifted modern philosophers like Maritain.

What he had done very really, and not merely in a manner of speaking, was to build a gigantic soaring ladder of all those questions. Laid end to end they furnished the sides. The answers which he furnished too were the rungs. On these rungs a man might mount to Heaven and the knowledge of it.

It was not all of virgin lumber. He had borrowed side-pieces and rungs for it. From Paul. Augustine. Erigena. All the old Doctors. Now an old abbot of Saint Denis. Again one from Saint Victor's. Also from Peter Lombard, his friends, Alexander, above all, Albert. But now and then he had had to go into some far mysterious deep forest, whither only the Voice of God, the whispers of angels led him. There, unseen, he cut and hewed his virgin timber.

The coventual compline bell now rang out. He did not go to the chapel; in his cell he was admittedly doing God's work. But he did go through the office there, much of the time kneeling, though of late, when he was still in his prime, he had an unusual stiffness and aching in his bones. Cell floors, prayers, vigils made for arthritis and rheums. The old scholars did not mind this too much. They had a compensating health that came way in the interior, sharpening their minds, intensifying their souls.

Now one might have guessed from an opening sentence that this little supposed scholar's help would take on more. His purpose, he had said there, "had been first to discuss God's Nature, then the progress of creatures toward Him, finally Christ, the way by which we approach God." It was a large order. In any age. Particularly then when God was not being patronized, diminished, banished, as in a later day, but when He was Source, Cause, Effect, everything.

Try some of the ladder rungs and sides. See how high that heavenly ascent reached. The sublime Creation—seven days? Seven aeons? What matter? The dramatic, symbolic, or very real Fall, through the failure of man to measure up to his heritage. We do not care for that now. Less for what came thereby—original sin. All the result of physical and psychological conditioning? Thomas would have admitted that, but would have added more. The more that counted. These old fellows were not escapists. They faced up to sin like men, wrestled with it, threw it, or recognized it by humble confession and crying aloud for the mercy of God. Curiously historians would back them. They have seen so much of this original sin, this incorrigibility which leads whole bodies of men, races entire to try, through curiosity and perversity, the very evil they have seen and known to have brought ruin on other races, their very ancestors.

But Thomas would not do what others after him did (Calvin, for one, who would study on that very hill, across the way from where Thomas sat at his sloping desk now): have God deliberately, calmly damning people. He leafed through the periwinkle questions. No, he had thought over that for many years. A moth played like a disembodied spirit around his candle flame. People were like that moth, but God desired to save them. For this He had a consuming passion. The Divine would have felt itself lost without the union with the human that had sprung from it. The foolish moth was singed in the flames. Thomas took up the quill. Predestination? Premotivating? Foreknowledge? Knowing all, God knows each man's nature and the way it will lead a man? With all these eternal soul problems Thomas had wrestled through the years.

The deep convent bell seemed to channel into sound the reverberating depths of his thought. But man undeniably, forever, had free will. He would stake everything on it. God, so great was that passion for redemption, was eternally whispering a cue to the right road. Divine grace? *And* free will? Yes. One thing a man had to learn—that truth was made up of paradoxes. The paradoxes were the twin legs that held up the torso of truth. Until a man had learned that, until he had learned not to be bewildered by but to accept paradoxes he never would be adult. The exact answers he would know when he climbed after death even beyond his high heavenly ladder. Grace there was, and free will there was. A man *could* choose the Good. He would fight for that. And so eternally would the Church.

And there was that magnificent unraveling of the universal problem of what to do with man. In spite of some worthy accomplishments, the mass of him had undeniably failed. God came to earth to save him. If genius is a little glint of God in an individual, here was the greatest bursting forth and illumination of genius in history. God came to earth in Christ and took over the sin which must in a balanced universe be requited, and the consequent agony.

Here in his cell, as so often, Thomas Aquinas felt surcharged by the glory of it. So truly and actively did it express itself in him that often he turned aside from his eternal questions to compose hymns like his beautiful and memorable *Ave Verum*—"Behold the True Body." At night he wrote these, and he wrote them singingly.

But if he had, like Saint Teresa, his ecstasies, and his mind soared to Heaven with his visions, he kept his strong body and legs firmly planted on the good earth. He kept earth and heaven linked by a superb sanity and common sense. That is the way with the greatest saints and it is proof of their belief's validity. Stout shoes. Angels' wings. Abbey budgets. Absolution, missals and scrub-brushes. Soap and Immortality. The soaring soul and the humblest bodily functions. Choir sheets, alms, fevers, chives, cabbages, water organs, confession. Fertilizers, the flowering graces, baptisms, scapulars, the primitive abbey sanitation, rosaries, lead for roofs, wood for crosses, firewood and fagots, extreme unction, God's love and His justice (which the lesser-spined would leave out). All, all these were in the saint's picture.

Another bell. It was midnight. He saw ten corded brothers going into the chapel for the midnight matins. On his knees again he said the office. He felt a little faint; he drank a little water. Always he was grateful for God's water. On it He had brooded at the Creation; with it He baptized men's souls, set His seal upon them. Always too, even when through lack of food he was faint, it refreshed Thomas.

There were so many questions, so many rungs, which on midnights like these and long after, he put together. The Trinity was analyzed, the Resurrection. The final curtain of the Last Day, of which they sang sometimes in the *Dies Irae*. The Judgment, the ultimate lore they call eschatology.

The vices, virtues too, and the Sacraments. Everything pertaining to God, which means everything. Even science. No scientific fact ever befogged Saint Thomas; all with religion could be squared for him. An effect cannot quarrel with its Cause, a result negate its Source. As it would be for his great successors from Pascal through Pasteur to Du Noüy down. It is rather silly, all these would have said, to put the versus between science and religion, to pit science against God.

No other man any time—and this too must be taken into account, that Thomas lived up to what he wrote in that cell—ever prepared so profuse a storehouse for the mind part of the soul of man. We can be grateful that in that same age one lived who performed a service that matched his in influence if not in kind: little Brother Francis who left an example that vitalized the world. Thomas would have been the first to stoop and tie Francis' shoe, if the little friar would have let him. As a matter of fact, they would have stooped and tied each other's.

He rose and walked to the window which he was fortunate in having in his cell. What a little community it was! Almost corresponding to the body with its organs. The heart, the chapel. Chapter house. Refectory where they ate. The calefactory, or heated sitting room. The great kitchens and cellars. The "necessary," as it was then politely called. The various craft shops. Infirmary. Porter's Gate. Watch Tower. All lay stilled and inactive in the light of the moon which gave to the humblest buildings lines of silver as in the Temple of old, or the loveliest old ivory.

Save where some brother prayed in his cell or before the altar, all the corded citizens were asleep. Too heartily some of them, he could tell from the snores. Abbot and sub-prior. The precentor-librarian who trained the choir boys, kept the choir sheets and rare manuscripts in the aumbry. Sacristan entrusted with vestments, candles, crucifixes, plate, who was always worried about the mending of worn sacred clothes and having enough candles and wicks for the abbey entire. Kitchener who had to see to the food, that it did not fall too far below the abbey standard of frugality or extend too far in the direction of luxury; his emptor, or buyer. Both had considerable trouble in keeping accounts accurate and neat to present of a Monday to the abbot. The infirmarian, who watched over the sick, tended to the healing of their bodies and as ordained priest, said masses for their souls. The refectorian who saw that this communal dining-room had sufficient platters, jugs, ewers, cloths, napkins and that these came back white from the washing. The all-powerful cellarer who saw to the supplies, that the flour was good, provided food, drink, and fuel, and even had the roofs mended. The almoner, who superintended the distribution of charity to the poor and the washing of the beggars' feet, the daily maundy, and kept the mortuary statistics.

He sighed. Perhaps if he had had less duties of the brain, more of these with the hands, he would have slept like them. He would try pruning those pear-trees in the morning.

He went back to the sloping desk, then took up his quill, but suddenly knelt down and looked among the notes in an old coffer in which was kept the rapidly growing body of his book. Yes, there it was among the R's.

This was another principle which Bishop Cyril of Jerusalem and his friend Albert had touched on, but which he was consolidating, making a part of the eternal platform of the Church. Two sources of knowledge there are:

Revelation.

Reason.

The first, Revelation, came through the Scriptures, sacred addenda to it, later light from the inspired writers since.

Faith, born of Revelation, counts more than knowledge acquired through Reason. It is more important to know God with the soul than with the mind to apprehend Him. Revelation is a burning glass focusing in the soul and kindling in it the fiery flower of faith.

But Reason had its divinely appointed place! He had a lecture disputation in the morning at the little "College of Eighteen" whose carved gate and portals he had always admired. And he must not forget to tell the young *messires* that the great Saint Bernard, watchdog of doctrine, had always been suspicious of Reason. Childlike faith for him had been enough; he feared greatly the evil rationalization that with some might grow out of this same Reason.

But—he must be sure to tell them this—while Saint Bernard was one of the truly great souls of the Church, later developments showed him to be slightly in error. Now, of course, he himself would not have every last person engaging in Reason. All were not equipped for it. A Christian should, of course, enter the Kingdom of Christ as a little child. But it was no design of God that, if he had the capacity, he should not grow up in spiritual things, become an adult Christian, and so enter into the joy that comes with the increasing knowledge of the riches of God.

Summing up—yes now he would tell them, "It was the blessed disposition of a merciful God that the very things Christian doctors can examine are also to be accepted of Faith. So one can say that all share in the knowledge of God."

Thus he joined the two points, Revelation and Reason, of his great arch pointing up to God.

While he was at it, and sleep would not come, he would take up a theme for a *quodlibet* day after next for the College of the Sorbonne as well as for his tiny favourite, the "College of Eighteen." Sometimes he liked these tiny colleges to express his big thoughts in. What he was going to say there is important for us to know as well as for those *jeunes messires* with whom the great man took such pains. It was thought developments like these that quite as much as the more tangible towers and spires, all the illumination, carved work, and goldsmithy, and the minstrels, alchemists, armourers, and crusaders, made the Middle Ages what they were.

What he had decided on (while we wait to go with him into the garden for the pruning and a remarkable discovery there; it will not be long now for the stars are ghosts, pale as moths, and the East is all palpitating serpentine and rose) was this refreshing thesis: The nobler pagans, those that came before the Christian era, thought their wonderful thoughts, surveyed well the universe and devised lofty moral codes, also had "light"; and they left this behind for our use and illumination. Albert, and long before him Dionysius, had touched on this theory. But it was the skilfully-directed, powerfully-impelled sledgehammer mind of Thomas Aquinas that now drove this truth, for the indelible remembering, home. It was nice to see that the fine B.C. men were not out.

These great early souls and minds, he would show the budding thinkers of the Hill and the Isle, were in line with Christ. (This long effort to find the common ground between Christ, the summation sun of these early dawn philosophers, and these philosophers themselves, was infinitely touching.) From both the pre-Christian and the Christian streams flowing from the All-Consciousness, one could drink in truth. He would take two guests with him when he talked with these Sorbonne and "Eighteen" young gentlemen, two guests by whom he would prove his theory of that pre-Christian light. From the stream of all the illustrious ones with their big books or papyrus rolls in that endless parade up the Paris hill, he had picked them out—two very live ghosts—had shown them around the colleges until they felt very much at home in the best university circles. And he had taken them to lodge in the convent, much of the time in the cell here with the pallet, large crucifix, sloping desk and coffer of writings which one day would prove as immortal as the two guests.

It was one of the most curious intimacies in the lives of Thomas and the schoolmen. This was not the first visit of these ghost guests to Paris. They had spent some time here in the twelfth century. We watched them then in our earlier story of the Cathedral: Plato with his pale look, over-all patterns, and orotund phrases; Aristotle with his penetration and bedrock reality—invisible coaches both of teams captained by William of Champeaux, Abelard, Roscellin, in the old Cloister below on the Isle.

"Is the idea of the object or the object more real?"

That was the idea they worried like terriers. Sometimes they called it the hunt for "universals," the "universal" being what is left of a substance after all distinguishing characteristics are pared off.

Plato fought every second of his life for the idea, Aristotle for the object. Aristotle admitted the existence of Plato's over-all arch-pattern, but called it more or less inconsequential. The true reality lay in the object. Plato declared the pattern, the grand negative in the mind of God from which all print objects were made, was all that counted.

Thomas, naturally, would have to speak to his young men of Abelard, and his attempted reconciliation: idea and name were real but not until they were tied up with the object. He would not speak to them of Heloise cheering Abelard on, mutely but with kindling colour, from the edge of the crowd. Really, when one came to think of it, these earlier hosts of the illustrious Hellenic pair had the advantage. These new ones, Thomas and the rest, were not high-lighted for the crowd by any lurid light of a hectic love-story, redeemed later by the man's remorse, three superb love-letters and the essential nobility of the girl. The flames these thirteenth-century scholars tended shed a serener, steadier glow. Thomas' lamp for one was never to go out.

Tomorrow, for the Chollets boys, Thomas would bring out the old "man" argument again. This young people always understood. Platonists believed "manness" was distributed through all human beings; differentiation meant little indeed. Aristotle would insist that he and Plato, for examples, were very different, that while there might be up aloft somewhere those cherished master patterns of Plato (which might make groups and species homogeneous) each individual varied widely in characteristics, qualities, size, shape, colour, and so on. Any universal idea, Aristotle had always said, only mattered as soon as it was expressed by an object.

But Thomas would have to give Plato his day in court whether it was in tiny Chanac or Chollets he loved or in any of the biggest colleges on the Hill. After all, the man could express himself. There had been times in Thomas' own life when he had been immensely taken with the idea of the elder scholar, Messire Plato, that objects were but pale reflections of the vital live ideas and patterns aloft in the mind of God. That universal man did exist apart from any man walking about the world, the universal ship from anything that sailed the Seven Seas. The philosophy was not only ringingly expressed in eloquent phrases, but had its abstract appeal. What was his main argument now? Plato's? Objects were but the bringing out of a previous existence a recollection of ideas which were renewed by the sight of the object. And, as a young man he had been very much enamoured by Erigena's expressing it even better for Plato, in sheer poetry: "The Universe is but the shining through of God."

And he must stress further, for the young gentlemen of Cluny, Constantinople, Picardy, and all the Four Nations colleges, and for us too who with all our activities may not have spent much time on this great history of the past, this difference between the Plato who for so many centuries prevailed in the eastern churches, and the Aristotle now being cultivated by the Church of the West.

Plato had conceptions of undeniable grandeur, in language beautifully clothed. He magnificently expatiated on a Goodness beyond all goodness, a Beauty beyond all beauty. In such a soothing sea his soul was rocked with all the waves of his types and patterns which did not have to be embodied, given existence below.

Aristotle might toss one look over his shoulder at these vague archetypes and patterns and universals. Of temples, statues, flowers, ships, stars, stones. But what mattered was that life below, tied up, implicit in, expressed only in, those temples, statues, flowers, and so on all around him. He event went so far as to conceive of the earth and its matter as eternal. So far Thomas could not go. Nor the Church. He could not, Copernicus and the rest not having come, take issue with Aristotle's once advanced system of spheres revolving around our central earth.

But what he would point out to them tomorrow on the podium, or as he, in his eagerness to get over what was so richly overflowing in him, walked up and down the room before the students, was not Aristotle's array of facts, though for the times this was astounding. It was the way he used his mind, his habit of exploring the world, the universe, his following all its processes, and trying to bind them up link by link. His effort to "see the whole" was magnificent.

The thought of the great Greek was not identical with the "Revelation" of Thomas. Never does he speak of any specific act of creation like our Seven Days or Seven Ages. He dwells so constantly on the indestructibility, the eternality of the earth, that he seems to conceive of a time continuity without beginning or ending. Yet he always has in mind a First Cause which started the universe in motion. This motion, for him, appears to have been going on forever. But the very starting of it seemed, to many Church doctors, to indicate in his mind a creative act.

This First Cause and Supreme Intelligence started motion but is Itself immovable, ever in eternal repose. It is at once a vast primal calm, at the centre of things, and a motivating pool of energy. It gave the first motion to the heavens, which were drawn to It because It was all-desirable, All Good. This First Cause was the first mover of the heavens, the universe. It became their goal and end.

It extended its motion first to the heavens, its stars, and the planets which revolved around the earth. These celestial bodies passed on the motion then to the earth and all that in it was. Motion leapt into, passed through, all the universe.

Homer had played the body up and had had a very dim idea of the "shade," or soul. Pythagoras thought of the soul as superior to the body. Plato sublimated the whole idea. But only the Hebrews as a race had consistently had a monotheistic ideal. Aristotle, as he developed, personalized and made warmer his First Cause. And he made himself an admirable pre-Christian ally of the Church when, in the surrounding darkness, he raised his "pagan" head, and cried: "God is a living being, eternal, and most good, so that Life and its unending continuance are good, and that is God."

This effort to support the Church (which already, in its Founder, had an indestructible foundation) by the subpoenaing of ancient witnesses, was the most curious of historic rationalizations. The schoolmen appeared to think that by the greater rounding out of knowledge, the supplementing of Revelation by classic thought, their belief was proved to all as impregnable. But instead of the once prevailingly popular Plato, most of the schoolmen of the Hill had taken Aristotle to their hearts, which meant into their books and disputations.

How should he explain it to the young minds? Say that Aristotle had built up a grand system of morals, and out of it written a great book on ethics? He had, but this was not what counted most.

First, of course, there had been his acknowledgment of an all-sovereign God. But further than that had been his all-out intransigeant reality. Plato was apostle of the abstract, Aristotle of the real of life. Christianity was nothing if not real. Oh, it has its archetype of archetypes, its ideal of ideals above, but it had here its stark, naked reality. That of suffering, of martyrdom. Of the blood of Christ. Of the living reality of His Body everyday on the altar for the true and very real nourishment of men's souls.

There is no history greater than that.

For the Paris students then.

For the gropers of today.

But the dawn pageant appeared now above the convent watch tower. The bells rang for Lauds, first office of the day. Thomas never failed to attend and he loved their beautiful canticles about light. Always, after it, he would go into the abbey gardens.

Sometimes at night he went there too, and would sit on the portal steps, looking at the infinitely bright diagram of the sky. His mind would range from the immeasurable to the minute. From the great wheeling planets to the tiny voyaging fire-flies, flashing their love signals on and off with their little udders of intermittent light. There was always a coolness there like that of the gardens of long ago when the first saint (uncalendared), Enoch, walked with God, and in the words of one of the most beautiful of epitaphs, "was not because God took him."

In the early morning, on the way from chapel, he would stop at the cow barns, greet the blind milking lay brother, pat the animals on their flanks, calling them by name. Sandalled, he would continue through the dew into garden where he had, he said, the feeling of coming into the Song of Solomon played out in reality before him. He would raise his great head facing the East, now a great tidal wave of blood, again a soft tremor of opal, peach, orchid, rose; and he would repeat aloud all the canticles he had heard at Lauds, the lovely ones about light and the greater Light of Resurrection.

Then he would stretch out his great arms. In part this was to shake out the kinks of his sleepless night's vigil of writing. More especially it was to take unto himself all the life and stimulus and refreshment of that little abbey paradise. To drink in all the exhalations of the flowers, the fruit, and the growing things, with the dew incensing them with its sweetness.

Paris was like that even then in the morning. Often Thomas would go out of the gate and climb to the city wall and look down upon the pent-up city. She did not have the great parks of today. But the massed fragrance of the morning offerings of the royal and nobles' gardens and particularly those of the great abbeys, springing up sweet and green among the massing towers and roofs, descended on and washed clean for the moment the most densely packed mediaeval quarter, even as this dawn breath of Paris sweetens Lepic, Wooden Sword, Venise, Sebastopol, all her mean streets today.

Thomas had spoken truly of the Song of Solomon. It was like the sweet breath of a woman when she gives herself to her beloved. So century, after century, Paris gives herself to her people in the morning, as there arise each dawn these waves, these distillations of fragrance, of beauty, of renewal of life, this purification, this soul reassurance, welling up from the growing things of God's good earth, the precious parts of it still left in the crowded city by the Seine.

As Thomas stretched forth his arms as though to gather in all this life and beauty, the bigness, solidity, ox-like strength of him were more than ever apparent. New gardeners or lay brethren working there would exclaim, "What a big man!"

And thinking that all-embracing gesture was taking them in, they would smile back and bow. They were right. It was for them. For all life. As he passed the little squad of workers wearing mediaeval leggings, with their skirts tucked up, he had a greeting for each. He asked this old man about his back and jokingly said his own back was worse than the others; he had discovered a certain new kind of pain. He gave his blessing to a boy who was about to leave and would not complete his vows because he wanted to marry. "A good gardener," he said to him, "should marry, for that is one way to replenish the earth." He got down in freshly turned soil and helped the little boy left as a foundling at the convent gate to fill his little container with worms for fishing in the Bièvre.

For a little while then he watched them at their various tasks. The abbeys had never let their knowledge of cultivation die out even in the Dark Ages. They were ever careful about rotation of crops, which, indeed, Virgil had commended long before them. They were skilful with ditching and hedging. Here some lay brethren were scattering lime on sour, overworked soil, and others were trundling in manure fresh from the cow sheds he had just visited. Veteran monks were moving with a regular, rhythmic cultivating swing beautiful to watch, working their bill-hooks with curved heads like those the Jacquerie would use on human skulls. One saw them among rows of turnips, lineal descendants of those which the Roman generals had loved; the onions the Egyptians had once worshipped as gods; the Phocan peas; and cabbages and beets bred from wild stock the abbeys had taken over from the Mediterranean, so increasing the larder of all Europe.

The orchards of apples, pears, almonds, and plums backed up against the city gate. It was very convenient for the fat warders who, when the reading friars were circling the paths, the gardeners busy, could so easily lean down from the crenels and machicolations and spear the choicest fruit. There was a suspicious movement among them when he went over to look at some specimens he was grafting and budding.

There was no earth detail but what was dear to Saint Thomas. When he sat down not on rocks or steps but where he felt at home, on the good soil, with his sinewy calves revealed with their good earth hue, he himself seemed to be a product of the garden. He watched the little snake which too, he knew, had its use in the garden, slither, a little ripple of yellow, among the débris of the once gay lily-iris.

Lovingly he picked up a nest which one of the rare windstorms of Paris had dislodged from a crotch in a laburnum. A Frenchman who was a poor mayor but a first-water essayist and wrote on rafters and walls, left a very good sentence, something very like what must have been in Saint Thomas' mind: "Our utmost labours cannot," said Michel de Montaigne, "attain to so much as to recreate the nest of the tiniest bird, its contexture, its beauty, and practicability."

But he was headed this morning for that great discovery of science in the world of the bees. He had always been fond of them ever since he had learned that hives had been so thick around Bethlehem where the Rose, the Sweetener of all the World, had come into it.

Seated under an almond tree, by a pencil-thin silver fall of water into a moss-green, cool-lipped bowl, he surveyed the gold-banded, fuzzy, black-bottomed squadrons and the infinite number of other gossamer-winged entities of the air as they darted and zoomed and zigzagged and then swooped down on their bright-petalled prey with ecstatic quiverings. Especially now he was interested in what he had discovered—their cargoes—the minute gold siftings, the pollen on their eager hurrying little bodies and vibrating wings. He pondered on it and on all the commerce, the creating of life it implied.

Everywhere among the flowers there was the constant humming undertone, but it became a vast thrumming fortissimo by the beds of fennel, rue, thyme, and the other herbs. The banded armadas hovered thickest where the rosemary showed its bright green and added a delicious pungency to the massed floral fragrance. Rosemary—*Ros Maris*—Rose of the Sea, it was first called because of its unusual abundance by Mare Nostrum, the Mediterranean. And the rosemary was the most plentiful supplier of the gold ore that could be minted into the honey so necessary as a sweetener for food in the Middle Ages.

As he surveyed the manoeuvrings of the bright pirates amidst a wealth and glory outmatching Solomon's, his eyes, which so often had the absorbed, rapt expression of the scholar, one going very deep into the heart of things, had a happy boy's, out-on-a-treasure-hunt look. Children often hold up a buttercup under the chin to see "if you like butter." When Thomas bent over the lilies to watch the mysteries at work in the gold chalices, that yellow of his complexion, which contemporaries said was like "ripe wheat," was brought out more strongly by the reflection of the gold of the lilies in the basic brown hue of the good earth in the pleasant broad planes of his face.

Here—it suddenly dawned upon him—was a great secret of life. If others had discovered it before him, well and good; it was none the less an authentic observation and study discovery of his own. It was the great secret of life, of nature, and nature's God, thrillingly demonstrated in this intricate world of anthers and antennae. Male and female had He created them! Not only man and woman; not only the animals that went into the Ark. But the very flowers of the field!

Quickly, by the unending silver falling into the mossy green bowl, Thomas Aquinas seven centuries ago wrote down on his blue paper the lovely miracle of ovary and ovule and golden life-giving pollen, of flower chalice and the little carriers with the vibrating wings: "In though sometimes the active quality is found in the one plant, the passive in another, so that the first plant may rightly be called masculine, the second feminine."

So Saint Thomas went on with his science as well as with all his philosophy and theology and visions for his book, the *Summa Theologica*—which in design and logic and far-reaching influence would prove to be one of the six very greatest books in the world—as he had for its companion book the *Summa Contra Gentiles* and the rest.

And all this science was doing more than what on the surface appeared. His great neo-disciple of the twentieth century—and it is a pity Thomas could not have had his help as Elijah had Elisha's, for example—Jacques Maritain had this to say about the bees, which well applied to Saint Thomas as he knelt by the flowers examining into the great life secret: "The external fact fertilizes the inner intelligence as the bee fertilizes the flower." It could apply, too, to so much of Saint Thomas' life besides his happy hours by the rosemary in the abbey garden.

Thomas did not always stay in the Convent of Saint Jacques on the Paris Left Bank Hill. He often fared forth to lecture in Cologne, Rome, Naples, and distant points. He spent some time in London and years in trying to unite the long-split churches of the East and the West. He corresponded with great men everywhere and was a helpful councillor of the pope. Offered the abbacy of historic Cassino, Saint Benedict's capital, and the archbishopric of Naples, he refused both.

He was the great codifier and coordinator, the Blackstone of the Church when the Church meant everything directly or indirectly to all. So he is still when after seven centuries the Church means at least half of that to the world. And he has affected, though they know it not, half of the skeptics. He made a grand summing-up of what that Church is, what Christ's kingdom is, to the sons of men: "When a man is building a home and goes away, the building remains. But what would remain of the world if God withdrew His support?"

Often in the evening, when the day drew to a close, while the sounds of the city came up to him, gradually with the deepening night being muted, he would leave off disputation and notes and *quodlibet* and turn to the company of the grand hymns. It was a great age for song. Sacred as well as profane or innocently secular. The Provençal poems thrill with the "breeze of April," with its "glittering showers." Every bird has his "familiar language known and beloved of all." They sing of the "ranked flowers," "the embroidered field," "Golden Hair and Freshredrose," "the little feathered chatterers of the bough."

But destined for longer life were the great hymns. Thomas was very fond of the *Veni Creator Spiritus* of Bishop Rhabanus of the ninth century. In the twelfth, Bernard, not of Cîteaux, but of Cluny, had written the resonant "Jerusalem the Golden." The direful but magnificent *Dies Irae,* which brought into ringing, rhythmic life the sculptured tragedy of the Last Judgment portal of the Cathedral, had been composed by a Franciscan, Thomas of Celano in Thomas' own time. An Italian, presumably Jacopone da Todi, would, in this thirteenth century, give birth to the *Stabat Mater* which radio concerts are playing still.

Thomas himself wrote several, which like the *Pange lingua gloriosi,* were intincted with the very grace of the Eucharist, of whose office the Pope later made him the grand patron saint. A Scotch nobleman has left us a quaintly translated example of one of his living verses which are unforgettable for all who truly value the Cathedral and that for which it stands:

> "In birth Man's fellow Man was He;
>   His meat while sitting at the Board;
> He aimed his Ransomer to be;
>   He reigns to be his great Reward."

While he was on a diplomatic mission for the Church Thomas was taken sick, not in a convent of his own Dominicans, but of the Cistercians at Fossa Nuova. He had a presentiment of his death, for he said to his monk hosts, to whom he showed a touching gratitude for one so renowned, "This is my rest forever and ever."

He wrote to a friend about the mystic experiences he had here: "Such things have been shown to me here, that all I have hereto written seems of little value." Once, toward the end, he, out of a reverie, as though he had not devoted all his years and strength to Christ, made this last prayer-declaration: "If there is any stronger knowledge of sacraments than that of faith I wish now to use it in affirming that I believe beyond all doubt and know as certain that Jesus Christ, True God, True Man, Son of God, Son of the Virgin Mary, is in this sacrament."

With his last breath he said this as he took the Viaticum, the Host, the *Panis Angelicus,* the transformed Body of His Lord, and, on the threshold, looked into the other world. He made this affirmation with almost his last breath for the sons of men, as though he were standing up before all of them that had ever been, were, and would be, and wanted to breathe the saving truth of it, the life it would give them into all their souls.

There are great statesmen.

And great generals.

And great scientists and inventors.

Also those who perform an even greater service.

Word of his passing almost broke the heart of his great and good friend, Albert the Great. He wept. These were no cold didacticians, but warm emotional warriors of the mind and soul.

We have noted several epitaphs about the great men who climbed the Paris hill in that immortal parade. Albert now added another—for Thomas Aquinas. It has been borrowed often since for our modern celebrities; he was before them in using it: "The Light of the Church and the World has gone out."

XVIII

*The Handsomest King in All the World. . . . He faithfully attends
Mass but quarrels with the Head of the Church. . . . England beats
him and he beats England. . . . Three Over-dressed but Clever Corporation Lawyers. . . . Philippe goes off the Gold Standard, gives
"Fireside Chats" in his Palace, mobilizes a Corps of Horsemen to
spread his Propaganda. . . . A High Head-dress and a Rose, Gable,
Voice, All of Gold. . . . Sparrowhawk Knights, Tax-gatherers even
in the Woods, People running naked through the Streets, Men
hanging at the Street Corners. . . . Absolutism and Absolution. . . .
The High-tide of the Gothic has gone. . . . Cropped Ears and Feet,
Ninety-foot Blood-red Banners in the Channel. . . . Four Thou-
sand Gilt Spurs on Church Walls. . . . The First States-General in
Notre Dame. . . . Philippe rides down Notre Dame Nave after
Mons-en-Pévèle Battle. . . . Beyond the Ile de la Cité he burns
Templar Knights. . . . Having done the World Some Wrong but
Much Good for France, Philippe passes on to his Fathers.*

1314 A.D.

PHILIPPE THE FOURTH WAS DYING. IT WAS, SOME SAID, OF
typhoid. But he had fallen in the forest while hunting. He was
far from the sounds of the Seine, its river traffic, the boatmen's
songs, the hum of the travel on the north bridge by his palace. There
is where he should have died, but no one can dispose his own death
place. No more than had his grandfather, Louis the Ninth, who died
in Africa. Philippe the Fair was at Fontainebleau, not in the later
Renaissance chateau but the original hunting lodge buried in green.

De Molay had foretold this. But Death the dark destroyer could
not dim the King's beauty, though he had wilted his superb strength.
He could scarcely raise his hand to cross himself. The ministering
abbot in his sacramental stole, remembering the strength of the once
mighty arm, thought it pathetic.

283

Drops of oil from the administration of Extreme Unction lay on eyelids, nostrils, mouth, the ears and wasted fingers. The intonations of the seven penitential psalms, the beautiful words of the "recommendation of a departing soul," sounded in the room, in unison with the mournful, multiple-branched harp of Fontainebleau Forest.

He had spoken the last words to his son. Though this Philippe the Fourth, the Fair, was not the pure soul his grandfather had been, he seemed to have taken a cue from him now. For he said something very like what Saint Louis had said to Philippe's father, in Algiers, and which we heard almost at the beginning of this story. "Louis, I love you above all others," Philippe said to his son. "So live, my boy, that you may earn the love of all others."

This was very beautiful, coming from Philippe the Fair who had been called by his critics "the devil." But then he had just been shriven, and doubtless he meant it.

There is a popular illusion that there are no tall Frenchmen. In spite of Napoleon and all his stature-shortening wars, there still are Girauds and De Gaulles. In the last half of the twelfth and in this thirteenth century, there had been four tall kings, all very powerful. Now that Philippe was going so fast, there would be two or three more tall ones. But none so mighty and able as the four of which Philippe the Fourth, here in the green heart of Fontainebleau Forest dying, was the last. What a magnificent family!

Great-great-grandfather: the mighty city-wall and Cathedral-builder, crusader and victor over the English and Lionheart, Philippe Auguste;

(Great-grandfather Louis the Eighth was shorter, but a very competent soldier.)

Grandfather: the incomparable Louis the Ninth who, in actual inches as well as in moral stature, towered over court, the battlefield, and all Europe;

Father: Philippe the Third, the Bold, the one we saw taking his knighthood vows, tall and strong and conscientious like his sainted father if not quite with his personality.

Son: Philippe the Fourth and Fair, lying here now, of great height too, even more stoutly-thewed than his grandfather, and of a prodigious competence, with all his politics.

A grand quartette (quintette it almost seems it should be, for except in cubits Louis the Eighth was a very strong fighting king too!). 1165 to 1314. All of the same blood. We won't throw in the two or three very tall ones to follow, for they would not be of the same kingly calibre. But this succession of the five was another and human by-product of the now vanishing Gothic power and glory. You cannot match them in any royal line. Five kings following each other, all endowed with great physical strength, two of them able, three of them truly great.

This Philippe the Fourth had been the strongest of all in body, as gifted as any in brain. He probably had had more to pour out from his soul in the confession of the hour before here in Fontainebleau Lodge than ever had any of the others. Over that soul, historians were to quarrel mightily. Some agreed with the soubriquet "Devil" which the Pope, and also a later Renan, gave him. Others, good churchmen among them, while admitting his harsh measures, placed him high as the father of an emerging modern France. There was one quality about which all agreed. He had been the handsomest of all five. Since we have no portrait of King Arthur in paint, only in words, we might add that Philippe was the handsomest king of any anywhere, before or since.

Candles stood now at his feet and head. A hunting horn in the forest sounded a careless call. The motif, at the moment, was appropriate for a busy king whose only relaxation had been the chase. Also for one who had done many worldly things. It wove eerily, elfinly, through the chords of the impressively chanted petitions, the gravely melodious measures of the *misereres*.

The priest assisting the abbot left the room. His hands, crossed over his breast, protected the draped ciborium containing the Viaticum, the consecrated Host for the dying, the Bread of Life. The ancient Greeks always gave a little farewell supper to their friends when starting on a journey. In the Latin the word for the provisions donated to them then, the clothes, money, food, utensils needed for preparing the food on the way, was *Viaticum.* The Church took the old custom and made it lovelier still as she had done with so many things of this earth. The term at first was figuratively applied to the soul supplies needed by the struggling Christian on his pilgrimages here below. Later the word was reserved for one sacred essence only. The Viaticum was the bread celestial for sustaining the soul on the last of journeys. The little earthly supper had become a heavenly one.

The Viaticum had passed Philippe's lips. "Fair Lord, God, into Thy merciful hands I commend my spirit," he had brokenly said. Then the pulse showed no beat, the mirror passed in front of those lips, no mist.

Even in death, he was exceeding fair. One was impressed by his size as he lay there unmoving. His passing had not taken a fraction from his six foot four inches. It lay, arms and legs razor-edged from the illness, under the silk coverlet embroidered with the lilies of France. Nor had death taken the silken life out of his profuse golden hair. It made him resemble one of the Gallic chiefs who had once ruled his land. For so strong a man, Philippe had always been oddly pale. Death had deepened this pallour to its own ultimate whiteness. The Dark Angel, who is something of a classicist, had sharpened and brought out the modelling of his features. In life they had been beautiful and a little hard. They were so still. It was the abbot himself who had sheathed the cold, keen, blue swords of the king's eyes under their ivory lid scabbards.

When one has loved the departed, that is a hard thing to do. The closing of the eyes seems such a final gesture, placing on the once breathing clay the Death's seal. When you close the eyes of a king, you seem to be doing more than sealing them. You are drawing too a curtain over a section of time, a phase of national life, putting another period in history.

With Philippe it was more true than when most kings pass. Not only was ended the life of that tall, vigourous, competent quintette of kings. They were pulling down the lids over the bright eyes of the Gothic era, putting up the shutters on its shining mansions. Not that Philippe the Fair, except in height, drive, getting things done, in his look of some magnificent statue in a Cathedral niche, was exactly Gothic. After him, those bright Gothic eyes would open now and then with a gleam here and there. The shutters would come down to show a little of the old spaciousness. Pucelle would be painting his exquisite miniatures. They would add some beautiful stone lace to Rheims. And so on through some very fine etceteras. But the crest had passed. As an evidence, the meagre vinegary prodigy of a Duns Scotus would replace the noble theology of Aquinas and Bonaventura and declaim that good was only good because God had made it so, that He could have pronounced the darkest evil good and that it would then have been good. Of course he added qualifying statements. But such a spirit was not Gothic. Even though all did not succumb to it, it was an evidence that the heart had gone out of the Gothic. And it is the heart that gave the impulse to throw up those mighty and beautiful fanes, to cut out and impress the infinitely lovely things that so abundantly had flowered.

As a further and now physical evidence that the heart's blood had been impoverished, the rich crimsons and violets of the cathedrals' glass would, not so far on, turn an anaemic silver white. The integrity, simple aspiring lines would curl up and turn flamboyant, as though the Gothic itself were going up in smoke.

As a matter of history, the great tide of the Gothic had spent itself by the time Saint Louis passed on, in 1270. Philippe the Fair had brought in the materialistic, the opportunistic, if in an extremely capable and truly regal way. Saint Louis had character superb; even so, the irresistible Gothic carried him on as the highest of its top waves. The tide had left Philippe high and dry, on his own.

Though he twisted conscience, ways and means, he was never sneaking about even his deviousness. He was rather forthright and royal even in his wrong. To have been anything else would scarcely have fitted this godlike, powerful and beautiful man at whose bones they have been picking ever since.

It would help us a good deal in judging if those bone-pickers are right, could we have heard that confession of his of the hour earlier. That is properly forbidden of God and Church. Undoubtedly, some things we would imagine he should have confessed did not appear to him, even in the quickened conscience retrospect, as culpable. From his point of view, even in death he may have looked quite differently from the historians upon such events as his expropriations, his riding down Notre Dame nave, having the Pope slapped, even on the fiery accents of those flames burning the Templars below his palace windows, just beyond the Isle. But let us see if we cannot find on those picked bones a shred of flesh, say, of patriotism.

For one thing, Philippe was always talking with his people. With ulterior purpose? Positively. Also with something else. If he did not have a burning passion for France, he was following the dictates of his nature, functioning perfectly when he was working for her as well as for himself.

These conversations occurred in the hunting lodge, the Louvre. In the Hall of the Lost Footsteps in the Palace. In the Cathedral—with great throngs of the people. And in the garden, that old haunt of Saint Louis, where he had spread his little carpet among the almonds and peaches, the onions and fennel, marjoram, and thyme. Sometimes Philippe even buttonholed folks on the street.

In that garden he looked, and was, slightly taller than his grandfather had been, broader across the shoulders and bigger around of biceps, though it is doubtful if his battle-axe fell with more devastating conviction. Also he was more golden in thatch than Saint Louis, if not so golden in spirit. His grandfather had tried to extract from these open-air assemblies among the flowers and herbs and fruit an abstract justice, a pure result about which one could almost write hymns and psalms. This grandson, in calling his "beloved of Paris" together, had his weather eye cast to windward. The observing could see what they called designing, mercenary, meretricious, in this beautiful cold, calculating eye, which, however, had melted in his address and welcome to them. Of course, Paris was bigger, but he was getting proportionately even bigger crowds than had his grandfather.

Philippe had no mother like the White Queen, to whom the saint had looked for sympathy and support. He had not chosen, and perhaps could not find, counsellors like Boileau, De Joinville, Louis' upright *baillis* and seneschals, who had caught a noble disinterestedness from Louis. But in garden, palace, Cathedral, he ever had at his shoulder three counsellors, all birds of a very different feather from the eagle and dove intimates of the saint. In fact, some said, they were crows. And these Three Sharp Ones were all lawyers, most curiously dressed up.

Philippe should have been a lawyer himself. He would have made a hard-driving, ruthless, resourceful as well as imposing prosecutor for the Crown. In fact, he was just that. And he was very litigious, forever engaging in suits. With princes, kings, even with the Pope. But he could put on his mail and fight ferociously too.

The Three were not Gothic at all. They dressed ferociously. As we would say, they "came from the wrong side of the railroad tracks." It is an illusion that only in our West do people rise from the ranks. Think of Napoleon's "base-born" marshals. School-teachers, bus-drivers, coopers have become latter-day presidents, premiers, generals of France—that is, after following the French rule and getting, with sacrifice, the best sort of education before starting their climb. Philippe's Three Sharp Ones had been law-school instructor, plain soldier, pantryman for a queen. Now they were decidedly on the track's right side, had the biggest houses, the most expensive households and clothes, though not just the right ones, in town.

Flote, very small looking against the King's height, had but one good eye, saw with that more than the rest. He wore the most elaborate and worst clothes of the three on his chubby person, had an extravagantly outfitted band of retainers which, for effect, he saw were always disposed in the assemblies in a conspicuous position. He was an able ghost-writer of proclamations for the King. When he spoke for him with his harsh but carrying voice, under the spell you forgot all about his grotesque appearance. Once sergeant, now he was Chancellor of France.

De Nogaret, the school teacher, was a sinister, scheming *intrigante* for the King, with an acid-thrower's face.

The third, Enguerrand le Portier de Marigny—what a tongue-rolling name!—had been the pantryman. He had some curious fancies. He had put a golden gable on his house. Perhaps that was because the Pope, in admiration of his talents and his voice, too of gold, had sent him a golden rose. When he spoke for the King his voice was all harmony where Flote's was dissonant. But he was no more effective than the chubby chancellor. De Marigny, too, in order to tower over

Flote and be nearer on a level with the King, wore a lofty *altour*, or headdress, a sort of folded-around hat. But no one ever loomed above Philippe's impressive six foot four. Even when he let Flote with his harsh dynamic voice, or De Marigny, with his mellow one, have the floor, it was the King who dominated all, in Notre Dame, among the fennel, rasps, and roses of the garden close, or over against the gold lilies and the blue on red of his newly decorated palace hall.

The four, often with him, made up a curious group. The eye-filling King. Little Flote, just up to the royal armpits, striding with extra long steps and a grotesque dignity yet a real power in his chubby over-decorated clothes-horse of a body. Dark De Nogaret with schemes, pugnacity, a new-risen arrogance in his lined face, at the left. De Marigny, with the golden rose, the smile that went with his mellow voice, looking over the royal shoulder, but with that tall top piece on a level now with the King's golden thatch. Royal counsellors they were for a king, reaching out for themselves, but helping an absolute king to strengthen France for her long sickness of the Hundred Years War.

But into what a mess had this tall young King walked! Most rulers on their accessions do that. Rarely is there a truly settled age. Saint Louis' was one. Victoria's, reputedly so, was not. She was all right for the barons of the smoking chimneys, some merry villagers. But under that upper crust of stately homes, gilt, plush, little children worked seventeen hours in dark holes. Karl Marx was right there. If only he hadn't aroused the horse that didn't know its own strength to kick out the good barns. If only he hadn't banished the Christ who has the only formula!

Far past Philippe now and all the rest was that vast forward Gothic ground-swell which bore the majority of the people forward to a true content, an interesting, even thrilling general employment, and lofty achievements in which all had a share. It is usually the lot of decent rulers, as soon as they have cleared up a vexing set of problems, to leave for their successors another set.

What had happened then was this: Saint Louis had put together a pretty fair puzzle picture of France. Under Philippe the Third the pieces had been disturbed. They were all awry for Philippe the Fair. He would put them together with adroitness again. Then it would become, after his death, a piled-up mess again—though, to change the figure, as one must now and then with the baffling problems of history, he would leave France with *a hard core to get through!*

There are abundant witnesses in text, De Weerde, a Fleming, for one: "As the thirteenth century drew to a close, entire regions were ruined by the lords, all siding with this faction or that. When they weren't at swords' points with each other, they perched like hawks up on their donjon tops, and pounced down on any convoys of cattle or merchandise coming up the highway. Stock or goods they would pilfer, torture the owners, and then hold them for ransom." Though the Flemings dug pits for the French on the battlefield, and murdered them in their beds, and might be considered a trifle partial, there is much of truth in the picture.

Adds a popular preaching friar: "As the wolf invades the cote to carry off the sheep, the king's men carry off what does not belong to them."

Numerous as well as silly were the private wars starting up all over again. It seemed as though the Pope would have to invoke once more the pious but grandly sagacious "Truces of God," which cut fighting down by over three quarters.

And now Saint Louis' once able *baillis,* provosts, seneschals, had become outmoded, inept, if not corrupt. Tax gatherers were swarming all over. They collected imposts at city gates, toll bridges and in the most unlikely places at road crossings. If you sat on one of those castle tops you could even see the collectors popping up at the entrances to the woods. All over France the flowing merchandise was being stopped for tithe, tax, impost.

It was only to be expected that the towns and the little people should revolt. Ypres, Lille, Douai, Arras, Provins, Châlons, Cahors, Bordeaux did. What now was the mess of the century's turn into which this golden-haired boy had walked, what were the pieces, segments, slivers of the fair puzzle picture that had and should again be France? Well, swiftly, scatteredly, necessarily confusedly, it was all something like this (not, of course, all over, but in too many towns and rural regions of France):

>   Ermined nobles putting screaming merchants to the rack;
>   Crow-picked men hanging from the corbels;
>   Hawk knights pouncing down from their castles on poor drovers;
>   Tax collectors stopping people even at the entrances to woods;
>   Town grandees stripping the little folk, driving them through the streets naked; the little people doing the same for the knights;
>   Mobs tearing off church roofs to get at "aristocrats" (not the "best rule" ones of the ancient Greeks, but the titled exploiters);
>   "Aristocrats" chasing mob leaders down the church aisles, violating "sanctuary" to murder them. The small people doing a bloody vice versa at the altars.

These were not all of the disarrayed picture segments. Just a few more:

The Three Sharp Ones and their great corps succeeding the old upright *baillis*, building up a tremendous bureaucracy, very, very
expensive for Philippe;

The Pope adding to the deficit by ordering the clergy to pay no taxes
to Philippe; Philippe cutting off the Vatican revenues by banning all coin exports from France;

His calling out of more friendly assemblies, his summoning and putting the squeeze on the not so friendly bankers of the Rues
Lombard et Venise;

(Then Edward of England had to horn in. He wanted to pick up
segments too, through marriage and feudal claims, or bribery.
He thought he could make a fairer picture of France than
Philippe.)

He (Edward) invaded Guienne, the Gironde;

He assembled a fleet, two hundred and twenty-five sail, built castles
on fore-decks and poops, streamed prodigious ninety-foot blood-
red banners from the masts, cracked down on a hundred Norman
fishing smacks, cut off the ears of the crews, and hanged half of
them from his yard-arms;

French sailors cut off captured English sailors' feet, set them adrift
(the English beat the French *to* the cruelty, not *at* it).

Edward bought with English pounds half the counts contiguous to
France and the German king, all to make war on Philippe;

The Flemings, owing allegiance to Philippe, began to dig pits and set
stakes for him.

Of course, some men were constructively and happily engaged in
making good shoes, gloves, hats, beautiful illuminations, and carvings.
Quite as Wordsworth wrote on Immortality, Beethoven his "Eroica,"
Keats his "Grecian Urn," Stendhal his *Red and Black* in all the hectic
Napoleon excitement.

Still, there had been altogether too violent an upsetting of the
segments and pieces. There were altogether too many of them for a
seemly fitting and a happy solving. And the old system of feudalism,
which once had done much to strengthen the world, though now outmoded cut up these pieces further. Titles to lands were tangled.
Marriages snarled them up still more. This nobleman owed fealty
of the bended knee and the more negotiable revenues and military
services to a neighbour on a bit higher caste rung, the latter to a man
still farther up. So on up to the swayer at the top, King Philippe,
who should have been dizzy but kept his gold head, which is to his
credit.

This seemingly logical order was itself often upset. Who should be
the renderer, who the receiver of these feudal services became a moot,

and more frequently a fighting question. Those left of the old *baillis* and provosts, the new-caste Flote, De Marigny, De Nogaret, mediaeval "Johnny-come-latelys," tangled with the local lords too. France was full of jurisdictional disputes and strikes. Long the nobles had sat on their steps leading up to their donjon keeps and heard the appeals or condemned their farmers, hired hands, the dependents and "inferiors" of their fiefs. Now often the King's Men claimed the right to sit in the assize. Everywhere ducal and royal authorities clashed or confusingly interarced.

The feudalistic complications were especially hurtful through England. When Queen Eleanor of the fetching ankles and roving eyes went over from France to a Plantaganet, she had long ago given England not too far-fetched claims to certain large sections of her native country. Philippe had made a great mistake in emulating his grandfather in trying to make peace. He had further strengthened England's claims by giving the hand of his daughter to Edward. For a while the latter acknowledged his fealty to Philippe. He even went up to Paris and in Philippe's great hall, newly decorated with the lilies of France, blue on gold or red, placed his hands between Philippe's as any leal vassal. But the sword can cut feudal ties, sacred as they are supposed to be. Edward had taken it out.

Even after these wars were—temporarily—called off, France was always going to have trouble because of this feud on through the Hundred Years War and after it. England was forever stretching out her long arm to pick up more pieces, when she wasn't on the wrong side of the Channel and with both spurred feet stamping on them. And she was acquiring a lot more with clever purchase, seducing this prince and that away from the lilies.

If, in confused historical times, one is allowed to mix figures for "clarification," the feudal state in France might have been likened to an acrobatic pyramid. Anchor men below. Upper tier men. These in turn supporting others higher up on their shoulders. Edward was persistently trying to entangle the legs of the anchor men with those of the upper tier people. Now and then he would try and steal away an anchor man for his own act. It was a wonder the pyramid that was France stayed up at all. Much credit is due to her innate solidity and balance, the legerdemain of Philippe and his three base-born, odd over-dressed Sharp Ones.

Basically, England had a very bad idea that France did not like at all. England did not own any Canada, Australia then. France would have made, say, a good India. But France did not want to be a colony at all. She longed to be just herself, and was having a hard time being that.

Other feudal tangles complicated matters. That Count of Flanders, for instance. Of all people he should have been loyal to Philippe. Once comrade-in-arms in the Crusade to Louis the Ninth, he was also godfather to Louis' grandson. And he was the feudally legal, if not now leal, vassal of that grandson. The trouble was that he was a champion. The Flemings were expert in building fine houses and furnishing them richly, in giving sumptuous feasts (valiant trencher-men all), and in weaving, also in continuous concupiscence and copi-ous copulation. Though in such an activity open contests could with difficulty be staged, it was at this that the ancient, white-beard Count of Flanders was a recognized champion. He had a good score: of many dozen children born, twenty-five still surviving. Providing for these kept him at least land poor. The English gold was too enticing.

But Philippe was not asleep. He captured the aged but prolific procreator and locked him up, far away from his harvest bed, in the Louvre. And he outbought England in the end, won back with livres most of those counts on his borders, in his own kingdom south, even the King of Germany. These people greatly profited. For the livres they rendered service to Philippe. They rendered none to England, but kept the pounds. Philippe further succeeded in lining up with himself, through lining their pockets, many Italians southwest, hordes of Genoese sailors. The Scotch some say (the Scotch claim libelously) are not too averse to money. Philippe got the Scottish king. Even the Norse who once had sent fleets down to attack Paris now got under way to defend her. If history teaches us any lesson it is that the allies of today are not those of tomorrow.

Confused, unhappy as it all was, it was not too different from the times of Caesar, the Carolingians, Disraeli, Roosevelt. From most eras, in fact, excepting those rare golden times of Saint Louis.

Philippe, considering the times and weapons, was not much more the politician than the others. There have been purchased American senators and French papers, also other compensations, appointments, favourable legislation. There have been modern disingenuousnesses so adroit as to be dazzling on the part of idealists. Philippe's methods, though mediaevally harsher, and his aims were not so different. Not with any patriotic heart-throbs, but with the natural carrying-out of his nature, in his cold but efficient way, he did much of permanent good for France—beside the wrong.

Other parallels occurred: he went off the gold standard. He put what some critics would call a good New Deal face on it. "We have been forced to issue coins which fall a little short in weight. But I shall accept them for all levies due me. So shall you, my people, be reimbursed(!)."

He started the slow long decline of the livre or franc, the equivalent of the English pound; the sou which paralleled the English shilling; the denier which matched the penny. To be sure, his neighbourhood wars, the staggering governmental expense run up by them, the new bureaucracy and all his means of propaganda, did not ruin French money as global wars and popular fronts would today. How then would the franc, symbol of hard work, soundness, of industrious lives, and of higher values too, shrivel up! Into almost an emblem of defeat, an infinitesimal fraction of its former worth, a fifteen-hundredth, in fact. It had bought many yards of good wool in mediaeval times or two good farm horses. After the Second World War, it would not purchase a strand of that wool or two hairs from the withers of a horse. Tragically representative would be the decline, tumble, dwindling, shriveling, of something magnificently worth while.

Often of nights, with his comparatively hard troubles which gave his golden head a financial migraine, for the bankers were not coming through, having been squeezed until their tongues hung out (and the Pope did not help that exchequer headache at all), he would glance through a long slit between the crowding towers at the Right Bank Castle of the Templar Order. *They* had money to burn. He did not know the excuse, the device yet. The Three kept whispering to him about it. He had not become the Prince of Expropriators so far. He would soon.

The moderns who would give universal history a purely economic slant have lost the "whole" view. Man is not only a bargaining, but a fighting animal. His is a lust for women, power, and blood. With his quart of wine he should have one of blood each day. It will continue so as long as tourists in times of peace go to see grown strong men pit fighting cocks against each other, and, in a larger way, men plot their wars. Over six centuries on, they would be firing mortars at each other in—of all places—Gethsemane's Garden.

There were battles now besides those amputating engagements in the Channel. Some unusual, some very picturesque, if the imagined suffering and blood does not blur out for you the martial glamour. Between his cash contrivings, his proclaimings, propagandizings, and verbal duels, Philippe sometimes had to put on his mail. He had strength to spare, no fear, and he did not mind. But it was rather a bore.

Sometimes the English won. Sometimes did he. If the English would only forget for a little Crécy and Trafalgar, and remember the victories over them of Charles the Fifth of France, Philippe Auguste, to say nothing of the immeasureable Jeanne; if Americans would not dwell so long on Braddock and Yorktown and think of the English chasing the troops to Washington in 1812 to burn the White House down; and also take into account the French moneys, armies, great fleets that really turned the Revolutionary trick; and if, by the same token, the French would overlook Napoleon, Rochambeau, Lafayette for the moment, we might see things whole, and get over this silliness of the sword and turn it into a plough-share and pruning-hook soundness. No race has a corner on either triumphs or common masculine bellicosity. But then, all those affairs are blotted out in the oncoming totalitarian night.

In any event, the Britons won sometimes and Philippe beat them very badly at Bonnegarde and in a couple of naval battles. He even landed at Dover, being one of the several French kings that proved that English soil was not, as legend has it, sacrosanct. That is, after the first 1066 rape by the Norman and Ile de France knights, which fertilized the great womb of England and helped make her what she so greatly is. However, English history is in the main right. These late invasions were merely technical, not of long duration.

The Flemings, who later were to fit into the French pattern as though they were made for it, hated that pattern at first. They did something in return for the English gold and made a fight of it. Philippe defeated them at Furnes and then put some garrisons in the households of the cities of this province which, after all, was his own fief. The citizens, particularly those of Bruges, did not relish having roomers, though they sang gay songs. One morning, not long after matins, they got up in the dark and murdered the sleeping French in their beds. There was a tremendous washing that day of dirty and bloodied linen under the famous bridges of Bruges. The capable fecund and ferocious housewives had helped, not only in the washing but in the actual dirtying. They had knifed many of the slumberers on their pillows. On those that escaped to the streets they tumbled down candle-sticks, chamber-pots, their heavy wedding plate, even wrenched-off coffer doors. Brains galore spattered the streets. They called it the "Matins of Bruges." It matched the bloody "Sicilian Vespers" famous in history and opera.

> Kill,
>   Kill,
>   Kill;
> Then breed,
>   Breed,
>   Breed,
> To kill some more.

That seems to be the way with the beings we call human.

At Courtrai the men then did their part. If Edward had been staging a little preview of the Hundred Years War in the see-saw struggle with Philippe, the Flemings in this battle staged one of Crécy. In a marshy, canal-channeled land, they dug Roman-like pits and covered them with branches. If the French aristocracy was to go down before the Crécy grey goose shafts, here they went down, tumbled into the pits. Out of these the Flemings got arms and armour, a tremendous junk booty, and the four thousand gilt spurs they hung on their church walls.

Philippe was to get back, and double, at Mons-en-Pévèle (Pouelle). Unhorsed in this battle, his cavalry running away, he regained his seat, and with his great height laid about him with sword and battle-ax, so that some thought Saint Louis had come back again. Seeing this, the French cavalry too came back, and splendidly was an initial rout turned into a stunning victory. It was decisive, and despite the seeming see-saw nature of the various struggles, Philippe was forging ahead—for his own reign, that is. Lille, Douai, all the Flanders cities he returned to the fold, a large part of Lorraine, the region around Lyons; and by marriage he had won over Champagne and Navarre.

After that striking victory, he made a spectacular entry into Notre Dame. This was in 1304. If every incident here recently narrated is not set down precisely according to the calendar, they rather fit that way into the general picture. Dates are indispensable to the perfect scholars to whom we are immeasurably indebted. But for many readers, dates are like telegraph poles which rise up every other split second or so by the railroad tracks to disturb the landscape's easy flow. What we need principally to know is that all the occurrences of this chapter came in the seven years before or the fourteen years after the thirteenth century turned into the fourteenth.

The great-great-grandfather of Philippe the Fair, Philippe Auguste, had too gone up that nave to celebrate a great victory—at Bouvines. That celebration had been in somewhat better taste than this of Philippe the Fair after Mons-en-Pévèle. But then Philippe, who looked every inch of his seventy-six inches the king and royal gentleman (especially when he was out of that old dressing gown he preferred when not showing off for France) did not always show good taste. He didn't here or when he baited the Pope.

Philippe Auguste had marched his men-at-arms in columns following one after the other to the altar, there kneeling, receiving communion, and circling out of the Cathedral again. They did not have on any good clothes for church. Their banners had been torn. They were heavily sweated and bloodied. But at least they knelt humbly and thanked God for their victory and begged forgiveness for their sins, which so long as we will have wars is considerable for a soldier.

Philippe did not give such warm thanks. He gave the lip service of his beautifully-cut, cold, somewhat ironically smiling lips. Still he was grateful. He was glad that victory had perched on his banners, on the oriflamme of France. It was "just and meet" that God should benefit him as the beautiful head and front of fair France. He was not a humbly devout or a highly intelligent mystical, but a rather mechanical main-chance Christian. But he most thoroughly believed.

The trouble was with the way he came in. He did not march in as a penitential soldier at the head of his stained columns. He came in alone. He played a lone hand. Also he came in not on foot, but (had it not been for the records, none would have believed so arrogant and absurd an entry) on his horse. In short, he was showing off. Whether or not this was showmanship for France—and in a king who preferred old clothes, watered his wine, and assisted at mass it probably was—it was scarcely a pious or reverent way to come into this tall, beautiful, shining house of Our Lady and of God and His Son to which pilgrimages are made from all over the world.

Thus mounted he entered through the Last Judgment Portal which many think should, for his punishment, have fallen down on him then and there, instead of waiting for the *Dies Irae* it depicted. All Paris had gathered in the lovely place to watch. But they hadn't counted on this, which had no precedent. Under the arches and between the two sixty-foot-around pillars directly under the towers, he went unperturbed. If it had been, say, a "Miracle" performance in a theatre, instead of this place, it would truly have been a spectacular performance. Half the crowd thought that, even so, it was.

But it was scarcely a holy picture, his riding down that aisle, a straight line of shining arrogance from crest to pointed steel toe, with the white silk and gold-costumed horse every now and then lifting his tail to drop straw and feed balls on the sacred pavements. The charwomen would, of course, sweep up, and the crowd did not mind. Their spiritually tangy admixture of piety and earthiness and acceptance of Nature's facts prevented any objections except from those who got too near.

Some thought a strained look and a lifted eyebrow on the face of the Bishop of Paris indicated he did mind. Worse than any temporary defiling by an innocent horse, was that implicit in Philippe's gesture by his pose, this stage-play, his assertion of his own, the royal authority, in the face of God's. It was all in keeping with his seizure of the Pope at Anagni, and his later transfer of the papal seat from the holy city of Peter and Paul and the martyrs to agreeable and beautiful but unconsecrated Avignon, so that he might have it near at hand, the Pope under his thumb.

The Bishop could contrast this ride down the nave with another picture: Philippe's humbly helping at mass, acting as royal assistant to the deacon in vesting the priest. Again, like any altar boy, he had genuflected on the steps behind the priest at the *Introibo,* had placed the gospel properly, and had rung the little sacring bell. Even if these gestures did not generate much warmth under the skin, they as truly expressed one part of his nature as all his dispassionate manoeuvres for France expressed another. If in any man these inconsistencies, disharmonies, this split nature, would have been baffling, they were particularly so in a powerful king. He would pose a problem for that *Dies Irae,* that Judgment Day, under the portrayal of which he had ridden with such arrogance of showmanship. The Bishop had best leave it to that great event itself.

Typical of these complexities, this great king who watered wine, played altar-boy, also wore a hair shirt under chain links, breast and back plates and the bright embroidered lilies of his surcoat. But the crowd did not know that. All they saw was his eye-filling six feet four inches of steel and links and the gay embroidered surcoat lilies. It was a picture made grander when he took off his casque and revealed the gold of the hair which seemed to set off so well the shining armour and to go with the lilies and the perfect chiselled marble and very strong features, the hard, shrewd, world-wise eyes, now like unsheathed blue-steel swords flashing right and left.

If you could only have melted out the hardness, he would have done perfectly for a Galahad. But there he was, showing off before Paris, the crowd, and God. He decided to leave the picture there forever in Notre Dame. It went up soon near the right aisle crossing, a giant mounted statue of Philippe le Bel, astride his lily-covered horse, with bright gold spurs, embroidered surcoat and a golden ventailled casque on his head. It would not, however, stay up forever, only until 1772. Most people are glad that it is not there now—in Notre Dame.

There was another great living picture which he and his three Reinhardts stage-managed in Notre Dame. A portrayal of it should hang up in the Louvre alongside of David's inaccurate but picturesque Napoleon coronation scene, also stage-managed. For the new, the first States-General, they had packed into the Cathedral Parisians, provincial folks, high, middle, and low. The delegates held the nave. The lookers-on were shuffled, sardined back around the pillars and to the farthest walls. From the banner-hung triforia galleries, armies of faces, looking white up above, gazed down. Throngs crowded over into the west organ spaces, and the circling second story aisles above the rood screen, the bishop's throne, the canons' seats, the horizontal tombs of kings and queens, and the high golden and white altar. The exquisite tinted motley of the panes lighted the variegated motley of the crowds.

Why had nobles, clergy, the new third, the commoners' estate, been gathered, manipulated into Notre Dame? For nothing less than to try the Pope, in this great capitol church of the Church of which he was head. Unhappy and incongruous it was; and the situation needs a trifle of explaining:

Two policies—not ideologies precisely like ours now, but theories—battled each other in Europe. Should Empire or Papacy prevail? The struggle was not always ignoble. Europe needed unity then as she does now. The only institutions in sight capable of effecting the union appeared to be the two. But which would turn out the strongest welder? Over this, on the continent, there was a vast cleavage. In the earlier story of the Cathedral we saw how a conscientious and strong Hildebrand, or Pope Gregory, had triumphed over a weak Hotspur of a German Henry. Philippe was no weak Holy Roman Emperor to kneel in the snow. He was the powerful and very shrewd king of a France just beginning to feel her oats. At any rate, while the Church might and should prevail here in church, she was not going to rule in temporal affairs in his kingdom. With his own brains, those of the Three Sharp Ones there beside him on the dais in an ill-fitting if Solomon-like magnificence, and with the *ouis* he could count on ringing out under the great pillars and arches, he was writing his own corollary to that Empire or Papacy thesis.

In the famous man now on trial, Boniface the Eighth, who was not there and was not even represented by counsel, he had a powerful adversary, even if Boniface did not possess the spirituality of the very great popes before and after him. The outer man was magnificent-looking. He filled the eye quite as well as Philippe. If the King would have made a perfect model for Giotto or Della Francesca, Titian would have been happy over the papal ripeness, the old-age splendour of Boniface. If Philippe appeared the Galahad with the idealism turned hard, Boniface seemed the pope turned a little worldly.

He had had a complete seminary and cultural education in Rome and Paris. If he was not in Notre Dame now he had been there before, very often. He was still another of the illustrious men in that endless parade up the hill. The conversation of highly intelligent people meant much to him, also painting and sculpture. A very fine art gallery he left behind him. Very fond of literature, he was a patron of poets and tried a little versifying himself, and sometimes the singing of little songs of his composition to the soft accompaniment of harp or lute. He could write eloquent bulls; was a master too of a peculiar kind of sonorous ecclesiastical billingsgate. With many kings walking barefoot (but Philippe not among them), he had been carried on a silver-shafted litter under a golden canopy in the jubilee of 1300.

Philippe was to blame. Boniface was to blame. And the moot issue of the times, "Church or Empire, which?" If Philippe had a monarchial chip with an ulterior purpose on his broad shoulder, Boniface was a living challenge. In disposition he was overbearing, and rode very high under his golden canopy. Also he had arranged to have borne before him in that parade two swords. These were symbolical, but they were to cause trouble, as we shall see.

The French King and his counsellors and manipulated subjects were far from being the only Catholics disapproving of Boniface. The friars he had repelled through his dislike of all religious orders. Franciscan Jacopone da Todi, creator of one of the Church's flaming hymns, the *Stabat Mater,* spoke vehemently against him. The poet Dante did more than that; he placed him in his "Inferno." And Dante was an eminent Catholic, having put into immortal verse the Church's mediaeval theology as Thomas Aquinas had framed it in prose.

And the great man who had taught Boniface on that Paris hill would never have approved of those two swords. Nor, as a matter of fact, would over ninety percent of the long line of popes. That long line is remarkable. Two hundred and sixty two popes! And most of them happily chosen, the vast majority with a very high degree of spiritual-mindedness with their marked ability. Never in any monarchial or presidential line will you find so high a proportion of mass integrity and selflessness or patriotism—in their case for the far-off country of Heaven, for the nearby kingdom of Christ which could so generally prevail on this earth if there were only men of good will. The preponderate number of pontiffs have not cared for temporal power. They see it as so temporary, the transient scaffold that will disappear when the enduring edifice of Christ is ready. While that scaffold still obscures it, the greatest popes have demanded only enough of state to keep the capital of Western Christianity respected by the purely political, to help their flocks in alien lands—not by armies but by the organized moral, yet outwardly earthly, prestige a holy institution may properly have.

This earth, which is God's, none will logically deny, should be run on Christ's Kingdom principles. The great body of consecrated

popes have realized that it will take some time. Meanwhile, the
Church, Body of Christ, should strive to pervade the souls of men
so that gradually they induce into the earth temporal more of those
Kingdom principles.

Now Boniface would hurry on Church hegemony. As politician
Philippe showed genuine patriotism for France, a none too spiritual
but highly gifted Boniface was a Church patriot. But he sought glory
for her here below. Church patriotism was tied up with personal
ambition. He fancied himself as a fine head and front. He liked the
perquisites he saw he could have: pomp, thrones, palaces, rare books,
the conversation of refined women and poets. Those two swords.

He had labelled them when they were borne in front of his golden
litter: spiritual and temporal power. For many of his predecessors
and successors among the two hundred and sixty-two, those two
swords would have shorn clean through the delicate web of their
conscientious general policy. They were spurs now to Philippe. He
saw one pointing directly toward his France.

But before looking in on that spectacular, outrageous trial, in—of
all places—Notre Dame, two attitudes of the Church must condition
your background: No one is so ready to admit human failings in an
administrant of the Church as an intelligent Catholic; they glory in
her record the more especially because she has survived all the storms
brought on by such frailties. This is, for them, incontestable proof of
her God-given authenticity, else this ship of the Church would long
ago have foundered. Secondly, no worldliness of culture or unwise
striving for temporal power in these frail exceptions can affect, in the
minds of any in the Church, their truth when they speak not in
temporal matters but on things spiritual, officially, in the sacred seat
of authority. There appears to be some spiritual, mystical law governing the Body of Christ that is the Church, by which, faulty as
may be some human cells in that Body, the minute one of those cells,
a too earthy celebrant, comes to the altar, he is surcharged for the holy
moment, and rises out of that earthiness into spiritual validity. So it
is with the larger suzerainty of the Pope. No more than he let the
faulty human disciple called Peter perish when he cried out in fear,
in the boat in the storm, will He let His Church go down.

Meantime, up in Paris, one sword of Boniface's—the left one—
pricked the King into action. Now the Franks had once called together conclaves on the Isle, the Hill, in the groves of Paris, but
theirs had been informal, gusty, roared-out affairs. This *Etats Géné-
raux,* ranking by degree, nobles and clergy, the new-commoners last
(in the Church where the first was supposed to be last, those of low
degree, exalted), was the first formal assembly or States General. One

would have supposed that this new admission of common folk or rather middle common folk—a great adventure in what had been a distinctly feudal world—would have made for freedom. And it would in the end. But as for this Notre Dame sitting, it was all too formal, too well coordinated. Philippe and his three corporation lawyers had seen to that. The King does deserve some credit as a parliamentarian pioneer, but he was, like so many today, able premiers and our very nicest presidents, an expert politician. Politics seem to be a sort of machine oil or grease that makes gears smoothly mesh; and sometimes grease is dirty.

If you can season your idealism with a little tang of cynicism to make it palatable, you would have found Philippe's political manoeuvring even prettier than his person. It would have delighted a Farley, Burleigh, Mark Hanna, Queen Elizabeth, or the last Roosevelt, could they have watched his clever use of propaganda. All to satisfy (it was probably like that with some of these last-named too) not any burning passion for his country, but a need of his nature, because he was made that way, to carry out her destiny. And he only functioned truly when he was acting the soldier, showman, politican, or higher statesman, for France. To this extent, he was to the manner —to the royal throne—born.

On the surface there had been much royally-decreed preparation for these grandee and clerical delegates and the commoners of the newly-fledged Third Estate. All through the preceding week you could have seen them from the walls, in trotting, walking, or mediaeval single-footing pace, with packs behind their pommels, making for the different city gates. A warm welcome had been ordered for them by the cold Philippe. Owners of inns and rooming-houses did not object. If it meant prestige for the King, it meant profits for them. For days there had been a great shaking out of beds in the town. Little curled goose-feathers like plumes from angels' wings had floated all over, settling in the most unlikely places, on concierge's shoulders, on old harridan's and the queen's as well as on the black soutanes of the friars.

On every street, up each lane, could have been heard the swish of scrubbing brushes, twig brooms and soap, the clink of iron, pewter, and copper, the foaming of the tap, and the hiss of the turned spit. Before every other great hinged door, dusty horsemen were dismounting to engage in colloquy and European bargaining with some host.

The Square, then half its present size, which did not allow the beautiful proportions, the serene relationship of horizontal lines and vertical, the majesty of the towers of the Cathedral to be seen to such advantage as now, was hung with banners and painted hangings from every timbered façade, even from the old Romanesque Hôtel Dieu. This was not only the oldest-going hospital in the world; it is the finest of reviewing stands. It has offered more sights for the invalids and convalescents than any other. Down the centuries, from under the arches, through the panes from the balconies, bandaged and sick folk have been looking at pageants so full of colour that they should have poured some of it into their wan faces. They have been watching Clovis, Charlemagne, Geneviève, Napoleon, Mary of Scotland, Marie Antoinette, the Sun King, Hugo, Verlaine, Pasteur, Sarah Bernhardt, Foch, an illustrious host, pass by.

Never had the Square such need to be larger. There was difficulty in leading away the horses from which, this opening day of the States-General, many delegates were dismounting without looking for rooms. Stables on the Isle, across the river, were at a premium. The nobles entered the Cathedral with hauteur and decorum, the clergy with ecclesiastical dignity. The commoner delegates seemed very joyous, ebullient even. It was the first time in the ages-old history of France since the primitive conclaves that merchants, guild brethren, men of industry, of the joint head and hands skills, were to be seated with the nobility and clergy, or at least very near them, in the grand upper doings of their land, to have a voice in assembly, a say about how things were run for France. In a way they were to have that say. When they didn't, Philippe let them think they had. For a much profounder preparation had been going on than that of beds, drinks, pots and banners, and for years, not days.

It was really a rather beautiful thing to see, the way Philippe the Fair held the people of Paris and France by simply talking to them. Sometimes through his instruments, but quite as often all by himself. He appeared to take no important step at all without consulting with them. "Appeared to"? Yes. He and his Three Sharp Ones had predetermined them, moulded them beforehand into agreement with what he really had in mind. Forever he was holding these little consultative chats, as we have seen, in palace, church, square, on the cobbles, giving over the air his open-air little "fireside chats"; whenever he was going to make a levy, defy the Pope's bull, squelch an order, or make war. Forever too he was trying to keep his political fences mended. It was very important not only for himself and France then, but for the future, that he keep alive the monarchical idea. In the patchwork chaos of the times, it was the only bright thread that gave any design to the national pattern at all. Kinghood meant far more for the French then than for England now. It was actually the magnet that attracted enough of the elements to make France

somehow stick together, the magnet to which sufficient of the steel
of the arms of the chivalry and of the tools of France, still adhered
to leave the land with something of a definable identity.

His propaganda bureau was organized with enough forcefulness
and subtlety to have aroused the envy of a Cassius, Caesar, Cecil, or
that later Roosevelt and his Farley. His couriers could constantly
be seen riding in swirls of dust up and down the provincial roads. In
their scrips they carried proclamations and confidential communications from the King to his dear people. They also had trumpets. Once
through the city gates, they would blow these in what would be our
courthouse square but then was that of the main church or cathedral.
The people tumbling out into the square, they would unfold the royal
letters and read them aloud in tones as resonant and orotund as their
trumpets. Very well trained they were at this. Very well and sympa-
thetically they got across the King's concern and affection for them—
which, incidentally, if somewhat academic and rhetorical, was fifty
percent sincere. Cleverly slanted were all these communications.
Philippe's case was always presented in full. Edward's or the Pope's
had usually been deleted. One-sidedly his people were wonderfully
informed. Sizeable figures, too, went down in the palace "proclama-
tion budget"—we would call it "publicity"—for broken trumpets,
drinks for the overblowing throats, and spent horse-shoes.

It was astonishing, the numbers of "yes, yeses," the *oui, ouis,* he
always got. Not tallied, tolled, but oral, vivaciously *viva voce* when
not thunderously roared out. As in modern Russian towns, these *ouis*
outnumbered the *nons* a hundred to one. He was counting on ten
thousand *ouis* here in Notre Dame alone.

In the situation here, he had taken advantage of what is called the
French independence, somewhat controlled by him, though of this
they were not aware. Continually he played on their jealousy, their
fondness for "home rule," quite as local politicians and national ones
do today. Even in the Cathedral his emissaries this morning were
going from pillar to pillar warning the mediaeval "yes-yesers" to be
ready when the king's message to the new congress was read.

Now Philippe covered over these profounder preparations with
more of those that were superficial. For appearance's sake, with the
same showmanship that had put up banners around the Square, the
King who wore a hair shirt and watered his wine doffed in the
palace his old taffeta dressing-gown, which he loved for his few off-
hours, and strode into the Cathedral in a splendid ermine-collared,
blue silk mantle, lined with a just off the scarlet shade, all given
gold accents as he proceeded to the dais by the lilies, his spurs, and
his hair.

The dais stood on a platform erected in the transept crossing. It is true that he might, like Napoleon, have usurped the sanctuary. That he did not may add a little to his account to be balanced in that final assize portrayed on the portal tympanum under which he had just come. Of course, the great rood screen, in those days, stood between the sanctuary and the congregation spaces. He wanted to face his people in his half-apparent, half-real love for them, to talk to them, he said, almost face to face, in at least as much intimacy as the great reaches of the packed Cathedral allowed.

There were three tiers of bells that had to do with the service of Notre Dame. The little "sacring" bell was rung in the accented moments of the mass by priest or altar boy. Over the sanctuary, up about where the dead archbishops' hats hang by suspending threads now, was the *sanctus* bell swung by a rope. Above, in the towers, were the resounding many-toned bourdons that often melodiously thundered over the city and which had this morning rung for hours as a sort of tocsin to summon the people and delegates to this unhappy battle against the head of the Church in this capitol church that was the Cathedral. This Philippe, who had himself swung that little sacring bell at mass, was now politically thumbing his nose at the great Vicar of Christendom.

Under the great waves of sound coming down from the towers above to make all the Cathedral's still stone violently vocal, there had been much talking in the crowd, among the great nobles seated on the few chairs in front of the dais, the bishops and abbots nearby, and the commoners standing behind, with a vast audience all around. A great human agitation ran through the throng. It was most obvious in the incoming commoner delegation; they were both excitedly joyous and yet nervously anxious now that they were in the great Notre Dame of which they had heard, almost at elbows with the illustrious, and before the King, in their new-found position and estate. And a great people-smell rose to Philippe's nostrils from the low degree audience: the sweating, patched, lame, halt, whole, burly, pimpled mediaeval sardines packed in, around all the pillars, in the chapel bays, the circling apse ambulatory, in the run of the triforium galleries, crowding into the west organ loft, and even shoaled in the upper story aisle running around and above, giving a view down on the sanctuary.

Admittedly, the whole affair was dubious and unfortunate. On the one hand the King established an important parliamentary precedent for the world. On the other he defied the Pope, who if he had some very human failings including a difficult disposition and did not measure up to the greatest of his line, after all represented churchhood quite as much as Philippe did kinghood. It was a tremendous disservice to the Church.

Still, Philippe gave them a good show. Arrow straight, he made the most of his height, as he rose from the dais. No ermine or red-lined silk could subordinate the sheer strength of him now. The fifty-candled corona above picked out those lily, spur, and hair gold accents. He seemed himself a human accent, a sort of sword-thrust down into that Church where he should not now, on this errand, have been. He was the livest thing there. That is, except for the invisible ones: The gentle Our Lady (whose lovely statue which we know now would stand just back of the dais where Philippe had sat with his back turned on the high altar), the Christ Who might have chased him out as a money-changer, for all his prayers and his turning his country into a modern power.

But, "God in Heaven! what looks!" exclaimed some who had not seen him before. Graciously he welcomed the great throng, through aisles and transept, and up aloft. His voice rang grandly enough through the pile, helped by wall and high vault and arch acoustics. But quickly he sat down. It was his way to leave the oratory and haranguing to De Marigny, De Nogaret, and Flote. It is wise sometimes to sit back and be the exceedingly galvanic symbol. Though the king is permitted a liberally laudatory editorial "we," it is best to have fine things said by others about one than to say them about one's self. Especially when that symbol can spring to power and life the minute action is required. Besides, it is the part of wisdom to leave what is called by the moderns the "dirty work" to appear to be done by others.

Now Enguerrand le Portier de Marigny, with the mellifluous name and voice, arose. His lofty wound-around headgear he had not had the grace to remove, thinking thus artificially to match the King's stature. He would have liked too to have that gable for a heraldic device, a golden chevron, suspended over his head. He did wear the Pope's golden rose which, considering his attack upon him now, was adding to injury flaunting insult. He looked around on all the tiers and planes of the ten thousand faces, some mere blobs of white, others dark shadows, still others with the light of innumerable candles and the iridescence of the panes upon them. The exquisite motley of the glass brought out woolen motley as well as the gay hues of the silken garments of the delegates.

So Enguerrand le Portier de Marigny began to call names. It was no place to do that, with Our Lady, even in her invisible presence, so near. Though it was not so bad as the time when Robespierre and the rest would set up the Goddess of Reason here, we have known scenes in this mighty Cathedral much more to our liking.

"Execrable infractions, gross and unwarranted, heinous offences,

stinking to the nostrils," De Marigny trolled out, "the Pope has
committed against our Lord Sovereign the King. With the English
he has sided in their wars against France. He has done worse than
that. Why, he, the supposed champion of truth, has released the
vassals of our King from their sworn oaths to serve the King. For
what? So that they may make war upon him. So that they may turn
over the lands which they hold only in fief, as vassals to our King,
to England's support. Far worse is this sin than that even of the
riches Boniface has piled so high here on this earth below instead of
in the Heaven above, as the Christ of whom he is the supposed vicar
long ago directed.

"Again the Pope has struck at our King and France by excusing the
clergy from their just debts." Here those representing that order
moved uneasily in their seats in the nave. "From paying the levies
they too owe to the King for their rich lands. And this has been prescribed not only by feudal law but by all the just practices of Christendom.

"In this continuous attack, at every point, the Pope has tried desperately to undermine the King, our country, our beloved France.
Evidently nothing would please him better than to see France go
under and down. Where, you ask? Why, under the spurred boot of
England. It is the only way he knows, or thinks he knows, by which
he may get us to go down on our knees to him."

The orator continued scathingly, telling them that the Pope was
such an old, old man—perhaps too old, he added in a forensic
pianissimo that yet, through his technique, carried to the far-off
galleries. Knowing this, their royal master had tried to be patient.
It was only when this old, old man had been so intransigent that the
King had countered with his own edict banning the export of coin
from France. Thereby the Vatican has undoubtedly been deprived
of its revenues as he deprived France of hers. And why not? His royal
master would forgive the apparent rudeness of the phrase at the head
when he caught the scorpion tail of it: Sauce for the royal goose.
Sauce for the papal gander! No monies for Paris, no monies for Rome!

So the angrily haranguing Enguerrand de Marigny went on, with
his voice changing now and then to a soft, smooth eloquence which,
with its wooing and persuasiveness, was even more effective. He was
a curious artist of the vocal chords. The glow from corona and windows streaming down high-lighted and brought out the sharpness
of his acid-thrower's, his hatchet-man's face to which the high head-
dress added an oriental and sinister look. As adeptly as he played
on the many notes of his ranging voice he played with his glances.
Forever it appeared he was taking in intently, now with ironic smile,

again with appeal, each one of the dark blobs, the window-and-candle-sublimated ones of the ten thousand faces, ranked, ranged, packed, in every spacious Cathedral sector.

Now their beloved sovereign had even been threatened with trial, with excommunication, branded a heretic! But who now was the real heretic? Had not the King himself, with his wisdom, discovered that? Had he not already told them in assemblies in his palace and the Louvre? Why, the real, the false heretic was—he tossed this plummet of a charge into the shocked voidal silence of the Cathedral—nobody but His Holiness himself. His *false* His Holiness! The carrying-on voice gathered incisive, stabbing momentum now—by all that was holy, by the Blood of God! Boniface the Eighth was the heretic!

For a second he thrust a finger in around the Adam's apple of his throat above the golden irony of the papal rose, as though this irreverence toward the head of the Church would make him choke. It didn't and he recovered. As a matter of fact, there was a grave, sobering silence for ten seconds through the Cathedral now. It seemed as though the very walls of Notre Dame resented the assault from the way in which they angrily re-echoed De Marigny's charges. But after the ten seconds there was a gathering human murmur that boded no good.

Once Boniface had gotten out of his harsh truculence and had spoken Philippe very fair: "God has appointed us, unworthy as we are, over kings. Hear, oh son, the warnings of a father and open thy heart to the exhortations of the master who holds on earth the place of Him who alone is master. Do not allow thyself to be persuaded that thou art not subordinate."

There was little use in reading such communications, which expressed the whole premise of the Church now. Philippe the Fair was a now calculatedly angry bull. De Marigny, De Nogaret, Flote helped on by serving as picadors. The nationalistic spirit of France had gotten—or Philippe had seen that it had gotten—out of hand.

De Nogaret was not chosen, for orator this day. His impudent bellicosity was to be reserved for the slapping of the Pope, which would come soon. Little Flote rose, his square-block figure curiously encased in a gold and poppy coat; his single good eye taking in the delegates and crowd as amply as De Marigny's black two. The harsh, dry, dynamic dissonances of his voice egged on and irked the crowd even more passionately.

He read the excommunicating bull.

Then: "Gentle messires, before there were any clergy the King of France had the care of his kingdom!"

This slight exaggeration and grandstand gallery play extracted a three-tiered, three-way variety of assentings. From the nobles at the front came a decorous but nonetheless decisive acclaim. The clergy near-by, bishops and abbots from Saint Denis, Chartres, Sens, Tours, Orleans, two score cities, were in a hard way. They were clergy of the Universal Church but they were Frenchmen born. They wanted France independent in temporal things. This feeling among the clergy, Philippe, in his astute way, had played upon well. If only the Pope hadn't raised the two points of those silly, unnecessary swords! If only he hadn't, in his quick choleric way, at the banning of the coin exports, called all Frenchmen asses! Even forgiving bishops do not relish being called asses. And Philippe had not only branded him heretic, he had also addressed the Pope as "Your Fatuity." Why couldn't they have held their tongues? Also some had heard the palace tale that he had said to his sons: "If ever you are so weak as to admit the King of France holds his crown from any but God, you will be accursed. I will haunt you after my death." Philippe hadn't wanted either the Pope or himself to hold any tongue. The lack of self-control, temperamental on the part of the Pope, designed on his, had greatly helped. Perhaps the clergy did not think of this, though the cleverer must have. France, independence, nationalism was in the air. Their parchment-like or healthy outdoor rubicund and leathern faces over daisy beards nodded a reluctant, half-hearted, troubled assent.

The third acclaim came from the commoners and the spectators, stirred by a civic and patriotic resentment. A growl now gathered and spread surlily, throatily, around the gallery tiers, through nave and aisles, and even among the little people looking down from the triforium, the second story aisle by the library, and over the sanctuary.

Dubois was another of the *nouveaux riches* (it was notable how these tasteless, crafty, powerful base-born lawyers dominated the council around the King), and the nobles did not like it at all, though they swallowed it as they must, when this Dubois from Coutances rose and read a paper suggesting that the King of France take over the Papal States and—ahem!—manage them for a new Pope.

Flote, however, gestured him down. That could come later. For the main matter now! And, turning first to King, then to delegates and crowd, his harsh voice rising a nasal notch or two but never losing its power and savagery, he read this blast *for* the King and *at* the Pope, addressed by the people of France (though Flote alone had written it) to the King:

"To you, most puissant prince, for you our Lord Sovereign Philippe the Fourth of France, the people of your kingdom, one and all, beseech and exhort you to preserve the freedom and independence of your kingdom, which is such that you shall recognize no one sovereign in these lands in temporal matters over yourself, save only God."

Robert of Artois, son of the one whom we watched taking his knighthood vows in this place, rose for the nobles, and cried: "My lord the King, we are ready to shed our blood in defence of the sovereignty of France!"

The aisle and tribune and gallery roar became ominous now, fore-telling that of those who would one day race through this place destroying the angels and saints and setting up the Goddess of Reason. In the same way Philippe, with the absolutism he had established for half patriotic principles, foreshadowed the Louis who cried, "I am the State!"; and the very Third Estate he had gathered here for royal purposes would, through its successors, overthrow Philippe's own line.

More than ever it seemed an unhappy event.

Some said that even the candles grew paler, others, "Nonsense, there's just a shortage of them, that's all." But for many of the clergy, the very crimson panes seemed now to blush. Not only the delegates, but border counts of France signed the challenging protest, and all of the bishops save only two.

Then the crowd roared out to much feasting and drinking. De Nogaret was not sent at once for the alleged slap. The next year, in the palace, Philippe had Pope Boniface declared a heretic and shameless De Nogaret was on his way to Rome. Even in his evil designs, he watched out for his master. He did not quite make the assault himself. On his birthday the Pope had gone to his birthplace, Anagni. The King had planned to have Boniface kidnapped, brought back to France, and tried for his "heresies"! Someone not French must be persuaded to pull the French papal chestnuts out of the fire. De Nogaret, with all his experience, stage-managed this too. The Pope was the prey not only of those two swords and his harsh disposition, but of the old inter-family quarrels that made a mess of Italy and once in a while, as now, troubled the Vatican. Because of some appointments of cardinals that did not take in his family, Sciari Colonna longed to get even with Boniface. So King Philippe did not himself openly attack the Pope. He did not want to, and stayed in Paris; he let someone else do it. He knew that this human boil, Sciari, was just coming to a head. De Nogaret pricked it for him and let the pus of his insolence pour out on the Pope.

Six hundred knights, a thousand men at arms, Sciari Colonna had assembled. De Nogaret and a companion were somewhere in the crowd. But the Italian impulsiveness broke in the doors of the church next door to the abbey where the Pope was staying. The Pope heard them, indeed, had already been informed of their intention. As Mary Stuart perhaps did not always measure up to the best in queenhood save in beauty, but died nobly at the end, so Boniface the Eighth, who had quite a few human failings, showed himself the lionheart and followed the best traditions of the Vatican now.

He had a throne set up in the abbey, but on his tiara, and took the sceptre and Peter's keys in his old ivory hands. He looked very beautiful there with his fine brow, the coal-black eyes still burning above his flowing white beard.

The mailed rowdies broke in. Sciari told the Pope to get down off his throne—and out.

Majestically and bravely enough the Pope replied: "Here is my heart, here is my head. Betrayed as was Christ, if it is that I must die, I shall die pope."

It was then, some say, that Colonna struck the Pope; other witnesses that Nogaret, playing, crocodile-fashion, the judge, restrained Colonna. Anyway, the aged Boniface died a little while after from shock, in great suffering.

On another day, not any better—five years later, in 1308—Philippe manoeuvred it so that his man, the Archbishop of Bordeaux, was made Pope. So began the Papacy's long Babylonian captivity at Avignon, away from Rome. The only good that came from it was the spacious and beautiful palace at which the tourists marvel still.

So Philippe settled the leading issue of the day. Neither theocracy nor empire, emperor nor pope in temporal things prevails. He swung the centre of gravity for a while away from the Rhine and Rome to the Seine.

In the last years his itching palm bothered him most of all. Continually, when harassed by the ever-mounting war and government costs, he kept cocking his cold blue eye down that slit between the city towers to the four pinnacled one of the Knights Templar. And they seemed a threat to other orders, Church, and state.

Well they had fought for the Tomb, leaving, Matthew of Paris tells us, two thousand knights of highest degree dead in the Holy Land. But the Crusades having petered out, they were now without any first objective employment. They had turned bankers—and loan sharks, some said. Already they had ten thousand castles over the world with rich and beautiful desmenes. These castles had vaults and keeps full of gold. The sword and battle-axe they had given up for the account book and the gold scales.

Playing safe, Philippe had made some pacific advances to them. He had suggested that he be made the Templar head; and he would have made a beautiful-looking Templar. Also he made one of their knights godfather to his own son. The order took it all as a matter of course and opened up nothing to him.

Thinking hard now, Philippe remembered how the Templars once had made common cause with the Pope against himself. His Three Sharp Ones started some ugly rumours against them. There had been a true story, but how they made it grow! In a few castles, some Knights Templar, having been shorn of their original noble purpose and growing soft through riches and lack of decently hardening employment, had turned decadent. Witchcraft they practised and "celebrated" something very like black masses. There had been perhaps but a few, but whisperings in the garden assemblies, on the streets, in the very Cathedral, throughout the provinces in their town squares, had woven the few threads of dark truth into a great blanket indictment to cover the whole Order.

There were thus seemingly sound, if manufactured, pretexts for arrests. And for tortures on more pretty days. To do Clement justice, Philippe's new Babylonian Pope refused to accept this rack-wrung and iron-boot extracted testimony. Later the affair was manipulated so that the Order was brought to trial and in 1313 was suppressed.

Again this oddly mixed royal nature of Philippe showed itself in somewhat better light, but for the moment only. While he used much of the gold for the crown, he, heeding the Church decree, turned a great deal over to the Knights Hospitallers, or Knights of Saint John.

Then everything turned dark. The *sergents de ville* gathered fagots on tiny Ile des Javiaux (or Juifs) which was a few rods away from the Ile de la Cité's point, but which has since been joined to it, the great statue of Henry of Navarre standing guard over the filling-in. A few dozen Templars were tied to the stakes, the fagots lighted around them. Jacques de Molay was conspicuous for his hardihood, his gallantry as the flames rose up toward his heart. No wonder that an order of youths has since been named after him. But, just before he died, he cried out a very bitter thing. King and Pope, he said, would appear with him at the Tribunal of God, *before the year was over*. Like Hailie Selassie's prophecy it turned out true.

So Philippe had come here in the green heart of Fontainebleau Forest to fulfill his knightly victim's avenging forecast. Now red side, now black side, had been his account. He had ended the old see-saw rivalry of Church and Empire and substituted France as a candidate for supremacy in temporal affairs. This had its good points and its flaws. The world was not ripe for any identifying of the things of Christ's and Caesar's. World machine and spiritual machine would not mesh. Perhaps even the faulty Philippe was an historical check on certain popes. Lesser pontiffs not so wise as the magnificently great and spiritual ones, had a worse sense of timing. They would hurry things on too fast.

For weal or woe, he checked the Church of his time. It is a tart but flavoursome bit of history. And it must not be forgotten that he checked a useful but somewhat over-colonial England too.

If he choked gold out of people, and monkeyed with the gold standard, rode down Notre Dame nave, desecrating it into secularity, and if he so terribly, at the end, burned some pretty fine men, it was to his mind—able but torn, calculating as it was, in the confused fission of the times—all done for the sake of France. And he talked with his people, brought them in, which, no matter what his purpose, was a parliamentary step greater than his parliament.

Some internal reforms too he effected which would last. Perhaps what he did best, though when he died he seemed to leave his country a prey for the further cutting, was actually to harden the body of France. He had filled out and broadened that body. As a prize fighter's skin is toughened at times, so under him she was toughened by a sort of pickling in a brine of policy. That hard core he gave her so she would get through the Black Plague, the even worse sickness called the Hundred Years War.

With his riderless horse, banners trailing and bordered with black, and trumpets playing sorrowful tunes, all to a measured tread not varying the pace, they brought the beautiful king, not tall but long now, to his tomb in the little church at Avon near the hunting-lodge.

There was no battle this day between Philippe and the head of the Church. The *Agnus Deis, misereres, requiescats* were much more seemly and beautiful than his own words had been in Notre Dame in the great assemblies. He had served God better when he, a great king, had served as a little boy might, kneeling, placing the gospel for the reading, ringing the little sacring-bell at the altar. The Church had taken back her own cold, warm-cored, dutiful, rebellious son, magnificent achiever and doer and astonishing sinner too, for her own.

XIX

Dante climbs the Paris Hill. . . . He sits in the Straw with the College Students, and, Homeless, sleeps by Saint Julien's Well. . . . In the Dawn he drinks Goat's Milk on the Little Bridge. . . . He studies the Theology of his Poem as it is carved and painted in all over the Cathedral. . . . The Great Central Undying Fact of the Cathedral.

𝔅eginning of the 𝔉ourteenth ℭentury

𝕴NNUMERABLE HAVE BEEN THE HOSTS OF THE ILLUSTRIOUS, the obscure, that would come into the Square to look up at Notre Dame. If the footsteps that have followed hard on each other there through the centuries could have left any trace, had any substance, they would have lifted us, the latest comers, high as the Cathedral towers. For the swift second before we leave the City and the Cathedral, to come again soon—the God of the Cathedral willing —to see them in succeeding ages, we should glance at them now, to gain a true sense, a real awareness of time and its passage through this historic City and Square, of its flow, immemorial as the rhythmic, reassuring, never-ceasing travel of the Seine around the Island, under all the bridges, on to its appointed fulfilment and rest in the Sea of the West.

We saw the Gauls of the golden hair and helmets, once conquerors of Europe, intoning at their altars on the site of this choir. Caesar's legions, conquering them in turn, had here made obeisance to their merciless Jove. Saint Denis, by preaching here, had lost that head he carries under his arm on the southwest and river corner of the façade of the Cathedral. Geneviève, sweet woman, powerful leader too, had by the river tended her sick and aroused her city against the invader. Big-biceped, hair-chested Clovis, that Dark Ages dynamo Charlemagne had knelt here in the parent churches of the Cathedral that after hundreds of years had vanished into Notre Dame. Into them had gone Hugh of the little cape which, like a magic cloak, covered an extraordinary line of eight centuries of kings, and fat, fighting Louis. The lovable Louis, the sainted, the incomparably just, the kind, with

314

his old hat, all the tall kings who loved old clothes yet looked so well, had walked under those tympana with humility or pomp or an admixture of both into this last new, tall, shining house of Our Lady.

By the same token, to her arms would come an infinite variety of soldiers, philosophers, scholars, other kings, the splendid, the motley and the patched. Smooth, glittering Francis the First; Paré who eased the warriors' wounds; the two beautiful and unfortunate Maries, one of Scotland, the other of Austria; Napoleon who in this beautiful seat of authority owned to none beyond his own; Pasteur, with bent back, going in here to pray after performing a God-directed miracle of science in the Hôtel Dieu; Foch, rock of strategy and faith in God; Charles de Gaulle, high as any of those old kings, undisturbed by the bullets raining down in militant blasphemy from the towers, walking through the Square, and then down the nave, calm under the same hail from the triforia galleries above the nave, the west organ loft, the very second-story aisle above the high altar.

One had come here during the last part of Philippe's reign, the last of the very great men of the era to join in that immortal parade through the ages, climbing the Left Bank Hill. He was worth a place in it, this dark exile of a Dante, reputedly one of the quintette of the greatest poets ever to sing in this world. And he saw, too, that the Gothic, which was passing, would never die out of this Square.

He will not keep us, for he did not tarry long. So brief was his Paris stay that some do not know that he was ever there at all. Residents of the quarter of the Street of Straw, which is still there, have passed down to us stories as proof that he arrived (for a weekend—a night—no one knows); and he did not find lodging even for one night. Also in the white parchment paving of his greatest poem, one or two of his Paris footprints are indelibly traced.

First, then, as the whole quarter knew, he climbed the Hill. We might as well climb with him, for a farewell look down on the city outspread before we depart for the time to our homes in various cities, he to Ravenna, Sienna, who knows where. He had no home. Had he gone to his, it would have been to have had a rope placed around his neck, his clothes stripped off to be replaced with a shift, then to kneel, as suppliant felon, crying for mercy. Not for corruption, poison, incest, any of the commoner Italian crimes then, had he been barred from Florence. But rather because of the excess of family which smothered Italian life, and the internecine quarrels which half the time bespattered the city walls. Above all, because of the famous issue which some kept at that, but which with handsome dominating Philippe degenerated into a knock-down and drag out battle: on this green earth, footstool of God, should Emperor or Pope rule in the purely earthly things of that great footstool?

Dante, with his fine Italian hand—not that of the intrigant, but of the fine statesman and supreme poet—had signalled out the Emperor. The poet was not only a Ghibelline, opposed to the Papacy-espousing Guelphs, but, so complicated were the politics and statesmanship of the day, of a faction within the Ghibelline faction. The Emperor, Dante said, with tongue, pen and sword, should be earthly manager for the Pope. There would be unity then (here Philippe would have cut in) all over the footstool. The Pope would be left free to build the invisible kingdom on an earthly foundation. Dante even condemned to his Hell two of the popes we recently met who did not measure up to the noble papal standards. This condemnation was to be rather permanent, since his verse was to turn out immortal. But never, never, did he assail Church teachings.

So rope and gibbet, not of the Pope but of still another faction within a faction, awaited Dante. Which is why he was ascending an alien city wall to look down on a celebrated city, of whose beauties and charms and wisdom he would not, as Fate had it, stay very long to taste. There Saint Thomas had put the theology of his time—most of it of all time—into his soaring prose. Even as he wandered homeless, Dante put that theology into the immortal lines of his *Divine Comedy*. The builders of the Cathedral had already engraved, dyed it, deep into the long, high beautiful body of Notre Dame. A trinity expounding it beautifully were the three—the Cathedral, Aquinas, Dante.

Dante himself did not look like so much to the warders at the gate. His black mantle, shiny in spots, was ingrained with travel dust. Later he was going to be forever pictured with that laurel wreath around his brow. He did not have it then. Instead, a piece of cloth like a tippet had been turned into something that went for a hat, by being wound around his head, then puffed up. Under this not precisely modish mediaeval millinery, a set of strong harsh features looked abstractedly yet searchingly out on the world, and with a seeming perpetual disapproval of it. *"Voilà la grimace!"* someone (it has not been recorded who) cried as he passed under that gate arch. And that, in the modern parlance of tourists who pass through the quarter, was as much as to call him "Sour puss!" Those features, however, could be lifted at times, on the hill summit, before the Cathedral, into beauty and nobility.

Evidently he did not stop long the day of his arrival. For him too "there was no room at the inn." A knob of bread which he took from his pilgrim's wallet, with a cup of wine, was meal enough. Then, brushing the crumbs from his ingrained dusty cloak, rubbing the wine drops off his mouth with the back of his hand in the careless way of the times, he must immediately have gotten off on that climb! Of a hill as sacred as Rome's seven, or the ancient Acropolis. Shining with even greater and farther-traveling beams of light and intellectual splendour.

Accustomed to being chased out of cities, he would not mind being elbowed here, especially since the crowd was good-natured about it. There was the familiar sound of a somewhat northernly-intoned Latin from many students. These brothers of the text-book, the pot, the forge fires, the flayer's knife, the broom, the hammer, the pigment and pestle, the staff of life and the green growing things, the sword, the proffered body, and the cross, poured out joyously on the streets; they were energetic enough, but not so quick, as in his Italian cities, with the fighting word and steel.

The aroma of fresh ink, the gall that went into it, of pigments and gold leaf, recently unpacked parchment, of new womb vellum of the unborn calves, came pungently to his aloof nostrils—those of one who, the wits said, forever seemed to be smelling a bad smell. The gleaming book clasps, the gems imbedded in books, the delicately limned hues of the miniatures, tempted a poet as much as jewels do a woman. But he could not have stayed.

He told then every bead college in that rosary of learning looping around the hill, and stopped at Saint Jacques' Convent at the top to ring the porter's bell. He wished Saint Thomas had not died. Though they had never seen each other, they were long-distance friends of the soul. Now he could only kneel by the great crucifix of the vanished inmate, and pray for him in the communion of saints, then pass out among Thomas' beloved thyme and roses, rosemary and hives on his way to the wall.

Goodly was the ancient city, looked down upon from up there. Everywhere on the circling wall the cone towers stood out like pointed manicured thumbs challengingly thrust up in that great belt. With the palpitating rose of the sunset west, the sea of houses on which we have so often gazed seemed to move, to heave tumultuously with its roof waves and curlings of chimney spume. Palaces, mansions, merchants' guildhouse, stood out like galleys moored on that sea. Sweet and far the bell-buoys of those roof waves, the belfries of all the churches, rang their melodious brass in the eventide. Notre Dame stood up facing the red West like a great twin-towered beacon, reassuring and serene in her ageless beauty, an eternal lighthouse for the sons of men.

So, like some Helsingfors royal ghost, the stories convincingly tell, he walked the battlements above Paris in the gloaming. Everywhere, in Can Grande palace, shabby attic, at poorly swabbed inn table, by roadside olive-tree, in truces on the battlefield, or as the swords flashed, he was writing his lines. For Inferno, Purgatorio, Paradiso, this dark patrolling phantom figure must have been writing them high above Paris and the Cathedral, on the city wall.

He came down to the riverside college quarter, where the houses of the Four Nations were, and where traces of his brief stay linger still. Not only in the six centuries-old reminiscences, those immortal Paris foot-prints in the page pavement of his books they study here now, but in the street nearby named for him because of this stay, and in the statue of him now before one of the proudest institutions of the land, the Collège de France.

"Tous occupés" they were, all four. There he could not sleep. But he could look in on a lecture or two, if he cared. Picardy College, founded by the famous statesman, Abbot Suger, of Saint Denis, he chose. It was on the Street of Straw, *La Rue du Fouarre,* which with its memories of Dante and thousands of the illustrious still awaits us today, winding in and out of the quarter, in and out of the centuries.

Before he went up, he could see, through the shutters open for the spring air, students in all sorts of frenzied or lazy study poses. The mediaeval regimen was hard. Some had backs curved over books on tables. Others' cheeks were knuckled by their clenched hands. A few lounged on beds, their faces turned toward the fading light of the west. Others munched on bread and cheese, heedless of the little grey forms coming after the crumbs, although, when they slept, these intruders would weave soft patterns on their faces.

The straw of the lecture room wherein he looked had none of the trestles, benches and podia of the better-furnished cloister colleges up on the hill. All squatted in the straw. Old straw! It had not been changed very often, for Four Nations' funds at the time were low. Nor had the straw been any too frequently sanitized with incense. Flowers, sweet-smelling herbs, were often used for this, but the precious frankincense was ever the base. Castles used it to cover up the vomit of drunken guests, the insanitation of their hound dogs. Churches had used it at Offertory ever since the twelfth century, and now they were beginning to use it in the thuribles at the Benedictus in late offices. Because prices were high, the Picardy straw was not any too sweet for the great Dante when he sat in it with the poor scholarship, the bursar, boys. They could not have been any too immaculate, either. *Tyreteine* cloth was going higher. The public baths were charging a *denier* now. Water for surface ablutions had to be carried up six panting flights of stairs. In with these were the richer youths with too winy breath, too explosive regurgitation, pimples, mediaeval acne. Still, out of that poor crowd, eyes often glowed with learning's excitement, the adventure of the spirit. If the Christ of the Bethlehem inn, of Saint Thomas' great book, Dante's poem, and the Cathedral would gladly have given his frankincense (and far, far greater treasure than that) not only to tragic outcasts but to the utterly unprepossessing, Dante that night registered, in memory, a tribute to these students in lines that will never die.

So, always the exile, and he one of the very greatest minds in the ancient or modern world, homeless still even in this capital of learning, Dante went down the stairs. He passed over more straw on this Street of Straw. It not only lined the lecture halls within, but also the guttered middle of the narrow highway. It was better than modern cotton in the ears for the students, more or less deep in their studies above. It softened the steps of roisterers returning too late and too noisily rolling wagon wheels. He went over, or under, one of the chains stretched at night at the ends of the streets to bar out the rumbling, creaking market tumbrils. So carefully did their Alma Mater, the University of Paris, cushion her students.

It was a notable sight for Dante. It would have been more so had he a place for his weary head. He saw a court with a well-curb. All of the quarter told of this later—years later. This well, sacred, but used too for more secular purposes by the Street of Straw, still stands in the shadow of Saint-Julien-le-Pauvre, then the university chapel, now a church of the Melchite rite of the Mother Church. It was, and is, a fat-buttocked little edifice, with a round half-tun for a vault, a classic doorway and gable. But to seeing eyes it is also more than that: a grey little ghost fragment of the Romanesque, just across the river from the shining house of the Gothic.

The dark form of the exile stretched itself on the cold courtyard paving with the head in the tippet hat, bursting with all its thoughts, against the well-curb. The illustrious sleeper dreamed on, heedless of the usual sights of that corner: lovers in one glued line in the Châtelet commandant's doorway (also still there); cats with tails like fur question-marks electrified; the students throwing down a Peter Lombard or Robert Pulleyn (a Bergson, it might be now); a patrolling *sergent de ville* twirling his mediaeval night-stick, a baton with a fleur-de-lys in the point of it.

The moon, if the gossips can be trusted, was at the full. Melon-golden, pregnant-round, it chinned itself on the tympanum triangle. It shone on the body with legs foetus-like curled-up, on the lopped tippet hat, the tired head against the well-curb, on the features which would have gained an overlay of mellow ivory on the olive. The moon was an artist that could have lifted as he slept those aloof features out of their aquiline saturninity, their repellence and disapproval, into their full potential nobility. There would have been no need for the familiar laurel.

The great visionary was given to ordinary mortal night mutterings: a girl's name ending in "Tritche." A mediaeval *sergent de ville* would not quite have made it out. Beatrice now—1309 it is—had been dead for nineteen years! The love of many centuries, people would call it. For almost a child, another man's wife, but a very pure affair—almost wholly idealistic. It was rapidly being transformed into the love that does not count on either physical or spiritual giving, but the impersonal though mighty affection for one who is brother or sister in Christ.

"Francesca!" Another girl. A *sergent de ville* of Paris would have smiled as he walked on toward the Little Bridge nearby. But she was not in the dreamer's heart, only in his head. Even in his sleep he was forging more lines for his poem. "And in the book they dreamt no more that day."

So the sun came up, banishing the night's visions, ushering in the more galvanic ones of the day. A patched, all-colours fellow was stopping at the doors of the bridge houses, with a pitcher and full-uddered goat, daintily mincing as though walking on eggs. The poet held out a coin. Not French, but precious metal. The white jets spattered with some force into the ewer. So the weather-worn exile, who was to be esteemed one of the five greatest poets in this world, drank goat's milk for his breakfast in the dawn on the Little Bridge.

As he passed down the Cathedral south side, past the now-vanished Gothic Bishop's Palace, the Bishop's lilacs, his cook in the kitchen garden hanging out dish-cloths to dry and gossiping with passers-by, the choir boys as they awaited their canon singing master playing prisoners' base, even as they do today in the shadow of the flying buttresses, he would have had a smile that was not so aloof and disapproving in his eyes. Mighty was the stable of those gigantic winged horses, those gargantuan dragons, the flying buttresses ranged down the sides. They evoked the grandeur he often sought for his poem, lines for which, grave, sonorous, passionate or tender, he was ever composing as he roamed from city to city, fought on battlefields, or stood as now in the great overcast presence of the Cathedral itself. These little human "tie-ups" in the sacred environs which as today were thronged with grown-ups and children, were like little tender tendrils for his mighty poem, keeping it within man's range. Those "tie-ups" anchored the Cathedral to the earth, which too was God's own.

There was another little human "tie-up" in those days that was infinitely touching. Once in the Cathedral-building days a great encampment had surrounded the two sides and rear of Notre Dame. It had been a fascinating place with its army of artisans of varied skills and tongues; its forge fires and crucibles; cartooning tables and designs; the great *molle,* or wood model, which we saw in the early story of the Cathedral. The clink of the chisels shaping out fiend and saint, the painters giving them bright robes. The stores of manganese, the ochres, the ferrous reds, the "sparkles," the precious "sapphire" for the stained glass; designs in these being laid out in the tents, fitted to the armatures and soon to be hoisted into their empty places waiting for them up there on high, to fill them with glory.

But by 1225 the Cathedral had been, to all worshipping purposes and intents, finished, with choir, almost complete nave, aisles, and galleries. There had been little left for succeeding generations to do. A pillar or two had to go in the northwest corner of the nave. Northeast windows, near the organ loft, had been changed from single to double. A few decades before Dante came, De Chelles had finished the two lovely transept porches. Now the last ring of chapels, girdling the apse, were going up. Sculptors were already at work etching in scenes from the Bible under these chapel windows.

So the vast encampment and the invading army had gone. There were left but one or two tents and sheds, which would always be there, with a little company for the army of occupation. Two stonecutters in the *charbonnier,* or work-yard, were shaping a stanchion for this ship of the Church, a buttress for the last chapel.

About the time of Dante's visit, a child, daughter of some cloister housekeeper, playing among the old shard-piles of marble and limestone, had spied two pieces of seemingly dulled glass ground into the earth. Prying these up with her foot, she had polished them on her wool smock, revealing the old hues—an exciting blue, a thrilling crimson. Exulting, she had skipped into the Cathedral. Children can always skip or run into Our Lady's house; she gives them a warm welcome, however they come.

Our Lady of Paris stood by the crossing near the sanctuary. The statue was of the twelfth century then; the one there now is of the fourteenth. But she had the same draperies, blue and white, and the same gold lilies. The child loved them. Before her she knelt, crossing herself, clasping her hands but still keeping in them the bright pieces of stained glass, so thrillingly red, so exaltingly blue. Her prayers over, she reached up and placed them, her only treasures, her gold, frankincense, and myrrh, in the hands of the infant Saviour.

The Gothic had never come to Dante's beautiful but forbidden Florence in the supreme way it had here. It would not so come to many-pinnacled Milan Cathedral, which was not yet. The Ile de France was the birthplace of the purest, the highest of the high Gothic. Notre Dame was the great exemplar, the first to swing out of its already started Romanesque into the Gothic. The first in senti-ment and history, associations, in ranked flying buttresses, and the serenity of its noble façade. In its all-around assembling of its many beauties too.

The long roll of that Gothic tide, which Dante had come to see, as well as to observe his versified theology taught in the hill schools and wrought into that long, high beautiful body of the Cathedral, had gotten under way in the twelfth century. It had reached its flood crest here. Speed and pace had slackened now toward the ultimate spending and running out. There would be later bright specimens of it, some a little flamboyant perhaps, cast up by that tide. The high Beauvais chair, for example. Bourges glass. Rheims lace. The Butter Tower at Rouen. But never more would there be the absolutely pure, hand-in-glove, the simple-in-the-multiplied fitting of stone and iron and glass to the lofty Gothic purpose. Beautiful combers and breakers of that tide, the supreme cathedrals, seemed to have ended. Still, the ebbing tide had not dragged them down with it. Forever, like eternal beacons, they would stand up.

Dante wanted to see what the sculptors and painters had done with that theology in the façade, the great frontispiece of this mighty pic-ture book stood up on end in the Square. Forefinger in air, as though giving a blessing, following unconsciously the designs, as Saint Louis used to do, he backed out into the Square toward the striped toy-soldier house fronts on the other side. The open space was smaller then than now and he collided with some in the stream: housewives out to shop, merchants in miniver, flayers of steers, artisans with tools in their smock pockets, cooks dusty white, chimney-sweeps sooty black, girls with flowers, king's trumpeters on the march, a priest in lace alb and stole, a long box draped with a black cross, and a red swinging censer before, and all sorts of sinning men going in to pray. Some roughed him churlishly as he backed into them. Others, though he had been the offender, apologized courteously in the old Paris way. All curiously took in the stain and dust of his travel-worn clothes, the sharp edges and the distinctly modelled planes of his face. The congenital disillusion in it had vanished. It was rapt now, lifted up into its inherent nobility as he looked up.

When one simplified that theology of his poem, the *Summa* of Thomas, and the Cathedral-builders, it all came down to this: the Cathedral was the expression of the payment of a universal debt. This was written all over the pile. God had started man out very well, with a lovely estate and nearness to Himself. And He had given man his freedom of choice, free will. He would not force him into good. He wanted a real man, a true soul. Man had made his choice—to experiment with evil, explore the dark. The colourful tale of it, the fall of Lucifer in the great battle on the celestial plains, the Eden sets, in arch and portal and on pier were graven deep. Children of the catechism class could hear the old Bible tales from the priest's lips, look up and see them dyed in the panes, or gaze on the old heroes almost come to life under the magic of the sculptor's chisel. When they came out they could trace, with their grimy fingers, the thrilling episodes in the bas-relief.

There were things the children and Dante looked at there that were very lovely, and some very dark—quite as in his immortal poem. That, with the Cathedral, was built out of the mediaeval mind. This mind, at its best, saw visions, knew ecstasies, but it never overlooked the dark. At its most naive it saw, with alarm, grewsome fiends leading away the damned, in the Last Judgment portal, in his cantos. On that door the flames seemed to burn though they were only of stone. And they lasted forever. None then questioned that. Much later on, some good Catholics would try to mitigate the endless punishment. By annihilation! Some would think these fires but metaphors. Estrangement from God was hell enough. Sinners too might, after death, repent, and be forgiven. Of that, in a clause, Christ had given a clue. But wide is the embrace of Mother Church. These compassionate souls and the more severe and rigid together can kneel at the Notre Dame rail.

As Notre Dame was upheld by giant stone buttresses, and given glory and light by the bright glass, so the mediaeval theology was buttressed by one thing moderns leave out—justice, even as it was illumined by love. In a balanced universe, as in Dante's books, debts had to be paid. There was a supernal logic in this. Man given the best, had chosen the low and, though given chance after chance, had continued incorrigibly in that choice.

Oh, there had been hopeful and heroic incidents through his red pilgrimage. These too, tales of Moses, Esther, David, Ruth, the prophets, were vividly portrayed all over the Cathedral. And man, through his long errancy, had woven a golden thread of song about the coming of a Hero who would rescue him. And He did come just as the debt of sin, of wrong choices, a wrong sense of values, wanderings from God, was piling up crushingly around man's neck and he was going down. Man had wandered so far that it could only be a tremendous force that would bring him back. That force came from God—through His coming down. The tragedy of it was that man, who had expected militancy and pomp, not manger and angel song and star, did not recognize the Hero when He came.

Star and Stable, multiplied loaves and fishes, nets, village wells, wedding wine, healings of the stricken, all the idyllic incidents of the shortest of public lives and the greatest, came to be dyed, carved deep up there—turned into bright beautiful pages for all joyously to read.

All these made up the gravely beautiful prelude to the tragedy. This, the payment of that debt, the very greatest of all the facts of life, is in this Cathedral ciphered out. In all the crucifixes with their beads of red. In the crimson panes. In the cross form of that great memorial body of Notre Dame, the very bend of the axis which indicates the head hanging in agony under the burden of the piled-up guilt of man which He had assumed—under the despair of His seeming desertion by God which Christ, the innocent, endured for man.

His last despair was the payment of the uttermost farthing of the debt. It was not when the nails went in, the spear drove deep, but when out of His agony was wrung that heart-breaking cry, that the Hero indeed went down into the depths to rescue man. That "My God! My God, why hast Thou forsaken me?" was no capitulation. It was victorious drama at its highest. And its world-shattering dissonance was at once resolved in the two noble chords, "It is finished!" and "Into Thy hands I commit my spirit."

It all did not end then in collapse. This living Cathedral is no monument to defeat. There, in the Last Judgment tympanum, He sits outlined against a Resurrection sunrise. There, by the door, He stands, His hands outstretched. And before her door is His Mother, with her foot on the Serpent's head, grand denouement of the Drama. And this is another and corollary fact established by the Cathedral: This woman God had chosen out of all the world to perform the greatest of human services, to be the chalice that would bear the Divine Wine of Life, the bridge by which the divine would enter the world. It does not require any special tenet to realize that here we are standing before the House of God dedicated to the Mother of God.

Dante himself had a great love for her. This makes lovely his poem with all its dark pages, flowing through it like the emerald, azure, green, crimson, and gilt foliage which border the illuminated pages of some beautiful old book. Every once in a while she appears in it, in the way she appears in her house. There are so many lovely personalities of her there: That lovely triumphant one at her door. Another, with the angels and the Child, centred above the king row. The great one—alas! because of the Revolution, now without arms—so instinct with womanhood, by the north transept door. The official

Notre Dame de Paris, with the gold lilies and blue and white robe, with the little joyous flare as though she came of the people, which she did, to be the Mother of God. And innumerable little appearings of her, such as you would welcome in the hostess of a house, in little niches here and there, in the innumerable little scenes kaleidoscoped across the great rose.

Dante has gone long ago, to wear that laurel forever. And we stand here without him and look up. Much as we love all of this Paris of other ages and of today, with its mighty walls and towers then, its newer palaces and charms now, and that wise old river with its reassuring philosophy flowing by, it is here, in Notre Dame that we will find the heart of Paris that is the heart of France.

Another great poet, Victor Hugo, came here later. But instead of putting the Cathedral into his great verse, he put her into a melodrama. And he made of her a theatrical maze. But she is never that. The Gothic can never be that. Ten thousand integers Notre Dame may have, but they have been welded into a marvelous unity. Everywhere there are vistas, light and shadow play, colour interrayings, a magnificent variety that is infinitely fascinating, but no obscuring, no confusion. The high Gothic has here an arrow-flight directness from foundation pier to the tower summits.

Visit it yourself a few times—it will pay us in this last moment now—and you will see the singular unity of the many-in-one. You can go direct, without any of the Hugo melodramatic deviousness to any feature. Past the sixty-foot-around entrance pillars. Up the beautifully over-arched nave. Under its giant many-flamed corona. Through the many-bayed, many-chapeled aisles, ablaze with little lights—soon you will be calling those chapels by name. The sacristy then, the treasury now, with many-coloured vestments and gleaming precious shrines. Past the choir screen with its gilded and coloured chapters of man's life. Around the curve of the ambulatory with its tombs and saints, as the sacring bell sounds for a mass, which should intensify the delight of your soul in this expression of God here. Seeing the Bishop's throne, the ranged canons' carved stalls, the high altar with its buried royal dead.

You can climb then by a little winding hidden stair, past the flying buttress' concealed ball-and-socket, to the great second story, visit the old once-filled library room, range the gallery above the choir, cross by the invisible, spider-thin suspension bridges right across the radiant faces of the roses, from sanctuary gallery to those above the nave. Everywhere within is evident the clarifying and exalting unity gained by inspired pattern and design. In the shafted upshootings of the pillars. Now the magnificent gatherings of the wedlocked arches overhead. The bright window tiers. Their stone "traceries." The stained glass anthologies of little scenes from the great Drama in each rose. Everywhere is evident the miraculous application of Heaven's first law: order, symmetry.

You can see that result of composite genius, the perfect result, that superb unity, if you cross the river and go upstream, Right Bank or Left. There is no more exquisite sight of Notre Dame than that of her at the oblique. The flying buttresses then fall into pattern and place. They are not gargantuan shorers-up now, but magnificently-functioning factors. Never in anything structural in this world have external factors been so beautifully made to seem at one with the internal.

From upstream too one gets a grand review of the great aerial population of the Cathedral, of the grotesques, heroes, saints, around her outer galleries and towers, in infinite variety yet artistically regimented, ever in that perfect harmony and symmetry.

In these angled visions one sees her three lofty stories. Like three decks they are, with their devil's crews and angels. When one gazes on the bright beings on those three high decks, they seem to turn the Cathedral into some majestic transport come down from above, temporarily moored there and soon to take all the heroes, angels, and saints up to Heaven. The angle too gives one an exquisite dream-view of the great beautiful high body of her, rising above the dwarfed black roofs in all her length, exquisite proportions and creamy whiteness.

There is the one last, the farewell, prospect, of course. From in front. Of the great façade frontispiece of this majestic story picture book stood up there on end in our Square. That noblest of west fronts in all the West is characterized by a superb simplicity and serenity and the perfect relating of the vertical lines, the great upshooting accents of the vertical buttresses, to the horizontal cross bands of king row and galleries, way up to that exquisitely light one at the top, just under the towers, with the great rose and heroic statues—never too many—in the planes in between, and the grand Alpine height and whiteness of the towers.

Out of the visible the Cathedral has framed the invisible for us. Out of a thousand details of the natural it has brought alive the supernatural and anchored that supernatural to our earth.

So she stands, Notre Dame, pre-eminently for faith. For those following the precise teachings of those in the Cathedral. For those whose beliefs approximate hers and, indeed, in the large, coincide with them. For those too who own to—or fancy they have—no belief at all, except in man. If the Ten Commandments were written on little tables of stone, here in the large has been written in stone man's Credo. Even the unbeliever, or one thinking himself such, is gripped by an exaltation as he surveys that vast, genius-guided assembling of so many things, that incredibly lovely arrangement of height and strength and delicacy, of colour and singing lines.

Here man has reached his greatest height, in his reaching out toward God. But more than that, the Cathedral is the expression of God's reaching down. It is the living, shining seal of the debt paid. That great cross, Notre Dame, so still yet throbbing with emotion, is the beautiful receipt written there by man for God.

Index of Names

Abelard, Peter, 13, 43, 82, 83, 84, 89, 92, 112, 124, 156, 164, 273, 274
Aberdeen, University of, 80
Adam, founder of Paris college, 84, 86
Adelard of Bath, 156, 187
Ader, Clement, 49
Agnes, St., 214
Aigues-Mortes, 63, 73, 74
Aix, 80, 84
Alain de Lille, 156
Albert I, king of Belgium, 34
Albert the Great, St., 78, 98, 102, 105, 107, 112, 155, 156, 161, 162–4, 177, 180 et seq., 268, 273, 282
Albi, city of, 19
Albigenses, 10, 18 et seq., 166
Alcuin, 117, 156
Alembert, Jean le Rond d', 153
Alexander of Hales, 102, 105, 112, 161, 162, 163, 180, 268
Alexandria, Egypt, 111
Alfonso of Castille, 7
Alfred the Great, king of England, 34, 117, 248
Algiers, 75, 284
Almaric of Bena, 165
Almeric of Narbonne, 258
Anagni, 297
Angelico, Fra, 204
Anjou, 34
Anjou, Count of, 226
Anselm of Laon, 83, 112, 187
Anthony, St., 177
Aquinas. See Thomas Aquinas
Aquino, 173 et seq.
Aquitaine, 7
Arabs, 115–16, 153, 230
Ardre, Lambert d', 265
Aristarchus, 154
Aristotle, 18, 93, 154, 156, 164, 273 et seq.
Arno, river, 112
Arras, 290
Arsenal Library, Paris, 229
Arthur, King, 248, 285
Artois, counts of, 62, 232–3, 241, 310

Athena, Greek goddess, 201
Aucassin and Nicolette, 187–96
Augustine, St., 177, 268
Augustinians, 90
Autun, Paris college of, 90
Auxerre, 201
Avacinna, 93
Averrhoës, 165
Avignon, 298, 311

Bacon, Roger, 79, 94, 102, 105, 110, 112–13, 120, 129, 155, 156, 158 et seq., 180
Baldwin II, emperor of Constantinople, 58
Bar, counts of, 13
Barastre, Jean de la, 27, 88
Barbarissmus, 93
Barcelona, 234
Barye, Antoine-Louis, 130
Bastille, 56
Bayeux, cathedral of, 201, 249
Beatrice Portinari, 319
Beauvais, 322
Beauvais, Paris college of, 90
Becquerel, Antoine, 178
Bede the Venerable, 120
Beethoven, Ludwig, 158
Benedict, St., 175, 280
Béranger of Tours, 80
Bérenger, Pierre-Jean de, 41
Bergerac, Cyrano de, 90
Bergson, Henri, 178
Bernadins, Paris College of the, 90
Bernanos, Georges, 145
Bernard, Claude, 154, 178
Bernard of Clairvaux, St., 126, 180, 220, 258, 262, 272
Bernard of Cluny, 281
Bernard of Trillia, 156
Bernhardt, Sarah, 178, 303
Béziers, 18
Bibliothèque Nationale, 41, 116, 128
Bièvre, the river, 122, 278
Biography of a Cathedral, 3

329

Date Due